WHO
KILLED
JOHN
LENNON?

WHO

The lives,

KILLED

loves and deaths

JOHN

of the greatest

LENNON?

rock star

Lesley-Ann Jones

JOHN BLAKE

First published in the UK by John Blake Publishing
An imprint of Bonnier Books UK
80 – 81 Wimpole Street, Marylebone, London, W1G 9RE
Owned by Bonnier Books
Sveavägen 56, Stockholm, Sweden

www.bonnierbooks.co.uk

www.facebook.com/johnblakebooks
twitter.com/jblakebooks

First published in hardback in 2020

Hardback ISBN: 978-1-78946-140-4
Trade paperback: 978-1-78946-297-5
Ebook ISBN: 978-1-78946-170-1
Audiobook: 978-1-78946-324-8

1 3 5 7 9 10 8 6 4 2

© Text copyright Lesley-Ann Jones 2020

Every reasonable effort has been made to trace copyright-holders of material
reproduced in this book, but if any have been inadvertently overlooked the publishers
would be glad to hear from them.

John Blake Publishing is an imprint of Bonnier Books UK
www.bonnierbooks.co.uk

To Dad:
The fighter still remains.
Kenneth Powell Jones
11 October 1931 – 26 September 2019

CONTENTS

IN MEMORIAM
JOHN WINSTON ONO LENNON
9 October 1940 – 8 December 1980

'I hold a beast, an angel, and a madman in me.'
DYLAN THOMAS

'Blessed are the weird people –
Poets, misfits, writers, mystics, heretics, painters and troubadours –
For they teach us how to see the world …
… through different eyes.'
JACOB NORDBY

'It is better to go out in a blaze of glory, young.'
SIMON NAPIER-BELL

ECHOES

The rhythms of mind and memory are like tides. They change shape constantly. Even those who were there, who knew and experienced John Lennon first-hand, can be inclined to forget things. Some rewrite history to stopple the gaps, for which they might be forgiven. Forty years is a lifetime. It was to John. Yet he hardly seems distant. In 2020, a milestone year – the fortieth anniversary of his murder, the official fiftieth of the Beatles' demise,[1] the sixtieth of the band in Hamburg and when John would have turned eighty years old – it feels like time to reconsider and to retrace him. If you are under fifty, you hadn't been born when the Beatles broke up. If you are younger than forty, you weren't alive when John died. Unimaginable? Does it seem to you, as it seems to me, as though he's still here?

There are as many versions of his story as there are those of a mind to tell it. Where truth is a point of view, facts and figures can be an inconvenience. When reminiscence is distorted by supposition and theory, it can lead to confusion. If assumption is the root of all blunders, speculation is the thief of rational thought. All of which gets in the way. John coined it (or did he?) in a lyric line for 'Beautiful Boy (Darling Boy)' on the final album released during his lifetime, *Double Fantasy*: 'Life is what happens to you while you're busy making other plans.'[2]

John said a lot of things in his crammed, contradictory half-life. He went back on his words, re-writing his own history and thought processes constantly. His propensity for doing so confounds the chronicler as surely as the conflicting accounts and shifting recollections of those close to him, or who crossed his path. Keeping 'em guessing is so John. Confused? But I'm not the only one.

*

We know the ending. It happened in New York on Monday, 8 December 1980. A gusty night, otherwise uncommonly mild for the time of year. John and Yoko were driven home by limousine from an evening session at Record Plant recording studio, reaching the Dakota apartment building at around 10.50 p.m. Eastern Standard Time. They were confronted by a Texan-born itinerant clutching a Charter Arms .38-caliber pistol and a copy of J.D. Salinger's *The Catcher in the Rye*. The twenty-five-year-old, Mark Chapman, had been waiting for them, and calmly fired five bullets at John. Four hit him. He was conveyed by cops to the Roosevelt Hospital on 59th Street and Central Park, where a twenty-nine-year-old third-year general surgeon, Dr David Halleran, held John's heart in his hands, performing cardiac massage and pleading silently for a miracle.

Doctor *who*? Don't previous accounts acknowledge the efforts of Stephan Lynn and Richard Marks for having operated to save John's life? Dr Lynn has granted many interviews, his recollections ever more embellished. Lynn also claimed that Yoko lay smashing her head repeatedly on the hospital floor. But, in 2015, having listened for years to other physicians taking credit, David Halleran came forward 'for the sake of historical accuracy'. In an interview for a Fox TV 'Media Spotlight Investigation', he said for the record that neither Lynn nor Marks had touched John's body. His statement was supported by two nurses, Dea Sato and Barbara Kammerer, who worked alongside him in Room 115 that deadly night. Yoko stepped up, too, denying hysterical head-banging. She insisted that she had remained calm throughout for the sake of their five-year-old son, Sean. She has supported Dr Halleran's version of events. Why didn't he pipe up sooner?

'It just seems unseemly for professionals to go out and say, "Hi, I'm Dave Halleran, I took care of John Lennon,"' he said. 'At the time I wanted to crawl under a rock, I just wanted to go home. I was distraught, I was upset, you feel somewhat responsible, on what you could have done different.'

Were you in America at the time? Were you one of the twenty million viewers at home watching the New England Patriots–Miami Dolphins game on ABC's *Monday Night Football* that commentator Howard Cosell interrupted to deliver the bombshell that John had been shot? Were you among millions more who picked up the newsflash on NBC and CBS? Might you have been one of the thousands who headed for the Upper West Side to join the vigil? Or were you stuck elsewhere in the world, tuning in during the aftermath, to watch throngs of grief-stricken fans sinking in mud in Central Park, threading flowers through the Dakota railings, wailing 'Give peace a chance'? Did you hear that a background-music version of 'All My Loving' was playing out over the hospital's sound system, around the time Yoko was informed that her husband was dead? TV producer Alan Weiss heard it. He happened to be lying on a trolley in the hospital corridor at the time, awaiting treatment after a motorbike accident. Are there coincidences?[3]

If you were born by then and were in England when it happened, you were probably sound asleep. John died at around 11 p.m. Eastern Standard Time on 8 December (reports vary with regard to the precise time of death), which equated in the UK to about 4 a.m. Greenwich Mean Time on Tuesday, 9 December. The news was buzzed across the Atlantic by New York-based BBC reporter Tom Brook, who heard it from former pop mogul and songwriter Jonathan King, at that time based there. Brook tore to the Dakota. He called Radio 4's *Today* programme from a sidewalk phone booth. There was no breakfast TV in those days, most people listened to morning radio. They told Tom to ring back at 6.30 a.m., when the show, co-presented that day by Brian Redhead, would be live.

Brook unscrewed an office telephone receiver and wired in a lead to transmit his taped vox pops – no Internet, no email, no mobiles – and was interviewed on air by Redhead. By the time we got up for school, college, work, the dog, the unthinkable was everywhere.

*

Where were you when you heard?

That is the question. Echoing the opener of Prince Hamlet's eternal soliloquy, it is arguably the question of our times.[4] The Silent Generation, born mid/late 1920s to early/mid 1940s, together with post-war baby boomers, tend to recall their whereabouts and what they were doing when they heard about the assassination of President John F. Kennedy. 'The subject came up in conversation with my three children as I was beginning to research this book. 'What you have to understand,' I said, 'is that John Lennon was our JFK.' 'Why?' said my student son. 'What's an airport got to do with it?'

Millennials and post-millennials, or generations Y and Z respectively, sometimes interpret the question as referring to the death of Diana, Princess of Wales, even if they were babes in arms or as yet unborn at the time of her accident. It is those in the middle, the so-called Generation X-ers who started arriving at the turn of the sixties, who are most likely to connect the question to John Lennon.

This is a trinity of pointless deaths with more in common than might at first seem apparent. In all three cases, conspiracy theories persist. When the thirty-fifth US president was assassinated in Dallas, Texas, on 22 November 1963, speculation raged. Did alleged assassin Lee Harvey Oswald act alone? Was he working for the Mafia? Was the set-up linked to Cuba? How many shots were fired? From a sixth-floor window from behind, or from the infamous 'grassy knoll', ahead of the cavalcade? Even the physics of the investigation have long been disputed. Nearly sixty years since it happened, they still are. After Princess Diana and Dodi Fayed died in a Paris underpass on 31 August 1997, a mysterious white Fiat Uno became the emblem of the tragedy. One hundred and seventy-five conspiracy claims were investigated. The chief plaintiff, Egyptian tycoon Mohamed Al Fayed, was behind the most serious: that the princess was exterminated to order because she was carrying his son and heir's child. Many believe to this day that she was offed by the SAS. As for John. It has long been speculated that his death was connected to CIA and FBI surveillance as a result of his earlier left-wing activism; that convicted killer Mark Chapman was a brainwashed assassin, a 'Manchurian candidate'; that José Perdomo, the now-deceased doorman in his sentry box at the Dakota building, was a Cuban exile linked to the failed Bay of Pigs anti-Castro military invasion of 1961. Simple truth, in the end, cannot satisfy the conspiracy theorist. See also 'flat-earthers', 'Obama's birth certificate', 'controlled demolition of World Trade Center, 9/11'. Experts point at proportionality bias, explaining conspiracy theories as coping mechanisms for unbearable occurrences. Folk on a flight from reason need bigger things to blame.

*

Were you here by 1980? Are you old enough to remember Ernő Rubik's Cube, Margaret Thatcher, Ronald Reagan, whoever it was who shot J.R.? Can you recall the launch of CNN, the world's first twenty-four-hour news channel? Did you watch the Winter Olympics in Lake Placid? Did you read about Tim Berners-Lee, the computer scientist who had begun work on what would become the World Wide Web? Not that we knew it at the time, but 1980 was the year that gave us Macaulay Culkin, Lin-Manuel Miranda and Kim Kardashian; the year we were shaking a leg to Blondie's 'Call Me' and Jacko's 'Rock With You', to McCartney's 'Coming Up' and Queen's 'Crazy Little Thing Called Love'; a year dominated by Bowie and Kate Bush, by Diana Ross and the Police; the year that deprived us of Jean-Paul Sartre, Alfred Hitchcock, Henry Miller and Peter Sellers, Steve McQueen, Mae West, Led Zeppelin's John Bonham and Beatle John.

Did you nip out to a record shop on Friday, 24 October that year, to bag a copy of his new single, '(Just Like) Starting Over'? Might you have heard the track on the radio on your way to school or college or work and thought, is it me or does that sound a bit like the Beach Boys' 'Don't Worry Baby'? Launched three days later in the US, 'Starting Over' would become John's biggest-ever solo hit in America. It turned out to be the last single release of his life. Come 6 January 1981, there were three Lennon singles in the UK Top 5: the aforementioned at number five, 'Happy Xmas (War is Over)' at two, and the chart-topper, 'Imagine'. The achievement would not be eclipsed for three and a half decades.[5]

*

Thirty-eight years later, in December 2018, we are at the O2 Arena on London's Greenwich Peninsula to witness Sir Paul McCartney promoting his seventeenth studio album, *Egypt Station*. This is the latest stop on his thrilling Freshen Up tour. Where once upon a time Paul had been in the habit of falling over himself to lean away from the legacy and play his own music almost exclusively, tonight is a celebration of the whole back catalogue, Beatles, Wings and solo Paul. 'A Hard Day's Night', 'All My Loving', 'Got to Get You into My Life', 'I've Got a Feeling', 'I've Just Seen a Face'. The choruses soar, sent higher by a jubilant audience. Images of John and George loom hugely on the backdrop. Here's 'In Spite of all the Danger', the Quarry Men's first original song. This one's 'Here Today', Paul's sorrowful tribute to John. Out of the swirl, Ronnie Wood bounces on, and they 'might as well do a song together'. Cue appearance of a springy seventy-eight-year-old, who jogs on to join the Beatle and the Stone. 'Ladies and gentlemen,' rasps Paul, 'the ever-fantastic Mr Ringo STARR!' Who takes to the kit while Ron straps on a guitar. They hurl into 'Get Back'. The arena erupts. 'Photograph it with your eyes,' I whisper to my children. 'Half the Beatles on stage, half a century since they broke up. You'll never see this again.'

*

Did we who caught the sixties by the hem, but missed the real-time Beatles' magic because we were still kids, bother to lament that fact later, or did it all go under our heads? For me, the latter. I came in at Wings and discovered the Beatles backwards – but not until I was through college, and not before I'd fallen for Bolan and Bowie, had become enchanted by Lindisfarne, Simon and Garfunkel, the Stones, Status Quo, James Taylor, Roxy Music, Pink Floyd, the Eagles, Queen, Elton John and all those other disparate artists, groups and music, endless music, that consumed my teenage years. How challenging it must be for those who missed it to comprehend the impact the Beatles had on the world. Nothing remotely comparable has happened during their lifetime. Older generations are well-served by a plethora of tomes penned by writers revisiting their youth. With the exception of two memoirs each by John's first wife Cynthia and by his half-sister Julia Baird, every respected biography of Lennon has been written by a man. Re-imagining time in the company of the Beatles, sometimes rendering themselves more essential to the story than they really were (for few are left to question it), they have little to teach the younger, more emotionally revved reader who tends to expect rather more than endless facts and dates and portly opinion. It is so, is it not, that over the four decades since his death, the Lennon with whom younger fans have come to be acquainted is so far removed from the John who existed as to be virtually a different person?

Only after his death did I cross paths with individuals who had shared John's life. Paul, George and Ringo. Maureen Starkey, Ringo's first wife, who became, for a while, my friend. Linda McCartney, with whom I began collaborating on her personal memoir, *Mac the Wife*. That it was never finished or published remains one of my greatest regrets, for what a story it was. Then there was Cynthia Lennon, who asked me to ghost-write her second book. Her first, *A Twist of Lennon*, published in 1978, left a bitter taste. Frustrated by John's refusal to communicate with her after he left her and their son Julian for Yoko Ono, she wrote a 'long, open letter to him, pouring it all out'. With hindsight, she admitted, she would have done it differently. Now that the dust had settled, she was keen to have another go. But she became entangled in a doomed restaurant venture, and our publishing ambitions were shelved. Years down the line, in 2005, she offered us *John*, a take much bolder and more confessional than her first. As a journalist during the eighties, I accompanied Julian Lennon to the Montreux Rock Festival. Eventually, I met Yoko in New York.

*

More than half a century after the Beatles broke up, we are still wondering. What was it all about? How did they do it? They were the greatest cultural and social phenomenon ever. The impact of their fame and music throughout the sixties affected as many humans in every cranny of the globe as did the *Apollo 11* space mission and the July 1969 Moon landing. Neil Armstrong, Buzz Aldrin and Michael Collins were rendered superstars by their lunar expedition and toured the world to celebrate the achievement. Yet in the scheme, it was gone-tomorrow. What is their legacy? A faded flag on a distant celestial surface. Bootsteps in the dust. A plaque to inform future moonwalkers of an unprecedented moment in history. That 'we' were there.

But the Beatles are not history. Their songs live, they breathe. They are as familiar to us as our own names. The music ensures its creators enduring relevance. Despite having been recorded with elementary equipment, regardless of endless reworkings, remixes, re-packagings and re-issues, the glorious original sounds they made remain fresh. There was nothing manufactured about their music. Apart from a few covers, they wrote and composed their own songs. They played their own instruments. They were among the first musicians to establish their own record company, Apple, through which they also launched the careers of other artists. Of their own output, a billion units have sold, with more acquired via download every day. They scored seventeen UK Number One singles: more than any other artist to date. They sent more albums to the top of the British chart, and lingered there longer, than any other act. They have dispensed more albums in America than anyone, ever. Their popularity around the world appears undimmed. They were awarded seven Grammys, fifteen Ivor Novellos. The most influential artists of all time, they still inspire more musicians than anyone else can lay claim to: Three Dog Night, the Bonzo Dog Doo-Dah Band, Lenny Kravitz, Tears for Fears, Kurt Cobain, Oasis, Paul Weller, Gary Barlow, Kasabian, the Flaming Lips, Lady Gaga, and the Chemical Brothers, to name a mere handful, fell under the Fab Four spell. Compare Noel Gallagher's composition 'Setting Sun' (recorded and released by the Chemical Brothers) to 'Tomorrow Never Knows' from the album *Revolver*. Beatles songs have been recorded by thousands of singers of all ages and across every conceivable genre. Gaga has also suggested, incidentally, that, music aside, the Beatles were responsible for the birth of the female sexual revolution. Works for me.

*

The biggest question – why are we here? – has long stimulated artists and sparked scientists. It drove us to the moon. It compelled the Beatles to write songs. They may not have realised it at first, when they were still gooey over girls and scribbling lyrics inspired by the thrills of physical love. But they were getting there. We are no closer to solving the great philosophical problems, those aspects of life that might lie forever beyond the reach of human understanding. Existential awareness, the dilemma of determinism, the existence or not of God, the mystery of our future and the likelihood of life after death and of reincarnation, have, for millennia, precipitated exploration and prompted creativity. We should not forget that the Beatles, too, were explorers. They went out on a limb. They created in unprecedented ways, at first oblivious of their gift for doing so. They embarked upon their great adventure during the televisual age, when the dissemination of music and message could be maximised – but pre-computer revolution, without the Internet, when there was less information about everything. There were not yet 24/7 news channels. You had to read the daily papers to keep up, if only with headlines. Which is why, because the Big Things got noticed, the majority of people on Earth came to know about the Beatles. They were, and are, the perfect reflection of the culture and climate of their times. Even though the 1960s brimmed with gigantic personalities – Bob Dylan, the 'Mozart and Shakespeare of his age'; Muhammad Ali, three times heavyweight champion of the world and a conscientious objector to the Vietnam War; John F. Kennedy; civil-rights campaigners Martin Luther King and Malcolm X; and those ravishing purveyors of classic Hollywood allure, Elizabeth Taylor, Rock Hudson, Cary Grant, Doris Day, John Wayne and the rest – the Beatles obscured them all. Could it have been because they were natural unifiers, transcending class, race, generations and gender with their irresistible appeal? Because they provided the soundtrack to the decade? Because they were real, touchable, ordinary sons who together came to conjure some otherworldly chemistry, the sensation of which humanity clamoured to share? Are we ever likely to see their like again?

I honestly doubt it. Because it is not, and never was, 'just' about the music. Their effect was the result of a collision of factors that crystallised into an unprecedented episode in history. There being fewer opportunities for exposure, and fewer artists competing in the same arena, if you were famous during the sixties, you tended to be massively so – if only for a moment. In the UK at the time the Beatles emerged, there were only two television channels: BBC and ITV. BBC2 did not arrive until April 1964. In America, most homes had a TV set by 1960, but there were only three channels: ABC, CBS and NBC. So there were times when the vast majority of viewers were watching the same thing simultaneously. Now that there are endless channels in virtually every country, focus is less concentrated and viewing figures are fragmented. If you happened not to be one of the seventy-four million Americans witnessing the Beatles' first appearance on *The Ed Sullivan Show* on CBS on 9 February 1964, there wasn't much else to watch. So most people became part of the zeitgeist by default. Radio airplay was also limited. In the UK, there was the BBC Light Programme, but BBC Radio 1 did not launch until September 1967, to serve the youth market hitherto dominated by the offshore 'pirates' – Radio London, Radio Caroline, Swinging Radio England – and Radio Luxembourg.

'Radio London was the Beatles,' recalls BBC presenter Johnnie

Walker. 'Slick and neat, the radio station you could take home to your mother for tea. Caroline was definitely the Stones – scruffy, anarchic, non-conformist and rebellious … it was there to give freedom and expression to the creative artistic explosion that was the sixties.'

In the US, the Top 40 stations of most major cities were playing Beatles records from 1963/4. But FM changed the broad-spectrum landscape in 1967, resulting in many more minor outlets pursuing special-interest music. Although it happened for the Beatles, mass-popularity artists emerge rarely these days. Adele, Taylor Swift, Justin Bieber, Ed Sheeran, Stormzy, Lizzo and Billie Eilish are obvious exceptions. Hip hop is a huge influence now, and has thrown up a number of true global stars: Kanye West; Beyoncé, obviously; Jay-Z. It still means little when compared to what the Beatles did and what they achieved. They can produce numbers that might demonstrate otherwise, but I would still say that it is nowhere near as popular, that it hasn't had anything close to the all-pervading influence of the Beatles.

The oft-overlooked advent of the cheap transistor radio was also a vital development. Most kids could afford or were gifted one, which they carried around in their pocket or schoolbag and even took to bed at night, in order to tune in under the blankets. I did. The personal listening device proved a major turning point in music consumption. Today's children and teenagers routinely access music on smartphones via earbuds or headphones on public transport, never pausing to think that their parents and grandparents might once have sat on the top deck of the bus with one ear glued to a tranny, with little choice in the range of music they were able to hear. At least sixties kids could stay tuned, and become part of the collective loyalty towards their favourite singers and groups.

As for marketing and mass media, the Beatles were the first pop group to take advantage of these burgeoning industries to appeal to the new demographic: a vast and growing band of teenage consumers. The young ones, many incited to riot by the effect of 1950s American rock'n'roll, now adopted identities, fashion, music and other aspects of lifestyle at odds with those previously enforced by their parents. Victorian traditions and post-war austerity were rebelled against. Hemlines went up, pills went down, and youth culture became a dominant, turbulent force. The US boasted seventy-six million so-called 'baby boomers' – that is, people born during or after 1946 at the end of the Second World War, when there was a spike in the national birth rate. Half the entire population there was under twenty-five years old. The Beatles were marketed to them using the very same tools as for toys, sweets and jeans. With social structure changing in First World countries, many 'new' voices were now demanding to be heard, including those of women, the working class and ethnic minorities. Post-war technological advancement, impending nuclear doom, the lost cause that was Vietnam and other factors all played their part.

In a nutshell? Go on, then. The Beatles represented change. They heralded a new direction. They validated alternative thought. They cut the crap, said what they saw, presented as their bare-faced selves, scorned protocol, took the piss, and shunned pomposity and pretence. Their Scouse gab, wit and humour became addictive. While the world looked set to stumble through the sixties on a path of apparent self-destruction, the Beatles paid attention to the still, small inner voice. They got sentimental. They expressed real emotions. They spoke and sang their truth.

Some commentators have singled out the assassination of President Kennedy as the defining factor in the breakthrough of the Beatles in the US. Bewildered and distraught, Americans needed something to turn to, to wind their minds away from tragedy and to offset unbearable grief. On cue, in blew four lippy Brits with flagrant disregard for convention and authority. JFK's 'man of the people' stance, his personality, glamour and charm had seduced America. Now the Beatles had landed to bridge the gap and do the same, as part of what became known as the British Invasion. As their confidence grew and their songwriting developed, to encompass spirituality and philosophy along with disciplines and dimensions hitherto unaddressed by purveyors of mere pop, their fans grew with them. Every aspect of their image was pored over. Every nuance of their private existence (as 'private' as it could be, by then) was invaded and dissected. The personification of fearless youth and liberty, they were as good as beatified. Sounding far-fetched, all this? Reader, it happened.

Friends who remember those insane days still ponder the what and the how. Now late fifties to eighties in age, they gush about how lucky they were to have been born in time to experience the Fab Four first-hand. Some believe their generation to be 'different' and 'special' just because of that single random circumstance. There is among some of them an almost tangible condescension towards those who were 'born too late'. Fancy. Younger pop fans, my own children included, are often perplexed by the Beatles' global domination. Why, they ask, when the music industry subsequently served up Queen, Bowie, Jacko, Madge, U2, Prince, George Michael and all those other fantastic artists, and has more recently delivered One Direction, the Wanted, BTS (the South Korean outfit Bangtan Boys) and, let's say, Little Mix, are the Beatles still considered the quintessential and never-to-be-improved-upon pop-and-rock force? It's because, using their music, looks and personalities, the Beatles broke the sound barrier. They changed the course of history by becoming the first pop group ever to implant themselves in the hearts and minds of hundreds of millions of people around the world. They turned pop into a universal language. Via their recordings primarily, and to a lesser but still significant degree their films, live-performance footage and endless recorded interviews, they continue to influence and infect new converts. Perhaps they always will.

John Lennon, the chippy, clever, quick-witted one, the out-rageously talented one, was the Beatle most favoured. Arguably, blessed with the best voice – though he disputed this – he was the minstrel most reflective of their life and times. He was also the most complex and contradictory; the most disturbed by and at odds with what fame had done to them. More than that, though, he was all kinds of Johns. He was a snarl of contradictions. One minute a hilarious mischief-maker, the next a bitter fool. Both vicious brute and snivelling baby. Overconfident, gauche, phlegmatic, paranoid, he could be both wildly extravagant and surprisingly restrained. He was spiteful but gentle. Mean, yet generous. Uncertain, though discerning. Remorseless and self-reproachful in the same breath. He was infinitely envious of McCartney's vast melodic virtuosity. He was never as magnificently creative post-Paul (neither was Paul) as they were together, as they had been since their teens, when their chemistry was fresh and newborn-wondrous. John had what we once called 'attitude'. He embodied the *carpe diem* spirit. Damaged, dysfunctional and defiant, he made his way in the world warts and all. He seldom cared what anybody thought of him. He relished the unacceptable, the unpalatable, the unspoken truth. His life was extinguished at the very summit of his fable. He was only halfway through. In death, his mythology is complete, and is preserved for all time. Even though we now know most of his weaknesses, we are forgiving. His memory is sanctified. More than any other artist, John Lennon has come to be regarded as both the symbol and the conscience of his age. But who *was* he?

*

To me, he reveals himself most plausibly and reliably through the formidable females in his four-decade life, regardless of whether they cherished or neglected, repaired or damaged, fortified or weakened him. Whether they enhanced or emasculated him. Whether they gave to, took from or were indifferent to him. His allegedly 'reckless', 'bohemian' mother, Julia, who in truth adored him and with whom he was besotted, left him twice, he said. The first time was when his parents separated, his father deserted them and his mother 'gave him away' to her sister (did she really?) before he got to blow out five candles. He identified the second maternal 'abandonment' as having occurred when Julia was knocked down by a car driven by an off-duty policeman, and killed on the street where he lived. John was only seventeen. The scene of the accident was clearly visible from his bedroom window. He awoke to that view every day, and never stopped fantasising about her. He even found himself desiring her sexually at one point, according to therapist Arthur Janov, and wondered whether he should try to seduce her. His half-sister Julia Baird made public her disgust at this insinuation of incest. She need not have agitated: Freud introduced the concept of Oedipal fantasy back in 1899. Truth be told, few teenaged boys are immune to it. Most would die rather than admit to it. John just happened to wear his various hearts on his sleeve.

He was raised impeccably by his Aunt Mimi, Julia's domineering, roost-ruling elder sister. His first wife, Cynthia, a fellow art student, fell pregnant and 'had to' marry him when he was only twenty-one, long before he was ready for responsibility. How withered by guilt was John in later years whenever he thought of the ways in which Cynthia occupied herself after her meagre divorce settlement ran dry: penning tawdry tell-alls, launching eateries, designing cheap bed linens, shacking up with a chauffeur to make ends meet. His first unofficial manager-slash-enabler was a woman: Mona Best. His first secret love was pop sweetheart Alma Cogan, whose premature death from cancer rendered him suicidal. Yoko Ono, the alluring, ambitious, clingy Japanese artist, happened along just in time. She was John's natural soulmate, and made a formidable second wife. Their production assistant May Pang became his short-term companion and lover at Yoko's scheming behest. His stepdaughter, Kyoko, whom he adored, was kidnapped by her biological father when she was only eight. John had loved her as his own, but never saw her again.

He spent his half-life overcompensating for his vulnerability and building his armour. He discovered his gift for writing about his emotions early on. He composed 'Help!' when he was only twenty-four, for example, laying bare his fragile psyche but packaging it as an upbeat pop number. He dallied carnally with Beatles Svengali Brian Epstein. In the interests of research, nothing more. He declared his group to be more popular than the Son of God, and sent their stateside standing up in smoke.

John's secrets, lives and loves continue to draw the faithful on epic pilgrimages. In Liverpool, they visit Mimi's house, Mendips;

his schools and the art college; the venues in which he performed, including the Casbah and the Cavern (it's not the original, but it'll do); locations that inspired the Beatles' best-loved songs, including the roundabout, bus shelter and barber's shop of Penny Lane, the site of the Strawberry Field Salvation Army refuge, the bus route from Menlove Avenue to the city centre that John re-rides in 'In My Life'; St Peter's parish churchyard, Woolton, wherein lies the real grave of one Eleanor Rigby: a possible (though never confirmed) inspiration for their everlasting lament on the plight of the elderly, featuring one of the most evocative lyrics ever written: '… wearing the face that she keeps in a jar by the door'. The church hall opposite was where John first met Paul, at a garden fête in July 1957.

Fans still flock, too, to Hamburg, where the boys held residencies from 1960 to 1962, and where they notched up their vital ten thousand hours. Irresistible are the photo opportunities at Beatles-Platz, the Indra and Kaiserkeller clubs, and the sites of the old Star-Club and the Top Ten, where they played more live-music hours than anywhere else in the world. Down on the waterfront, the faithful congregate outside the building that once housed the old Seamen's Mission, where they went for morning cornflakes and for meat'n'two veg, and to launder their smalls. They stop for a swift half at the Gretel & Alfons, the home-from-home pub reminiscent of any street-corner boozer back home, where their idols were wont to wind down after hours and let fatigue kick in.

In London, the droves still lurk outside Abbey Road Studios, where they recorded almost all of their albums and singles between 1962 and 1970. They snap selfies on the most famous zebra crossing ever painted. They wander from the London Beatles Store to Marylebone Station, where the opening scenes of *A Hard Day's Night* were filmed; to 34 Montagu Square, Ringo's former home and a sort-of Beatles halfway house, which John and Yoko rented and were busted for drugs in, which belongs these days to friends of mine, and which is nowadays Blue-Plaqued; to the London Palladium, where the group famously performed, and to Sutherland House next-door, once the domain of their manager Brian Epstein, from which he ran his NEMS Organisation; and to 3 Savile Row, the old Apple Corps offices and studio, where they gave their last-ever live gig, up on the roof, on 30 January 1969.

In New York, the five-star St Regis Hotel on 5th Avenue, John and Yoko's first home there, still features on the Beatle map; as does 105 Bank Street in the West Village, their first formal dwelling; and the Dakota building at 72nd and Central Park West, their last. John was gunned down there. Yoko still lives there. I'm not sure I could, but there you go. At the site of the old Hit Factory studio on W48th and 9th, fans still hang to remember the recording of John and Yoko's final album together, *Double Fantasy*. Mr Chow's Chinese on E57th was the Lennons' favourite restaurant. In Central Park, across from the Dakota, lies John's eternal memorial, Strawberry Fields.

Even Japan has become a Lennon destination, offering echoes of happy family holidays that John spent there with his wife, younger child and in-laws. In Kameoka City, Kyoto, they visit the Sumiya hot spring resort 'because John did'; Karuizawa is home to the Lennons' favourite hideaway, the Mampei Hotel; fans also frequent the Ginza district of Tokyo, seeking out the better Beatles tribute bands – there are hundreds of them.

*

Who can imagine what it was like to be John? Perhaps not even John. At the height of the Beatles' fame and significance, he nursed a terrified awareness of his inner void. He was dogged by a deep sense of disappointment and dissatisfaction in the material things that fortune had afforded him. Neither recognition nor reward provided the answers to the questions that had tormented him since boyhood. Sickened by a fear that 'this is all there is', John even considered religion. At one point, he asked God for a 'sign'. When nothing was forthcoming, he withdrew into his imagination, concluding that 'God' was simply energy that vibrates endlessly throughout the universe, and that it was probably benign. Still, he longed for a theme, a code to live by, which would shape his existence and give it some sort of point. It was through drugs, principally LSD, that he landed on love.

An invitation for the Beatles to perform for the first live international satellite TV broadcast in June 1967, to an audience of four hundred million, provided the perfect opportunity to promote his new theme to the world. Having fallen for his own publicity, John embarked on a deluded mission to 'improve humanity'. This led to the song they performed for that historic broadcast: 'All You Need is Love'. You wanna save the world, you gotta fit your own oxygen mask first. For what is love but a yearning to be loved? John's stance chimed uncomfortably with the personality trait that had long kept him sane: his inherent cynicism. He clung to it anyway, a limpet to a rock, until Yoko perceived the gap in the market and became that rock personified. Despite both the world's and the Beatles' rejection of this curious Asian interloper, she became his constant, his one true thing. Into the sunset they waltzed, hand in hand, promoting world peace.

They might get laughed out of Dodge today. But those were different, pre-politically correct times. One could still denounce the self-serving great and good and expose them for corruption without incurring retribution. John the peace-seeking missile hailed the human imagination as the key to salvation both collective and individual. His signature song 'Imagine' was the distillation of both his personal luminosity and of everything that had hitherto preoccupied him. It reached for the stars in its attempt to inspire people from all walks of life, all over the world, and to transcend barriers of every kind. It made its point but was idealistic in the extreme. It didn't change anything. That still didn't kill his fervent belief that popular music has a far more important job to do than merely entertain.

Never less than an artist of integrity, John challenged the lot. Even his own songwriting. Perhaps especially that. He was the first to admit that his early lyrics were sexist. He re-adjusted his approach in later years to reflect his new feminist awareness. He took risks, and often fell short, but seemed always true to himself

... or as true as he *could* be. The Beatles excelled because they broke rules: in song structure, lyric-writing, personal presentation and countless other ways. The icing on their cake was John, whose sharp wit and sardonicism, whose talent for riddles and puns and plays on words, whose unique take on life lifted their music into hitherto unheard and unimagined realms. He experimented with the impossible, cramming songs with subliminal messages and layering them with clashing sentiments until they were almost too much to bear. Revisit 'Strawberry Fields Forever' and 'Across the Universe' for proof. The so-called 'White Album', *The Beatles*, may be John at his most bitter, furious, frustrated, committed, mad, sad, vituperative, political and reflective. Then again, what about *John Lennon/Plastic Ono Band*? Delivering his devastating denunciation of the Beatles – 'the dream is over' – it features the acoustic ballad 'Working Class Hero', John's gutted acknowledgement of what, thanks to global fame and unimaginable fortune, he was no longer able to be. If indeed he was anything like that humble in the first place. Mimi made a point of retaining the servants' bells over the 'morning room' door at Mendips, lest we forget. Finally, from the last LP of his lifetime, *Double Fantasy*, 'Watching the Wheels': admitting why he stopped making music during the truncated 'house husband' years. Having found his own heaven on earth – domestic bliss, a variation on the theme of, with Yoko and their son together – 'I just had to let it go.'

*

What if he were here today? What sense might the octogenarian ex-Beatle be making of our glacier-melting, eco-damned, COVID-clobbered, politically condemned world? What, if anything, would he be doing about all this? Would he matter now? Would he be relevant? Would he still mean something?

I think he would. Because he was a voice of conscience. He stood up. Right-wing populism, the leitmotiv of modern politics, is on the rise. I believe that John would have got off his arse and railed against it. Even at the age of eighty, provided he had been in good health.

We don't see McCartney getting involved in politics, do we? Which flags up a fundamental difference between the two. I reckon John would have been talking to this day about the things that piqued his ire. Would he still be making records? Possibly. Although one has to wonder whether he had run out of steam musically. *Double Fantasy* has a few good tracks on it – 'Watching the Wheels' and 'Woman', for example, while 'Beautiful Boy' is divine – but would the album have been the success it became, had he lived?

Had he not been murdered, would he still be alive?

'Maybe not,' ponders former *Melody Maker* writer and editor Michael Watts. 'And if he were, I think he would have slowed right down, although I'm sure he would have been a public figure in some way. He would have voiced his opinion about important issues. He was so famous and powerful, he and Yoko would have been all over television, making programmes and films, being high-profile on the radio, hosting podcasts, social media. I think he would have secretly hated that kind of role, but I think he would have given in to it. He would have absolved himself from seeming pious about anything. He would have said it all in a funny way. He would have demolished Trump. Newspapers and the media would have rallied around anything he would have had to say about "The Donald". That kind of voice is definitely missing, certainly in the British media, where I think, for example, the *Guardian*, which does report things from a liberal perspective and is anti-populist, certainly anti-right-wing, should be blaring things on the front page – TRUMP IS A CUNT, that kind of thing – rather than couching it in lighter terms. That's what John would have gone for. He wouldn't have held back. He would have served as a rallying point. Who's doing that now? He wouldn't have been a politician, he could never have toed the line. Imagine him in the House of Commons: you can't, can you. I think he would have dwindled as a writing, creative force, but that he would still have had this great potency as a spokesperson. Along with Yoko, yes: they would have been a formidable team. They would have spoken up. That's why we need him.'

Would John and Yoko still be together? Would he have returned to his Lost Weekend companion May Pang, as she and others believe, or might he have found himself a new model, because rock stars do? Would he have given peace a chance with Paul? Would the Beatles, as has been mooted, have reformed to perform at the Live Aid concert in July 1985, after fifteen years apart? Not that far-fetched a notion, is it? Bob Geldof's powers of persuasion were at their peak at the time. The Who did it. Led Zeppelin gave in. McCartney put in an appearance. Why not the greatest band of all time? So what after that? A comeback album? An Abbey Road reunion with master producer George Martin, who was still alive? A go-again world tour – which would no longer have been about the deafening screams of thousands of tweenagers (the primary reason they gave up performing live in August 1966 was because they could no longer hear themselves play, sing or think), but about adult fans listening, *really* listening, and about state-of-the-art technology and stage equipment, which they might actually have enjoyed? More Beatles magical mystery until George Harrison's death in 2001? I would give everything I own.

Would John have ridiculed such ideas? Might he have tried to hijack the Global Jukebox at Wembley Stadium that day, and turn it into a 'JohnandYoko' (as they took to styling themselves) peace rally? Would he have preferred the thought of being cut off in his prime and being preserved at forty, the age at which he will remain for the rest of time? Who knows. One thing's for sure: he would have taken no pleasure in the thought of becoming an exhausted old has-been with no new inspiration to share, nor in busting a gut to come up with still-relevant songs, rehashing the hits and traipsing out endlessly on exhausting last-ever, five-continent outings, rock-rock-rocking until he dropped.

We should go the whole hog. We should ask: who, or what, killed John Lennon – and when did the 'real' John Lennon die? Because the bullets fired by his assassin were only (so to speak) the final nail. *Why* were they? Was John's happy-go-lucky boyhood demeanour extinguished by the death of his mother Julia? Was he so dented by the demise of his Uncle George, who fetched his creativity to life in the first place, and so devastated by the loss of his best friend Stuart Sutcliffe, who died from a brain tumour (John having victimised, ridiculed and punished the pal who worshipped him) that he could no longer see the point of staying alive? Could his guilt over Stu and his inability to forgive himself have been the catalysts for John's tendency to self-sabotage? Having fashioned himself as a leather-clad rocker, what made him relinquish that edition of himself so readily, allowing the gritty band he had founded and honed to be restyled as a mop-shaking cop-out in matching suits? Why did he allow himself to be subsumed by a bubblegum popstar, a Thunderbird-puppet shadow of his real self?

At the height of the Beatles' fame, John jacked it in; rediscovered rock; and reinvented himself as a musical activist and peacenik. But was philanthropy no more than a cynical smokescreen for how little he really cared for mankind? Imagining no possessions while owning cattle herds, fur-coat fridges and multi-million-dollar homes in Manhattan, Long Island and Florida? Do those complex conspiracy theories that have gained traction down the decades hold water? Did John dump self-imposed house-husbandry and childcare after only five years because the traditional woman's-place-in-the-home thing turned out (as he might have guessed had he thought it through, which he probably did) to be a skull-numbing, soul-destroying drag?

*

The story has been written, revised and re-imagined ad nauseam. So relentlessly has John been regurgitated that certain fictions have been elevated to fact, while significant truths have become distorted and irrelevant. There are always details that could do with tweaking or ironing. Did anyone say to Sam Taylor-Wood, now -Johnson, 'You can't make that film *Nowhere Boy* because it's all been done before'? The greatest stories ever told – *Tyrannosaurus Rex*, Tutankhamun, Caesar, Dickens, Shakespeare – can always stand retelling. No less so the greatest rock star.

It's about perspective. Time passes. We wonder, we review.

There's always room for new opinion. There are encyclopaedias, libraries, university degrees, even, dedicated to the study and appreciation of the Beatles and their music, yet still the experts and historians pan for more. Memory, context and tolerance are not static. They never were.

I didn't fancy writing yet another conventional biography of John. This is not that. This is a roam of my own through John's lives, loves and deaths in honour of his big Forty-Eighty. It is a kaleidoscope, a musing, a reflection: who was he, anyway? How did he feel about this and that? It is driven by a desire to comprehend his contradictions; to find out when and why he died. Which is not gratuitous. We already know that there was more than one John, so who or what killed the original? His variations? Who was the John we came to know, and what does he represent in the twenty-first century? What might he come to mean beyond? Is it possible to envisage a time when John Lennon will no longer be listened to, discussed, debated, dissected? When we will grow tired of making pilgrimages to the places he remembered, the people and things that went before, the experiences that shaped his vision? When we can no longer be bothered with the Where It All Began?

There was obviously music, long before Lennon and McCartney collided. If that was the reason, music was always the reason. Few are blessed with the ability to create and express it. All can appreciate and be moved by it. Every life is enhanced by this most universal and accessible of art forms. Even the profoundly deaf feel the rhythms to which every heart beats.

Agonising though this is to articulate, John is now long enough gone and far enough removed to count as an historical figure. The saving grace is a sonic legacy as vital and magnificent as when he created it. I can't imagine a day when his lives, loves and deaths, his songs, his influence on music and musicians and upon billions of ordinary mortals across every earthly expanse, will no longer matter.

Tumbling blindly through broken light, I go looking for him.[6]

*

What is rock'n'roll if not mythology and hyperbole? Open the doors and let them in: the impudent, the aliens, the death-defiers, the plugged-in Peter Pans. The brooding scofflaws, the frozen free-fallers, the risk-takers, the seekers of success against the odds. The most spectacular originators, the most intense individualists, the darkest, boldest, most devil-may-care, eccentric, offbeat, bohemian winners and losers who take, who snatch, it all. Into rock'n'roll and the purveyors of its crafts we project, more than into any other genre of entertainment or category of performer, our most extreme dreams and fiercest fantasies. To millions, rock idols are the ultimate superheroes. They ignite the imagination, and they walk on water. They can obviously fly. But for our lack, we muse, of their plucking, thumping, squawking, scribbling genius, their backbeat, their melodies and harmonies, their ravishing, incendiary sex appeal, we too could have been participants in their frantic dance. We, too, could have been contenders. As if it were ever that simple. Nothing, least of all your oxymoronic average rock star, is ever as it seems.

I have been obsessed with rock stars all my life. I first met David Bowie when I was five, and started door-stepping him when I was eleven. I encountered, on the twinkling footpath that led to his legendary front door, the kind of fairy fellers who would grow into Siouxsie Siouxs, Boy Georges and Billy Idols. I went to the school once attended by Beatles producer George Martin. I studied at the London college that generated Pink Floyd. As a green-gilled sidekick to DJ Roger Scott at London's Capital Radio, I flew to Florida to rendezvous with born-again Dion DiMucci, the fifties/sixties teen idol who'd found his calling singing a cappella on street corners of the Bronx. Roger idolised him: Dion and the Belmonts' first hit 'I Wonder Why' had rendered them pioneers. Dion survived the tour that killed Ritchie Valens and Buddy Holly in 1959, and opened up about it. His solo hits 'Runaround Sue' and 'The Wanderer' were also Roger Scott classics. In New York, we accompanied Billy Joel to the doorstep of 142 Mercer Street, SoHo, where they'd shot the cover image for his rock-heritage tribute album *An Innocent Man*. In New Orleans, we immersed ourselves in the Neville Brothers. Keith Richards introduced Roger to them. The Stones played on their 1987 album *Uptown*. In 1989, they released *Yellow Moon*, which was perhaps the album, especially its track 'Healing Chant', that turned Roger inwards and lifted his soul when oesophageal cancer got the better of him. By this time, he was at BBC Radio 1, prevailing over the Saturday afternoon and late-night Sunday shows. He had packed in the relentless globetrotting and was hoping against hope. He died on 31 October 1989, having shared with me those 'Friend of the Beatles' stories with which he'd wowed America, and having divulged essential detail about the time he met John and Yoko in Canada towards the end of May 1969 and took part, on 1st June, in the recording of 'Give Peace a Chance' during their infamous Bed-In for Peace at Montreal's Queen Elizabeth Hotel.

As a Fleet Street journalist, I interviewed most of the rock stars most people can name. I accompanied many of them on the road. I spent hundreds of hours within touching, talking, breathing-the-same-air distance of A-listers. My exposure to and observations of them clotted into the dawning that there were common characteristics, personality traits, frames of mind and outlooks on life that could not be ignored. Despite the clashing sounds and visions, the myriad songwriting and performance styles, most of them had been cast in the same crucible. They had too much to prove. They were excruciatingly insecure, and craved approval the way the starving would die for a crust. When you delved a little deeper, the source of their art became all too clear. It was, to them, that deafening swell, the terrifying internal tidal wave. The yawning, unfillable chasm of adversity, abuse and/or dysfunction during childhood. Rock stars might be the most tormented, pain-stricken subspecies of all.

I've been studying these guys for years. I say 'guys', but of course as many female artists as male emerge as victims. For every Johnny Cash – who hailed from a background of hardship and abuse, who battled addiction and trauma throughout his early life and became so disturbed that he wrote, in his celebrated song 'Folsom Prison

Blues', about shooting a man in Reno just for the experience of watching him die – there is a Christina Aguilera, who suffered extreme physical and emotional cruelty at the hands of her father, and who turned to music to offset the pain. For every Prince, who survived his parents' split when he was two by cladding himself in contradictions, and who was a bullied epileptic and self-confessed sex addict before finding solace in religion – there is an Adele, who was three when her father dumped her mother. Mark Evans tried to worm his way back when he discovered who his daughter had grown into. Adele was having none of it. For every Jimi Hendrix – born to a single mother and an incarcerated father and raised mostly by family friends, for whom domestic violence and sexual exploitation were routine – there is a Janis Joplin, whose family never understood her, and who was bullied relentlessly throughout school for her weight, her acne and her adoration of black music. 'Pearl' was denounced as a 'pig' and a 'whore'. She and her Southern Comfort bottle were run out of town. Alcohol didn't kill her. Heroin did. For every Eric Clapton – who believed his grandmother Rose was his mother and that his gymslip mother Patricia was his sister until he was nine; was rejected again when Patricia married, moved to Canada, gave birth to further children but failed to send for her firstborn; who, while heroin-addicted, fell in love with the wife of his best friend George Harrison, eventually luring Pattie Boyd to be his bride. The couple could not conceive. The insult to injury was his impregnation of two other women. The greatest tragedy of his life occurred in 1991 when one of his children, four-year-old Connor, fell to his death from an open bedroom window in a Manhattan apartment block – there is a Rihanna, raised on Barbados by a violent, abusive, alcohol-and-crack-cocaine-addicted father, who escaped to the road to stardom at just fifteen. For every Eminem – a baby when he was abandoned by his dad, he was abused by his mother who also betrayed him in a book; despite which, when Debbie Nelson became ill with cancer, her son paid all her medical bills – there is an Amy Winehouse, who could never come to terms with the father she worshipped having dumped the mother she idolised for another woman. Amy sought refuge in self-harm, drugs and drink until she expired. For every Michael Jackson – accused of the molestation of minors, having endured abuse himself – there is a Sinéad O'Connor, who claimed that she was sexually violated by her 'possessed' late mother in a home torture chamber, who was forced to repeat over and over, 'I am nothing', and who has since suffered mental breakdown.

Richard Starkey was born to an often absent, drunken father and an overbearing mother, spent a year recovering from an appendectomy and, on the threshold of adulthood, was virtually illiterate and innumerate. He found his salvation in music, and fame and fortune as Ringo Starr. Paul McCartney and his younger brother Michael became motherless boys when midwife and health visitor Mary died aged forty-seven in October 1956.

You see. Rock stardom, in endlessly celebrated and lesser-known cases, has been an antidote to adversity since the beginning.

*

There is no single truth. There are no facts, and there are millions of facts. A contradiction? He was. Many aspects of his life remain open to interpretation. Theory, rumour, supposition and wishful thinking play their part. As does John himself. Barely a pithy comment, spiteful aside or pensive utterance leaked from his lips that he did not counter or revise down the line. No thought in his head was set in stone. There is no finished, definitive version of him. Reinventing himself constantly, often subconsciously, he tried on endless Johns for size. The phrase 'all things to all people' falls short, but that was John. Solipsistic, obdurate and frustrated by the circumstances of his early life – abandoned by his father and surrendered by his mother into the care of a severe aunt and mercifully mellow uncle, who expired prematurely – his outlet for emotion and frustration was the written word. Sex, rock'n'roll and then drugs soon seized control of him. His mother died violently when he was seventeen. Never would she get to witness or puff with pride over her child's effect on the whole world. Never would he overcome the loss of her. He felt cheated and deprived for life. Nothing could comfort nor compensate. He married too young, fathered his first child before he himself reached maturity, and too soon into his twenties was juggling global fame and fantastic fortune with run-of-the-mill familial responsibility ... with calamitous results. It was all, he must have said, too much. His saving grace was finding true love. For what a vast, simple, complex, propinquitous union his and Yoko's turned out to be. An uplifting, agonising, death-defying love from the Romeo and Juliet, Antony and Cleopatra, Venus and Adonis mould. A pair of soulmates re-emerging as one, just the two of them against a judgemental world, confounding critics and cynics as they went; confirming, to those of us desperate to believe it, that the One True Love thing exists. For what did John live for, in the end? Just for Yoko, and for their son Sean. This was to Julian Lennon's everlasting devastation.

The world turns. Decades accelerate. Is John now reduced to words and melodies, albeit those of songs embedded in our DNA, which we will never cease to play? He is not, nor will he ever be. The self-loving, self-loathing, self-discovering John, who belonged to the planet but who existed mostly within his own mind, is among us.

CHAPTER 1

COME TOGETHER

Historians can be inclined to hasten their readers through a subject's formative years, to rush to the point at which the 'interesting stuff' begins. Yet what could be more fascinating than the circumstances of birth, the challenges of childhood, the rough-cut squares of a patchy quilt that somehow expand and self-embroider into the character we seek to know? Even more so, the odysseys of their forebears?

For all the fierce, influential, indomitable men in John's life, it was women, for better, for worse, who dominated it. Paddle the shallows of his ancestry to find females on both sides of the family tree of great courage and resilience. Women who survived famine, estrangement from family, the hardship and upheaval of relocation, the tragedy of war; who were perennially pregnant, who bore a dozen or more babies; who died desperately in childbirth; who, broken by destitution and widowhood, relinquished care of infants to charitable institutions rather than watch their offspring starve.

While women were to rule John's life, to varying degrees and with conflicting consequences, there were no distinguished female forebears in either line. How far back do you want to take it, is the thing. Some biographers have trawled the DNA in an attempt to fish out beguiling ancestors whose own achievements might shed light on the origins of John's personality and talent. Eagerness to discover that genius is in the genes may have been what breathed life and colour into the notion that John Lennon's paternal great-grandfather James, described as a ship's cook and sometime singer, emigrated from Liverpool to America; and that James's son John, also known as Jack (John's grandfather), found quasi-fame stateside during the late nineteenth century as a pre-civil-rights, pre-abolition of slavery blackface minstrel. Robertson's Kentucky Minstrels was the troupe with which he is claimed to have toured, before about-turning to the land of his father's birth and settling on Merseyside, where his American first wife would die in childbirth. How enthralling if all that were true. Alas, birth certificates and the censuses of 1861, 1871 and 1901 indicate otherwise. Lennon lore, like that of any other family, had long danced the length of fantasy beaches. Fable can prove tough to contradict. Rumour and supposition are seductive. There are still those inclined to believe shimmering legend, despite the unequivocality of fact.

What is certain is that John's paternal great-grandparents James Lennon and Jane McConville were not born in Liverpool but in County Down, Ulster, in the north of Ireland, and that they crossed the Irish Sea with their families during the Famine Years of 1845 to 1849 at a time when Ireland was still part of Britain (it remained so until 1922). James, a cooper and warehouseman, married Jane in Liverpool in 1849 when he was around twenty years of age. His bride was only eighteen. They were blessed with eight or more children before Jane died in childbirth. Their son John, known as Jack, was born in 1855, and was our John Lennon's grandfather. Jack became a shipping clerk and bookkeeper, and was a bit of a fly-by-night. He was a popular pub customer, and often sang for his beer. He married Liverpool lass Margaret Cowley when he was thirty-three, and fathered four offspring, only one of whom, a daughter named Mary Elizabeth, survived. Her mother died during delivery of her sister, also named Margaret. Widowed Catholic Jack was soon 'living in sin' with Protestant Mary Maguire, an illiterate apparent psychic known as Polly. They produced fourteen or fifteen children (records vary), eight of whom they lost, and were at last married in 1915, three years after the arrival of their son Alfred, John's father. Jack died in 1921, from cirrhosis of the liver, when his little boy was eight (or nine) years old and afflicted with rickets: a childhood disease brought on by deficiency in vitamin D, causing the bones to soften and the legs to bow. Alf's own were for years encased in irons, which inhibited normal growth. Polly was too poor to support her family alone, and was forced to surrender Alf and his sister Edith to the city's strictly Protestant Blue Coat School Orphanage. Alf emerged the best-educated of any previous Lennon, and soon found gainful employment in a Liverpool shipping company.

On his mother's side, John's ancestors can be foot-stepped back to Wales. The blend of Irish and Welsh gifted him strong ancestry, the two Celtic nations and cultures meeting in the middle and commonly sharing significant characteristics of vivid imagination, sporadic gloominess, stubbornness, passion and ready friendliness.

John's obscure Welsh roots are now known. His great-grandfather John Milward (sometimes Millward) was the son of Thomas Milward, head gardener to Sir John Hay Williams, High Sheriff of Flintshire. This John was born in the stately surroundings of Dolben Hall in the mid-1830s, while his father was employed there. Milward Junior became, in his teens, apprenticed as a solicitor's clerk to the Williams family. During his early twenties, a terrible hunting accident necessitated amputation of his left arm. His recuperation in a guest house at Rhyl led to him into the embrace of twenty-year-old Mary Elizabeth Morris of Berth y Glyd, Llysfaen, near Colwyn Bay on the north Wales coast. Mary had recently been banished from the family farm after having fallen pregnant by a neighbour and having produced an illegitimate child. When she and her new lover conceived, they were anxious to dampen additional scandal and escaped to England. John Lennon's maternal grandmother Annie Jane, a future tailoress, was born in rented lodgings at the Bear and Billet Inn in Chester in 1871. The family moved to Liverpool soon afterwards, where mother Mary evolved into a fierce matriarch and refused to speak in any tongue but Welsh. The relationship collapsed. John died destitute and alone in his mid-fifties, while Mary lived into her eighties, until 1932.

Through Mary's line, it is suggested that John's great-great-great-grandfather was the Reverend Richard Farrington of Llanwnda, Caernarvonshire, the esteemed author of books on Welsh antiquities. Through him, John's ancestry may be traceable to Owain ap Hugh, an Elizabethan High Sheriff of Anglesey; and through him, several generations back, to Tudor ap Gruffud, brother of Owain Glyndŵr. The last native Prince of Wales during the fifteenth century, Glyndŵr was immortalised by Shakespeare in *King Henry IV Part I*. Which would make the Welsh national hero John's ancestral uncle. Thus is John reckoned to be a direct descendant of Llywelyn the Great, who ruled Wales during the thirteenth century; also, via Llewelyn's wife Joan, a descendant of kings John of England, Malcolm of Scotland, William the Conqueror and Alfred the Great. What would John have made of such grandeur, were it proved beyond doubt to be true?

John's maternal great-grandfather William Stanley was born in Birmingham in 1846. He had moved to Liverpool by his early twenties, where he met and married his northern Irish wife Eliza. The couple resided in Everton, north Liverpool. Their third son, George Ernest Stanley, who arrived in 1874, would become John's maternal grandfather. George grew up to be a merchant seaman, working years away at sea, and was also a sailmaker for tall ships and other ocean-going vessels. He subsequently worked for the London, Liverpool and Glasgow Tug Salvage Company, which carried out local marine salvage work. He met the aforementioned Annie Jane Milward during the late 1890s. The couple did not marry before starting a family. Despite conflicting accounts, John's half-sister Julia Baird maintains that their first- and second-born children, Henry and Charlotte, died soon after birth, and that their remains are interred at Liverpool's Anglican Cathedral. Their third was Mary Elizabeth, who was destined to become John's fabled Aunt Mimi, the woman who would raise him instead of his mother and who really had a hold on him. One living child born out of wedlock was evidently enough for George and Annie, who married towards the end of 1906 and went on to produce four more daughters who would call their father 'Dada', later nicknaming him 'Pop'. The fourth-born of the five redoubtable Stanley sisters was John's mother Julia, who arrived in Toxteth, south Liverpool, on 12 March 1914, along with the Great War.

If you know about her, who do you want her to be? Are you inclined towards Jezebel Julia, the tart-with-a-heart? A flibbertigibbet, an unvirtuous chit who acquired ideas above her station and pocket as the result of having overdosed on the Hollywood surreality that flickered her senseless from the screen at the Trocadero picture house where she worked as an usherette; who was sharp of cheek and of tongue, voluptuous of figure, pert in her trolley-dolly uniform and pillbox hat, and so vain that she'd go to bed in make-up; who, in her frillies and fragrant curls, frequented Liverpool's clubs and dancehalls to cavort with sailors, soldiers, dockers and waiters, giving the chaps what-for and holding her own with a brazen laugh; who could be casual with her favours; who gave birth to and gave away children with nary a care? Or is misunderstood, much-maligned Julia Lennon née Stanley your preference? Parking the fantasies along with the hundreds of thousands of words previously penned, spoken and presumed about her, can you concede, as I have to, that real-life Julia hovered between extremes like everyone else? That she was neither sinner nor saint? That she was nowhere near as devilish as she's been daubed? John's own journey begins with hers, in the city of their births. John idolised her, bled to her, castigated and longed for her in such wrenching songs as 'Mother' and 'Julia'.

Liverpool was by no means the only thing that mother and son had in common. Both had the Celtic light reddish-brown hair (though dissimilar eyes; Julia's were baby-blue, while John's were pale brown). Both were born on the brink of and lived through world wars. Both were musically gifted misfits, mavericks, daredevils and crowd-pleasers, the life and soul but essentially lonely people. Each married to the dismay and disdain of their families. Each would, in blatant, heartbreaking ways, become the other's muse. Each died violently at the hands of others, in their forties, leaving devastation and fall-out that would never heal.

Liverpool in 1914 was still a proud, prosperous, formidable city, a place of impressive architecture and phenomenal achievement. It was the birthplace of Cunard, founded in 1839, which spearheaded the oceanic revolution. By 1870, it has been claimed, every Liverpudlian either worked for that great shipping company, or knew a man who did. The city boasted a population which, thanks to the agricultural and industrial revolutions having mobilised the masses, had swelled from less than a hundred thousand a century earlier to more than eight times that number come the 1920s. Tobacco from Virginia and sugar from the West Indies were supreme among its imports. The industries developed to process those commodities were huge. Brewing, banking and insurance generated fortunes – as did the Atlantic slave trade. At the other end of the scale, thousands toiled as navvies, in manufacturing in the factories and mills, and laboured precariously in sprawling shipyards. The upper-working and lower-middle classes tended to be engaged in commerce, as managers, clerks and office staff. Skilled tailors, dressmakers, furriers and milliners served the sartorial needs of the moneyed elite. Gentlefolk of the North were as finely dressed as their counterparts in the capital. Although many working-class women were employed in schools, shops, factories and garment-making establishments, they tended to be on the single side. Huge numbers of humbler females slaved as servants – housemaids, cleaners, cooks and child-carers – in prosperous mercantile households. Many married and widowed women took in laundry at home to stave off starvation. Away from the dazzling facades of gigantic edifices, out of sniffing range of the prevailing air of affluence, the brickwork of the common man was soot-blackened, the atmosphere thick with the stench of coal smoke and excrement equine and human. Life limped to the clip along cobbles of hobnail boots under ankle-grazing hems, to the rumble and slip of horse-drawn carts. Deep in the slums, colonised by the forsaken, lay a Hades of deprivation and poverty.

Britannia no longer ruled the waves. Britain under King George V had ceased to be the world's foremost industrial power. Foreign competition was increasing. The status of Liverpool, formerly the maritime heart of a victorious nation with a superiority complex, was boosted by the Great War. With its miles of docks along the Mersey, its strategic position as a deep-water port just under 3,500 direct nautical miles across the Atlantic from New York, and its gateway-to-Europe location, Liverpool was in pole position during the Allied effort against the Germans. Essential cargo, food, fuel and manufacturing supplies, troops, medical staff, prisoners of war and refugees torrented her waterfront.

The city's young men leaped to enlist. More than twelve thousand Liverpudlian males signed up for the fight at sea. Three thousand more heeded Lord Kitchener's battle cry, and presented for the army. Nearly a million women manned the munition factories, ran public transport, police stations, Government departments and post offices, and swept the cobbled streets in their long, grimy skirts. Come 1918, some women had won the right to vote. But, by 1923, there were still only eight female members of Parliament, while women over the age of twenty-one would not become eligible to vote until 1928. Meanwhile, social change swelled in Liverpool during the 1920s. The workers were empowered, having sacrificed and suffered so much during the war. Social change was not so much sought as demanded. The provision of council housing commenced on an unprecedented scale. While the country would have to wait until 1948 for the Welfare State, the hopes and expectations of Liverpool's underclasses soared.

Julia would have had no detailed memories of her war-torn toddler years. The baby of the family to big sisters Mary Elizabeth (later Mimi), Elizabeth Jane (dubbed Betty, or Liz, and eventually referred to in the family as Mater) and Anne Georgina (Anne among the sisters, but who would come to be known as Nanny), she was doted upon. Dada played the banjo, and taught his fourth-born. Julia was soon strumming confidently by ear, and singing along to herself. She would also come to master the ukulele and the piano accordion. By the time the fifth Stanley sister, Harriet (Harrie) arrived, Julia had blossomed into the precocious 'pretty one' with a streak of black sheep. Tongues tutted. Blind eyes were turned. She was also 'the musical one'. For that, as well as for her effervescent personality, she was indulged. No academic, she left school in 1929 at fifteen with dim prospects. She happened upon Alf Lennon in the city's Sefton Park, near the lake. Banter ensued. If it wasn't love at first sight, it was an intro.

But Alf had heeded the siren call. The nautical wilderness beckoned. The youngster quit land for a life on the ocean wave, signing up as a merchant seaman and setting off in search of the world. Known variously as Freddie and Lennie, he took to the job and to its irresistible perks, the lucrative trading of contraband his favourite. Promotions danced his way. This wet-eared bellboy clambered the rungs to senior steward, pledging allegiance to the bottle and lurching his passage from scrape to scrape. Like his sweetheart, to whom he'd pen long, romantic letters that were never answered, he too was musical. Alf carried a harmonica in his pocket and a song in his heart. Julia was hardly smitten. She couldn't care less. Well aware that her family considered the Lennon boy to be beneath her, Julia – stunning, wilful, captivating Julia – kept her options open and her heart inside her sleeve. She would flirt wherever and with whomever she chose. It seems far-fetched that either could have remained faithful to the other during Alf's elasticated absences. Perhaps he kept a girl in every port, that old seadog ruse. Perhaps Julia succumbed to a few of the many slavering suitors reluctant to take no for an answer. Perhaps she taunted Alfie baby with a proposal of her own, as has been floated, or maybe he did do the proposing in the end, Julia having ridiculed her diminutive beau that he would never in a million be man enough. Whatever the truth underpinning the his-and-hers, the couple were married on 3 December 1938, at Bolton Street Register Office, some eleven years after they'd first met. Julia was twenty-four years old. No family

member from either side having been alerted, none was present.
They spent their honeymoon in a cinema and their wedding night
apart – she in the family abode, he back at digs – as if bracing
themselves for the wrath of the clan. The next day, Alf bolted back
to sea. He spent three months sailing to and from the West Indies.

*

With the exception of London, no British city was bombed more
than Liverpool. It was targeted because of its status as our largest
west-coast port, into which vital food supplies and other cargo were
delivered. To annihilate the supply route would have guaranteed
Britain's defeat. The German Luftwaffe made some eighty air raids
on Merseyside between August 1940 and January 1942. The raids
peaked in a seven-night blitz during May 1941. While the docks,
factories and railways were primary targets, vast sections either side
of the river Mersey were also devastated or destroyed. From the
airfields of conquered countries including France, Belgium, Holland
and Norway, German bombers took off for Liverpool, augmenting
their campaign with treacherous night raids. On 28 August 1940,
when Julia Lennon was six months pregnant with John, a hundred
and sixty bombers dumped on Merseyside. During the Christmas
Blitz that year, the city suffered its heaviest assaults. For the first six
months of John's life, the air raids banged on relentlessly. Come the
end of April 1941, greater Liverpool had sustained more than sixty
raids. Docks were damaged, and ships had been sunk. Corporate
buildings including the famous Cotton Exchange, Customs House
and Rotunda Theatre, hospitals, churches, schools and houses were
flattened. Roads, tramlines and railways were ruined. By 1942,
around four thousand people had been killed, thousands more
seriously injured. Much of the damage would take years to restore.

Despite the compulsory call-up of able-bodied men between the
ages of eighteen and forty-one, Alf Lennon, then twenty-six, was
excused from duty, having been deemed to be in reserved occupation
at sea. Julia's parents, Pop and Mama, together with daughters
Mimi, Anne and Julia, had retreated from the inner city and were

renting in the Penny Lane suburb of Wavertree at 9, Newcastle Road. When Alf's ship docked, he made a beeline for his wife, and would later claim that they conceived John on the kitchen floor of the Stanleys' terraced house. Can even the most experienced obstetrician-gynaecologist pinpoint the moment of conception with such accuracy? Off again Alf legged it, onto a ship now deployed in the protection of the North Atlantic's trade route, not knowing whether he would see his beloved again.

While his doting Aunt Mimi could have sworn blind that John was born during an air raid, it didn't happen. All was calm as Julia brought forth her firstborn and only son, at the Liverpool Maternity Hospital on Oxford Street – which is student accommodation today, and which still bears the scars of flying shrapnel along with the commemorative plaque declaring it to be John Winston Lennon's birthplace. To visit that building is a haunting experience. The memory of it left me unsettled for days, while many return trips to the Strawberry Fields memorial in Central Park have barely moved me. Ever been? Go and see.

Soon afterwards, patriotic Julia, who had flown the flag in her choice of middle name for him, carried her baby home to Newcastle Road.[1] Mimi, at long last married to the suffering suitor who had all but given up on her, was now Mrs George Smith. Her new husband was a local dairy farmer with an inherited cottage a couple of miles away in Woolton to which Julia and her child, and on occasion Alf, would sometimes escape. John was more than two before he knew his father. Julia had not exactly sat at home, nights, during her spouse's long absences, and had instead lived it up and down, round and about in the company of servicemen, with all the abandon of any war-zone good-time gal worth her sass. Not that Alf had been an angel: he'd compounded the fracture of desertion from one ship with getting himself arrested for having dipped his digits into the cargo on another, and was sentenced to detention in Algeria. Julia, accustomed to collecting a portion of his pay along with the rambling letters home, now found there was nothing for her at the Mercantile Marine Office. With no word from Alf, and with no idea of what might have become of him, she must have assumed that he'd callously deserted her and their newborn. She about-turned accordingly. Obliged to earn a crust, she bagged a barmaid's gig at a local tavern. It was there that she met a Welsh soldier whose name has never been more specific than 'Taffy Williams'. When Alf knocked on the door a year and a half later, it was to find his wife apparently pregnant with Taffy's child. A to-do ensued, of which John would have adult recollection. Julia changed her story to insist that she had been raped by an anonymous soldier. It's possible she didn't know who the father was. Williams dismissed out of hand the idea that it could be anyone's but his, and would have taken on mother and baby willingly. He killed his chances with Julia by demanding that she let her little boy go. Julia refused to abandon John, and that was the end of the Welshman. Alf pleaded with Julia to allow him to assume paternity of her unborn, and for the four of them to become a family. Julia turned him down. It seems reasonable to assume that her upright parents and mighty sisters, fearing social embarrassment, what'll the neighbours say, must also have felt anxious for the welfare and happiness of their adored little grandson and nephew.

Alf was not about to give up on his son. How he was able to talk John out of the Stanley fortress and off to his brother Syd's place in Maghull begs questions. What made Julia allow him to whisk their son away for several weeks, and later for months on the trot, to stay with Syd, his wife and daughter several miles north of Liverpool? Maybe depression played a part. Syd's wife Madge enquired into having John enrolled at their local school. So devoted to their nephew did these Lennons become that they seem to have dared hope for legal guardianship of him. Where were his parents? Syd and Madge saw neither hide nor hair of Julia for the duration. When the wayward Alf rocked up without warning during the spring of 1945, informing them that he'd come for his boy, the little family was left heartbroken.

Julia Lennon gave birth to her second-born on 19 June 1945, in Elmswood Infirmary, a local Salvation Army maternity home.

Under pressure from her family, who deplored her wanton behaviour and resisted the heaping of shame on the Stanleys' good name, she was coerced into agreeing to adoption. Her baby girl, whom she named Victoria Elizabeth Lennon, was yielded to a local couple, Peder and Margaret Pedersen, the husband being of Norwegian birth. The Pedersens changed their new daughter's identity to Lillian Ingrid Maria, and raised her in Crosby, mere miles from where Julia continued to live. But Ingrid, as she was known, never met her real parents, nor her half-brother John. Not until she decided to marry and needed her birth certificate would she discover her true identity. Ingrid was shocked and stunned, but resolute. She felt uneasy about reaching out to her birth family while her adoptive mother was still alive. When Margaret Pedersen died in 1998, Ingrid came out. At one point, she seems to have believed that she was her adoptive father's biological daughter, sailor Peder having allegedly had a liaison with Julia. No paternal name appeared on Victoria Lennon's birth certificate.

CHAPTER 2

FORSAKEN

D id Julia Lennon contribute to the war effort? She was not, as far as we know, ever called up. Which seems surprising, as most sane, able-bodied women during the forties were. From the spring of 1941, every British female aged eighteen to sixty had to be registered and interviewed, and the majority were asked to choose from a range of jobs. Motherhood was no guarantee of exemption. Women were expected and required to do both. The National Service Act of December 1941 legalised their conscription. Although only single females aged between twenty and thirty were recruited at first, by 1943 nearly ninety per cent of single women and eighty per cent of wives were active in the cause, working in factories, as land girls or in the armed forces. These included the WRNS: Women's Royal Naval Service; the WAAF: Women's Auxiliary Air Force; the ATS: Auxiliary Territorial Service; and the Special Operations Executive. Thousands drove ambulances, piloted unarmed planes, worked as nurses and served behind enemy lines. Even HRH Princess Elizabeth, the future Queen Elizabeth II, was serving in the ATS in 1945, when she was only nineteen. Having trained as a driver and mechanic, the princess progressed to the rank of Junior Commander. Prime Minister Winston Churchill's youngest daughter, Mary, destined to become Lady Soames, served too.

Eighty thousand joined the Women's Land Army to cultivate

and harvest food. The Women's Voluntary Service (WVS) was a force to be reckoned with in cities, especially the capital, where they manned the shelters in the London Underground, brewing millions of cups of tea. Former stay-at-home mums now donned siren suits and rolled up their sleeves along with their locks to toil in factories, making vehicles, aircraft, chemicals and munitions. They laboured in shipyards, on the railways, on the canals and buses. Three hundred and fifty women built London's Waterloo Bridge, dubbed the 'Ladies' Bridge', although this fact was not officially recognised for more than half a century. Nearly twenty-five thousand women were employed in the British construction industry by 1944, but were paid significantly less than men doing the same job!

If Julia managed to avoid the production line and the shipyard, did she sign up to the wartime 'Make Do and Mend' and 'Sew and Save' schemes? Although knitting became the national female obsession during the war, it is hard to imagine a glamorous barmaid at it behind the pumps of the local pub.

I think about Julia. She has preoccupied me for years. John was haunted by her memory, which makes her fascinating. I have, on the top shelf of my mind, an image of her as a Rita Hayworth-style[1] femme fatale in a petticoat at a dressing table, powdering her nose, slicking her lips red, applying scent; titivating ahead of another night of defiant fun. Justifying herself to her reflection with the excuse that in wartime, anything goes. The usual social mores and rules no longer applied. Existing as though the sword of Damocles were dangling over their heads, with the real threat of being bombed off the face of the earth at any moment, who could blame people for letting rip and throwing caution to the wind? Cases of venereal disease rose dramatically throughout the land, as did pregnancy rates. Abortion had yet to be legalised, and would remain a criminal act until 1967. Which didn't deter some desperate women from resorting to home remedies. Scalding baths, gin, knitting needles, knives, curling irons and squatting over a boiling pot of steam were all health- if not life-threatening, as were the barbaric practices of backstreet abortionists.[2] Although the having of illegitimate children was still socially unacceptable (and would remain so for decades to come), there was a huge increase in the number of children born to single mothers. Sex education developed as a result. For Julia and her ilk, the nag had bolted.

Mama, the adored Stanley matriarch, was dead. Pop would linger longer, until 1949. Little John is said to have shared a bond with his stern Victorian grandfather, the pair often jaunting around the docks or 'down the prom',[3] where they'd peer across the Mersey and pick out buildings on the other side. Aunt Mimi, a former trainee nurse at Woolton Convalescent Hospital (who had met her sweetheart George there, when he came delivering the milk), was the eldest sister who had always looked out for her siblings and their offspring; who made everybody's business her own and who was all too often at odds with her father. Mimi took it upon herself to observe proceedings with a beady eye. She was no doubt fearful of the impact on John of his mother's lifestyle. She was clearly determined to see to it that matters would be dealt with 'in the best interests of the child'.

What does it mean, really, that indeterminate, sinister phrase? Boiled down, it propounds the obvious: that when the mother of a small child takes a new boyfriend, flaunts her affections for him and lavishes attention on him instead of on her infant, the latter is bound to suffer. If the boyfriend is dismissive of the child – or, worse, is mean to him – the mother's blatant preference for her lover constitutes neglect and abuse of her kid. Julia would not have seen it that way. Such issues were rarely discussed openly in those days. In these more enlightened times, we have the advantage of extensive scientific research into childhood welfare. The Adverse Childhood Experiences or ACE Study, established during the 1980s, was one of the largest and most comprehensive investigations ever to assess the association between childhood maltreatment and an individual's health and well-being in later life.[4] It was instigated by Dr Vincent Felliti of the Kaiser Permanente Health Appraisal Clinic in San Diego, USA, and was replicated internationally. Its findings were devastating. We are now all too aware of the factors that threaten children's fundamental sense of themselves, as well as their healthy development. Young children experience the world through their relationships with their parents and carers. In a nurturing environment, they thrive emotionally and physically. The elements essential to positive child-rearing are basic: safety, stability, consistency; routine, continuity, discipline. The X-factor is affection. Let's call it 'love'. A child must not be pulled from pillar to post, nor caught in the crossfire between warring parents. He must not be used as a pawn. He must never, under any circumstances, be asked to choose between his mother and father. We know now that trauma in childhood often leads to depression and other mental illnesses in adulthood, as well as to disease. How so? Because stress is toxic. Extensive exposure to stress hormones inhibits the developing brain and compromises the connections of brain circuits, which are still vulnerable and still developing during early childhood. The immune system becomes suppressed, leaving the child prone to infection and chronic health problems. Stress hormones can also damage the part of the brain responsible for memory and learning, leading to deficits that can harm the individual for life.

Mimi Smith would have known little to nothing of all this. Which is to say, she may not have had the vocabulary or medical knowledge to help her articulate her fears, but she was shrewd. She had instinct. Her sense of right and wrong was acutely attuned. She may have been a bit too Hyacinth Bucket[5] for most, placing excessive importance on what other people thought. She could be prickly and judgemental. She was dutiful and proper, at least. She could see with her own eyes that her sister Julia was behaving selfishly, and that she was putting her own needs before John's. No one is suggesting that Julia did not love her son. By all accounts, she doted on and even worshipped him. But as a parent, she was disorganised. Her inclination was not to put him first. Mimi's gut told her that John was in need of better mothering. Although she had always insisted that she never wanted children of her own, her ego convinced her that she was the one to provide it. Thus did she set about 'getting John', and absorbing him into her own comfortable, well-ordered household. She and her husband George would bring him up quietly and respectably, would cherish him as their own, and would raise a fine boy of whom the entire family could be proud.

The Allies toasted Nazi Germany's surrender on 8 May 1945. Revellers tidal-waved the Mall all the way to Buckingham Palace to cheer King George VI, Queen Elizabeth and their daughters, princesses Elizabeth and Margaret. Rations had been saved, and street parties were thrown all over this land. Picture the jam-chinned, knee-scraped John in short trousers and a home-knit jumper among dozens of other children at tables laid end to end down the middle of the road, beaming beneath the bunting and the Union Flags as he piled into sandwiches, fairy cakes and jelly. Just four-and-a-half at the time, he later claimed no particular memories of VE Day. There were places he'd remember, but that was not one of them.

Julia having switched jobs, she took a shine to a patron of the pub in which she now served. John Dykins was a swarthy, brown-eyed, trilby-hatted door-to-door salesman. A local spiv who had avoided war duty on account of a respiratory condition. He was now flashing his cash across the bar to impress the pretty young barmaid. Julia's family disapproved, but what did she care? She called her new fancy man 'Bobby', perhaps to allow her child his name to himself.

In November 1945, a month after his fifth birthday, John started at Mosspits Lane Primary School. From the calling of the first register he was a fish out of water. He could already write, read, paint and draw, take care of his personal needs, think for himself, had an enquiring mind, and seemed streets ahead of his classmates. From the outset, he needed more than the standard state education was able to give him. Or, he needed less of it, but creative stimulation of another kind. It's possible that Julia didn't even notice. She would walk John to and from school, then work the lunchtime shift at the pub until it was time to pick him up. Within five months, she was moving out of Pop's place to set up home with Bobby ... in a tiny Gateacre flat in which she, her boyfriend and son would sleep together in one double bed, and where John would be well aware of what they got up to. Mimi, naturally, was outraged. She marched right round to give the living-in-sinners a piece of her mind. When Bobby showed her the door, Mimi flounced off to Liverpool City Council to report them to the relevant social services department. She clearly shot from the hip without stopping to consider the consequences of betraying her own sister. The public assistance people got the picture, and accompanied her back to the soidisant den of iniquity. Mimi was promptly awarded temporary care of John, pending further enquiry that probably never progressed. With what joy must she have collected his things, grabbed his little hand and marched him back to Mendips, her Woolton home at 251 Menlove Avenue. Where John would never have to share a bedroom, never mind a bed.

But what of cuckolded Alf, John's father, who by this time had been Julia's husband for seven years? Returning from sea on leave to find that his son was now living under the roof of his sharp sister-in-law and her amenable husband, he was round there in no time. He must have been confused by the revelation that Mimi had already removed John from Mosspits Lane and transferred him to Dovedale Road Infants'. He promised to return the next day, and did so, asking to take John out shopping. He did no such thing. Instead, he escorted his little boy to Liverpool Lime Street station, where they boarded a train to Blackpool and went to call on fellow merchant seaman Billy Hall. Despite oft-repeated accounts of the horror story that happened next, the truth is less melodramatic. Alf is said to have been planning to emigrate to New Zealand with his son, who would be sent ahead in the care of Billy's parents; Julia tore to Blackpool[6] to demand the return of her child; John was then forced to choose between his parents, at first opting to stay with Alf, but then suffering second thoughts and stumbling desperately down the road to cling to his mother. Or did he? Accounts conflict. Billy Hall has contradicted the drama. He remembered Julia arriving at the Hall abode with Bobby Dykins; a civilised summit being held in his mother's front parlour; and Alf emerging satisfied that the right decision had been made – which was that John would return to Liverpool to live with Julia.[7]

Which was all very well. But the way things panned out after that fateful day in June 1946 was far from ideal. Alf drowned his sorrows in the local boozers, returned to life on the ocean wave, and would not see his son again for twenty years … by which time, the Beatles had conquered the world and John had become an international superstar. As for Julia, she'd made her bed, and she would keep on lying on it. Besides, she was once again up the duff. Julia and Dykins moved in with Pop, to share the household bills and look after the ailing old man. Back John went to Mendips, into the care of Aunt Mimi and Uncle George. And that was that. From the age of five, despite the fact that Julia would continue to reside within walking distance, John would never again live with his mum or dad.

At forty and forty-three years of age, respectively – with their house named after a range of hills in south-west England, their leaded stained glass, their cardis, their musty, decent ways, their mongrel Sally and their Siamese cats – Mimi and George must have seemed more like surrogate grandparents than parents. The dairy business and land which had been in George's family for generations had been commandeered by the British government. George had been called up, was discharged from the army after three years, and had worked in a Speke aircraft factory until the end of the war. At one point he worked nights at Woolton Depot, cleaning buses and trams – in those days, where grass grows now, trams still ran the length of Menlove Avenue. George must have lamented the fading of prosperity and vanished prospect of easy retirement. Still, ends were made to meet. Frugality ruled. Rationing had not yet been lifted (and would not end completely until 1954). Mimi did all her own cooking, cleaning and laundry, but the air of gentlefolks' residence was maintained. Though the old servants' bells had long been disabled, the mouse-swing cubby hole off the kitchen where breakfast was served was still referred to pretentiously as 'the morning room'. Precious porcelain plates, freshly dusted, were proudly on display. Appearances were kept up, even indoors. In spite of which, the family had so little money that they would eventually be obliged to take in student lodgers.

John must have found the change of environment overwhelming. How did he cope? At five, he was still learning to manage his emotions; still acquiring self-control and still vulnerable to outbursts over minor mishaps, which Mimi would never tolerate. At five, he was still wrestling with the complications of dressing himself, of getting his fingers around buttons and trying to tie his shoelaces. He was still getting to grips with his toothbrush and fretting at the fall of each baby tooth. Did Mimi lavish him with the things he needed most – love, attention and approval – or was she more often than not reproachful and remote? Did she expect more of John than he was yet capable of? It seems so. Mimi was all about table manners and rigidly observed bedtimes; about speaking when spoken to; about enunciation and articulation: she would not be shown up by John yapping like a Scouser[8]. She also saw to it that he attended Sunday School at St Peter's Church, Woolton every week, where he briefly sang in the choir. What was a smarting little boy to make of all this? How was he supposed to process the fact that his mummy didn't need him anymore, because she had a new boyfriend? Why did his daddy let her fetch him from that man's house, only to take him back to his auntie's and leave him there forever? The thought of him lying there alone, pyjama'd and candlewicked in his narrow single bed in the narrow single box room over the forbidding front-door porch (the porch that is there now was added in 1952) wondering what he'd done to make Mummy and Daddy not like him anymore and decide to give him away, is heart-wrenching. If John became withdrawn, was easily distracted and started blurring the lines between reality and make-believe, is it any surprise?

Thank goodness for his uncle. Tall, grey-haired, pipe-smoking George was a kind, patient, fun-loving man who had done his share of long-suffering; who yes-deared his better half; who became John's most loyal ally during those confusing years when he wasn't exactly sure where he belonged. Tired out from school, sullen and niggly, scolded by Mimi to set the table and put his clothes away, John couldn't help but giggle at Uncle George pulling faces at him behind her back to ridicule the missus and lighten the mood. It was with George that John played ball games in the neat back garden with its apple trees, coal bunker and lawn roller, even though he had no interest in nor aptitude for sport; with George's help and encouragement that he learned to ride a bicycle; thanks especially to George that he became obsessed with books. Mimi and her husband were voracious readers. There were many volumes of all genres around the house. John's particular childhood favourites were the *Alice in Wonderland* and *Just William* tales, and *The Wind in the Willows*.[9] George also introduced him to newspapers, which aided his sketching, cartooning and storytelling, and taught him how to do the crossword. It could be entirely down to George that John learned, at a precociously young age, to harness the power of his imagination.

None of which is to denigrate Mimi's efforts to give her nephew the best possible start in life. For whatever else has been said about his aunt, she cared about John and she meant well. She assumed the role of mother, but would not be his 'Mummy': he already had one of those. She would accompany John to and from school, made clear that she would always be there for him, and did not leave him to go out gadding of an evening. Over her dead body would John become a latchkey kid. Things could so easily have gone the other way, had he remained under the casual care of Julia and Bobby. In such circumstances, early delinquency and worse may have beckoned.

What of Julia? She did visit her son. Did those visits grow fewer and further between, until she was mostly a memory? She did not withdraw completely. Her other sisters came too; all had a hand and a say in John's welfare. Five sisters is five sisters. It has been suggested that Mimi discouraged Julia from visiting, determined as she was to wield her own brand of discipline and authority. That may be stretching it. Whatever the truth, no one appears to have questioned the set-up. It seems that Julia never did try to take John back. She bore Dykins two daughters, little Julia and Jackie, and wound up with her own council house within easy reach of Mendips, at 1 Blomfield Road. There was room enough for John, but he was never invited to live with his real family. A distance between mother and son yawned. Thus did Julia begin to evolve into the unwitting focus of his fantasies.

A vital element of John's young life over which Mimi could exert little influence was his friendship group. A displaced child who is also effectively an only child is bound to go looking for surrogate siblings and playmates. In this, John got lucky. He fell in with an unruly little gang of bruisers: bookish Ivan 'Ive' (they called him 'Ivy') Vaughan, policeman's son Nigel Whalley and Pete 'Snowball' Shotton, so dubbed because of his almost white-blond curls. Their names are remembered because of their childhood connection to John and to the embryonic Beatles. Pete and John, soon renowned as the double act 'Shennon and Lotton' or 'Lotton and Shennon', became inseparable almost for life. John quickly usurped Pete's status to become leader of the pack, a role he was born to play. Pete soon got him back: at Sunday School, children were obliged to confirm their presence by stating their names in full. When Pete heard John say his middle name, Winston, he gleefully nicknamed his new pal 'Winnie'. He would use that diminutive whenever he thought John needed taking down a peg. Which was often. Despite which, the friendship blossomed and endured.

John and Pete wasted no time in bringing out the worst in each other. They soon evolved into foul-mouthed, risk-taking, piss-taking rascals who trespassed, vandalised and petty-thieved their way around Woolton. Partial to a dare, they swung on ropes from trees at oncoming buses, hurled clods over the railway bridge at steam trains and bricks at the streetlights, for the hell of it. Most of their misdemeanours were originated and orchestrated by John. Mimi would have had a fit. But this John was at odds with the boy she knew indoors. Had she known, she surely wouldn't have believed that her nephew was living a double life beyond her four walls, and even speaking what was as good as a different language.

'John instinctively gravitated towards the centre of attention,' remembered Pete in 1983, 'and his powerful personality always guaranteed him a large and admiring audience. As far as the rest of the gang was concerned, John was our resident comic and philosopher, outlaw and star. Like Nige and Ive, I generally found that I was happy to go along with most of his ideas and suggestions.'[10]

Pete would soon be indispensable to John as fellow mischief-maker, sidekick, Quarryman (Shotton grated the washboard in John's first proper band), business partner, driver, escort and co-songwriter: Pete assisted John in the writing of John's 'I am the Walrus', and contributed to the storyline of Paul McCartney's 'Eleanor Rigby'.[11] He and John even, by Pete's admission, shared girlfriends and casual bed partners, and not always privately or separately. From police cadet and supermarket owner-manager, Shotton would rise to become the Beatles' Apple Boutique chief and first managing director of Apple Corps. He would drop back easily into the position of John's personal assistant when it all 'went tits', before going on to create a fortune of his own, after he established the American-themed Fatty Arbuckle's restaurant chain during the 1980s.

According to Bill Harry,[12] a close friend of John's at Liverpool College of Art and founder and writer of the *Mersey Beat* newspaper, Pete was 'the closest friend John ever had, apart from the Beatles. John respected Pete because he stood up to him and could be a bit like John – a bit sarcastic and moody. John went to Pete for advice on lots of things, and their friendship from schooldays continued right through the 1960s. And I know they did meet up in New York in the 1970s.'

While it might at first seem unlikely and even surprising that a globally fêted rock star should hang on for dear life to his boyhood best friend, it's not unusual. This scenario has played out plenty of times. Notable is the case of David Bowie and his playground pal George Underwood, infamous for having 'caused' David's dilated pupil.[13] The pair found each other in the Wolf Cubs at a Bromley church when they were eight years old. 'We met and that was it: we were best friends from then on,' Underwood told me. 'Our first-ever conversation was about music – skiffle … basically a blend of blues, jazz and folk, and you played it on home-made instruments … all you needed was your mum's washboard, the flat, ridged, wooden thing you scrubbed clothes on, and a tea-chest bass.' Coincidentally, the instrument played by Pete Shotton in the early Quarry Men line-up (the band he himself named) was the washboard. Other examples include Bob Dylan, who as Bobby Zimmerman met chum Louie Kemp in 1953 when they were twelve and eleven, at Herzl summer camp, Webster, Wisconsin. They remained joined at the hip for fifty years. George Michael, Andrew Ridgely and David Austin, who had been best friends since they were boys, grew up to make world-class music together. Andrew and David were both devastated by George's death on Christmas Day 2016. And Prince met his closest childhood friend André Cymone in seventh grade, when they were twelve years old. They played together in the former's pre-Revolution live band. Prince later moved in with Cymone's family. The pair displayed a sixth sense for many things, from music to girls. 'You know what the other person is thinking without even having to speak,' commented Cymone. Which must be the crux.

Such friendships are a curious phenomenon, particularly when one rises to fame and fortune while the other remains obscure. The beauty of a relationship that pre-dates celebrity is that it exists on a level that is not affected by elements that might otherwise unbalance it. While it is mostly impossible (not to mention impractical) to be close to someone famous if one is not, a non-famous friend that a star has known all his life can prove invaluable. More than that, it could be regarded as almost vital for a celebrity to maintain relationships with pals who knew him 'before'. Only they know him as he really is. Only with them can he be his true self, and feel free to relax and let down his hair and guard. Recognition of this confers on the childhood chum a uniquely privileged status. It can also put him in a compromising position. It is often the rich, famous figure, the larger-than-life character, that he finds hard to accept, because he knows and appreciates the real person. The more revered by his fans an artist becomes, the more nostalgic for and desperate to revisit the pre-crazy days he can feel. Thus, he becomes all the more attached to the one or two who were there in the first place, with whom he can share the good old days. The childhood buddy, the silent witness, the original accomplice, becomes a precious conduit to simpler, 'happier' times. The backward glass through which the superstar peers is all too often rose-tinted. John's instrument of time travel was more sophisticated. In every direction, he appeared to see through kaleidoscopes.

Little did Mimi know, at that point, that she was fighting a losing battle. That all her efforts to make a respectable, dutiful schoolboy of John, one who would mature into a high-achieving grammar school student, earn a place at university and eventually distinguish himself, perhaps as a doctor, lawyer, accountant or teacher, would be in vain.

A dysfunctional infancy against which to rail. A stimulating but strict, stifling home environment from which to rebel. An admiring audience to play to, to strut before. John was on his way. All he needed now was an outlet for his anger and frustration. A means to express and relieve the pain he couldn't begin to understand or control. Was the music in him already? I think it must have been, if not embedded in the genes. Even without formal tuition, both Alf and Julia, his parents, had musical ability. Modern research suggests that musicality might be inherited, but also that early exposure to music can create and increase aptitude. It's possible that the first musical instrument John ever touched was a banjo or ukulele belonging to his grandfather, which Pop had taught his daughter Julia to play. It's equally possible that the first instrument John played was the humble harmonica owned by one of Mimi's student lodgers. Which is ironic, given that his own father carried and played a mouth organ, and could easily have taught John himself. The student, one Harold Phillips, promised John his harmonica if he could blow a whole tune on it by the next day. John obliged with two tunes. He was not allowed to have it until Rudolph did the rounds, but boy, what a thrill when it came. He would never forget it. He later described Christmas morning 1947, and the stocking treat it delivered, as 'one of the great moments of life'.[14]

Seven-year-old John, who had inherited his mother's myopia, wore nerdy specs and buzzed a credible harp. He kept his tools of sound and vision tucked tightly in his pocket, mindful of the big boys, and sharpened his fists, feet, sarcasm and wit in preparation. He was going to need all four and more in big school.

Down the garden and up a tree, John had a clear view of a grand Gothic Revival mansion dating back to the 1870s, set in grounds where wild strawberries once grew. The house had been donated to the Salvation Army during the thirties, and re-opened as Strawberry Field, an orphanage for girls. John would hear them all shouting and playing. Their exuberance got the better of him. He was soon climbing the wall, jumping over and joining in.

CHAPTER 3

JULIA

Too bright for his own good, John was already bored with education by the time he passed his 11-plus exam. Being forced to commit useless information to memory and learning times tables by rote were pursuits that he found pointless. Despite his apathy, he gained a place at one of Liverpool's most venerable academic institutions, Quarry Bank High School for Boys, and began his secondary school education there on 4 September 1952. With a gasp of relief, as separation would have been unbearable, Pete also made the grade. Waving farewell to fellow gang members Ivan Vaughan, who was off to the Liverpool Institute in the heart of the city, and Nigel Whalley, who had been accepted at the Bluecoat School, black-blazered Shennon and Lotton started cycling together daily during term time from the junction of Menlove Avenue and Vale Road, Woolton, to Quarry Bank School, a mile and a bit away. There went John on his pride-and-joy Raleigh Lenton, business as usual. Early promise predicted A-streaming, but both boys soon tumbled down the charts, as documented in their termly and half-termly reports. Fortunately for them, their marks perished in tandem, so that the comedy duo was not dissolved for the entire half-decade that they spent there. Had there been an O Level in pranks and mischief, both would have excelled. There was no end to their ability to torment masters, no limit to their propensity for getting up to no good.

Lateness, truancy, cursing, impudence, splattering teachers with ink, sabotaging classroom equipment and smuggling in pupils from other schools, outrageously, was all routine. Frequent detentions were the wages of sin. John and Pete found themselves being kept behind after school most days. When the japes failed to subside, infuriated Sirs, at the end of their tether and tearing out hair, could do little other than condemn them to summits with the Head. Which translated as 'six of the best', an almighty thrashing across the buttocks with a cane. Insult to injury was the recording of the incident in the Punishment Book, and sometimes the assignment of the writing by hand of hundreds of lines of the 'I Must Not …' variety.

Spankings, lashings and canings across the rump and palm, though akin to torture, were still legal and commonplace throughout British schools during the 1950s. Though unthinkable now, violence inflicted by teachers on children for 'grave offences' where other correctional methods had failed was allowed and was deemed acceptable. Educational staff were regarded as in loco parentis, figures of authority with the same rights as parents. Corporal punishment in state schools would not be outlawed for thirty more years. Although it was banned in the mainstream in 1986, it took until 1998 for it to be eliminated from private schools in England and Wales, 2000 in Scotland and 2003 in Northern Ireland. The mere thought of which makes the mind bleed. It was never OK to hit children, was it. Pain inflicted by an adult upon any part of the body of a minor was never right. Where does the line fall between acceptable corporal punishment and child abuse? It doesn't.

Extensive studies by UNICEF, the United Nations and other organisations have led to the identification of corporal punishment as a pervasive form of violence, and to its prohibition in many countries throughout the world. The UN Secretary-General's Global Study on Violence Against Children, launched in 2001 and published in 2006, documented the immense scale of the problem. The evidence is unequivocal. Physical correction leads to aggression, vandalism and destructive behaviour; anti-social and disruptive conduct; lower intellectual achievement; poor social skills, and mental health problems including but not limited to anxiety, depression and diminished self-esteem. It causes lethargy, and can result in a poor attention span, school avoidance and eventual drop-out. It can give rise to attention deficit disorders, substance abuse and even brain damage. Adolescents subjected to physical punishment are more than three times as likely to grow up to abuse their own children and spouse. Hitting teaches children that it is OK to hit; that the best way to solve problems is by lashing out.[1] Taking all this into account, it is not difficult to understand John's loathing of school and teachers, his relaxed attitude towards authority, or the personality and demeanour he developed during his teens. The natural precociousness that led to boredom and misbehaviour, which was punished with violence, provoked him to behave in negative and savage ways. He would even go for those closest to him, including his best mate Pete.

John's saving grace was a prodigious talent for drawing and writing. Inspired by Lewis Carroll, whom he parodied, he took to sketching wicked caricatures of his teachers, and dashing off deliciously offensive rhymes to match. Pete was amazed by his friend's talent. He egged him on to churn out more. John was soon in the habit of creating new ones every night, which led to the launch of the *Daily Howl*, his own satirical newspaper. This was in fact no more sophisticated than a humble school exercise book packed with devilish delights, which would be passed round the class, and of which to get a glimpse there was soon a waiting list. There was a surreal quality to those weird words and pictures. They revealed a possibly unhealthy obsession with physical disability, the disadvantaged and the grotesque. John clearly identified with the afflicted on some level. Whatever may have caused this would have gone over the heads of fellow classmates, who naturally found his scribblings vomit-inducingly hilarious. Schoolboy humour and its obsessions with the ridiculous, the lavatorial and the sexual is in a class of its own. The *Daily Howl* was a peep into John's contorted mind, which clearly had a dark and sinister dimension.

'People like me are aware of their so-called genius at ten, eight, nine,' said John in 1971. 'I always wondered, "Why has nobody discovered me?" In school, didn't they see that I'm cleverer than anybody in this school? That the teachers are stupid, too? That all they had was information that I didn't need. I got fuckin' lost in being at high school. It was obvious to me. Why didn't they put me in art school? Why didn't they train me? Why would they keep forcing me to be a fuckin' cowboy like the rest of them? I was different, I was always different. Why didn't anybody notice me?'[2]

John's apparent arrogance, which he displayed from an early age, was almost certainly born of low self-esteem. This personality trait is usually forged during childhood. It has prompted endless speculation as to his state of mind, and whether he was afflicted by some syndrome or disorder that in those days may not even have had a name. We know that John was never formally diagnosed. Countless commentators have played amateur psychologist down the years, describing him as having had narcissistic personality disorder, borderline personality disorder, multiple personality disorder, attachment disorder, and more. Some declare with staggering conviction that he 'must have been bipolar', or that he was a 'classic example of congenital familial Asperger's syndrome'. How do they *know*? Yet, you name it, John Lennon apparently had it. Throw in his addictions – to heroin, sex and alcohol – along with immense wealth and global fame, and you can well see his problem. He was needy, neurotic, erratic, unstable, childish, self-centred and cruel. He did everything in his power to attract attention to himself. He overcompensated for his weaknesses. He did not take criticism well. He would present as a charismatic extrovert, and seduced others easily with his charm, talent and wit, but would all too soon reveal his lack of empathy, not to mention contempt. He couldn't help himself. We know that he was a wife-beater, an emotional abuser – especially of his son Julian – a hypocrite and a pathological liar; and that he rewrote his life as he went along, often contradicting himself in the process.

But any attempt to distil John's complicated character into having been 'due to a lack of self-esteem' prompts more questions than it answers.

'I would describe Lennon as "narcissistically wounded", says psychotherapist Richard Hughes. 'A lack of self-esteem is an outcome of that, but it is not binary.

'Describing someone as "narcissistically wounded" is not a diagnosis. It is more a "character style", which is not a pathological term but one which is used by psychotherapists and psychiatrists to explore character from a developmental and relational perspective. It is important to remember that we are all a bit borderline, that we are all a bit narcissistically wounded.

'We should not try to diagnose John. To do so would be to pathologise, and even in retrospect I would argue that it is unnecessary. In general, people only get diagnosed with a "disorder" if they have had a serious breakdown and need psychiatric care. To be diagnosed as being "on the spectrum" is extremely difficult due to the shades of the spectrum and the fact that resources are not adequate. The modern conception of Asperger syndrome only came into existence in 1981 anyway, a year after Lennon's death.'

While the tendency can be to focus on a person's developmental and relational background, we should not forget his context, points out Hughes. Growing up in post-war Liverpool, for a start: a tough immigrant city that was Catholic in spirit, shattered by bombs and deeply traumatised.

'There is evidence that when developmental needs are not met or if there is inconsistency, the child does not develop the ability to self-regulate,' explains Hughes. 'As an adult, he consequently vacillates between overestimation of the self and feelings of inferiority or low self-esteem. A history of inconsistent attachment can lead to defences such as dissociation, splitting and self-soothing strategies – including alcohol and drugs – which may lead to a deep sense of alienation and the inability to maintain meaningful and intimate relationships. Of course, for the narcissistic character, that is always someone else's fault.'

It is well known that people with narcissistic deficits often find it hard to empathise. They can be highly social, seductive and charming as adults; and, in the same breath, they can push people away when relationships call for vulnerability or intimacy.

'Despite this,' says Richard Hughes, 'narcissistic people are often "merger" hungry. Lennon was. He idealised. He needed to "twin", and he "mirrored". I think about his significant relationships with Brian Epstein, Paul McCartney and Yoko Ono in particular, and there is definitely a sense of where does one end and another begin?

'Being a celebrity adds another layer of complexity, because so many people projected onto John. He stood for everything modern and post-war. They wanted him to be the pin-up and the philosopher. This was as much about his context and about their own deficits as about him. It just played into his adapted self. It encouraged his narcissistic wounds. At the height of the Beatles' success, it must have seemed like a price worth paying.'

Still, we may continue to be curious about his growing self-awareness; about his fear that what he was and had was not enough. We can reasonably speculate that he needed something else: for himself as well as for the world. After all, as he wrote, 'All you need is love.'[3]

*

Back to the blackboard. Certain teachers did pay him attention, John conceded, and would encourage him in his drawing and painting, the means via which he was best able to express himself.

'But most of the time they were trying to beat me into being a fuckin' dentist or a teacher ... I didn't become a something when the Beatles made it or when you heard about me; I've been like this all me life.'

As for Mimi, she felt that John was disrespecting her by not toeing the line, by not applying himself to his studies when she had given him every opportunity in life. The daily reminder of this so infuriated her that she felt compelled to punish him. She did so by dumping his drawings and writings in the bin.

'I used to say to me auntie, "You throw my fuckin' poetry out, and you'll regret it when I'm famous," and she threw the bastard stuff out,' he later complained. 'I never forgave her for not treating me like a fuckin' genius or whatever I was, when I was a child.'

*

On Saturday, 4 June 1955, when John was fourteen, his beloved Uncle George haemorrhaged violently and was ambulanced to Sefton General Hospital, where he died the next day. He had shown no signs of serious illness, and was only fifty-two. The cause of his death was given as non-alcoholic cirrhosis of the liver and a ruptured abdomen. There is confusion about John's whereabouts at this time. Was he already away on his customary summer holiday, staying with his 'Edinburgh aunt' Mater, her second husband Bert and cousin Stanley on Bert's croft at Sango Bay, Durness? His half-sister Julia insists so, it being her belief that John was sent away by Mimi each summer on those long trips to Scotland 'to keep him away from his mother'.

'John had to face another ordeal after returning from that holiday,' Julia said. 'His Uncle George, Mimi's husband, had died while he was away, collapsing as he came downstairs one Sunday [*sic*] afternoon to go to work on the nightshift. Mimi and one of the lodgers, Michael Fishwick, called an ambulance ...'[4]

Whether or not he was there at the time of Uncle George's death, John was no reluctant visitor to his relatives in the Scottish capital. He adored his trips with them to that place of stark beauty in the remote north-west Highlands, with its unspoilt beaches, caves and waterfalls, seals, whales and all kinds of birds. It must have seemed like paradise to a Liverpool city boy.[5]

Cousin Stanley's father had died young, and Stan had been despatched to a boarding school in Peebles in the Scottish Borders. His mother Mater remarried, and was now the wife of an Edinburgh dentist. That city became their new home.

'It was then that John started coming up on the bus to visit us in Edinburgh,' recalled Stan, who was older than John by some seven years, and highly protective of him. 'There were six cousins altogether, but John, our cousin Liela and I were especially close.'

The adults and children would all pile into the family car for the six-hour, nearly three-hundred-mile trip northwards, which

John would make with them from around the age of nine until he turned sixteen.

'He loved his holidays up there,' Stan remembered. 'He would race around the hills, build dykes, pick things off the sand, and do sketches of the crofts and scenery. He never forgot those times, and still talked about them when we got together as adults.'[6]

The family's croft cottage where John stayed is still there. A poem that he penned there was the original inspiration for the Beatles song 'In My Life' on *Rubber Soul*.

Was it not, as has been noted, the done thing in those days to involve children in the rituals of death? Was it simply a case of John being nearly five hundred miles from home and uncontactable except by letter, which might have taken prohibitively long to reach him? Did Mimi not try to let John know that he'd lost the uncle who had been as good as his father for the past nine years? Or was John not yet in Scotland at all at that point, but would make his way there during July, after the end of term, while poor Mimi was being treated in hospital for stress and depression? Was he simply not in the house that fateful Saturday when Uncle George fell ill? The facts are not clear. While the first week of June does seem rather early for John to have been away on his summer break – although in those days it was still possible to apply for and receive permission to be absent from school for the purpose of a trip that fell during term time – one explanation for the possible timing could be that the half-terms and holidays of Scottish schools do not coincide with those in England and Wales, and may well have been even more out of sync during the 1950s.

Is it true that Mimi didn't summon John back to Liverpool for the funeral and interment, and that by the time he returned home, his uncle was cold in the family plot in St Peter's Church graveyard? Or was he in Woolton all along, and did he attend? We know that he wrote Mimi a tender poem of condolence on the day of her husband's funeral, which she treasured for the rest of her life. We don't know where he wrote it. We know that John was devastated and didn't know how to process his grief. As he would later recall, he and his cousin Liela fell about laughing together over George's demise; there being a thin line between comedy and tragedy, laughter and pain. John's suffering was so terrible that he felt completely helpless. He laughed to express his hurt. Liela was so incapable of helping him that she couldn't help joining in. But John wept bitterly for his uncle by himself. It was understandable. How was he supposed to cope with this loss on top of everything else? Abandoned by both biological parents, and now this? Who was going to stick up for and be there for him now? How much more cantankerous was Mimi going to get, now that she was wearing widow's weeds? John took to sporting George's old overcoat, as if to envelop himself in his kindly compadre's essence; as if to shield himself with George's stale middle-aged male aroma and absorb his DNA.[7] He refused to discard it even when it became shabby and frayed. He would insist on wearing it all through art college. As for Mimi, whose upper lip remained stiff, she was too brusque and no-nonsense to allow herself to be seen to be wallowing in grief. But she did reveal her pain in subtle ways. Never again would she use the sitting room where she and her husband had been accustomed to relaxing and reading together. Confining herself to the kitchen and her little morning room, she allowed that once cosy front parlour to grow stale. Although John continued to live with Mimi at Mendips, without George life was never the same again.

*

While the circumstances that led to it are unclear, the devastation coincided with a furtive rekindling of John's relationship with his mother. Unbeknown to Mimi, John had started taking a detour on his way home from school and was spending secret quality time with Julia. Pete Shotton recalled that when he and John were suspended simultaneously for some dastardly deed, they were too terrified to go home and confess, admit that they'd been excluded, and face the music. So, they got up every day as usual and stuck to their normal routine. They buttoned their uniforms, scoffed their Shredded Wheat and set off on their bikes for school. Only they never got there. Instead, they went to Julia's house in Allerton, which all this time had been less than a couple of miles away, certainly not too distant for regular visits. She welcomed the likely lads with open arms.

John adored and was in awe of Julia. Mimi, the crusty 'It's for your own good' stoic with her strict personal behaviour and morality, her regimented ways and polished china, could not compete with her beguiling younger sister. Julia was warm, welcoming and bohemian, with a cheap but appealing glamour that teenage males could not resist. Unashamedly sexy and flirtatious, with a naughty sense of humour and a chortling laugh, she would totter down the shops in high heels, prance about with a feather duster, and dispense sugary treats and forbidden fizz with a wink. Hers was a female, feminine, fun-loving household, the model of chaotic family life. All were welcome, the more the merrier, and meals could always be stretched. Even better, there were two dear little girls, John's half-sisters Julia and Jackie, to play with. By all accounts, he was delighted by and adored spending time with them.[8]

Julia and her son were each other's other half. Both were daring, spirited, carpe diem sorts with a disdain for authority and a dislike of convention and rules. Each was eccentric, naturally funny and seemed almost to need to make others laugh. Crucially, both harboured a great love of music. It was largely down to Julia that John's passion for it flourished. Not only had she hung on to her banjo, which she taught him how to play, but she also owned a record collection and a gramophone, which even had speakers extended in to other rooms around the house. In her way, Julia was 'with it', as we used to say: a dedicated follower of fashion. Not too many households yet owned a gramophone. Mimi's certainly didn't. The 33⅓-rpm 'LP' – or long-playing record – offering twenty-five minutes of music on each side had only been available since 1948, while the 45-rpm 'single' (with a capacity of eight minutes) landed the following year. No doubt, there were a few Big Band recordings in Bobby's and Julia's collection, including Glenn Miller, Benny Goodman and Artie Shaw; a bit of forties jazz, blues and Dixie; perhaps a handful of the big-name country music stars such as Patsy Cline and Chet Atkins; certainly the crooners of the day, including Pat Boone, hugely famous for his covers of black R&B hits. Bobby Darin, Frankie Avalon, Neil Sedaka, Connie Francis and Rickie Nelson are all artists to whom John would probably have been exposed, as were Carl Perkins, Jerry Lee Lewis, Perry Como, Nat 'King' Cole; Tony Bennett and Doris Day; Julie London, Jim Reeves and Harry Belafonte. Then there were the groups, endless groups – the Penguins, the Crows, the Turbans, the Weavers, the Fontane Sisters among them – and the Platters, whose 'The Great Pretender' was a 1955 stand-out.

If the 1950s was the era of uncooked blues and world-weary R&B finding its way onto America's airwaves to encounter a fresh lease of life and whetting the appetite of a restless demographic, it now reached a turning point. This 'new' music (which had been around for ages) gained momentum as if out of nowhere to become the springboard of an explosion of teen subculture, the like of which had never before been witnessed. Millions of kids heard the clarion call. They also flocked to consume the rebellious role models that Hollywood was now dishing up – Marlon Brando in *The Wild One*, James Dean in *Rebel Without a Cause* – which led to a connection between the behaviour of young tearaways and the music known as R&B. In fact, the film industry rushed to mine the gold. In 1955, it delivered a watershed with *Blackboard Jungle*, its immutable theme Bill Haley and His Comets' 'Rock Around the Clock'. So thrilling to its audiences was this unprecedented film that fans could not contain themselves. Drape-jacketed, drainpipe-trousered Teddy Boys armed with blades would go berserk and tear out cinema seats during screenings.

From the convergence of blues and country, of black and white, had risen rockabilly. Out of rockabilly via minstrels with names like spells – John Lee Hooker, Muddy Waters, T-Bone Walker, Bo Diddley – and filtered through the audio prisms of the wireless and the make-believe visuals of the silver screen, the culture shock of rock'n'roll emerged. Embracing and absorbing infinite influences as it advanced, from African drums and dance beats to gospel, hambone rhythms and Hawaiian-inspired steel guitar, its adaptability, exuberance, propensity for mutation and refusal to sit still promised endless and perpetual appeal. Thus, the breakthrough of Little Richard and Fats Domino. Thus, Buddy Holly and Elvis Presley. When the latter stepped up to the mic in his chequered jacket to give his debut performance for *The Ed Sullivan Show* on 9 September 1956, the first rock'n'roll generation experienced a Second Coming: 'Don't be Cruel', 'Love Me Tender', 'Ready Teddy' and 'Hound Dog' reached 82.6% of the combined US TV audience on the show's season premiere that night. Although Presley's ovary-igniting hip-swivels and smouldering gaze were camera-censored, the screams of the beside-themselves studio audience ensured that the viewers at home got the picture.

There prevails in legend the line that all four future Beatles owed their early exposure to the songs and musicians that would inspire their own writing to American transatlantic sailors who plied a spin-off trade in the casual import of vinyl. Hauling their stashes of the latest US releases through Liverpool's port to offload for a profit locally, Yank seamen are credited with having introduced exotic and obscure artists into the British mainstream. If they were offloading such records, where were they selling them, and what kind of outlets were buying them? American imports were not available in Liverpool's shops at that time. If there existed any black market it was by no means obvious. The city was in those days still a musical backwater. If anything, it was the popular rather than the more obscure American musicians who inflamed John's imagination initially. Artists such as Johnnie Ray, the celebrated jazz and blues pianist and singer, and Frankie Laine, one of the biggest recording artists of the late 1940s and early 1950s, who was dubbed 'America's Number One Song Stylist', 'Old Leather Lungs' and 'Mr Steel Tonsils'. Laine not only belted the theme tracks to well-known Westerns, but he could sing in virtually any style, from pop and gospel to folk and blues, eclipsing Bing Crosby and Frank Sinatra. Ray's 'Walking My Baby Back Home' and Laine's 'Cool Water' were the kind of songs with which John began serenading his friends on the 'harp' he now never left home without.[9] During the sizzling summer of 1955, yet another boring six weeks of eff-all to do, no spare dosh to do it with and no particular place to go, the wayward gang would gather in the park to loll about in the sun, smoke and get off with girls, most of whom had eyes only for John. Boys and girls alike would be harmonica'd into rowdy singsongs. He was getting there. It was, as things turned out, a summer like no other. One that heralded a great sea change. Safe, family-friendly music was under threat from the impending onslaught of threatening, thrilling, parent-riling rock'n'roll. From the aural smorgasbord now theirs for the taking, a single track changed John's life.

'Arguably the first rock'n'roll record, "Rock Around the Clock", was loud, crude and sexy like nothing we'd ever heard before,' said Pete Shotton. 'Both John and I identified with it almost at once. The only thing wrong with the song, in fact, though we could hardly have realised it at the time, was the singer's image. Bill Haley was fat, married and utterly conventional in his appearance and demeanour.'[10]

But hot on Haley's heels came Elvis, delivering on the chief Comet's promise at every turn. The latter's look, attitude and sound epitomised everything about that vast, fabled realm experienced only through movies that flogged the American Dream. Presley fetched the Promised Land close in tantalising ways, and at a level that appealed to every teenage rebel. Not even John had the nerve, at that stage, to believe that he could ever follow in the King's footsteps. A nowhere boy from the back of beyond? He didn't even own a guitar.

But he could listen. He could dream.

The other attraction of his mother's household was that Julia, unlike Mimi, still had a partner around the place, whom as it happens John didn't mind. Lacking male role models now that Uncle George was gone, it didn't take much effort for Bobby Dykins to win John's confidence. No longer doing the sales rounds door-to-door, Dykins was now a dry-land version of Alf's ship's waiter, working the big Liverpool hotels. He was partial to a drink, which John clocked and of which he was warily respectful. He also had a couple of unignorable facial tics, which caused John and Pete much mirth. They had soon rechristened him 'Twitchy', though not out of spite. The boys were well-disposed towards the chap, not least because he was in the habit of sliding them a share of his tips.

'Julia's' was now the boys' home from home. It was to hers that they would head whenever they felt the urge to play truant. They knew that John's mother found them a welcome distraction from the drudgery of housewifery between walks to and from school with her girls. She would never scold, punish nor tell on them; would never go running to the Head, nor to stomping, yelling Mimi. Her home was relaxed, a refuge, where they would get well-fed and watered and where they could put their feet up and do as they pleased without disapproval or retribution. Little wonder that John and Pete started spending more and more time there. Now that arguments with Mimi were frequent and fierce, John even started stopping the night at his mother's. When rows at Mendips became intolerable, he taunted Mimi that he was running away and never coming back.

'In retaliation,' said Pete Shotton, 'Mimi once went so far as to get rid of John's beloved mutt Sally. One of the few times I ever saw John cry was after he returned home from Julia's house and found Sally missing. Mimi justified her drastic action by reminding him of his vow never to come back to Mendips. Since John wasn't going to be around to walk the dog, she argued, he'd left her with no choice but to have it destroyed.'[11]

'Aunt Mimi killed John Lennon's dog'. Ah, Mimi, could you really have done such a thing? It does seem unthinkable. If you did it, as Pete says, what searing anger and instability in your own mind would have induced you to commit such an atrocity? To deprive a child of an innocent creature he loves and cares for, in whatever circumstances, is a monstrous thing. Sally had long been a lifeline to John. She was something to come home to, an uncritical best friend, a wonderful source of comfort and unconditional love. She was a link to Uncle George, whose loss was still raw and at times unbearable, and to how things at home had once been. As psychologist Elizabeth Anderson observes, 'Nothing less than alchemy is involved when animals and children get together, and the resulting magic has healing properties that work well.'[12]

In turmoil as a result of his troubled relationship with education, confounded by raging hormones, less certain of his place in the world than ever before, and confused by rapidly-changing views of himself and of life in general, John had had Sally as a constant to whom he'd long needed to cling. She was no more, and John was shattered. That he leaned away from Mimi and gravitated increasingly towards Julia was inevitable. To neither sister can this have come as a surprise.

John and Pete sometimes talked, when life got the better of them, about running away to sea. Indeed, Mimi had long feared it, anticipating that her charge might try to follow in his ne'er-do-well father Alf's footsteps. It was the obvious escape route for sons of seafaring cities. Thankfully, to these joined-at-the-hip pals, it would remain a last resort.

*

So then the pair discovered sex. Like all adolescents, they had been talking and wondering about it for years, though little information had been forthcoming. Only the rudiments were taught at school, the details received with red-faced embarrassment. Pete's parents hadn't seen fit to enlighten their son, and John certainly wasn't going to get a hint out of Mimi. Pete reckoned that John would have been about eleven when he discovered the thrill of self-gratification. In that, of the two of them, he was well ahead. He wasted no time in giving his friend a personal demonstration of this mind-blowing new skill, by which Pete was amazed but at which he was a little slower on the uptake. Before long, masturbation gatherings had become the latest craze, and at times attracted a large and enthusiastic crowd. Shyness doesn't seem to have come into it. Most of the boys appeared eager to get a look-in, measure each other up, compare shapes and sizes and results, fantasise together and learn from each other as they went. John made no bones about the fact that he favoured beating around the bush to the image of French screen goddess Brigitte Bardot. He was unashamed of boasting to his friends that he kept small magazine posters of his ideal woman stuck to the wall and ceiling of his tiny bedroom, where he could indulge to his heart's content.

The next step towards the offloading of his virginity was taken at the Abbey Cinema along from Penny Lane, where Saturday afternoons were spent fondling anonymous local girls in the stalls. From these sessions, they would soon graduate to friendships with benefits – at which cocky, confident, wise-cracking John excelled. Considering the level of his northern chauvinism – the fairer sex were regarded as good for one thing only, and were hardly worth bothering with otherwise – he got away with murder. Once he had won the heart of his first proper girlfriend, Barbara Baker, he was dismissive of her and gave her the run-around. Unless there were an opportunity to bend her into playing the blanket hornpipe[13] – often literally in the company of Pete and his latest squeeze, or other chums similarly engaged – he'd go so far as to pretend he wasn't at home when she called round. The more elusive he was, the more ardently his sweetheart pursued him. Even though we are talking the mid-1950s, his attitude at that time still seems shocking. John came from a female-dominated family. His four indomitable aunts and feisty mother were no pushover. He maintained a grudging respect for Aunt Mimi, who had sacrificed so much to bring him up, and was so mesmerised by the enchanting woman who bore him, no one would have been surprised had he had her cemented to a pedestal. So why did he have such a low opinion of females? That low self-esteem of his was rearing its ugly head again. By his casual, controlling and dismissive stance, with all his swagger and lip, was he able to assert the upper hand, enhance his status and augment his popularity within his clique.

*

Meanwhile, John's musical tastes were growing. Both he and Pete were devoted to Radio Luxembourg, which they listened to under the covers in bed at night – in John's case, through Bakelite headphones on an extension lead – devouring Gene Vincent,

Elvis Presley, Bill Haley and the rest. Through their mutual friend Donald Beatty they met Mike Hill, a lad who was willing to share his record player and stack of American records. Thanks to Mike, they discovered Little Richard, Chuck Berry and Buddy Holly. While miffed that he hadn't found his way to such rare, cool artists of his own accord, John let his resentment go. He allowed the music to consume his life.

'It was the only thing to get through to me after all the things that were happening when I was fifteen,' he told *Rolling Stone*'s Jann Wenner in an interview years later. 'Rock'n'roll was real, everything else was unreal. And the thing about rock'n' roll, good rock'n'roll – whatever "good" means – is that it's real, and realism gets through to you despite yourself. You recognize something in it which is true …'

Along with the sound, the boys just had to adopt the look. Supported by Julia, who coughed up for his purchases, John reinvented himself as a Teddy Boy. 'Teds' were unruly gangs got up in a cartoon take on preening Edwardian male style. In velvet-collared coats, brothel-creeper shoes and bootlace ties, they patrolled and terrorised neighbourhoods. Not that John or Pete were paid-up gang members. Far from it, they just wanted to look the part. John was soon a shoestring mirror image, complete with Elvis-esque quiff. Pete, on even more meagre funds, did his best to keep up. But that craze soon gave way to another, when the pair of them fell for Lonnie Donegan. They weren't the only ones. Kids all over the land heard Donegan's skiffle group covering Lead Belly's 'Rock Island Line' on Radio Luxembourg, and millions of pennies dropped as the war-cry went up: '*We* can do that!'

'Rock Island Line' was the first debut recording to achieve gold status in the UK. It shifted more than a million copies worldwide. It kicked off a trend that quickly became a national obsession. At one point, there were reckoned to be between thirty and fifty thousand skiffle outfits in Britain. Chas McDevitt's Skiffle Group, Johnny Duncan and the Bluegrass Boys and the Vipers were among the most prolific. When *Six-Five Special* produced by Jack Good launched on BBC TV in 1957 – the first British youth music programme with a skiffle recording as its title track, and featuring skiffle acts as well as pop artists such as Terry Dene, Petula Clark, Marty Wilde and Tommy Steele – John was already thinking about forming his own group, the Quarry Men. His 'first guitar' was borrowed. Had an inexpensive instrument been acquired from Hessy's music shop, an eventually legendary establishment that stood coincidentally on Stanley Street? Was it Mimi or Julia who furnished John with his 'first guitar', which was actually, strictly speaking, his 'second guitar'? The consensus is that it was Julia, but the mythology is rich, here. John's first 'proper' guitar was purchased from a mail-order company based in south London via the mass-market periodical *Reveille* (pronounced 'Rivalley'). 'Rock'n'Roll Guitars' were advertised in a March 1957 edition of the magazine for outright or hire purchase, for which Julia appears to have signed up. The guitar that John received was a cheap and cheerful, three-quarter size Gallotone Champion acoustic. He wasted no time in composing his very first song, 'Calypso Rock', which alas was never recorded, and which, in later years, he could never remember. Its melody and lyrics were lost to the ether, leaving behind only its name.

While Mimi is so often credited for that critical first-guitar acquisition, Pete Shotton was adamant that Julia paid for it. Either way, it was Julia doing the teaching of the banjo chords, such as they were, and encouraging her son through his first attempts at 'Ain't That a Shame' by Fats Domino, while his Aunt Mimi was the one doing all the disapproving. It was Julia inviting him to do his guitar practice at her place, while Mimi was shooing him out the back with a growl for winding up the entire street with that racket.

Despite Pete Shotton's reluctance – by his own admission he was not the remotest bit musical, and couldn't for the life of him see that his inclusion in any group could be to its advantage – the Quarry Men skiffle group came together, with John on guitar and Pete on washboard. Fellow Quarry Banker Bill Smith was enlisted to pluck tea chest bass. Bill's unreliability soon saw him replaced by gang member Len Garry, whose understudies were vintage muckers Nigel Whalley and Ivan Vaughan. Another classmate, Rod Davis, came in on banjo. A second guitarist, Eric Griffiths, also joined, and threw a drummer, Colin Hanton, into the line-up. Although often written as 'The Quarrymen', Pete insisted that their band's name always comprised three words. Nigel Whalley was soon elected 'manager' and went about advertising for gigs. None was forthcoming. Then, just as they were about to leave Quarry Bank School for good, Pete's mum fixed it for them to wow the throng on 6 July 1957, at Woolton Village's annual happening, St Peter's Garden Fête.

It was the fête that sealed John's fate. For here, in a field beyond the graveyard where the remains of Uncle George were interred; where stood the gravestone of real-life Eleanor Rigby, in the shadow of the red sandstone, buttressed, gargoyled Gothic Revival church on Liverpool's loftiest point, where John had once attended Sunday School and where he had sung in the choir, he would meet his match. Here, following the afternoon show for which the Quarry Men – John on guitar and lead vocals, Eric on the other guitar, Rod with his banjo, Colin at the kit, Pete scraping at his washboard and Len going at the tea-chest bass – had played on the back of a lorry, cheered on by a crowd that included John's mother and half-sisters Julia and Jackie; after the Rose Queen had been crowned, the cakes polished off and the police dogs led back to their compound; after the sideshows had been dismantled, the hoopla packed away for next year, the fancy-dress paraders were back in plain clothes; and when the skifflers had relocated to the church hall over the road to practise for that night's grand dance, sharing the bill with the Band of the Cheshire Yeomanry, Ivan Vaughan wandered in with a mate from school, James Paul McCartney.

Posterity has processed, analysed, revisited and rewritten, must be millions of times, the occasion that would only later be considered of world-shaking consequence. There is no formal record of this 'pivotal day for the history of modern music'; nothing to prove that it happened or what was said beyond the first-hand recollections and the eye-witness accounts of those present. While there does exist a snatch of a recording of John and the Quarry Men performing 'Puttin' on the Style' and 'Baby Let's Play House' that afternoon

– the vocal on which, even at that nascent point, is undeniably, quintessentially John Lennon – there is no taped evidence of the first words exchanged between sixteen-year-old Lennon and just-turned fifteen-year-old McCartney, nor of the debut notes that they played each other.[14]

Unbeknown to John at the time, Paul had watched the Quarry Men in action that afternoon, and was blown away.

'I remember I was amazed, and thought, "Oh, great," because I was obviously into the music,' recalled Paul.[15] 'I remember John singing a song called "Come Go with Me".[16] He'd heard it on the radio. He didn't really know the verses, but he knew the chorus. The rest he just made up himself.

'I just thought, "Well, he looks good, he's singing well, and he seems like a great lead singer to me." Of course, he had his glasses off, so he really looked suave. I remember John was good. He was really the only outstanding member. All the rest kind of slipped away.'

They had each other at hello. They also circled each other like sharks. John was aloof and silently provocative. Paul was deferential, a little in awe. John was check-shirt casual and greasy-quiffed. Paul was scrubbed, white-jacketed and drainpipe-slacked. John was playing banjo chords, apparently tuning his guitar to the A string while leaving the bottom E string loose. Southpaw Paul turned the instrument upside-down to strum it, and showed John how to tune it properly before launching into 'Twenty Flight Rock' by Eddie Cochran. He also played Gene Vincent's 'Be-Bop-A-Lula' and a few numbers of Little Richard's. John was prone to forgetting lyrics. Paul committed them easily to memory. He impressed the group by scribbling down, off the top of his head, the words to some of John's favourite songs. John was grudgingly impressed by this big-eyed, bush-baby-faced upstart, but seemed to know instinctively that something special was happening. He both respected and resented Paul for being all that he was. That the group would undoubtedly benefit from this lad's inclusion must have occurred to him more or less immediately. But if he invited Paul to join, would John find himself eclipsed by him?

'I half thought to myself, "He's as good as me,"' John later admitted.
'I'd been kingpin up to then. Now, I thought, "If I take him on, what
will happen?"'[17]

A few years on, John was able to articulate his predicament more
coherently: 'I had a group,' he said. 'I was the singer and the leader.
Then I met Paul, and I had to make a decision: was it better to have
a guy who was better than the guy I had in? To make the group
stronger, or to let *me* be stronger?'[18]

John's quandary was about ceding control. It was as if he knew
intuitively, from the first encounter, that if Paul were to come on
board, it would have to be in equal partnership with him rather
than as just another member of the band. As much as he wanted
to remain the leader of the group he had founded, John knew how
much better it could be with Paul jointly at the helm; and that this,
in turn, would reflect favourably on him. Although John would take
his time over it, his acceptance of Paul as the vital and inevitable
next step for the Quarry Men was as good as a done deal that same
day. Had they been able to see into the future and glimpse the power
struggles that lay ahead of them, the fallings-in, the fallings-out, the
highs of their most supreme collaborations and the lows of their
most vicious hostilities, chances are they might have taken their
leave there and then. As things stood, there was everything to play
for and nothing to lose. As young as they were, they knew it.

Clinical psychologists and scientists engaged in the study of
human potential have pondered for more than a century the secret
of the creative partnership. What alchemy occurs between two
talented individuals that sends their artistry soaring and makes
their collaboration hugely more productive than anything they can
create individually? Whatever it is, Lennon and McCartney could
be the ultimate example. If a partnership works because of the way
in which the individuals in question are able to enhance each other's
strong points while disguising each other's weaknesses, forging
opportunities as they go for each other to shine, there is no need to
look beyond them. Set Paul's kissy face, his cutesy lyrics and melodic
flourishes against John's frowning, snarling ferocity and bluesy riffs

and licks; take John's angst and rage and blend them with Paul's coy charisma and whimsy; corrupt Paul's sentimental innocence with John's lasciviousness and cynicism, and what do you get? We can call it magic. In essence, it is. Each being coaxed by the other out of his comfort zone. Each bringing out the best in the other, and rounding the other off. Unafraid of censoring and even ridiculing each other, they naturally spur each other on. The dynamic is staggeringly simple in its complexity. As a singing and songwriting, recording and performing duo, they are greater than the sum of their parts.

*

Rewind … to John's 'it's a yes from me' to the shy but musically confident new boy. Consider the feelings of Pete Shotton, whose nose was well out of joint now that John was spending all his time learning guitar chords and practising with this pretty little clever Dick. But whence had clever Dick sprung?

From Speke, south Liverpool, originally. James Paul McCartney had been born in Walton General to Roman Catholic Mary and Protestant Jim. Both parents were sweet, well-mannered and hard-working people who went about their business and kept themselves to themselves. Paul's father had worked for a cotton brokers and banged piano out of hours in his own informal line-up, Jim Mac's Band. His mother had been a nurse and midwife, for whom accommodation came with the job. They had got together and married during the war. Their firstborn arrived on 18 June 1942. A little brother for Paul, Peter Michael, happened along eighteen months later, who, according to tradition, would be known as both Michael and 'our kid'.[19] Like John, Paul was used to family gatherings and endless doting, indestructible aunties. He had learned piano by observing his father play. Formal lessons had been arranged and paid for, but Paul lacked the patience for 'proper' teaching, and protested that he was better off figuring it out himself. He would never learn to read or write music. He had acquired rudimentary trumpet-playing skills on his own second-hand instrument, and had found his way to the C, F and G/G7 chords on the guitars of friends long before he ever owned one himself. This bright, open-faced, once chubby, now lean and charming child had already found his first smoking pal on the top deck of the bus to and from school, a boy in the year below at the 'Innie' (as the Liverpool Institute was known) by the name of George Harrison (one of the aforementioned friends-with-guitars). George, a youngest-of-four and another council house lad, was the son of ship's steward turned bus conductor Harold and singing shop assistant Louise. He had fallen for Elvis Presley at the same time as Paul and John, having heard 'Heartbreak Hotel' in 1956.

Which was a life-changing year. Paul's family had relocated from disintegrating Speke to yet another council house in a more salubrious area, this time Allerton – 20 Forthlin Road is only a ten-minute walk from Mendips on Menlove Avenue. It was from there that his mother Mary would now operate as a health visitor, the humble but neat rented property having become theirs as a perk of her employment. It was there, just before his fourteenth birthday, that Paul began to write his own songs, which he discovered that he could do without effort. It was there that he composed 'When I'm Sixty-Four' on the family Joanna.[20] It was there that his forty-six-year-old mother first felt what she chose to dismiss as early symptoms of impending menopause. She popped a few indigestion-relief pills and got on with it. Her elder son acquired his first record – Gene Vincent's 'Be-Bop-A-Lula' – which he carried home so proudly from Curry's record shop. Because she had taken the decision to keep the awful truth from her children, Paul was none the wiser when his mum was diagnosed with a tumour and was admitted to hospital for a mastectomy. Too late. Her breast cancer had metastasized to the brain, and could not be controlled. Her sons saw her one last time, still unaware that they were on the verge of losing her. She died on 31 October. Paul was not yet fifteen, while his brother was only twelve. Neither was taken to her requiem mass, nor were they present at her burial. Their heart-broken father had no idea how he was supposed to cope. In anticipation of his domestic cluelessness, his wife had left detailed notes of instruction all over the little house before she departed that final time for hospital. The clan rallied. Paul retreated into his shell, lost himself in music, and wrote a song that may, subconsciously, have been inspired by his mother's death: 'I Lost My Little Girl'.[21]

*

Young trainee Liverpool stockbroker and jazz fan Alan Sytner launched the Cavern Club in an old warehouse cellar beneath Mathew Street in January 1957: 'eighteen slippery stone steps leading down to a set of fetid brick catacombs', as the *Daily Telegraph* described it. Sytner had visited subterranean jazz joints during his European travels, such as the famous Le Caveau de la Huchette on Rue de la Huchette below the Seine in Paris's Latin Quarter and decided to create something along the same lines.[22] Mathew Street lay at the heart of Liverpool's wholesale fruit and vegetable market. Its cellars echoed the rough construction of Le Caveau's sixteenth-century building, with bricked arches and labyrinthine tunnels. The passages had served as air raid shelters during the Second World War, and would accommodate six hundred or more music fans. While the first musicians to perform there were exclusively jazzmen, the bill soon expanded to include skiffle groups, of which there were hundreds in the Liverpool area. It just so happened that the Quarry Men's 'manager' Nigel Whalley, who had quit school to take up an apprenticeship as an assistant golf professional at Gatacre's Lee Park Golf Club, found himself doing the rounds with Alan Synter's GP father. Seizing the moment, Nigel asked him for an introduction to Alan with a view to securing a slot for his charges at the Cavern. Sytner Snr generously proposed an audition at the golf club, following which the Quarry Men were invited to fill in between jazz sets at the Cavern. Their first, historic performance at the club took place on Wednesday, 7 August 1957. The group were under firm instructions to keep it skiffle. John, naturally, had other ideas. On the night, after easing in gently according to instructions, he launched brazenly into a rendition of Elvis's 'Don't be Cruel'. His gobsmacked fellow Quarry Men had no choice but to follow suit. Sytner was enraged by the defiance. He barged through the throng to thrust a hastily-scribbled note into John's hand, telling him to 'Cut out the bloody rock'n'roll!'

Alan Sytner would sell the Cavern in 1959 to promoter Ray McFall, who would expand its remit to include blues and rock'n'roll, demand for which was on the rise. Down the years, however, Sytner was never slow to claim credit for his pivotal role in the advance of Liverpool's most celebrated sons.

'Without me, no Cavern. Without me, no Beatles,' he asserted in 1998. 'Without me, none of those bloody things really. Oh, obviously Lennon and McCartney became geniuses and great artists, but answer me this: would they have flourished without the Cavern? If the Beatles had only been playing church halls in Maghull, would anyone have taken any notice?'[23]

Articled accounts clerk McFall bought the Cavern for £2,750 in 1959, and re-launched it with a performance by Acker Bilk and his Paramount Jazz Band. Already aware that the beat boom was stealing a march on trad jazz, he began booking the new bands. Rory Storm and the Hurricanes played there in May 1960, with Ringo Starr on drums. After they were brought to his attention by the club's DJ Bob Wooler, Ray booked the Beatles, who made their debut appearance as such during a lunchtime session there in February 1961 – having just returned, in disarray, from Hamburg. It was McFall who ordered them to smarten up, for the sake of attracting a cleaner clientele. Brian Epstein visited the club in November 1961, and signed the group that December. They would go on to play the Cavern two hundred and ninety-two times, until August 1963, apparently earning – according to McFall, although reports conflict as to whether Epstein later negotiated various rises – twenty-five shillings (£1.25) for each performance. After Beatlemania erupted during 1964, the Cavern became a shrine to them. It even had its own weekly show on Radio Luxembourg, and would attract the biggest acts of the day, the Who and the Kinks among them.

Unable to cover the cost of extensive drain repairs, McFall sold the club and declared bankruptcy in 1966. It did re-open under new management, but was demolished in 1973. Today's Cavern, which is one of Liverpool's most-visited and most popular attractions, is situated several yards along Mathew Street from the original club.

*

After being invited to join the line-up in October 1957, nearly three months after he and John had first met, Paul made his first public appearance with the Quarry Men at the New Clubmoor Hall – a men's Conservative club in north Liverpool – on Friday, 18 October. They played there again on 23 November, almost matching: white-shirted, black-trousered and bootlace-tied. Their repertoire of covers included Elvis and Gene, Buddy and Carl and Little Richard. The skiffle element was fading. They travelled to and from engagements by bus. Paul's Cavern debut with the group took place on 24 January 1958.[24] He was five months short of his sixteenth birthday. John was just seventeen. You know what I mean.

The pair were now joined at the hip, seeing each other as often as schedules allowed, and carting their guitars wherever they went. Thanks to Paul's painstaking efforts, at Mimi's Mendips, at Jim McCartney's 20 Forthlin Road, at Julia's 1 Blomfield Road and wherever else they could come together, a competent guitarist was coaxed out of John. Paul's school marks were now on the slide, he had incurred his father's wrath by hanging around with this hoodlum new best friend, but a future was emerging that he liked the look of. They dared to dream. Thanks to Nigel Whalley, the bookings kept coming: social club dos, shindigs and dances back and forth across the city, plenty of these on school nights. Pete Shotton was still around, though he had quit his role in the Quarry Men. In spite of which, he and John remained best friends. Pete and Paul were now competing for John's attention and affections. John couldn't be arsed with the simmering aggro between two lads coming on like lasses. He grinned and let them get on with it. Besides, there were more important things to worry about. The group clearly needed another guitarist. One who could manage the kind of complicated solos that defeated both him and Paul. Come the turn of 1958, Paul's old school chum George was finding his way to their live engagements. He was introduced to John by Paul at the beginning of 1958, and performed an audition. The follow-up took place on the top deck of a bus. The kid could play, all right, but how was this supposed to work? John was a man, Paul was a boy, but little Georgie Harrison, not yet fifteen, was just a kid. Not for much longer. In February 1959, George turned sixteen, left school, and became an apprentice electrician in a department store. Maybe John would take him seriously now that he had a job.

*

Titillated by John's intimations, in private recordings never intended for publication or broadcast but which found their way after his murder into the public domain, some commentators have inflated the implications of John having possibly experienced sexual feelings towards his mother, which were probably no more than fantasy. Some have gone so far as to suggest that actual intimacy occurred. There is no evidence of it. Julia herself never commented. That privilege, along with all others, would be denied to her.

Did anyone expect, given his lack of interest in formal studies and his overt disdain for school, that John would have done anything other than hopelessly in his O Level exams? Mimi must have prayed that he would pull himself together at the eleventh hour and yank something out of the bag, making the most of opportunities she herself had never enjoyed, and remodelling himself into something that would have made her efforts and investment worthwhile. His mother didn't give a toss, recognising in John a maverick after her own heart, an echo and reflection of herself, a 'special', 'different' 'someone' who would make his mark regardless; who was far too clever, bright and talented to toe any line. Mimi could probably have crowned her sister for not supporting her own more conventional point of view, and for encouraging John to go his own way. But John had made his obsessions clear: girls and music.

Music and girls. Rock'n'roll was all that mattered. Sooner or later he would get 'picked up', you mark his words.

Aunt Mimi, meanwhile, was determined to salvage something from the wreckage. Despite the sorry fact that John had even flunked Art, at which he excelled, she went and convinced Quarry Bank's headmaster, Mr Pobjoy, to put in a word for him at Liverpool College of Art. Her ploy worked. She could now at least comfort herself with the thought of him forging an eventual half-decent living as a commercial artist. On 16 September 1957, three weeks ahead of his seventeenth birthday, John became an art student. He could hardly wait. He seized the opportunity to stand out from the crowd from the start, prowling about in a series of eccentric get-ups that defied categorization, invariably topped with Uncle George's old overcoat. Still officially part of Mimi's household, where 'his' music was disapproved of and where practise was tolerated only in the back garden or front porch, he spent at much time as possible at Julia's, where he could strum, sing, play records and leap about to his heart's content. It was at Julia's that he composed one of his earliest songs, 'Hello Little Girl'.[25]

*

Consumed as he was by music and obsessed with developing the group, John was not exactly applying himself to his art college studies. While his natural talent was obvious, and while his flair for the quick fix in order to back himself out of a corner when work was due in was impressive, come the end of his debut student year he was bored. Apart from alley-catting about with the kind of women you didn't take home to meet Mother, let alone Mimi, swilling his fill in the coffee bars and the local pubs, and finding like-minded souls to do nothing with, he achieved little. He was an art student by name and in image only. Which was a shame, given his ability. Meanwhile, his group were not as in demand as they had once been, largely due to their 'manager' Nigel Whalley having had to step down through long-term illness, and there being nobody else to take on the procurement and orchestration of their bookings. The Quarry Men needed a rethink.

They were not the only ones. Things were not going so well in Julia Lennon's life. The culmination of a series of unfortunate events was the arrest of her partner Bobby Dykins, who was done for drink-driving, fined heavily and subsequently relieved of his job. All of which led her to seek the heart-to-heart with her sister Mimi that she wished she didn't have to have, on Tuesday, 15 July 1958. She left John back at her own house, 1 Blomfield Road, to go and face Mimi with the ultimatum that Bobby had given her. Money being too tight to mention, he had insisted on Julia informing Mimi that they would no longer be putting John up. Nor would they be feeding him. Given that strapping teenage boys can consume more than the rest of a family put together, one could well see Bobby's point. How it must have hurt and humiliated Julia to have to put this to Mimi, however – especially after all that her sister had done for John already; after the way she had relieved Julia of the burden and expense of bringing him up. Mimi herself was not exactly rolling in it, and was still working to provide for lodgers to make her own and John's ends meet.

Once her unhappy mission was accomplished, Julia sadly took her leave at almost quarter to ten that evening. Though it was late, complete darkness had not yet set in. Mimi was just saying goodbye to her sister at the front gate when up rocked Nigel Whalley, looking for John. Julia teased him into accompanying her to the bus stop. When the pair reached the corner, they bid each other good evening. Julia made to cross Menlove Avenue while Nigel turned to head off in the other direction. At which point his blood was suddenly curdled by a screeching of brakes and a horrifying whomp that could mean only one thing. He turned to see Julia flying. She had been hit head-on by a Standard Vanguard car driven by unaccompanied learner driver and off-duty officer Eric Clague, aka Constable 126 C of the Liverpool City Police. The life was lifting out of her before she hit the ground. She was dead on arrival at Sefton General Hospital, killed by extensive damage to her brain caused by fractures in her skull. She was forty-four. The Coroner at her inquest returned a verdict of death by misadventure.

Did John attend his mother's funeral, which was held a week later? He never spoke of it. His cousin Liela, by this time a student of medicine in Edinburgh, would confirm that she attended with John. His half-sisters Julia, who was eleven, and Jackie, eight, were not even told that their mummy had been killed. They were removed from their home and made to 'go on holiday' in Scotland with their Aunt Mater and Uncle Bert whom they barely knew. Not that they were aware of it on the day they were taken away, but they would never see their home again. On their return to Liverpool, they were made to live with their maternal aunt Harrie and her husband, Uncle Norman, in a cold and unaffectionate home, and were deprived of their father too. No reasonable explanation was ever given. The girls had no idea until years later that they had been made wards of court. Julia was later moved to describe this awful situation, and I can only agree with her, as 'child abuse'.[26]

Did John rant and rave, gnash and wail? Did he go on the lash and drink himself stupid, becoming even more disruptive and offensive? Did he take to his bed and grieve hopelessly and silently? Did he grow harder, more vicious, more bitter, more cynical, more warped, more rebellious than ever before? Did he wash his hands of authority and spit on 'the establishment', condemning both once and for all – a stance that would in later life make a fully-fledged agitator of him? History has him doing all this, and more. The contradictions seem appropriate. All are true.

'It was the worst thing that ever happened to me,' said John, ten years after the tragedy. 'She was great. I thought … I've no responsibilities to anyone now.'[27]

A dozen years later, just before his own death in 1980, his recollections were as raw as ever:

'I lost my mother twice,' he said. 'Once, as a five-year-old when I was moved in with my auntie. And once again, when she actually, physically died … and that was really a hard time for me. It just absolutely made me very, very bitter. The underlying chip on my shoulder that I had as a youth got really big then. Being a teenager and a rock'n'roller and an art student and my mother being killed, just when I was re-establishing a relationship with her ... We'd caught up on so much in just a few years. We could communicate. We got on ... it was very traumatic for me.'

He raged against the dying and the loss. This was bound to come between him and Mimi, whom he now found unbearable to live with. He awoke each morning to draw his curtains on a view of the exact spot where his mother was killed. Imagine it. I have stood at that front window in John's childhood bedroom, looking out just as he looked out. It was unbearable. How did he hang onto his mind? Isolated in his anguish, he was unable to articulate his grief, even to Pete, for fear of how it might affect their friendship. He was deprived of access to the lovely little half-sisters who might have afforded him sibling comfort. He now shared with his closest musical partner the worst experience of all, but couldn't talk to Paul about it. John was in desperate need of someone to cling to. Who would be his rock?

CHAPTER 4

LUNA

He found two. Both had been under his nose for a while, being fellow students at art school.

Cynthia Powell is often described as 'prim and proper'. She was 'posh totty'. Pretty, demure and sweetly spoken, she went about her work in a dignified and unassuming manner, never drawing attention to herself. She hailed from Hoylake, the well-heeled seaside town on the Wirral Peninsula with a war memorial designed by a Jagger,[1] prominent old lighthouses, many listed buildings, a sailing club and a lido. Also home to the Royal Liverpool Golf Club, with the second oldest links in England, it still takes turns at hosting the Open Championship.

Born in Blackpool in September 1939, Cynthia was the youngest of three. With two elder brothers, she was not dizzied by young men. Her father Charles had been an employee of the General Electric Company. While her mother Lillian was carrying her daughter, she was evacuated to Blackpool with many other pregnant women so that they could have their babies safely away from the bombs. When Cynthia was born, her parents decided not to risk resuming family life under constant German air raids. They relocated to the coast, where Cynthia grew up. She showed early artistic promise, won competitions and a place at the city's junior art school, and was expected to progress to Liverpool College of Art. She might never have made it, and history would have taken a different turn, after her father fell terminally ill with lung cancer and ordered her to forget about college. He wouldn't be around much longer to support her mother, he said, so Cynthia had to get a job and provide for them both. He died when his daughter was seventeen. Her mother did an Aunt Mimi, taking in lodgers so that Cynthia could follow her dream. She joined the college, like John, in September 1957. As a student of Graphics, she may never have met him, but for the fact that they overlapped in Lettering.

'Cyn' was a year older than John, and it showed. Disorganised and detached, he was usually empty-handed and unequipped when he lolloped along to class – if, that is, he could be bothered to turn up at all. With his customary cheek and sense of entitlement, he took to helping himself to her pencils, pens, rulers and other instruments. He never returned them, and she never dared ask for them back. Late as usual, and all too often hungover and unkempt, John was the last student in the building with whom anyone would have matched squeaky 'Miss Hoylake'. Was he really only in the Lettering class because other tutors had banished him from theirs? Shades of Quarry Bank. Would John ever learn? Guess not. Who knows what attracted Cynthia to him. He wasn't nice to her. While he couldn't resist making fun of her accent, her outfits, her 'properness', her apparent snootiness, there was something about her that he couldn't quite put his finger on. She wasn't his type. Never could he be described as hers. But there was chemistry, and there was Cupid. They were powerless. Their courtship began. John couldn't wait to introduce her to Pete, who had, of all surprises, become a trainee police officer. He was baffled by the chalky-cheesiness of it all:

'I was immediately struck by how different this attractive, well-bred young woman was from all the lowlife scrubbers John had lately been associating with,' he said candidly. 'Cyn proved to be exceptionally polite and almost painfully shy, and I couldn't help but think she was perhaps too fragile a flower to be in John's hands.'[2]

Opposites attract? The latest science dismisses the notion, but Cynthia certainly subscribed to it when we discussed this and other aspects of their relationship during our interview sessions in 1989, for a memoir that in the end did not progress. This was shortly before the opening of her ill-fated restaurant, Lennon's, on the edge of London's Theatreland. Despite the fact that she and her business partners invested heavily in the venture, and that she had even poached Peter Stockton, the flamboyant general manager of her Upper St Martin's Lane neighbour Peter Stringfellow, to run the place for her, the venture was short-lived. She invited me to the restaurant one afternoon during the week of its showbizzy launch.

Cynthia had divorced twice more since John. She said 'I do' to second husband Roberto Bassanini, an Italian hotelier, in 1970. They managed three years. Her third husband, John Twist, was a Lancastrian engineer. The couple were wed in 1976, but divorced seven years later. When we met, she was living with Liverpool chauffeur Jim Christie, four years her junior, based in Penrith in the Lake District.

She had reverted to her first married surname. It was 'good for business', she said. She had designed home furnishings for the Viyella fabric company under the family name, and had launched her own perfume, 'Woman', in response to the 1980 hit song of that name that John wrote for Yoko. An enthusiastic cook, Cynthia had also owned a restaurant/bed-and-breakfast establishment, Oliver's Bistro, in Ruthin, North Wales. She was candid about her money-making schemes. 'Needs must,' she said with a shrug. 'My divorce settlement from John was very modest (£100,000 and custody of Julian), and of course it's all gone now. I'll do whatever it takes to get by. I have to pay the bills like everyone else.'

Paul McCartney's late wife Linda orchestrated our encounter. Linda and I had collaborated briefly on a tentative book, *Mac the Wife*, but she decided midway not to publish. Paul had retained ties with Cynthia after the demise of the Lennon marriage, and had written the Beatles' 'Hey Jude' for Julian[3]. Released by the Beatles in August 1968 when John's firstborn was only five years old, and still one of their best-loved hits, it had been composed by Paul to comfort the child through the agony of his parents' break-up.

I was there to discuss a new memoir that Cynthia wanted to write. Her first, *A Twist of Lennon*, published in 1978, had left a bitter taste. She was so frustrated by the way John shut down on her and refused to communicate after he left her for Yoko that she wrote the book as a 'long, open letter to him, pouring it all out'. With hindsight, she admitted, she would have done it differently. Now that she had come to terms with John's murder in December 1980, she was keen to try again. She needed to tell her side of the story for the record. She no longer lived in fear of recrimination from John. She had sought advice, and decided that she needed professional help. But she became immersed in her new restaurant, and the project was shelved. Years later, in 2005, she wrote and published a second memoir herself. Entitled simply *John*, it was much bolder and more confessional than her first.

Sitting at a corner table in her monochrome eaterie that day in 1989, Cynthia chain-smoked and kept the wine glasses filled.

'It all began with the death of John's mother,' she said. Her chocolate eyes glistened behind huge gold-rimmed specs. She flicked often at her thick blonde fringe. Her pleasant voice bore a whisper of Scouse. In her fiftieth year, and no temptress, she was still turning heads. Once a Lennon.

'It was complicated, the way it all happened,' Cynthia explained. 'The effect of his mother's death on John's psyche was profound and damaging. He was seventeen years old, and I don't believe he ever recovered from it. It disrupted his ability to have normal relationships with women.

'He never sat me down and explained it all in any great detail. I'm not sure he could have articulated it, come to that. I had to piece the story together from remarks he made, from bits and pieces that slipped out, and from comments made by other people. I knew that his mother was what they called "bohemian", an uninhibited sort, and that she had given up her little boy at around the time he started school. John said that he'd gone to live with "Aunt Mimi and Uncle George", his mother's elder sister and her husband, who I know John was particularly close to. He never said a lot about his dad, who some people referred to as "Alf" and others as "Freddie". I got that his mother was estranged from John's father, had been living with another man called Bobby Dykins, and that they had a couple of kids. I know that he idolised his mother, that she taught him to play the banjo, and that she'd got him his first guitar. Mimi was a different kettle of fish. I'll have to be careful what I say here, as of course she is still alive (Mimi died two years later, in December 1991, aged eighty-five). She brought John up very strictly, with lots of rules and expectations. She was hard to please, easily disappointed, and she would make it known, let's put it that way. Her sister Julia, from what John said about her, was nothing like her. She was less rigid, more fun, more laid-back. John obviously identified with her. It seemed to me that he was very much his mother's son. Although Mimi obviously worshipped him, John was clearly a disappointment to her. In her eyes, he never fulfilled his potential, and he wasted his opportunities.

'I knew that John had underperformed at school, even though anyone could see how bright, sharp and ahead of the game he was. I got that a lot of his troubles stemmed from boredom, which would explain why he just couldn't apply himself to his studies. He got into the art college by the skin of his teeth – he probably shouldn't have been there at all, really – and we met when he sat behind me in class. He would poke me in the back and ask for a lend of my pencils and things, which of course I never got back.'

By Cynthia's own admission, none of her friends or family could understand what she saw in him.

'We didn't even look as though we went together,' she grinned. 'His "wardrobe", if you could call it that, was almost tramp-like. Actually, I'd seen better-turned-out tramps. He stopped just short of lacing his boots with bits of string. He'd do things like rip the pocket off an old school blazer and go around in that, even though it was far too small for him and the frayed sleeves only reached to just below his elbows. He moped about in this really shabby old overcoat that belonged in the dog basket if you ask me. I only found out later that it had been his Uncle George's and that he couldn't bear to part with it. He must have felt close to and comforted by his uncle when he was wearing it.'

John was a challenge to Cynthia from the first moment.

'He was sullen and moody most of the time, and his rages could get out of control,' she said. 'And he would swear constantly. Really crudely and badly, the sort of words you ought not to say in front of a lady. I wasn't used to hearing language like that – my parents certainly never cursed – and I did used to find it embarrassing, I don't mind admitting. I used to go bright red a lot in those days, but John never seemed to care. I think he enjoyed making me feel uncomfortable. It gave him the upper hand.'

The thing that bothered Cynthia most was his lack of ambition and drive.

'OK,' she concedes, 'we were still very young. But I couldn't help feeling baffled by the way that John would never plan anything. I mean, he tended to know what he was doing at the weekend, and that didn't usually involve homework, of course. But he'd never talk about his future or his life. Those were definitely no-go areas with John. I sometimes had the impression that he didn't expect to live a long time, and that bothered me. He didn't seem to have any respect for life, put it that way. Perhaps because of everything he'd been through. When your mum gives you away and your dad walks out on you, then the uncle who brought you up dies, and then you're dealing all the time with this very complicated, cross and disapproving auntie without the uncle there any longer to take the edge off things, and then that truly awful thing about his dog, and then your mother dies, just as you're starting to get close to her again … well, it was all so much tragedy, wasn't it. No wonder John was the way he was. He was very vulnerable, and he obviously needed mothering. He was only a kid himself, of course, when you think about it, though in so many ways he seemed like a middle-aged man to me. He really did, at times. But most of the time he was just a boy. A confused and vulnerable little boy inside that gruff, swaggering exterior.'

Cynthia supposed that he did bring out her mothering instinct.

'I felt very protective of him, and I was always telling myself that other people simply didn't understand him,' she told me. 'I often felt like his mother, in more ways than one. I was independent, and quite driven. I worked, I studied, I met my deadlines. I liked to keep busy, and I enjoyed having a goal to work towards. John seemed to have no motivation, apart from when it came to music. It was as if his mother's death had caused him to put his own life on hold. I used to think to myself sometimes, he doesn't actually care whether he lives or dies.'

Did she want to change him?

'Yes, of course. And no. I secretly adored the way he was. All the stuff he got away with. I wasn't brave enough to throw caution to the wind and behave like John did, though there were definitely times when I would have liked to. So John's behaviour was a vicarious thrill for me. He was dangerous. He attracted attention, in ways that I would never have dared to. There was something about him. He was irresistible. He was a rebel. He could get the attention of everyone in the room without doing anything at all.'

So the baddest boy in the college bagged the most butter-wouldn't-melt girl? To see if he could?

'I don't think it was as calculated as that,' Cynthia countered. 'There was something about being "his girl" because it was the last thing that anyone expected. I confess, I did bask a little in his limelight. I can't explain it, really, I just did. I was shy and low-key, and me being with him did shock people. Being around John, being one of his inner circle, made anyone more interesting. There was also the fact that my mother couldn't stand him, and she made her feelings plain. She warned me that he was a very bad influence, and that no good could come of our relationship. Of course, that just made me want him all the more. It's fuel to a fire, isn't it, warning your son or daughter off some undesirable they might be falling for. It was exactly the same with Mimi. She was blinkered to the truth about him. She simply didn't see what everyone else saw. He was the apple of her eye, and no female was ever going to be good enough for her John. Not even a nicely brought-up girl like me, even though

I say it myself. Mimi couldn't bring herself to accept or approve of anyone who was closer to John than *she* was.'

Did Cynthia know the minute they were in it that John was The One?

'What do we know, at eighteen?' Her smile was rueful. 'And don't forget, he was the youngest, and girls tend to be much more mature than boys at that age. But of the two of us, he was the 'old' jaded one, while I was the shy, innocent, starry-eyed one. The entire time we were together, there was never a moment when the mere thought of him didn't set off the butterflies in my tummy, when I didn't feel all gasp-y and hot-cheeked. John literally took my breath away. It was as if I didn't have a choice: I *had* to be with him, and that was that. There's something incredibly sexy about the power that one person can wield over another, don't you think? It's that rush of adrenalin when you see them or even just think about them, I suppose. That confusing mix of confidence and vulnerability in a person is a truly intoxicating thing. It was not so much that he believed he was better than everyone else, but that he really didn't care either way.

'John could have had any girl he wanted. He could have had any of us, but he wanted *me*. In truth, there isn't anything that I wouldn't have done for him. I still felt that way long after we were divorced. Despite all the blood that had flowed under the bridge. John was complicated. More screwed-up than most people ever knew. I wanted more than anything for him to be happy. I don't believe he ever was, and that kills me.'

John could 'have any girl he wanted'. The female after whom he had long lusted was a siren of the silver screen who was blonder, more pouty and more voluptuous that most ardent young men could dream of. In a move pre-empting that of Olivia Newton-John in the fifties American high-school nostalgiafest *Grease*, when her character Sandy sheds her squeaky Sandra Dee image to get leather-clad and dirty with the danger girls, Cyn reached for the peroxide and the lippy and shamelessly Bardot'd herself up. Mimi's eyes nearly fell out. Her blatant disapproval of the harloting of Miss Hoylake was loudly voiced. Cyn ignored her. If her Sunday School teacher image hadn't been sufficient to win John's auntie over, she had zero to lose by turning full tart. Whatever it took to keep hold of her John, Cyn was game.

*

Sisters are one thing. Be they step-, half-, full- or part-time, they tend to be ignored by brothers at worst, tolerated at best. They can be taken or left. But a boy needs brothers. He who is without any will seek substitutes, which John did. He had male cousins, but his interactions with them were occasional, given geography, and tailed off as he matured. His neighbourhood gang had boiled down to a band – who metamorphosed, briefly, into Johnny and the Moondogs. Pete Shotton had seen him through school, had done a half-hearted turn in the group, and was to remain John's devoted friend forever. But now that Pete had pledged allegiance to the boys in blue, John needed to find someone else on his wavelength. Someone who would not only raise his game, which he must have known, subconsciously, that he needed, but also someone whom he could dominate.

It may at first seem odd that he singled out Stuart Sutcliffe; perhaps more significantly, that Stu caved in to John. Neither was the other's type. There was Lennon, big, fierce-looking, vaguely thuggish, appreciably Ted-ish, suffering no fools, scowling about, thumbing his nose at authority and getting away with it. Then there was Stu: a small, brooding, bespectacled Scot, fine-boned and delicately fingered; the least-likely dustman imaginable (he worked the trucks part-time to pay his way as a first-year student); a dedicated, gifted artist who impressed John no end, and who generally wouldn't say 'boo'. Who looked the younger but appeared the elder. Who at one point cultivated a modest Van Gogh-style beard-ette, presumably to render himself more mature-looking. Who suffered for his art, being possessed of true artistic talent. Who lived bleakly in a chilly, unglamorous garret, a one-room, mattresses-on-the-floor-type gaff with an old coffin and a Belisha beacon for furniture. When John moved in at the beginning of 1960, and shared the flat with him for a while, Mimi was beside herself. She begged Cyn to talk him out of leaving home. When Cyn explained that she couldn't make John do anything he didn't want to, Mimi insisted on at least being allowed to carry on doing John's washing, so that he'd come round once or twice a week and get a hot meal down him.

While John fancied himself as an artist, his own efforts amounted to little more than sketches and cartoons. He liked to say that art was his 'first love', but his output could never live up to the affectation. Mind you, it is no surprise that his lithographs and limited-edition prints change hands today for considerable sums. His whimsical drawings, intimate portraits and caricatures exploring 'peace', 'love' and 'truth' (many of them since hand-coloured by Yoko) are massively popular today, and have in recent years soared in value. Always the way, when a famous artist is no longer around to produce more. In 2014, Sotheby's New York scored an auction record for a Lennon drawing entitled *Untitled Illustration of a Four-Eyed Guitar Player*, which sold for $109,375. The scribbly ink sketch, which more than quadrupled its generous estimate, was part of the most extensive collection of John's original artwork and scripts ever to come to auction. Billed as 'You Might Well Arsk: Original Drawings and Manuscripts 1964–65', the show was 100% sold and fetched close to $3 million. John the artist has an undeniably strong following – but how much of that is down to the fact that the offerings are by the world's greatest rock star?

We are familiar with the concept of 'musician as visual artist'. Bob Dylan's Picasso-esque paintings and pastel portraits, John Mellencamp's huge oils and 'mixed-media pieces', Cat Stevens' bewitching album covers, the abstract expressionism of Jim Morrison, the graffiti-style paintings of Dee Dee Ramone, Ronnie Wood's hewn-looking studies of the Stones (and other artists), drawings and photographs by Patti Smith and artworks by Brian Eno, Joni Mitchell, Grace Slick and David Bowie – he who drew and painted 'the sound of the music' – are only a few. Nor was John the line-drawer the only Beatle to get his hands smudgy. Macca started painting during the 1980s. Ringo experiments in pop art. George Harrison collaborated with fellow musician Keith West in

1986 to produce pieces based on his best-known songs. There have been exhibitions featuring the collective art of all four Beatles.

Was John a musician who made art, or an artist who made music? Is it not better to resist the urge to pigeonhole and acknowledge him as a creative capable of expressing himself in more than one medium? The same imagination, heart and vision that conceived and created sublime music were simply channelled through another medium. It's not unusual. Picasso wrote poetry and surrealist plays. Salvador Dalí co-created screenplays with Luis Buñuel and produced a novel, *Hidden Faces*. Neo-expressionist Julian Schnabel also made narrative films, including the celebrated *Basquiat*, about fellow artist Jean-Michel Basquiat, which features a blinding soundtrack and co-stars David Bowie as Andy Warhol. The King of Pop Art himself created hundreds of films and penned a disjoined novel: *A: A Novel*. If we're doing this, we ought not overlook conceptual artist Yoko Ono, who wrote her fairy tale *Invisible Flower* when she was only nineteen (it was not published until 2012, at the insistence of her son Sean); who in 1964 published the curious book of instructional poems called *Grapefruit*; and who created music with and independently of her husband. Nor should we ignore the fact that some rock-star painters produce artworks that eclipse the very best of their own music. John might find today's so-called celebrity art movement rather up itself, a bit Emperor's New Clothes. That galleries are falling over themselves to exhibit artists already famous for non-visual work while they might not look twice at an unknown fine artist of similar ability does little to uphold the purity of 'art for art's sake'.

*

Not only did Stuart Sutcliffe help John with his homework. He also opened his friend's eyes to the French impressionists. Pierre-Auguste Renoir, Claude Monet, Édouard Manet and Henri de Toulouse-Lautrec were some of the painters he adored and was inspired by. The movement that swirled out of minute, delicate brush strokes flickering suggestions of light, time and substance was perfected by Paris-based artists who rose to prominence during the late nineteenth century. It offended artistic convention of the time. This more abstract, less-defined approach to art, in which moods and emotions were conveyed and atmospheres evoked, seeped down into music and literature. It also inspired Vincent van Gogh, who moved from the Netherlands to Paris to learn at the knee of Gauguin, Pissarro and Monet, and experimented with colour to express emotion. He figured out how to work pain, depression and anguish into his art. To gash his veins, figuratively speaking, all over his canvasses. For an artist to expose his soul and feelings through paint was revolutionary. Van Gogh invented this new style that would come to be classified as expressionism. It probably cost him his sanity: by the age of thirty-seven, he'd shot himself dead.

We can know too much. The most appealing aspect of any art form is its mystery. The blank spaces between the brush strokes, the silent notes unplayed. The artist of whatever discipline is not so much striving to show us something of himself as struggling to make sense of his own existence. It is a viewpoint with which John agreed.

'If I had the capabilities of being something other than I am, I would,' he commented in 1971. It's no fun being an artist. You know what it's like, writing, it's torture. I read about Van Gogh, Beethoven, any of the fuckers. If they had psychiatrists, we wouldn't have had Gauguin's great pictures. These bastards are just sucking us to death; that's about all that we can do, is do it like circus animals.

'I resent being an artist, in that respect, I resent performing for fucking idiots who don't know anything. They can't feel. I'm the one that's feeling, because I'm the one that is expressing. They live vicariously through me and other artists …'[4]

*

Although he, like John, was mad about rock'n'roll, and despite having fashioned a cool-rocker look for himself, there was nothing fledgling-rock-star about Stu. The extent of his vocal ability had been exhausted during a short-lived stint as a choirboy. Although he'd endured piano lessons, blown bugle in the Air Training Corps, and his father had shown him a few chords on the guitar, he was none too impressive an instrumentalist either. His acquaintance with Paul McCartney and George Harrison had been facilitated simply by geography. While still pupils at the Liverpool Institute next-door to the art school, they often came over to rehearse with John in empty college classrooms. Stu was impressed by the boys, was drawn to the band and took to pitching up at parties to watch them play.

A pivotal moment came when a canvas of Stu's, *Summer Painting*, was chosen for the John Moores Painting Prize exhibition at Liverpool's Walker Art Gallery. It would be on display there from November 1959 into the New Year 1960.[5] Moores himself purchased the painting, for £65, which would have been seen as a major turning point for this as yet unqualified young artist. Not to mention a serious windfall. John, Paul and George wasted no time in helping him spend it. Currently devoid of a drummer and drumkit, a bass player and a bass guitar, it was decided that Stu could step into the line-up as either one, provided he was prepared to invest in his own instrument. Unable to imagine himself as a credible thumper, he was persuaded to give the bass a go. A Höfner President 500/5 model bass was duly acquired from Frank Hessy's Music Shop.

'The trouble was,' commented Paul McCartney, 'he couldn't play well. This was a bit of a drawback, but it looked good, so it wasn't too much of a problem.'

When Stuart joined the ever-evolving group over Christmas 1959, Paul confessed, he and George were beside themselves with jealousy.

'It was something I didn't deal with very well,' said Paul. 'We were always slightly jealous of John's other friendships. He was the older fellow; it was just the way it was. When Stuart came in, it felt as if he was taking the position away from George and me. We had to take a bit of a back seat. Stuart was John's age, went to art college, was a very good painter and had all the cred that we didn't.'[6]

The group was at this point known as the Silver Beatles, no doubt inspired by the plethora of 'creature' R&B and doo-wop groups who dominated a variety of US charts during the 1940s and 1950s. Many of which were 'bird' groups: the Crows, the Flamingos, the Orioles, the Robins, the Ravens, the Larks, the Penguins, the Swallows, the Wrens. There were the 'animal' groups, such as the Spaniels, the Rattlesnakes (Barry Gibb's skiffle/rock'n'roll outfit that would become the Bee Gees in 1958), the Impalas, the Teddy Bears and notably the Spiders. Most crucially, there were Buddy Holly's Crickets – who themselves emulated groups named after birds. Warming to the theme of insect-inspired names, Buddy and the boys overlooked the existence of Bronx R&B vocal group the Crickets, having chosen but changed their minds about calling themselves the Beetles. A little way down the track, the actual Beatles coined their moniker (partly) in honour of the Crickets. What goes around.

CHAPTER 5

GIOCONDA

To what extent did John's coercion of Stuart Sutcliffe into a band he was barely equipped to play in have to do with John's own insecurity? Accustomed as he was by then to being able to get virtually anybody other than Mimi to do anything he wanted by flaunting bullishness sugared with charm, it wouldn't always have been obvious to those around him that his was a smoke-and-mirrors act. Reluctant Stu was no more a musician than Pete Shotton, who, keenly embracing his limitations, abandoned the DIY-band washboard almost as soon as he'd been talked into scratching it. But Stu had artistic talent. He was going places. He looked the part, and would entrance the chicks. Music came so easily to John, he probably assumed that anyone could get their head round it, especially one with creative inclinations; that all it took was determination, dedication and a few perfunctory practice sessions. Stu would be in his group, and that was that. The more subliminal, perhaps even sinister aspect of this is that John needed him there. Threatened from the outset by Paul's precocious virtuosity, John was in danger of being overshadowed in his own band by the younger, more angelic, more visually appealing, more musical one. There was already toxicity in the set-up, which the others may well have sensed. For Stu's primary role was to make John look good.

Though he would have derided the suggestion, and had such

diagnoses been available at the time, John was even then displaying signs of what we now refer to as narcissistic personality disorder. He was instinctively critical and judgemental of others, at times ad punctum saevitia, as if the only point to their existence was to enhance his own standing and significance. He was given to lashing out and to belittling others, in ways that conferred the delusion of superiority. He would not have understood at that time and at such a young age that it was his own extreme lack of self-esteem that was driving him to seek control and to put down others. His relationship with Stu was a prime example. He wanted him in his band, but would ridicule him for poor musicianship and for falling short of the standards he expected of him. Instead of trying to help him to improve his 'bad' habits or working constructively with him on his bass-playing, John would go out of his way to berate him, injure him and dent his confidence. John could be terrifyingly passive-aggressive, even outright aggressive, causing those in his circle to tip-toe on eggshells when they were around him, so fearful were they of what he might do or say next. Prone to lavishing them with sarcasm and spiteful witticisms, he shot from the lip and kept the others on their toes while remaining in denial of his own feelings and shortcomings. He was also inclined to withdraw and sulk, leaving his sidekicks wracking their brains as to what they might have said or done to anger him.

We have all encountered narcissists. We know to our cost how damaging relationships with such people can be. Coming on like God's gift, looking down on us from their polished pedestal, refusing to compromise, needing always to be the centre of attention, being one minute affectionate, the next acidic and cruel. They tend to bathe all with whom they come into contact in negativity, often subliminally. Biographers and psychologists have had a field day with John on this level. While it is impossible even for those with the requisite professional qualifications to diagnose an individual they've never met, and who is in any case deceased, we are at liberty to reflect on the experiences that shaped him. His deeply complex, dysfunctional childhood was, we can reasonably assume, the root of his problems. He was the ultimate tangle of contradictions, a bunch of both good and bad guys. Much more is known today about brain development during the early, crucial years and about the formation of the adult self than was ever imagined during the 1950s and '60s. We can conclude, from a distant, detached but informed viewpoint, that John the abandoned, needy child was Peter Pan by another name.[1] He had never grown up. He hated himself. The yanking-on of the heavy leather jacket that he adopted as his 'look' at around this time was symbolic. It concealed and protected a thin skin. Anyone who scraped, scratched or got under it would become the target of his rage and brutality. He was compelled to behave this way by his low self-esteem. He couldn't help himself. It was fine for him to hurt and reject others, but woe betide he or she who did similar to him. While he was capable of sustaining close personal relationships, he would invariably put himself first in them. He would all too soon sabotage the partnership in some way, in blatant acts of self-harm. A little down the line, throw in fame and fortune on a vast and barely comprehensible scale, stir in substance abuse, sprinkle infidelity and domestic violence, light the gas and stand well back. Perhaps John never stood a chance of living a 'normal' life. If there exists such a thing.

'Like all great artists, he was damaged goods,' reflects Simon Napier-Bell, the fabled rock manager, songwriter, filmmaker and author; caretaker of the careers of Marc Bolan, Eric Clapton, Jeff Beck and George Michael upwards; who knew John personally during the early sixties.

'He was extremely aggressive, angry and upset most of the time,' says Simon. 'He was very good indeed at disguising that some of the time. I never saw Paul like that: he survived their phenomenon in a different way. He was always the politest Beatle. John always had to make a sarcastic comment, had to say something that would make him look good and put you down. Or he ignored you. He didn't like himself, and he had a death wish. But listen, you are describing *artists*. These are not normal people. Given that my personal weakness is for difficult, intelligent people, I was never daunted by him. We were the same age. I saw him in a way that perhaps others didn't. He was fine by me.'

That he was driven, from his late teens, to destroy virtually everything that came good for him, from romantic relationships to professional success, is the key to his lives, loves and deaths. Who killed John Lennon? *He* did.

*

No one bats an eyelash these days at the thought of a female rock manager, club promoter or entertainment guru. We are more than used to the Sharon Osbourne effect, to Apollonia Kotero and Tina Davis, to Janet Billig Rich and Dianna Hart.[2] Back then, such a woman was a rare sensation. At a later time and in different circumstances, Mona Best's personal story, and her major part in theirs as 'Mother of the Beatles', might have steered them down an alternative path. She may even have moulded a group better-equipped to deal with the vagaries and madness of fame, that might not have disbanded at the zenith of their global popularity, that might have carried on performing and recording towards the twenty-first century, John's death in December 1980 and George's in November 2001 notwithstanding.

Sultry, raven-haired Mona was the owner of the Casbah Coffee Club, which she opened in the cellar of her large, rambling Liverpool home in August 1959. She was inspired by an item she had seen on television about the 2i's on Soho's Old Compton Street, launched three years earlier by the Irani brothers, hence the name. It was a hang-out for 'beatniks', a spin-off of the American Beat generation popularised by writers Jack Kerouac, Allen Ginsberg and cohorts. New York's disaffected youth and downtrodden hipsters had whirled themselves a following that would expand to become the global hippie movement. London's beatniks flocked to the new coffee bars to recite poetry, discuss music and art films, trawl Italian magazines for style tips, swap records and jive to those played on jukeboxes. Such joints attracted hordes of youngsters initially for the simplest of reasons: they stayed open later than pubs. The 2i's, which despite its erroneous apostrophe would later acquire legendary status as 'Europe's first rock club', was something of a crucible. It was where Ian 'Sammy' Samwell met Harry Webb, who metamorphosed into Cliff Richard, for whom Samwell wrote 'Move It', Cliff's first hit record in August 1958. Four months earlier, the Marquee Club had opened at 165 Oxford Street. Four years later, in 1962, the Rolling Stones would play their first ever gig there. The Marquee would move to 90 Wardour Street in 1964. Stock Records on South Molton Street was a crucial element of the scene because it imported R&B, blues and rock'n'roll records unavailable elsewhere. Brian Jones, Eric Clapton and many other young, fledgling rock stars became residents of Soho. Mona's pennies jangled.

Her Casbah Club would be membership-only, to prevent bombardment by riff-raff. Two shillings and sixpence (half a crown) a year guaranteed entry to about three hundred clubbers that first season. She installed an espresso machine (like hen's teeth), provided snacks and non-alcoholic drinks, and would spin discs to her eager punters on a tiny Dansette.

John's Quarry Men bagged the opening-night gig by default, after another outfit pulled out. Not only had George Harrison been due to play guitar with the Les Stewart Quartet at the launch, but one of that group's line-up had been helping the proprietress to spruce up the venue. She needed not only a replacement act, but extra hands wielding paint brushes. John, Paul, George and Stuart Sutcliffe obliged. A bunch of artists were never going to leave a blank wall. They took it upon themselves to embellish the space with stars, rainbows, dragons, spiders, even a beetle. Those cave wall images, together with a silhouette of John added by his girlfriend Cyn, were of course preserved for posterity. As were the stories. According to Mona's family, when she discovered that nineteen-year-old John had carved his name into the wall of the cellar, she lashed out at him with 'a crack around the back of the head'.

'It sent his glasses flying on to the floor and then he stood on them,' said her son Roag.

This left the short-sighted John desperately trying to fathom how he would make his way home. Mona saved the day.

'That's how John Lennon ended up wearing my grandmother's glasses for the next month,' explained Roag, suggesting that it was their own family-heirloom 'granny glasses' that would influence John's image in years to come.[3]

In 2006, Grade II Listed status was conferred upon the old coal hole beneath 8 Hayman's Green. It was subsequently relaunched as a tourist destination and established itself as a popular stop on the Beatles Liverpool tour.

John's group, who had by this time gone through several name-changes – Johnny and the Moondogs, Japage 3 and Los Paranoias, before reverting to the Quarry Men – performed some seven Saturday-night concerts from 29 August into October 1959, featuring Ken Brown from the Les Stewart Quartet alongside John, Paul and George, on fifteen shillings a head. They did so without a drummer, or even a PA. Despite which, three hundred-odd local teenagers crammed in for their debut offering, and danced and sweated the night away in the suffocating cellar. It was John who talked Mona into engaging an amateur guitarist called Harry to open for them, so that they could borrow his little amp. Encouraged by the success of their first night, Mona proposed a residency and negotiated a marginally more attractive group rate. She sat back, counted the shillings she charged in admission, and watched the queues snake the distance to the corner of the Green. After every Saturday-night show, 'Mo' threw open her private quarters to her young musicians. Her seductive talk of Eastern philosophy and Indian traditions particularly impressed George Harrison.

The postscript is delicious. Paul and George were friendly at the Liverpool Institute with Neil Aspinall, who would become their first roadie. He drove the band's gear to and from shows in and around Liverpool in a second-hand Commer van bought by Mona. By March 1960, Stu and John had renamed the group the Beatles, though they were often promoted as 'the Silver Beetles' by clubs who couldn't understand the 'weird' name. Neil and Mona's son Pete became such close friends that, in 1961, Aspinall started renting a room in the Best abode. Aged about twenty, and vulnerable, he became entangled with Mona, who was some seventeen years his senior. Mona fell pregnant. Despite its phenomenal success – she had built the club's membership to more than a thousand – she closed her hugely successful Casbah for good with a final performance by the Beatles in June 1962, just before the birth of her third son. Vincent 'Roag' Best arrived in July 1962. Aspinall carried on working for the Beatles, and would remain in their employ for the rest of his life. When former telephone engineer and part-time Cavern Club roadie Mal Evans began lugging for them, Neil was upgraded to personal assistant. Mona and Neil separated in 1968. Neil would rise to become chief executive of Apple Corps. He died of lung cancer in 2008, aged sixty-seven, with Paul McCartney at his bedside.

Mona's Collegiate Grammar School son Pete had also made his way as a musician. Soon after she bought him his first drum kit, he launched his first band, the Black Jacks. After a falling-out over fees, John and the Quarry Men walked. Pete's Black Jacks replaced them as the Casbah's resident band. Being the only local venue that would give new amateur groups an airing at that time, there was always plenty of interest and competition. Most of Merseyside's emerging bands played there at one time or another, including Gerry and the Pacemakers and the Searchers. The Quarry Men soon returned, and would perform there from time to time. It was in Mona's cellar that John and Paul talked Stu into buying his bass and joining their line-up. In that basement, too, Mona's son Pete was added to the Beatles' line-up as their much-needed drummer. Soon after his half-brother Roag was born, Pete would be dumped by the Beatles. But we have Hamburg to visit first.

When her son became a Beatle, Mona assumed responsibility for their career and effectively became their first manager. It was she who lobbied Cavern Club owner Ray McFall to try to get them a lunchtime residency. McFall was committed to jazz at the time, but eventually revised his stance as rock began to come to the fore.

Mona might well have continued to manage the Beatles, had not record-store manager Brian Epstein turned up, kitted and witted, like a seasoned entrepreneur. Mona was probably intimidated by him. She ceded control. But even after they signed to Epstein, she retained an interest. She had opened her home to them, fed them, tucked ready cash into their pockets, tucked ideas into their heads, and later claimed to have taken more of an interest in them than their own parents ever did. She became such an irritant to Epstein that he came to refer to her as 'that woman'.

Peter, Paul and George would find themselves deported from Hamburg in November 1960. It was Mona who reassured them, and got their equipment back: no mean feat in those days of limited communication and language barriers. It was she who pestered Granada Television the following year, to try to secure them a spot on producer Johnnie Hamp's popular show *People and Places*. In 1967, when the Beatles were preparing the artwork for the cover of the *Sgt. Pepper* album, John cheekily asked Mona if they could borrow her father's war medals, awarded in India, to wear for the photo shoot. Still smarting from the way they'd dumped Pete from the line-up, Mona nevertheless agreed. It was always clear that the Beatles respected her enormously. In their gauche, bashful way, they remained eternally grateful for all that she had done for them. Even after they had rocketed to fame, the boys kept in touch and sent her gifts from the road. Was she stung by her involvement with the biggest band in history? Put it this way: she never opened another club; never attempted to manage another band; never immersed herself in any other business, beyond the welcoming into her hallowed home of a handful of paying guests. That she never moved out of that huge Hayman's Green house suggests a strong emotional attachment to the place, which represented her part in their extraordinary story. A heart attack took her eight years after John died, on what would have been his forty-eighth birthday. She was sixty-four.

CHAPTER 6

INFERNO

It was former singer turned Jacaranda coffee bar/strip club/ nightclub owner and beat-scene booking agent Allan Williams, a squeaky little Welshman, who fixed it for his Beatle regulars, sometime performers and occasional painters to perform in Hamburg. The now infamous Indra and Kaiserkeller clubs exist to this day on the Grosse Freiheit in St Pauli, an unholy dominion in the shadow of St Joseph's majestic Catholic church. The venues were owned by Bruno Koschmider, a German entrepreneur with a thirst for British groups. 'Kosch' also owned the Bambi Filmkunsttheater, known as the 'Bambi Kino', a small cinema on Paul-Roosen Strasse round the corner from the Grosse Freiheit.

Neither London's Soho nor Amsterdam's De Wallen could hold a candle to the Reeperbahn red-light district, which was, at the turn of the sixties, Seamen Central. Its proximity to the city's extensive docks and its cluster of brothels, strip clubs and nightspots infested with prostitutes, pimps, transvestites, gangsters and drug dealers guaranteed a nightly influx of punters seeking beer, bands, babes and brawls, probably in that order. Make your way there today and you'd be forgiven for mistaking the still-seedy neon-lit enclave for an anti-Disneyland for brides and grooms. Its streets now brim with suspended hens in tutus, veils and porn shoes; with green-gilled stags staggering from live sex shows to leak and vomit in the cobbled streets. Nothing fancy about it. But still, a kind of magic. Hamburg has been written about all these years with a reverence bordering on religious worship, on account of its pivotal place in Beatles history.

It was here that they would be dropped in the deep end to serve the most arduous of apprenticeships, performing, it is said, more gigs than anywhere else in the world during the course of their career. Though estimates vary, and though the total is rivalled by the number of appearances they are calculated to have made at the Cavern, the consensus is around two hundred and eighty. However many shows – the actual number barely matters, who cares, it's enough to know that it was a lot – they upped their game, tightened their act, rocked the crowds with their extended interpretations of songs by Little Richard, Elvis Presley, Carl Perkins, Fats Domino and so on, and 'did their ten thousand hours'.[1] It was here, too, that the boys would meet and connect with Ringo Starr, heralding an end to Paul's part-time duties on drums; here that the Beatles would expand their repertoire, and make their first-ever commercial recording as backing band on Tony Sheridan's 'My Bonnie' – which would draw them to the attention of Liverpool music-shop owner Brian Epstein and prompt him to offer his services as their manager; here that they would meet the cool new friends who inspired a collective, collar-grazing, androgynous haircut that would earn them the moniker 'moptops'; here, in this fetid, forsaken sewer that John would give unbridled vent to his misanthropic streak, coming on a full-pelt menacing, arrogant, sneering yob. He would abuse and insult his hosts with on-stage goose-stepping, 'Heil Hitler!' salutes and cries of 'Nazis!' 'spazzies!' 'retards!' and 'Krauts!' He would also hold a black pocket comb to his upper lip as a fake Adolfian moustache and fall about impersonating cripples. Kosch has gone down in history for commanding that the Beatles must '*Mach schau!*' John, in his element, took him at his word and then some, going so far as to start fights from the stage. On one occasion he even appeared wearing little more than a toilet seat. Far from taking offence, the punters lapped it up.

A Caribbean steel outfit sowed the seed. They had jumped from 'the Jac', a dank subterranean hang-out on Liverpool's Slater Street near the art college, to do a couple of gigs in the German port. They penned cards home to Williams, raving about the scene there. Spotting an opportunity, Williams offered his services to Koschmider as a booking agent for Merseyside groups. After failing to engage Rory Storm and the Hurricanes because they were committed to a summer season at Butlin's, and getting a 'no', too, from pre-booked Gerry and the Pacemakers, Williams sold Koschmider the Beatles. With nothing to stop them – Paul, Pete and George had left school, while John had failed his year-end exams, and had been kicked out of art college – they were raring to go. They convinced themselves that this opportunity to consolidate and build on what they'd made of it so far could lead to their big break. On 16 August 1960, still revved from a fortnight-long tour of northern Scotland in support of Larry Parnes protégé Johnny Gentle, an epic voyage was undertaken. John, Paul, Stu, George, Williams, his wife Beryl, her brother Barry Chang and 'Lord Woodbine', aka Trinidadian music promoter Harold Adolphus Philips (with whom Williams co-owned a Liverpool strip club) sardined into Williams green Austin van. They belted a detour to London to collect waiter Georg Sterner (who would act as interpreter and 'Beatles spy' while working as a waiter for Kosch at the Kaiserkeller) and looped back up to Harwich to take a ship across to the Hook of Holland. They drove like the clappers through the Netherlands into Germany, arriving during the next day with only a few hours' respite before being hustled on stage. They performed several hours a night thereafter into the early hours, eight days a week for six weeks, while billeted in cramped and filthy accommodation behind the scenes at the Bambi Kino.

Rory Storm and the Hurricanes arrived in October, and soon fell into a routine of five or six ninety-minute sets each day, alternating with the Beatles. Hello Ringo.

The shenanigans that ensued during the five Hamburg trips undertaken by the boys between August 1960 and December 1962 are books and films in their own right. Their visits comprised forty-eight nights at the Indra, followed by fifty-eight nights at the Kaiserkeller after complaints were made about the noise at the former; three months at the Top Ten; and a seven-week opening stint at the Star-Club. They returned to Hamburg in November and December 1962 for their fourth and fifth engagements, booked by the Star-Club months in advance. During those final two visits, Ringo drummed, having replaced Pete Best that August. The Beatles had been reluctant to honour their final two-week booking commencing 18 December 1962, as they were now in demand in the UK thanks to the success of their first chart single 'Love Me Do'.

John said famously that he'd been born in Liverpool but had grown up in Hamburg. They all did. They could hardly have done otherwise. Dragged from the relative luxury of home, they endured a baptism of fire and learned quickly to fend for themselves on some of the toughest streets in Europe. They made new friends, including former flyweight boxing champ Horst Fascher, a beacon among the lowlife. A former jailbird employed as a bouncer by Koschmider, he fancied himself as a crooner and saw his new chums as a stepping stone to the spotlight. It never happened, but, hey. Their initial encounters with him were hostile. When George Harrison asked him if he was a Nazi, Horst belted him one. When John persisted with the insult, Fascher dragged him into the men's room and pissed all over him. His anger was perhaps justifiable, given that his family had embraced and aided Jews during the Holocaust. But he softened, took a shine to the grubby gobsters, and started looking out for them.

Bearing in mind that John was not yet twenty and Paul and George considerably younger when they made their debut in Germany, the thought of them hanging with strippers, hookers and trannies, violent thugs armed with flick knives, and drug-touting, cosh-wielding security bruisers and bar staff would have been more than sufficient to see Mimi into an early grave. Unaware that John had already started down the path of substance abuse while still a student, she would have been horrified by what ensued. Whatever gets you through the night. To help boost their stamina during several sets each evening, playing to marauding gangs only there for the beer and the fisticuffs, to begin with, at least, they began to neck Preludin, dubbed 'prellies'. The brand name of the drug Phenmetrazine, it was known on US streets as 'Bam'. Preludin was a powerful stimulant with few unpleasant side effects that could be used to suppress the appetite. When they swallowed the pills with beer, the boys would sometimes froth at the mouth, and could stay awake for days. When high, their shows were a riot. John, naturally, overdid it, at times ingesting four or five prellies to Paul's more restrained single dose. Pete is said to have barely touched the drug. Which could account for something.

'In Hamburg the waiters always had Preludin – and various other pills, but I remember Preludin because it was such a big trip – and they were all taking these pills to keep themselves awake, to work these incredible hours in this all-night place,' remembered John. 'And so the waiters, when they'd see the musicians falling over with tiredness or with drink, they'd give you the pill. You'd take the pill, you'd be talking, you'd sober up, you could work almost endlessly – until the pill wore off, then you'd have to have another.'[2]

Before long, they found themselves in need of something stronger, and graduated to speed: highly addictive amphetamines prescribed as antidepressant/anti-anxiety drugs, with street names such as Black Bombers, French Blues and Purple Hearts.

Within no time their reputation had soared beyond the thousands of ratings on shore leave to reach the ears of a handful of Hamburg's sophisticated young intellectuals more attuned to trad jazz; in particular, those of a group of cool, black-clad graduates of the Meisterschule, a tertiary educational establishment of art, fashion and photography. Klaus Voormann came first, and soon brought his girlfriend Astrid Kirchherr and their mutual friend Jürgen Vollmer. Others of their ilk followed. When I interviewed Klaus for this book, he had just turned eighty-one.

'People have been asking me for decades to analyse my good friend John Lennon,' he said. 'But I won't. I can't do that. It's too difficult.

'What I will say is that the time before they became famous is

the most interesting incarnation of John, for me. He wasn't happy,
you see. Oh, no. I'd say the opposite. John was always very, very
frustrated. He was very sarcastic, very funny, trying always to cover
over his problems with a joke or a prank. He didn't know what
or who he was, this was obvious to me. It was about his mother,
the problems that arose during his childhood. Her death was very
recent, she'd only been gone a couple of years, and that's what he
hadn't worked out when he came to Hamburg.

'John pretended to be a rocker, but he wasn't one really. What he
was, was a very hard person. He was the first one in the band who I
met, and I didn't know what to make of him. I was scared, I thought
he would hurt me, but there was something very strong that drew
me to him.'

Klaus's own in-crowd, he admits, had little in common with
the Beatles.

'We were the arty people. We wore suede and leather, floaty scarves
and funny hairstyles. We were very different from them. Because of
the way we looked and the kind of people that we were – quite deep,
intense and questioning – it was difficult for us to go to those clubs.
There were always so many fights. But we were fortunate that the
waiters saw that we had become friends with the band, and they
protected and took care of us. We started going down to the Grosse
Freiheit most nights to hear them play.'

The Berlin-born dyslexic son of a physician was two and a half
years older than John and about twenty-two when he discovered
the Beatles. A graphic designer and commercial artist, Klaus's first
professional record cover was for the Typhoons' reworking of the
Ventures' 1960 instrumental 'Walk Don't Run'.

'I was proud of it. I could talk a little English, and I took it along
and showed it to John, who told me to go to Stuart as he was the arty
one in the band. That was our opener to get contact with the Beatles.
Stuart and I sat around talking about Kandinsky and other favourite
artists, and everyone else just joined in. Even John – who didn't on the
whole tend to enjoy any scenario that wasn't directly about him.

'They were unlike anyone we'd met before. Everything about

them was completely instinctive, they were completely fascinating to us. I think that we were fascinating to them in return. We'd had the education that had moulded us into sensitive, enquiring beings. We were sort of existentialists at the time, following that philosophy, and it was John who decided that we should be called "Exis".[3]

'I definitely expected them to make it,' Klaus insists. 'I certainly knew by seeing them on stage, from the earliest moments. I just knew that they would be big. With them, you had everything. John's unique rocker voice and energy. Paul's strong, melodic vocals. Sweet George, in his way very cocky, doing Eddie Cochran and Joe Brown songs. Each individual with his very strong personality. Put together, their blend was magical. I never analysed it at the time I was experiencing it, I just felt.'

But John was a puzzle to him. For all his showiness and larks, Klaus laments, he would never let his friend in.

'He did come round eventually, and he would reveal to me bits and pieces, but he'd always cut the information short, and would rarely give away much of himself. Only much later on, when our friendship had existed for many years, when he was living in America and working on his solo projects, I would go to see him and he would really open up to me then. In Hamburg, however, he said little. I longed to know him.

'I remember one night we got really drunk together, we went into a strip club and got thrown out. It was around five in the morning. He and I went to the fish market and sat on a bench shivering in the open air, just talking. It was a strangely intimate situation, but still he could not open up to me. He wouldn't let go. He really wasn't in tune with himself at that time. I was a little older, and I had my own problems, for sure. But it hurt me to observe John in such agony. He would get so angry that he would do things like smash the door of a cupboard in with his fists, and rip his precious leather jacket. He was a good friend, a dear friend to me, but I couldn't help him.'

The primary issue with the Beatles at that time, reflects Klaus, was that they had no adult there to guide them.

'This was the fundamental problem. They were not old enough

to be in Hamburg by themselves. They were really just kids, but they had no one there to take care of them. There was no mum, no auntie to take care of domestic things, which is what they had been used to until they went there. They were just youngsters pulled out of Liverpool to be exploited in a foreign country; to live in these terrible digs, you can't imagine the squalor, and forced to work like dogs night after night, hour after hour. They had to take drugs to keep themselves awake. We felt so sorry for them. Those digs at the Bambi Kino were just awful. You wouldn't keep an animal in there. The room they slept in was just a broom cupboard. There was no wardrobe, no proper bed to sleep in, just camp beds. Filth everywhere, they were using a pot for a toilet, there was nowhere decent to wash, they had to put their feet in the sink in the public toilets in the cinema. They would have kept on doing that, too, if we hadn't come along. It was so terrible, so disgusting, that it shocked us. It made you want to cry. We weren't like these big saviours or anything, we simply wanted to make it nicer for them. Astrid and I invited them to her mother's home so that they could have a bath, wash their hair and eat proper food. They just desperately needed mothering, and this is what Astrid did for them. We became their family. Astrid and I were like parents to them. We took care of those boys, and made them feel good again. We took them on trips to the cinema, all over Hamburg and the surrounding areas, and to the Baltic Sea. They were very open to new experiences, especially Stuart.'

Astrid, then also about twenty-two, was a photography graduate and lensman's assistant. She captured some of the most iconic early black-and-white images of the Beatles, which have since been exhibited in the UK, Germany, Austria, all over the USA and in Japan, and published in limited-edition books.

'It was like a merry-go-round in my head, they looked absolutely astonishing … My whole life changed in a couple of minutes. All I wanted was to be with them and to know them,' she said in 2005.[4]

She was a stunning, heart-melting blonde. In John's view, a 'German Brigitte Bardot', a give-or-take perfect reincarnation of the object of his pubescent dreams.[5] Every Beatle was smitten. Astrid took them to the historic Heiligengeistfeld (Holy Spirit Square) the site of the Hamburger Dom, the city's most famous funfair, to photograph them. Jürgen Vollmer photographed them too, as a group and individually, around Hamburg. Astrid took them home for tea to her widowed mother Nielsa in Altona, a well-heeled western suburb of Hamburg that had once been a flourishing Jewish neighbourhood. They were goggle-eyed at her bedroom, a candlelit fantasy chamber painted black with a silver-foiled ceiling and black satin sheets. They got on so well with Nielsa that they were soon rocking up at her house most days for dinner. She was soon persuaded to obtain supplies of Preludin for them from her friendly local pharmacist, as they were officially available only on prescription. Another regular supplier was Rosa Hoffman, one of the club toilet attendants.

Even cynical, hard-hearted John was enchanted by Astrid. He wrote home to Cyn about her in such glowing terms in his annotated, illustrated up-to-ten-page letters that his girlfriend grew wildly jealous. She had nothing to worry about. When she travelled to Hamburg to visit John on a fortnight's holiday, accompanied by Paul's sweetheart Dot Rhone, Astrid welcomed them, behaved beautifully and even put Cyn up in her mother's house (while Dot was consigned, with Paul, to Rosa the toilet attendant's houseboat). Cyn saw for herself that Stu and Astrid had got engaged: they were wearing each other's gold rings. Stu had fallen in love at first sight. But their marriage, for a tragic reason, was never to be.

Twice-divorced, childless, reclusive Astrid retained her beauty and integrity to the last. She continued to refer to her first fiancé Stuart Sutcliffe, who had died in her arms at just twenty-one, as 'the love of my life.' She herself died alone in Hamburg on 12 May 2020, fifty-eight years after him, and eight days ahead of her eighty-second birthday. Her pioneering images of the baby-faced Beatles, captured around her hometown on her humble Rolleicord, remain suspended like stars across their universe. But she was always modest about the part she played in the shaping of their image and style.

'The most important thing I contributed to them,' she insisted, 'was friendship.'

Meanwhile, the Beatles returned to Liverpool under a cloud towards the end of 1960. They had dumped on Koschmider by quitting his employ to work at a rival club that was bigger and more professional: the Top Ten. Returning to the Bambi Kino to retrieve their meagre belongings, Paul and Pete found themselves fumbling in the dark. Hanging a condom from a nail in the wall and setting light to it was always going to incur Koschmider's wrath. No permanent damage, but Koschmider wasted no time in alerting the police that they had tried to commit arson. The offenders were arrested, questioned and deported. George, still only seventeen, permit-less and not old enough to be working there in the first place, was ejected in November. Paul and Pete followed in December. John brought up the rear shortly afterwards, wending his way on the train by himself, truly fearful that he would never again find England.

Stuart had tonsillitis and remained in Hamburg until he was well enough to travel, on a plane ticket paid for by Astrid. But his heart was no longer in Liverpool, nor in the Beatles. He abandoned rock'n'roll for love in July 1961. After moving in with his fiancée in Altona, he enrolled on a scholarship at the Hochschule für bildende Künste Hamburg with the intention of seeking eventual employment as an art teacher. But he had been plagued for some time by severe headaches, light sensitivity and even intermittent blindness. After he collapsed unexpectedly in class one day, Nielsa Kirchherr called in specialists. Although tests were inconclusive, Stu's condition worsened. On 10 April 1962, Nielsa urgently summoned Astrid from work to accompany him to hospital in an ambulance. He died in her arms before they arrived. The cause of his death was later given as 'a ruptured aneurysm resulting in cerebral paralysis due to bleeding into the right ventricle of the brain'. He was twenty-one. Astrid collapsed in grief. Yet it fell to her to go to the airport to meet Paul, John and Pete when they returned to Hamburg to commence their next stint there. George jetted in on a later flight with Stu's mother Millie and the Beatles' new manager Brian Epstein. The boys were beside themselves. George and John did their utmost to support Astrid, who had all but lost the will to live. As she recalled in a later interview, John told her she must decide if she wanted to 'live or die, there is no other question'.[6]

Neither Astrid nor John attended Stuart's funeral in Liverpool. Missing, or being forced to miss, the funerals of his nearest and dearest had already become a feature of John's existence. He appears to have been haunted by his friend for the rest of his life. Yoko Ono would later acknowledge that John spoke often and fondly of Stuart, describing him as an 'alter ego' and as a 'guiding force'. 'I felt I knew Stuart because hardly a day went by that John did not speak about him,' Ono said.[7] Was it John's own guilt and even fear of repercussions that prevented him from turning up, as he should have done, to pay his last respects?

There has long been speculation that John may have been directly to blame for Stuart's death. The shocking claim was regurgitated ahead of the launch of Pauline Cronin Sutcliffe's book about her late brother. Pre-publication coverage distorted what the Long Island-based psychotherapist and art dealer had to say about John's alleged physical attacks on Stu. She was vilified by the media for her 'fervent belief' that the fatal brain haemorrhage was generated by one of John's unprovoked assaults during a jealous rage in 1959. Pauline was said to have declared Stu's barely legible scrawlings and exclamations in his sketch book during the last year of his life to be 'a reflection of a slow decline in his mental health'. The post-mortem did flag up a skull indentation that could have been caused by a kick or a blow. But in July 2003, ahead of a Bonhams London auction of more than a hundred of her brother's personal effects – his birth certificate, diplomas from Liverpool College of Art, photographs, poems, letters written by Astrid to her fiancé's family, billets-doux from Stuart to her, some lyrics to 'lost Beatles songs' allegedly co-written by Stu, and his sketchbooks – she admitted saying that a fight between John and Stuart that happened weeks before the Beatles bassist died 'could not have been helpful', but denied having blamed John for causing the injuries that killed him.

'I did not say what was quoted in the papers, and I am shocked by it,' she said. 'I'm distressed for John Lennon's family and for my own family and for millions of Beatles fans worldwide who would be deeply offended by it.'

Ms Sutcliffe had dedicated forty years of her life to collecting memorabilia and writing about her brother. The Sutcliffe estate did not earn any income, she said, and had proved prohibitively expensive to maintain. She believed that fans would clamour to own a piece of Stuart Sutcliffe history because it was he who gave the Beatles their distinctive image.

'I always believed Stuart was not only the central force behind the Beatles – but also the member who most influenced their public image, making style statements that still reverberate throughout the world to this day. More importantly, though, he was an artist who chose to put his affiliation with the Beatles to the side in order to pursue his first love – his art.'

Whatever the truth, biographers and fans have long been deeply divided over it. Stuart's injury has been attributed to a range of occurrences and conditions, from a street brawl during which John flew at him, not to hurt but to protect, to Stuart's own excessive use of amphetamines.

'My brother had been beaten up more than once,' stated Pauline in another interview. 'In fact, many of them had been. It was part of life for rock'n'roll bands in late fifties, early sixties Liverpool. There were always gangs out to get them … it's just part of that world at the time.'[8]

Ms Sutcliffe, who contributed to the 1993 film *Backbeat* starring Stephen Dorff, based on her brother's life with the Beatles, also discussed the rumours of a possible homosexual affair between the two. If Stu and John had been carnally close during their tenure at Liverpool College of Art, she said that she would not be in the least surprised. 'John said himself at one point that this happened,' she pointed out, neglecting to reveal her source. She described John as 'a very brilliant young man, but very complex and not properly understood'.

John adored Stuart because he was the only person who truly got him, was Pauline Sutcliffe's professional analytical assessment. Stuart comprehended that John's violent rages were eruptions of disappointment and ventings of hurt, which stemmed from the fact that nobody understood him. None but Stuart. So why turn on *him*, then? *Because. You always take the sweetest rose, and crush it till the petals fall.*[9]

Still, their friendship endured, and even flourished.

'I read some of the letters that Astrid has,' Klaus Voormann told me. 'Stuart and John kept up their intimate conversation in writing after Stuart quit the Beatles to be with her. I had the feeling at the time I knew them, and was reminded by reading the letters, that John looked up to Stuart, and considered him to be the superior being. John was so insecure in himself that he always needed someone better than him to hero-worship. In all his days beyond, he never found a better hero than Stuart.'

*

In July 1962, another celebrated bass player was having a Grosse Freiheit moment, and anticipating eagerly if naïvely the point at which his and John's paths would cross. Nineteen year-old Frank Allen would soon achieve international fame as one of the Searchers, but was at the time a guitarist with Cliff Bennett's sensational Rebel Rousers. Bennett's band was playing at the newly opened Star-Club opposite Bruno Koschmider's Kaiserkeller.

'The Star-Club, owned by Manfred Weissleder and managed by Horst Fascher, was a converted church nestling amongst a string of bars and sex clubs,' remembers Frank.[10] 'It was a much bigger deal than the Kaiserkeller, employing not only dozens of bands from the UK – in particular a flurry of unknown acts brought over from Liverpool – but also major attractions from the US. During our several stints there, we shared the stage with such legends as Bill Haley and His Comets, Joey Dee and the Starliters, the Everly Brothers, Bo Diddley (I ended up playing bass in his set), Gene Vincent, Vince Taylor, Ray Charles, Fats Domino, Jerry Lee Lewis and many more. On that first trip, we found that the talk around the club was all about a band from Merseyside called the Beatles. Their pictures were everywhere, along with those of other hitherto unheard-of musical outfits. The bar girls, Bettina, Goldie, Rosie and the rest, obviously adored them.'

Given that the Beatles were by now being hailed as the finest band in the land, Frank and the lads were intrigued, and hot-keen to meet the competition. On their return to Hamburg on 30 December that year, they were more than looking forward to checking them out.

'Back home,' recalls Frank, 'they had managed a low entry into the charts with "Love Me Do": not the most impressive of disc debuts. Anyway, word was that their manager Brian Epstein had purchased a huge number of copies of the record himself, to help it on its way up the charts. Which was a scandalous practice, but all too common. In the end, it stalled at the number seventeen position in the UK best-sellers.

'That year delivered the most horrendous winter. Heavy snow closed Heathrow airport for most of the day. We were booked to play the Star-Club the same evening we were due in. Given the weather, it didn't look as though we were going to make it. Eventually, however, the airport opened for a time that evening, and we arrived late to be picked up by Horst and driven directly to the club. There was no chance of us performing, but at least we could check out these other wannabes.

'Cliff Bennett, a man with the most impressive R&B voice and not someone to deliver praise lightly, watched the Beatles intently. He was mightily impressed. I too was quite taken by them, although I must admit I didn't fall over with excitement. Not exactly sophisticated, they were rough in both manner and presentation. I think it was their black polo-neck era. But there was something about them. An attitude that made them stand out above everyone else. It was quite magical, the way they took command of the whole event. They were hugely impressive.'

Frank and the band caught the Beatles' New Year performances.

In return, the Beatles had the opportunity to check out the highly-rated Rebel Rousers.

'The following day, the Beatles were due to fly back to England. It must have been a late flight, because I ran into John Lennon coming out of the dressing room area just as I was going in, shortly after midday. There we stood, face to face. I introduced myself, said how much I'd enjoyed their show, and mentioned that I'd heard they had a new record coming out. I wished him and the band every success with it. John stared at me intently, not exactly warily, more in the manner of a snake sizing up a defenceless rodent before killing and devouring it whole. It was incredibly intimidating. I was a very nervous lad in those days, and in many ways still am.

"'Ah, yes, it's Frank, isn't it," said John. "Yeah, I enjoyed your show, too. I've been talking to people in the club, and it seems that, next to Cliff, you're the most popular member in the band." He paused, before going in for the kill. "I can't think why," he sneered. "Your harmonies are fuckin' ridiculous."'

Frank was blindsided. 'I wasn't sure if I was being insulted or if this was some typical friendly if off-the-wall Liverpool banter,' he says. 'I had no idea how to respond. I just about managed to blurt back, "Well, good luck with the new record, it was nice meeting you." To which John replied, "Yeah, nice meeting you, too, Frank. See ya."

'The Beatles left for the airport, and a bunch of us were hanging about on the stage listening to some very rough tapes that Kingsize Taylor had recorded of their final show from the previous evening. With the help of Adrian Barber, a previous member of another great Merseybeat group, the Big Three, who had quit playing to become the Star-Club's sound engineer, they had managed to retain for posterity a significant moment in pop history – although no one realised at the time exactly *how* significant.[11]

'Horst Fascher then rocked up with a small disc, an acetate that John had given him of the already-recorded new Beatles single. Adrian played it over the club's sound system. It was utterly mind-blowing, from the brilliantly ear-catching opening instrumental phrase right through to the finish. There was no doubt. "Please Please Me" would take them where "Love Me Do" had not.'

The two young musicians ran into each other many times after that. There was never any reference to their initial encounter. 'Any subsequent meeting with him went without any discomfort at all,' said Frank. 'He could be Mr Nice or Mr Nasty, and change from one to the other in a heartbeat. You never quite knew what you were going to get with him, and you learned not to let it bother you.

'Many years later, we played at The Cutting Room, a club in New York. May Pang, she of Lennon's infamous Lost Weekend period during the seventies, was in the audience. She came to chat after the show. I recounted to her my Hamburg story, adding my theory that, despite all his apparent confidence and bravado, John was just as riddled with insecurities as the rest of us. His way of dealing with that, I said, was obviously to get the boot in first. "You've hit the nail on the head exactly!" she exclaimed. "That was John."'

CHAPTER 7

SVENGALI

B rian Epstein once remarked that he felt like an old man at twenty-one. Booted, besuited, impeccably spoken, respectably employed since the age of sixteen and still only in his mid-twenties when he awoke to the Beatles, the former RADA[1] student likely perceived in them a vehicle for his own unfulfilled ambitions. The thwarted thesp of Russian-Jewish descent was a closet homosexual at a time when to declare one's orientation would have been to risk imprisonment.[2] An unsuccessful public-school education had compensated him with the consolation prize of a position in the boring, staid but prosperous family business. Brian was deprived of his teenagehood and seemed to have progressed straight from puberty to middle age. The Beatles personified everything he'd missed out on. He was seduced by a vicarious thrill.

He first became aware of the group while managing the new NEMS music store, which was part of the Epstein clan's empire. He read about them in *Mersey Beat*, Bill Harry's music magazine in which Brian took ad space, which he stocked in the shop and to which, in August 1961, he began contributing his own column. John would soon start writing for it too. Brian's interest was piqued when customers started coming in asking for a record from Germany called 'My Bonnie'. When he discovered that it featured the Beatles, local boys who had visited his shop many times, he resolved to check them out. No stranger to the Cavern, which Brian had been known to visit occasionally, he got wind of one of their midday sessions, which was chalked for 9 November. He and his PA Alistair Taylor came on down, to find themselves mingling with schoolgirls and office workers on their lunchbreaks.

'I was immediately struck by their music, their beat and their sense of humour on stage – and, even afterwards, when I met them, I was struck again by their personal charm,' he said in a televised interview featured in *Anthology*. 'And it was there that, really, it all started.'

Despite their tangible chemistry, infectious humour and surprisingly honed musical ability, this bunch of rough rockers had an unfortunate image. Ill-clad in jeans and leather jackets, they were stale, uncouth, looked vaguely threatening and were oblivious of stagecraft. They smoked, drank, scoffed, cussed, gossiped and larked during performances as though heedless of their audience, or as though they were an inconvenience. Brian might have bitten off more than he could chew, here. Yet he was enchanted by them. He returned to see them again and again. He wanted them. It was agreed the following month that he would become their manager, despite having no previous involvement in artist management.

'It's the easiest thing in the world to pass comment and criticism on historical figures from the position of hindsight,' reflects Ed Bicknell. With twenty-six years' management experience of Dire Straits to his name, as well as significant spells in command of the careers of Scott Walker, Gerry Rafferty and Bryan Ferry, the candid Yorkshireman does not mince his words. 'In pop music terms, only one manager of note had come along prior to Brian: Colonel Tom Parker, the manager of Elvis Presley. Back in 1961, precious little was known about him. Even less was known about what he did. Parker's background was in carnival shows: he certainly wasn't a "Colonel". We didn't have carnival shows in Britain, the seaside funfair was about as close as it got.[3]

'Unlike today, there were no books, no documentaries, no biographies, no academic courses, and definitely no one to ask. So

Brian's offer to "manage" the Beatles didn't really mean much to either side. It was going to be a case of making it up as they went along.

'At that time, "pop music" was seen as a passing phase. Careers might last two years and then, if you hadn't progressed to being an all-round entertainer, you were back on the railways. The business "establishment" was made up exclusively of middle-aged men with a background in "variety". Men with names like "Lew", "Leslie" and "Bernard".'[4]

Pop music was indulged, explains Bicknell. Its audience was patronised. Cliff Richard and the Shadows soon found themselves in pantomime, summer season, and on every MOR TV show imaginable: almost as a novelty act paying lip service to 'The Kids'. Which is pretty much how TV and radio regarded 'that awful American noise'. To begin with, at least. Not much later came the films. Rock'n'roll was rapidly diluted, to be replaced by 'family entertainment'. Teenage angst was reduced to 'The Young Ones' and 'Summer Holiday'.

'In due course,' says Ed, 'the Beatles found themselves in the same boat, making what were effectively extended videos to sell albums and singles, with not a hint of danger in sight.

'Such was the mindset of the time. It was called "pop" music because it was popular. That was the point. The idea that it might be "art" was a little way down the line.' Certainly, the Beatles themselves were not looking at a place in cultural history. They were young and they were having fun. They weren't looking to the future, or dreaming about becoming 'the Fabs'. All that was on the distant horizon.

'But Epstein did have the quality that *all* managers must have: belief. He had that in spades. For that belief to work, it has to turn into a kind of pig-headedness. To the point that the word "no" actually means, "well, maybe". So you keep going in spite of every rejection, until you hear "yes". George Martin told me that a major reason he wanted to sign the Beatles – other than the fact that it wouldn't cost anything – was Brian's relentless persistence and belief in "the boys".'

A five-year contract was duly drawn up and signed at Mona Best's house on 24 January 1962. Because Paul, George and Pete were not yet twenty-one, Epstein required parental consent. As John was already of age, Mimi's protests were gleefully disregarded. Although she had long picked holes in and disapproved of virtually everything he did, diminishing him and shredding his self-confidence, no way was she going to get a chance to ruin this.

But was 'this' what John wanted? The mould into which Brian sought to pour the Beatles, to package, market, commercialise and, yes, exploit them, could not have been more at odds with the way John saw himself. He had already made it known that he was no-way-José up for the matching-suits-and-ties look. He then confounded himself by putting the clothes on and going along with it anyway. He is famously quoted as having said, 'I'll wear a suit; I'll wear a bloody balloon if somebody's going to pay me.' So he compromised. He sold out. He relinquished control of his individuality, the essence of John Lennon, the elements that made him unique. *Why?* To spite Mimi? To give her what-for? To show her that he was not the chip-off-the-old-block, good-for-nothing loser she'd written him off as, hurling his uselessness in his face at every opportunity? That he would airbrush his true nature out of existence and knock himself into someone else's shape in the pursuit of fame and fortune, seems a step too far for a man like John. Until you analyse it. Minor acts of rebellion, such as tying his tie incorrectly or leaving his top shirt button undone, were subtle clues. He didn't like what was going on here, clearly. But he could see the point, and obviously felt that he had no choice. Even though it was John who objected to the four of them being packaged in twee, matching stage suits and urged to flaunt almost identical haircuts, he went along with it because that was the way things were done then. The artist deferred to the manager. The biggest of the predecessors, Cliff Richard and the Shadows, sported tuxedos and bow ties and made a mint. It had worked for them … so fuck it. He'd make his feelings felt, then shake his hair as hard as the next guy. But what was this if not his first act of self-sabotage? The first killing of John?

*

If you're making it up as you go along, of course, you are going to make mistakes. But errors are only errors when you come to look back. It is doubtful that any of the current crop of rock and pop managers, those who have devoured all the books, attended the courses and got the qualifications (and the tee shirt) would have done very much of it differently had they been making their way in Liverpool in 1963.

'Did Brian make mistakes? Sure,' says Ed Bicknell. *'Everyone* does. And managers like to think they make much more of an impact than they actually do. It's the talent and drive of the artist that drags everything with it. Brian has been hugely criticised down the decades for the notorious merchandising deal he did for the Beatles, effectively yielding control and earning power of most of it, all with the benefit of hindsight. It certainly was disastrous, but what information did he have to go on? Our old friend the Colonel had initiated it almost single-handedly with Presley. But there were no rules, no precedent, no history that decreed that, well, you should get X% or Y%. In the case of the Colonel, he was taking such a big chunk before Elvis got his share, that Brian Epstein's deal doesn't look so bad in comparison.

'When you're a manager, you have a split responsibility. Firstly, you do the business – and back then, the record companies and song publishers had "standard" deals. "Take it or leave it" was the mantra. Promoters were not dissimilar. So, until you had the manager's greatest gift – leverage – you'd be boxed in, as Brian was. In many ways, technology has brought us full circle. And one thing is certain: corporations will always take the shortest route. In other words, the cheapest route.

'Secondly, you "manage" the act. In Brian's case, that meant the four Beatles – and don't forget, before long, he was taking on many other artists, almost all of them from Liverpool. This is the difficult bit. It's part psychological, part devious, part political, part dictatorial.

'In every band, there is the one who wants to be leader. They usually get there via a combination of force of personality and being the angriest, the least willing to compromise and usually the biggest shit. Talent plays a role occasionally, but is not always a given. Democracy in bands never works, which is why they all collapse eventually – the shit inevitably being the first to leave. Because part of being a shit is to have an ego the size of a small planet, with self-obsession to match. It goes with the territory.'

George Martin told Bicknell that John could be a horrendous bully: 'Especially towards George Harrison, whose early attempts at songwriting were treated with utter disdain at best, and with dismissal bordering on contempt at worst. It took several years before Lennon would begrudgingly acknowledge that "Something" was by far the best song on *Abbey Road*.'[5]

*

So Brian drilled some manners into the Beatles, instructed them in the art of the synchronised bow to be taken at the conclusion of every number and smartened them up. It is recorded that he conveyed them to the Wirral to meet his friend, master tailor Beno Dorn, who would make their first matching suits. It was London scenester Jeff Dexter, a professional dancer, singer, DJ and fixture of the Lyceum Ballroom on the Strand, whom Epstein consulted regarding the group's ongoing image.

'Yes, it was me who got them to Dougie Millings, who made their classic collarless Beatles suits,' Dexter confirms. 'He was the rock'n'roll tailor of the day.

'They also picked up on my après-ski boots from the dance footwear store Anello & Davide – easy on, easy off. We called them "après-ski" because the "piste" was what the dancers called the dance floor – as well as "rug", as in "cut a rug". Actually, I think the Beatles bought Anello's Baba boot first. I also took them to Star Shirtmakers on Wardour Street, direct from Dougie's workroom.'[6]

Epstein's next step was to set about landing them a recording contract. While it was somewhat round the houses and not as simple as he may have anticipated, his NEMS business connections to the major labels eventually enabled him to land them a deal with EMI's Parlophone, where their producer would be George Martin.

The other major consideration was exposure. The Beatles were already, thanks to the relentlessness of Mona Best, on the radar of Granada Television. An important regional TV station in the north-west of England with a vast reach at the time – from the Lake District in the north to the Potteries in the south; from north Wales all the way to the Yorkshire coast – an appearance on a Granada show constituted a mighty plug for any act chosen to appear. Producer Johnnie Hamp, eighty-seven years old at the time of our interview, was crucial to the evolution of the Beatles, and would later create a major TV special on the music of Lennon and McCartney. Paul confessed in the Beatles' *Anthology* that they didn't really want to do it, incidentally, but did so out of loyalty to their mate Johnnie. He travelled regularly to Germany to catch American acts at the big military bases, and had watched the Beatles perform on the Grosse Freiheit in 1962.

'I was very impressed with them,' he told me. 'They were so much better, musically, than the other acts playing at the time. I didn't know Brian Epstein very well in those days. He was the Beatles' manager and that was that. They were with him a long time, at a time when people changed their managers frequently. There came a time when he and I started meeting regularly for dinner: at the Caprice in London, one of his favourites, and at a nice, small hotel with a very good restaurant behind the Empire in Liverpool. He always seemed a bit scared of the Beatles, who he referred to as "the boys". Of John in particular. It only occurred to me later that he must be in love with him. But he never confided in me about his feelings for John. He was trying to be a good businessman.

'There was a group of researchers at Granada making a programme about acts in the north of England. Leslie Woodhead was a researcher and fledgling director for us at the time, and in 1961-2 he directed the first film of the Beatles in the Cavern Club, just before they made their first record. The Beatles' clip wasn't shown in the end, because it wasn't broadcast standard. But it's a wonderfully historic piece now. Brian Epstein rang me a few times to ask why it hadn't aired. I couldn't tell him. But they did bring the Beatles in to perform "Love Me Do" as a kind of compensation.'

After Granada asked Johnnie to revamp the show *People and Places*, the Beatles were invited in to perform 'Please Please Me'.

'John always stood out, to me,' Johnnie remembers. 'This was one of the first bands that didn't have an "official" front man, yet to my mind John was exactly that. He was the one to whom my eye was drawn, and the one I always talked to. I thought he looked like a prince. He had an almost regal look about him. There was a dignity, an elegance to him, even in black leathers, whereas the others at the time just came across as kids.'

The producer was acutely aware from the first moment of John's dark side.

'It was unavoidable,' he affirms. 'It stared you right in the face. He was an angry, flippant, objectionable person most of the time. He would get quite annoyed with me, especially when the "secret cameras" were following them around the studios – into the dressing rooms, into Make-Up, around the props department. We knew even then that the footage we were shooting would be historic material. John soon changed his mind when he saw the potential. He'd pose about and walk around like a bloody cripple. Like the Hunchback of Notre Dame.

'What we know now is that John was several people. The secret to dealing with him and to getting the best out of him was recognising which John you were faced with on any given day, and then interacting with that version of him accordingly. If I say so myself, I had a gift for recognising star quality, the so-called "X-factor", and for treating talent with respect. The effect on me of true talent was that it reduced me to tears. That was how I knew when I was witnessing something special, something wonderful. John recognised that in me, and we bonded because of it. I got him, and he got me. We met in the middle.'

Was there a pin-point moment?

'There was when he screeched "Twist and Shout".

'They talk about the "Mersey sound" [aka Merseybeat],' ponders Johnnie, 'but I don't think it really existed. Cilla Black had her first hit with a Burt Bacharach number ["Anyone Who Had a Heart", lyrics by Hal David]. Gerry and the Pacemakers ["How Do You Do It?" by Mitch Murray, originally offered to Adam Faith and then earmarked as a debut for the Beatles] and Billy J. Kramer and the Dakotas' 'Little Children' [by John Leslie McFarland and Mort Schuman]: their hits weren't their own. The so-called "Mersey sound" was something that was conjured in hindsight. If the Mersey sound was anything, to me it was the Beatles. So it was very easy to understand, as far as I'm concerned, why the Beatles went global. It was because of their songs, primarily, together with their personalities and the chemistry between the four of them. They were unique.'

A kind of friendship evolved between Johnnie and John over the years, not that they socialised extensively. Hamp remembers the Beatles hanging around after coming in to do a show, and that they tended not to shoot back to London or Liverpool immediately. They'd go and have a drink. John was especially interested in the blues and gospel one-off special that Johnnie made, 'I Hear the Blues', featuring Muddy Waters, Sonny Boy Williamson, Willie Dixon, Memphis Slim and Alonzo 'Lonnie' Johnson, from whom Lonnie Donegan pinched his name.

'John wanted to talk to me about all those great acts. He also loved my Little Richard special in 1963, and my programme about Jerry Lee Lewis in 1964. And the *Blues and Gospel Train* I did with Sister Rosetta Tharpe, the grandmother of rock'n'roll (check out "Didn't It Rain?"). Our conversations were mostly about music. Those were the kinds of artist that he himself longed to be, of course. That he felt he was, in his deepest inner self. There's the rub. It touched me. I loved him for it. "I'm one of *those* guys. I'm a real musician too, Johnnie," was what he seemed to be trying to say to me. He didn't need to spell it out. Nor did he need to convince me. I was already aware that he was so much more than a Beatle; that sooner or later it would all blow up in their faces. Yes, I knew.'[7]

*

Still there was Cyn. Who would say that she went to 'all' the gigs, but couldn't have. Especially not those after which John and his old partner in crime Pete Shotton, by this time an ex-policeman, sloped off with pairs of girls to while away stolen afternoons all in bed together. Cyn's mother having moved to Canada to care for a cousin's baby, Cyn had moved into Mimi's as one of her paying guests. As John's aunt had no time for his girlfriend, while the latter as good as despised the former, the only real beneficiary of this eccentric arrangement was John. Who returned from Stuart's old digs to live there too. Mendips is neither as big nor as grand as has sometimes been painted. It has fewer rooms than have at times been counted. I have been there and seen them. With two lodgers besides Cyn also installed – i.e., five adults, with only one toilet and a basic separate bathroom, the modest semi would have been cramped, to say the least.

John set off to celebrate his twenty-first birthday during the first week of October 1961, in Paris, with Paul, on a hundred quid that his aunt Mater had gifted him. Wouldn't Cyn have been a more appropriate choice of travel partner? The trainee art teacher was busy with both her finals and with school-placement work experience. So it was with his songwriting partner and bandmate that John ran into Jürgen Vollmer on the streets of the French capital. Vollmer escorted his old Hamburg pals back to his hotel to cut their hair for them in the distinctive 'Exi' style.

*

Their Decca audition in London on New Year's Day 1962 came and went with recrimination and embarrassment. It was a legendary 'thanks but no thanks'.

'But Decca's A&R manager Dick Rowe never turned down the Beatles, as was claimed for years,' insists Simon Napier-Bell.

'It was utter rubbish. They recorded two groups on the same day: the Beatles, and Brian Poole and the Tremeloes. Rowe asked staff producer Mike Smith to choose which one to sign. Smith had been up to watch the Beatles play at the Cavern, and was excited by them. It was later put about that he found them nowhere near as good when they were not playing in front of an audience. That's not true either. Mike just didn't want to hack all the way up to Liverpool every time he needed to meet and work with them. So he chose the more local Tremeloes. Who had hits with covers of "Twist and Shout", already released by the Beatles on *Please Please Me*, and "Do You Love Me".'

*

Back to Hamburg the Beatles slogged that April, to the terrible news of Stuart Sutcliffe's death. Cyn packed up and moved out of Mimi's, up to here with her criticisms and sneering, and lodged with an aunt of her own while seeking a central bedsit. Two days after the boys' return to Liverpool, Neil Aspinall drove them to London for their audition with George Martin at EMI. Which led, a month or two later, to an offer they couldn't refuse. The Beatles were on their way. Everything John had ever wanted? There was more. His girlfriend was pregnant.

Women have choices today because women like Cynthia didn't. In the 1950s and early sixties, nice girls refrained from sex before marriage. Promiscuity was frowned upon, primarily because of the risk of pregnancy. Although the contraceptive pill was introduced in the UK in 1961, the NHS prescribed it mainly to older women who had already completed their families. The Pill would not go on general release until 1967, when girls were effectively granted control over their own bodies and when the dynamics of relationships would change. Until then, girls were expected to get married and raise a family. Most did so at a young age, stayed at home to look after the kids, and cooked and cleaned while their husbands went out to work: a lifestyle that was idealised as the 'perfect family'. In reality, it was a form of imprisonment for the woman, who surrendered her right to any personal power and independence – few women even had bank accounts in those days – in order to become a servant to the 'head of the family' and a slave to the stove. Yet it was the life that Miss Prim had been looking forward to with the man she loved. Thanks to the fact that her boyfriend was now teetering on the brink of global superstardom, it was not the life she got.

Brian Epstein had already made clear to his boys that serious relationships would dent their popularity with their hordes of female fans, and were to be kept under wraps and denied. Cyn understood when John told her why she had to be a secret, and managed to keep her head down when out and about and in the audience at Beatles gigs. She had no idea how to tell him she was up the duff.

'I think I dreaded telling John more than I was afraid of having to tell my mother,' she admitted.

'Mum was coming over to see me from Canada, and there was no way I was going to be able to keep it from her. One look at me and she would have known straight off in any case, I felt sure. As for John, I was terrified of how he was going to react. I was afraid we'd get into a terrible row about it, as if it was somehow my fault. I cried and cried, all on my own, and eventually I made a decision. John was almost certain to dump me. Things were really beginning to happen for the group, and he couldn't be held back by a thing like this. An abortion was out of the question. It was still against the law. Women could and did go to backstreet abortionists in those days, but you risked your life if you did. Of course girls still agonise today over whether or not to keep their babies, but at least it is their decision to make.'

There was only one thing for it.

'I was going to have to go it alone,' said Cyn. 'I knew I'd be made to feel ashamed, that I'd be stigmatised, but I couldn't bear the thought of the alternative. I still had to tell John. He had a right to know. I couldn't bring myself to do it for days, but eventually I took a deep breath and I went for it. I still remember that day so clearly. I watched the blood drain from his face, and I flinched and squirmed. I might have convinced myself that he was going to hit me. But then when he said, 'We'll have to get married,' it was like all my Christmases had come at once. I could hardly believe it. I told him he didn't have to, that I would understand if he didn't want to do it. No, he insisted, he loved me and that was that. "It took two of us to make a baby," he said, "and it'll take two of us to bring it up. I'm not having you going through this on your own." I cried and cried, with happiness, gratitude and relief. We were going to be a proper little family.' He loved her, yeah, yeah, yeah.[8]

Brian Epstein, true to form, tried to talk John out of marriage. But once he was convinced that his boy was serious, he did everything possible to help. It was polished, pinstriped Brian who obtained the marriage licence, who booked Mount Pleasant Register Office for 23 August, who escorted the bride through a deluge in his own chauffeur-driven car, who coughed up for the modest wedding breakfast at a local café called Reece's, and who provided the couple with their first marital home: temporary residence of his own flat in the Georgian Quarter of Liverpool that he maintained for dangerous liaisons. There had been no flowers, no gown, no pictures, no wine, no speeches nor any kind of spectacle. But there were Beatles, japes, genuine happiness and a gig that night. Mr Lennon kissed the bride and went off to work. Mrs Lennon stayed in.[9]

Mimi, of course, went berserk. She refused to give John her blessing, and called his girlfriend everything under the sun. While her rage was, to some extent, to be expected, Cyn told me that Mimi's unleashing wounded John more than anything she had previously done or said. She had been as good as a mother to him. Despite the years of carping and fault-finding, he still craved her approval when it came to milestones as significant as marriage and fatherhood. He wanted Mimi there, beaming with pride and showing her support. Not only would she not attend, but over her dead body would the rest of her family. It was insulting. It therefore took guts for Cyn to suggest that they go and see her a few months into the pregnancy, after she had suffered a near-miscarriage. They found a Mimi softened by the Beatles' burgeoning success, and bewilderingly keen to help the expectant young couple. Perceiving that the arrangement regarding Brian's flat was temporary and less than ideal, and that John and the band were about to return to Hamburg, Mimi invited them to move back to Mendips. They could rent the ground floor while she would occupy the top floor, once the last remaining lodgers had moved out. In the circumstances, it seemed ideal. Until you took Mimi's temper, her ongoing contempt for Cyn and the fact that John would be absent most of the time into account.

*

At the turn of 1963, the Beatles were the darlings of Liverpool but had yet to seduce the UK. A February tour supporting Helen Shapiro helped their new single 'Please Please Me' to Number Two (Number One on the NME and Melody Maker charts). They were on their way. John stole a little time at home to be with his wife, their baby due within weeks, and was horrified to find that she'd sliced off her flowing blonde locks. His reaction of rage and spite was out of all proportion, and made even Mimi's temper seem mild. Cyn was shocked and heartbroken. By the time we got to talk about it, she had forgiven him.

'Poor John, it was all too much for him,' she said. 'Even though the Beatles' success was thrilling, and was the answer to all our prayers, there was something about the way things were going that wasn't right, for John. He wouldn't talk about it, and I was able to piece it together only over time from bits and pieces that were said. They were recording their own songs and having hits with them, which was what they desperately wanted. But Brian had insisted on imposing a whole new image, which John was finding very hard to come to terms with. It was all about a "look" and an "attitude" that simply were not John. He had to toe the line and behave himself now that they were in the spotlight. It was such a strain for him, concealing and repressing his true self, and he was bound to react against it every now and again. Me going and altering my "image", too, was more than he could take. He couldn't handle it. He wanted the old Cyn, the one he'd fallen for. He just wanted me to stay the same. I was too young and self-preoccupied to realise that at the time. I must have thought that I'd become dowdy and unattractive the minute my baby was born, and just wanted to zap myself up a bit. Whatever it was, it was a mistake. If I could, I'd have given anything to go back to the way things were.'

*

They recorded their debut LP *Please Please Me* in London, and promptly went back out on tour. Cyn was forced to endure her long, terrifying labour in hospital alone. The frightened twenty-three-year-old gave birth before breakfast on 8 April without even Mimi to hold her hand. By the time the crotchety aunt deigned to pitch up to inspect the newborn, she had already called her nephew to inform him that he had a son. John Winston Lennon did not meet John Charles Julian for three more days. Three weeks later, he left the worn-out nursing mother and their tiny baby at home by themselves to swan off on holiday with Eppy.

CHAPTER 8

QUINTUS

N ot that John had ever been faithful to Cyn. Not once, not ever, perhaps not in his tamest dreams. From coming on to other students under her nose at college parties to behaving like a sewer rat while far from her in Hamburg – where anything went and everything did, where the frauleins were the kind who carry pistols and where barely a night didn't end in an orgy – keeping it in his pants was never a John thing.

As Pete Best remembered, even John described himself as a 'randy sod': 'John was the one who set the breakneck pace at which we lived,' he said, of those early Hamburg days. 'Maybe he felt less inhibited than the rest of us; he had no parental ties and was well away from the scoldings he used to say that Aunt Mimi gave him. He could do exactly as he liked, and be as outrageous as he wished. In those hectic days, we all had a healthy appetite for sex, but Lennon's was stronger than most … even so, John would find energy enough to masturbate as well, never trying to keep it a secret. He would lock himself away for five minutes with some soft-porn pin-up studies and then rejoin the rest of the Beatles with a satisfied grin on his face.'

John also delighted in regaling the others with wig-raising tales of his wilder pursuits, many of which involved multiple partners and gravity-defying gymnastics. 'The more, the merrier!' he would laugh.[1]

Pause … to reflect on the fact that we are less judgemental and more accepting today. Aren't we? So sanctified are the Beatles that certain factions of fans, usually too young to have experienced the band first time round, seem to think that they walked on water. Such devotees can grow enraged, vitriolic and abusive on social media and elsewhere whenever anything even mildly unfavourable about their boys appears. The idols in whom such people believe, and whom some invest with Disneyesque innocence, supernatural talent and quasi-magical powers, are sanitised caricatures. They are a fantasy. Those jesting, jostling, clean-cut, butter-wouldn't-melt, take-them-home-to-meet-Mother Beatles never existed. It was an *act*. Some artists are more human than others. The Beatles were more human, more hardcore, more fallible, more susceptible, and had infinitely more sex, than most. Even Paul? You bet.

So, the issue, if that's what this is, is not whether John experimented sexually with other men, nor whether he batted and bowled – whatever – but infidelity. By all accounts and recollections available, John was only a husband and father when tucked up at home, and even then half-heartedly, resentfully and distractedly. Cyn admitted to me, and also confirms in her second memoir, *John*, that he confessed to extra-marital liaisons and that she assured him she didn't mind. Not that she knew the half of it. Was her turning a blind eye, her tolerance of his adultery with groupies (of which there must have been hundreds if not thousands down the years) indicative of Cyn being willing to do whatever it took to hang onto him? What torment must have burdened her heart and soul. So fearful of divorce, which in those days was still both dirty word and shameful status, she was prepared to put up with almost anything. *Almost*. She drew the line at 'wicked' insinuations that Brian Epstein and John had a sexual relationship. She would have been exposed to rumour and gossip at the time, because 'everyone' was talking about it. But what was shocking then is not shocking now. Maybe it's hard for us, in our enlightened age – in much of the First World, at least – to get our heads round what a scandal this was. Homosexual activity between consenting adults was not yet legal. The rumours raged, down the decades, beyond the deaths of the two men allegedly involved. They were, whatever anybody says, the only people in the room at the time. The only ones who could have told us either way. Cyn remained adamant that it never happened.

'Nothing could be further from the truth,' she insisted in her memoir. 'John was a hundred per cent heterosexual and, like most lads at that time, horrified by the idea of homosexuality.'

Paul has pointed out, perfectly reasonably, that he (McCartney) and John spent so many years living on top of each other that surely John would have made at least one advance towards him had he been that way inclined. He never did. He also revisited the episode in the *Anthology*, reiterating that John saw that short holiday together as an opportunity to establish with Epstein exactly which of them was boss. Which was ironic, given that John had stood back, kept his trap zipped and allowed Brian to make the decisions thus far.

But John was well aware that Epstein was gay. Why, then, accept an invitation from their manager to accompany him to Spain for an almost two-week break, just the two of them, rather than hot-foot it to the Canary Islands for a fortnight of the four 'S's with Paul, George and Ringo? Klaus Voormann saw the dark clouds gathering a mile off.

'It was just like a marriage,' he said. 'There was the honeymoon, then, slowly, because of the incompatibility of the partners, the friction began. Unlike the Rolling Stones, where Mick leads and the others follow happily – which is why they've been able to keep going all these years – with the Beatles, there were three leaders and only one follower: Ringo. So it could never work in the long term.

'Although Paul was the friendly one, within the setting of the band he was always slightly apart from the others, on his own. It was triggered by the fact that Brian Epstein was in love with John, so Paul felt isolated. Even after Brian had gone, it was something he always felt.

'I remember after they had a Number One hit with "She Loves You" in 1963, they came out to stay with me in my father's house in Tenerife. Paul, George and Ringo. But no John: he'd gone on holiday with Brian. While George was busy trying to befriend the girl in the shop down the road, showing her the cover of the single, and Ringo drifted through the days, Paul resented John going off. It showed.'

He could see the end of the Beatles coming from a long way off, Klaus says.

'The rows were getting more aggressive and more frequent. There were physical fights, and the tension between them just got worse and worse. It was just like a marriage going wrong. Divorce was inevitable.'

Looking back in 1980 on his relationship with Epstein, John had this to say:

'Well, it was almost a love affair, but not quite. It was never consummated. But it was a pretty intense relationship. It was my first experience with a homosexual that I was conscious *was* homosexual. He had admitted it to me ... We used to sit in a café in Torremolinos, looking at all the boys, and I'd say, "Do you like that one, do you like this one?" I was rather enjoying the experience, thinking like a writer all the time: *I am experiencing this*, you know.'[2]

He also said (getting his dates mixed and overlooking the fact that his wife had already given birth to their son before he departed), 'Cyn was having a baby and the holiday was planned, but I wasn't going to break the holiday for a baby and that's what a *bastard* I was. And I just went on holiday. I watched Brian picking up the boys. I like playing a bit faggy, all that. It was enjoyable, but there were big rumours in Liverpool, it was terrible. Very embarrassing.'[3]

Brian Epstein never commented on the subject, for obvious reasons. Nor has the Shadows' Brian Bennett OBE. Until now.

The first-ever backing band to break through as stars in their own right, the Shadows are still revered as one of the UK's best-selling singles-chart acts. Brian joined the line-up in October 1961. The Beatles loved them.

'I had three memorable close encounters with John Lennon,' Brian recalls.

'The first was in Sitges, the so-called "Saint-Tropez of Spain", where we were taking a break and working on a Spanish album. John had driven down to Spain with Brian Epstein, and they were staying in the same hotel as us, on the beach. All John did all day long was sit in the sea wearing various pairs of blue jeans, to get them to shrink to fit and nicely faded. I honestly didn't give a second thought to the two of them being down there together without the others.[4]

'The second occurred when I was working in EMI's Studio 2, and he was in Studio 3. We bumped into each other. "Hi, John," I said, "What's happening?" "Trying to make a fookin' record!" was all he said, before disappearing, presumably to get on with said record. It made me think of a line he was supposed to have said: "I wouldn't go and see the fookin' Shadows if they were playing in me back garden!" Whether or not he actually said that, I'll never know. But it's a typically caustic Lennon line that I can just hear him saying.

'The third time was actually *in* a back garden: the garden belonging to Paul McCartney's Auntie Gin.[5]

'The occasion was Paul's twenty-first birthday party in Liverpool, on 18 June 1963,' says Brian. 'We'd been playing in Blackpool. Paul and his then girlfriend Jane Asher picked us up in his Range Rover from Lime Street station. We drove to his auntie's house, and when we arrived the party was already in full swing. They had a marquee, but it was a small house, so it was all a bit tight. A group called the Fourmost were the entertainment for the night. We saw a few people we knew there, including Billy J. Kramer, and I had a good chat with Paul's dad, Jim.

'Cynthia was talking to my wife Margaret, and asking her how she managed being left at home while the Shadows were away on tour. Towards the end of the party, an argument started up. A lot of alcohol was consumed, and things began to get really loud. When differences of opinion are mixed with booze, it almost always ends badly. In those days, if you called someone a "poof" or a "queer", you were usually asking for trouble. I think someone called John a "queer", and that was it. Whoever it was got hit hard and was carried out.'

History asserts that John was the attacker, and that his victim was Cavern Club DJ and Beatles champion Bob Wooler: the mildest man by all accounts, and one who had always gone out of his way to support and promote the Beatles. He jokingly enquired after John's and Brian Epstein's recent 'honeymoon'. He was by no means the only one to have done so, but for John it was the proverbial last straw. He lost control, leaped at his tormentor and laid into him so viciously that Wooler had to be rushed to hospital. Unfortunately for John, the story made the local rags, and reached Fleet Street the day after. His remorseful telegram to the DJ can't have done much to heal the wounds. Eight years later, in 1971, he addressed the subject during an interview:

'Obviously, I must have been frightened of the fag in me to get so angry. You know, when you're twenty-one, you want to be a man, and all that. If somebody said it now, I wouldn't give a shit. So I was beating the shit out of him, and hitting him with a big stick, too, and it was the first time I thought, "I can kill this guy." I just saw it, like on a screen – that if I hit him once more, that was going to be it.'[6]

John's friend Pete Shotton, as was his wont, went full-throttle with his own remembrance of sins past. According to Pete, he called on his pal at Mendips post-vacation, teased him a bit, OK, a lot, and got the full-and-frank in response. Because John always told it exactly as it was with Pete. Brian had propositioned him, John confessed. The suave manager's relentless pestering got on John's nerves. In the end, he called his bluff, disrobed, and invited Brian to do the necessary. At which point, Eppy had recoiled, spluttering that he 'didn't do that kind of thing'. John was bemused … and intrigued enough to enquire as to what Brian *did* like.

"And so I let him toss me off," shrugged John.

'Well, so what?' Pete responded. 'What's the big fucking deal, then?'[7]

The pair agreed that Brian was suffering enough as it was, on account of the routine batterings he received from Liverpool dockers

– which was exactly the kind of after-hours R&R that Brian went looking for. Because refined, cultured Epstein's sexual preference was, as they say, a bit of rough. John had indulged him on that one occasion because he felt sorry for him. Pete empathised and sympathised. They left it at that.

One occasion? Paul Gambaccini offered further information during our John-related conversations.

'What is your take on John's holiday with Brian Epstein?' the celebrated BBC broadcaster and 'Professor of Pop' asked.

'They obviously had a relationship,' I replied.

'You think? Do you have a quote on that?'

'Not from John.'

'Well, I can tell you, the person to whom John Lennon spoke about that is John Reid [the former manager of Elton John]. John Reid told me personally what John Lennon had said about it. I'm going to tell you what he said, but I don't want you to put it in the book unless John Reid gives you permission.'

'I will ask him,' I said.

'OK: John Reid said that when we were in Boston with Elton and John in 1974, he couldn't resist asking John whether the rumours about him and Epstein were true. This was in response to John having said to John Reid, "You're the most intimidating man I've met since Brian Epstein." And so John Reid, never knowingly one to miss an opportunity, said, "Did you ever have sex with Brian?" And John said, "Twice. Once to see what it was like, and once to make sure I didn't like it."

'All these years, by the way, I have not wanted to be the guy who declared, "John Lennon and Brian Epstein had sex." You can appreciate how I feel about this. Do we want the historical record to be accurate, or does John have a right to privacy? And would it upset Cynthia [by now deceased], or Julian? I don't mind about Yoko, she'd probably think it was a great idea. Bisexuality, *wooh*.'

'Simon Napier-Bell said that both Epstein and John told him they did it in Spain,' I said.

'Ah, I'm not the only one. Good,' replied Paul.

But then there were John's liaisons with David Bowie, which David himself told me about. According to him, it happened on several occasions. He didn't go into detail, nor did I press him, but he was perfectly open about it. About Mick Jagger, too, I told Paul.[8]

'Huh. I feel sort of left out,' said Paul.

Me, too. Yes, John Reid gave me permission.

*

'Brian Epstein had no reason to lie,' points out Simon Napier-Bell. 'It makes sense: if John *was* gay, he needed to get on and try it. As it turned out, he wasn't. John tried things out. He didn't shy away from experiences. Anything at all, whatever it was: a new drug, a new religious idea. John was the leader in all the things they did that were new and experimental. Was Brian in love with John? I don't know. What I know is that Brian was *obsessed* with the zest of the Beatles. He adored that camaraderie that he could never be part of: the whole concept of being included. That's what Brian fell in love with. He understood it, he sold it to the public, and he marketed it brilliantly. That's what the success of the Beatles was all about.

'There's hardly a man on the planet who hasn't tried another man at some time or another. Especially the ones who insist that they haven't. John Lennon didn't go to public school, where everyone was at it, so this was about him trying something that he'd never tried before. He obviously respected Brian, and Brian loved what the Beatles were. So there was mutual admiration, which can turn very easily into lust between two men, especially entertainment industry types, who have gone out, had a few drinks and find themselves alone together. What I don't understand is why people have made such a big deal of it all these years. It's no different from trying Japanese food. Try it, you might like it. Inquisitive, that was John. Why *wouldn't* he try it?'

*

There have been many contenders for the unofficial title of 'Fifth Beatle'. Media references to such a character kicked off as early as

1963, pre-global fame, and irritated John no end. When quizzed on the subject by the editor of *Rolling Stone*, he left his interrogator in no doubt that he was not only opposed to the concept but enraged by those who went swaggering about assuming credit for the Beatles' existence and achievements.

'I'm not the Beatles,' John insisted, 'I'm me. Paul isn't the Beatles. Brian Epstein wasn't the Beatles, neither is Dick James. The Beatles are the Beatles.'[9] He also sensationally undermined the contribution of producer George Martin. Paul, however, singled out their producer for the privilege, as well as their manager. George Harrison begged to differ, insisting that if anyone were entitled to call himself 'the Fifth Beatle', it was a toss-up between Derek Taylor – the Liverpool-born former Fleet Street journalist, columnist, PR, producer and author who became head of publicity for Apple Corps – and former driver/road manager/publicist and eventual chief executive of Apple, Neil Aspinall.

As for musicians, original bass player Stuart Sutcliffe was technically the 'fourth' Beatle, given that he was in the line-up ahead of drummer Pete Best, who was technically 'fifth' – thus rendering Ringo (even more technically) 'sixth'. As for significant contributions, Stu had plenty to do with the group's definitive name, and was the first of them to sport the moptop haircut.

Although not strictly speaking a musician, John's childhood mate Pete Shotton, who went on to manage their Apple Boutique and became Apple Corps' first MD, scraped washboard in the Quarry Men, provided percussion on several studio recordings, and came up with ideas that enhanced the lyrics of 'I Am the Walrus' and 'Eleanor Rigby'.

But it was George Martin, really, wasn't it. Plain as any 'Fifth Beatle' could be. Not only did he produce most of their music, he created orchestral, instrumental and vocal arrangements for much of it, and played piano on various tracks, including 'Misery' and 'In My Life'.

He was born George Henry Martin in Holloway, north London, on 3 January 1926, to 'skint, non-musical' parents Henry and Bertha.

His carpenter father was often jobless, selling newspapers on the street to feed his family. When the Martins acquired a disintegrating upright, his elder sister was allowed piano lessons. George copied her and bagged a few tuition sessions of his own, but mostly taught himself. By the age of fifteen, he was running a dance band. He attended several schools, including St Joseph's Elementary, in Highgate, and St Ignatius College, Stamford Hill, before his family moved to the suburbs, and George reached Bromley Grammar.

He worked as a quantity surveyor and as a clerk in the War Office before joining the Fleet Air Arm of the Royal Navy in 1943. He trained as a pilot, but never saw active service. Demobbed in 1947, he resumed his education at the Guildhall School of Music & Drama, where he studied piano and oboe.

'I couldn't read or write music,' he confessed, 'but they still let me in. I crammed composition for three full years.'

His oboe teacher was Margaret Eliot, whose actress daughter Jane Asher would become Paul McCartney's girlfriend. Jane's brother Peter Asher, half of the pop duo Peter and Gordon, would become Apple Records' head of A&R, and discovered, produced and managed James Taylor. In 1948, on his twenty-second birthday, George married Jean 'Sheena' Chisholm, whom he had met in the bride's native Scotland while the groom was stationed there. His fifty-three-year-old mother was beside herself with grief over it. She died of a brain haemorrhage three weeks after the wedding, for which George never forgave himself. Sheena and George had two children, Alexis and Gregory.

Employed briefly by the BBC's classical music department, George landed at EMI in 1950 as an assistant to the head of minor label Parlophone. He inherited his boss Oscar Preuss's job five years later, and forged a reputation as a producer of comedy and novelty recordings,[10] working with Flanders and Swann, Peter Sellers, Spike Milligan and Rolf Harris. In 1962, Brian Epstein brought him the Beatles. It was a last-ditch endeavour on the part of the tenacious manager, who had been shown the door by virtually every other record company. The match was obvious. A shared sense of humour

Above left: His mother's son: ten-year-old John with Julia Lennon. © *Getty Images/Icon*

Above right: John in his first year at Quarry Bank, aged eleven. © *Getty Images/Hulton Archive*

Middle left: Mendips, Woolton, John's childhood home. © *Edward Phillips*

Middle right: 'Auntie Mimi' Smith, with David Stark, in Dorset. © *David Stark*

Below left: John's bedroom at Mimi's Sandbanks home. © *David Stark*

Below right: Harbour's Edge, Sandbanks. © *David Stark*

Above left: 'Stu', modernist painter turned bass player. © *Getty Images/Mirrorpix*

Above right: Stuart Sutcliffe with Astrid Kirchherr. Hamburg, 1961. © *Getty Images/Popperfoto*

Below: The Silver Beetles onstage in Liverpool in the 1960s. From left to right: Stu Sutcliffe, John Lennon, Paul McCartney, Johnny 'Hutch' Hutchinson (filling in on drums) and George Harrison. © *Getty Images/Michael Ochs Archive*

'Story of my life, stuck between two Johnnies . . .'

'Come on, Paul, give us a "cheese"?'

'I think we got away with it . . .'

With Granada's Johnnie Hamp, the first producer to put the Beatles on television.

JOHN HAMP   PRODUCTION   10.12.63

P387/216	25.11.	Ent. Beatles & Manager.		15	0
P387/218	26.11.	Visit Whiskey Club re: Elke Brookes.	1	2	0
Late/9 7	23.11.	Lunch on Train.		17	6
P387/219	28.11.	Meal Pat McKeegan.		8	6
	28.11.	Ent. Agents Gene Vincent /Odeon	1	5	0
Late/8	29.11.	Ent. George Melly, Joan Sims, etc. and			
		musicians.	3	5	0
P387/221	2.12.	Meal Adam Faith.	1	3	0
	3.12.	Petrol Manchester/London. one way.	2	5	0
			11	1	0

Above: The Beatles, posing for a postcard. © *Getty Images/SEM*

Below: Johnnie Hamp's Granada TV expenses claim, 10 December 1963. Entertaining the Beatles and their manager Brian Epstein cost him 15 shillings: less than £20 today.
© *Johnnie Hamp Collection*

Above: 'Fabs Keith' Altham interviews John for Fabulous magazine *(© Keith Altham)* – and (*right*) KA still has his copy *(© Lesley-Ann Jones)*.

Below: All about the bass with Ed Sullivan: (L-R) Brian Epstein, Ed Sullivan, John, Ringo, Paul. *© Getty Images/Popperfoto*

Left: Domestic bliss and the love of a good woman: John at home with Cynthia and Julian, trying to convince himself . . .

© *Getty Images/Robert Whitaker*

Below: . . . but he has eyes only for her: John with Alma Cogan at the Ready Steady Go! studio, 1964. Host Keith Fordyce can hardly get a look-in.

Below: Cyn and John.

© *Getty Images/Keystone France*

Above: Alma Cogan beams before a portrait of herself. © *Getty Images/Popperfoto*

Left: The NYPD try to restrain hordes of teenagers from crashing the Beatles' hotel on 12 August 1965.

© Getty Images/Bettmann

Right: Three days later, the Beatles take the stage at Shea Stadium.

© Getty Images/Michael Ochs Archive

Left: The deafening hysteria inside the stadium is hard to imagine – luckily video footage is available online.

© Getty Images/New York Daily News Archive

'The best view in the house!': the Fab Four perform in *A Hard Day's Night*. 1964. © *Getty Images/John Springer Collection*

'We don't just play our own instruments, you know . . .'

© *Getty Images/Popperfoto*

was what did it. George would spend the rest of his life declining credit for having 'created' the group, and always dismissed the notion that he was ever their 'Svengali'.

'A lot of nonsense was written and said,' he once remarked. 'It was a myth that they were uneducated guttersnipes and that I was this toff who knocked them into shape. In fact, the Beatles and I came from very similar backgrounds. I went to the same sort of schools. Musically, we were all essentially self-taught. As for our accents, mine was as working-class as theirs before I became an officer in the Royal Navy. You can't hang around with such folk without absorbing a bit of posh. I had also belonged to a dramatic society, which helped. As for the music, I muddled through. I experimented and learned on the job.'

His chemistry with the Beatles arose from the fact that they were enthusiastic Goons fans, he said.

'They worshipped Peter Sellers, and knew that I'd recorded him. They weren't exceptional when we began. The magic wasn't instant, it had to emerge. But when they hit the jackpot, it was chaos.'

With a backlogged schedule and barely time to go home and sleep – George was also recording Cilla Black, Billy J. Kramer and the Dakotas, Gerry and the Pacemakers, Bernard Cribbins and Matt Monro – something had to give. Now that he was embroiled in an affair with Parlophone secretary Judy Lockhart Smith, his marriage was the casualty. He divorced Sheena, and married Judy in 1966. They produced a son and daughter, Giles and Lucy.

Also that year, the Beatles would quit touring, and would retreat into the studio. *Sgt. Pepper's Lonely Hearts Club Band*, widely raved about as the greatest album ever made, would appear in 1967. Brian Epstein would die shortly afterwards. The Beatles needed George Martin more than ever. But they rebuffed him for *Let It Be*, which was produced by Phil Spector, returning to him sheepishly for their *Abbey Road* swansong. George, who had challenged EMI over the injustice of producers not receiving royalties, produced the Beatles' later recordings as a freelancer. With his business partner John Burgess and two other producers, he launched Associated

Independent Recordings: AIR. Post-Beatles, George worked with a wide range of artists, including Jeff Beck, Neil Sedaka and UFO. He likened the experience to 'having been married for decades and suddenly finding myself free to have affairs'. He and Paul resumed their relationship in 1982, when George produced McCartney's *Tug of War*. When the lease ran out at Oxford Circus, George established alternative world-class facilities, Lyndhurst, in a deconsecrated church in Belsize Park. Just as he was enjoying work as never before, life dealt a cruel blow. George was diagnosed with progressive hearing loss, a condition from which he would never recover.

'The damage was done in the sixties,' he said, 'when I was working with the Beatles. For twelve to fourteen hours at a stretch, I'd be listening to loud sound levels. Nobody told me I was damaging my ears. I later told all my engineers, "Don't do it! Put plugs in!" I didn't really notice until well into the nineties. By then, of course, it was too late.' The title of his 1979 autobiography, *All You Need is Ears*, was rendered a horrible irony. His deafness hastened his retirement from the studio. He stopped recording, but didn't stop completely, his son Giles stepping in to act as 'his ears'. He conducted orchestral concerts of Beatles music around the world, annotated classical recordings, and gave lectures on the making of *Sgt. Pepper*. Knighted in 1996, George helped organise the live concert to mark the Queen's 2002 Jubilee and escorted Her Majesty to the stage.

In 1998, the Martins released *In My Life*, a compilation of Beatles songs performed by George's favourite stars including Goldie Hawn, Robin Williams and Sean Connery. In 2006, father and son scored a show with Cirque du Soleil, which became the celebration album *Love*, 'a mash-up of the Beatles' musical lifespan'.

He was the world's most celebrated producer and I was an office dogsbody when I met the 'Fifth Beatle' in 1980. He stopped me in the lobby of Chrysalis Records, off Oxford Street, where I worked in the art department. George ran AIR Studios from there. The recording business he'd co-founded owned a huge facility overlooking Oxford Circus, and had been acquired by Chrysalis for a fortune. My leather mini-skirt, tee shirt and battered boots were no match for his dapper get-up. George, into his fifties and still an upright six foot two inches, was tidy in a striped shirt and navy tie. Grey hair fringed his collar, and his crinkled blue eyes shone.

'Come into my office and see someone you know,' he said, grinning.

John Burgess, Managing Director of AIR and former record producer for Freddie and the Dreamers and Manfred Mann, played alongside my late father, retired professional footballer Ken Jones, in charity soccer team the Showbiz XI. It featured former athletes, entertainers, agents and artist managers. Sean Connery, Jimmy Tarbuck, Des O'Connor and David Frost turned out for them during the sixties, when the crowds regularly exceeded 30,000. John had joined EMI's press and promotions department in 1951. After the company acquired Capitol Records, he was made responsible for Frank Sinatra, Dean Martin and Peggy Lee. But what he really wanted to do was make music, and eventually he became an assistant producer. George and John had been colleagues for years, having met at the studios on Abbey Road as EMI employees. I hadn't set eyes on John, who died in 2014, since I was small.

They took me to lunch. George was as I'd imagined him: quietly funny, endearingly shy. John was the crowd-pleaser. They were quite the double act. It emerged during the meal that George and I had attended the same school, Bromley Grammar in Kent. Rockers Peter Frampton and Billy Idol went there too. George recalled our school motto, 'Dum Cresco Spero': 'I Hope When I Grow'.

That December, John Lennon was murdered in Manhattan. George had weathered with silent dignity the former Beatle's vitriol during the seventies. John dismissed and belittled their producer's 'influence' and input, while Paul, George and Ringo 'were always sweet'. Implacably loyal, George was of course distressed by the news of John's murder. There was not even a funeral at which to pay his final respects. George flew to Montserrat, where he had opened his dream residential recording studio the previous year.

He sat staring at the ocean and listening to Lennon in his head, he said. The studio complex, the whole island, would be flattened by Hurricane Hugo within the decade.

I left Chrysalis for Fleet Street, and asked George for several interviews down the years. He never refused. I hadn't seen him for some time when we convened at the BRIT School in Croydon, south London, in September 2011. George was a founding governor of the establishment that produced Amy Winehouse, Adele, Katie Melua, Jessie J. and Lola Young. The opening of a state-of-the-art studio in his name was to mark the BRIT's twentieth anniversary. Then the fire alarm sounded. Everybody out. George and I caught up and stood reminiscing in the car park.

The last time I saw him was at the Savoy, on the occasion of the Gold Badge Awards in October 2012. Doddering, deaf, a rather old eighty-six, George was honoured by the British Association of Songwriters, Composers and Authors (BASCA). For the man world-famous not only for the Beatles but for film scores, Bond themes, orchestral arrangements, best-selling books, thirty Number Ones – his final chart-topper was Elton John's reworked 'Candle in the Wind' in 1997, his tribute to Diana, Princess of Wales – innumerable albums and almost half a century in the studio with more household names than any other producer in history, it seemed an understatement.

'I've had a great innings,' he said. 'I know I look decrepit and past-it. But the brilliant thing about growing old is that while you fall apart on the outside, you don't feel any different on the inside. Isn't it the Irish who say we all have an age at which we 'stop'? I have been thirty years old all my life. I'm with George Bernard Shaw: "We don't stop playing because we grow old; we grow old because we stop playing".

'I've been so lucky, I really have,' he went on. 'I've worked with and enjoyed relationships with great people, and not only pop stars. And I've never worked for any length of time with anyone I didn't like. Life really *is* too short.'

Modest George had always shrugged off any claim to the much-disputed title, typically declaring that, as far as he was concerned, there was only ever one 'Fifth Beatle', and that was Brian Epstein.

Paying tribute to their producer in a press statement after his death, Paul said,

'I have so many wonderful memories of this great man that will be with me forever. He was a true gentleman and like a second father to me. He guided the career of the Beatles with such skill and good humour that he became a true friend to me and my family. If anyone earned the title of the fifth Beatle, it was George.

'From the day he gave the Beatles our first recording contract, to the last time I saw him, he was the most generous, intelligent and musical person I've ever had the pleasure to know.'[11]

CHAPTER 9

AMERIGO

In this game, during the so-called Swinging Sixties, provincial acts and artists had no choice but to head for the epicentre of the British entertainment business if they intended to survive. The Beatles were no exception: their relentless touring, recording and filming schedules would not allow them to be based anywhere but London. Luxurious dwellings down south were duly acquired: John's, George's and Ringo's in stockbroker-belt Surrey, keeping the group close together and interdependent. Only Paul branched out, relocating to Cavendish *Avenue*, St John's Wood. Walking distance from the studios on Abbey Road is the home he retains to this day. Such a central, elegant mansion would have suited John infinitely better than 'Kenwood', his somewhat graceless mock-Tudor abode on Cavendish *Road*, St George's Hill, where the first alteration made was the digging of a swimming pool. But there was family to consider. Cyn must have had some say. As for the boys, they didn't change. Not much. Not really. They kept their accents, at least. You could divert the lads from Liverpool, but you would never extract the Scouse. Were they really the first working-class artists who remained working-class? John reckoned so.[1]

Respected rock publicist Keith Altham, who represented the Who, the Rolling Stones, the Beach Boys, the Small Faces, Van Morrison, Marc Bolan and Uncle Tom Cobley on the side was a pop journalist and scenester during the sixties, employed by *Fabulous* magazine: the forerunner of *Fab 208*. When the publication featured the Beatles on the cover in January 1964, it shifted a million units. That one-shilling journal changes hands today for £75 a copy.

'After I got the editor to agree to it,' recounts Keith, I phoned Epstein: "Good news, Brian. *Fab* have agreed to run a campaign featuring the Beatles over a three-month period. The photoshoot is on." "Oh, good," Eppy replied, "you'll send a limo for the boys, then." *What?* We didn't even send cars for Cliff Richard!

'He was dapper, well-educated and a gentleman of the old school, was Brian. He was never less than sweet, polite and well-mannered, but he could be a bit naïve. He didn't get it. And yet, he did. He'd predicted that the Beatles would be bigger than Elvis, and, for a while, they were. He produced *four* Elvises. Not only that but they were writing songs, which Presley never did. Songs that people of all ages and from all walks of life could appreciate. Their music really did appeal to everybody. Everyone was singing or whistling those songs. What was their secret? That winning combination of Paul's sweetness and John's acidity. John was the more challenging, pithy and thoughtful one. He managed to give an edge to Paul's sentimental stuff, although Paul was the more obviously commercial writer. They were such a great team. They fused beautifully. They had chemistry. Brian perceived how to package that, and make a fortune out of it. That was what he brought to the table. Which wasn't nothing.'

The aforementioned photoshoot was good news for 'K.A.': 'I had the Beatles for a whole afternoon, down at Fleetway Publications (which metamorphosed into IPC Magazines). I *did* pick them up from the Westbury Hotel in Mayfair in a limo! And I learned that day that John would be the Beatle who'd preoccupy me the most. The one I would spend many years of my life thinking and wondering about.

'He had just fallen out of bed that day, and was all over the place, but it didn't take the edge off him. He called me "*You*, Fabs Keith". I knew from the off that he was testing me. He'd say something sneery, to get a reaction. After he'd made the initial confrontation, he'd have the measure of you, and he'd relax. I must say, I liked the early John immensely. Though, even in those days, there were typically two Johns. He could be a bit Jekyll and Hyde. After a few drinks, he was inclined to be unpleasant. Almost as though he couldn't help himself. I'd run into him in clubs like the Speakeasy, and he'd either blank me or say something nasty.'

John was the self-styled leader of the Beatles, observes Keith: 'He left you in no doubt that it was *his* band. He was immensely damaged and disturbed by his childhood, and too sensitive for his own good. I think he was looking for windmills to tilt at.[2] By taking the piss out of spastics and so on, which he even did on stage – imagine *that*, today – he was testing people. To see if he could upset them. Watch the performance footage now and it's excruciating. He got a kick out of that. Because when John couldn't deal with things, he'd make fun of them. He wasn't really laughing at disabled people. He was terrified of being seen as a soft touch, or of winding up that way himself. It made him hideous company at times. The quick-witted, razor-tongued joker who shot from the lip could not have been more different from the private John. Few people ever got to see him. I did, and I saw that the bereft little boy was always in there. His sarcasm was a frailty. He probably needed psychiatric help when he was quite young, but of course he never got it. By the time he got around to doing primal therapy with Arthur Janov during the seventies, it was all too late.'

*

By now the Beatles were household names all over the country and across Europe. More than fifteen million viewers caught their performance on Val Parnell's *Sunday Night at the London Palladium*. Shows sold out. The teen legions swooned. It was a turning point. But they had yet to achieve recognition 'where it mattered'.

'America mattered because, quite simply, it was the biggest record market in the world,' affirmed George Martin. 'In January 1964, when "I Want to Hold Your Hand" reached Number One in the American charts, it opened that market to us.'

If their exuberance would later appear over the top, George made no apology.

'It is important to remember that no British artist had got near to breaking into that market in the same way,' said George. 'America had always been the El Dorado of the entertainment world. In the glory days of Hollywood, we used to worship the British stars who went over there and managed to make it …' He mentioned long-forgotten screen idols before coming up with '… Cary Grant, Ray Milland and, of course, Charlie Chaplin. To make it big in the world, you had to make it big in America.

'In England,' he went on, 'imported American records dominated the market, and we could never break that stranglehold. American records used to outsell the home product by five to one. It was hardly surprising … the roll-call ran from Sinatra, Presley and Crosby to Mitch Miller, Guy Mitchell and Doris Day. There were scores of huge names, and of course most of the jazz players – Ellington, Armstrong, Basie and the rest. Against that traditional background, any idea of reversing the trend had been almost unthinkable.

'What the Beatles were about to do was unprecedented and, to us, almost unbelievable. To be there, and to see all those famed American stars queueing up to see the Beatles and pay homage to them, was an extraordinary experience.'[3]

Their first two American releases, 'Please Please Me' and 'From Me to You', had failed to dent the charts. Capitol, the US division of EMI, were unimpressed by them. But things changed after US TV host Ed Sullivan, who was making a connection via Heathrow Airport, came across thousands of beside-themselves teenaged girls. His curiosity was piqued. What was this about? Some pop group flying home from Sweden? He'd never even heard of them. Still, something told him he couldn't ignore this. Oh, yes, he agreed with Eppy, these guys actually *could* be bigger than Elvis. In a blink, he had them booked to perform on his show. It was the kick in the butt that Capitol needed, the label having dragged its heels and having passed on further releases. When CBS News TV presenter Walter Cronkite dipped a toe in the tears of 'Beatlemania' and referred to the 'British Invasion'; and when kids began scribbling to local stations pleading to hear these Beatles on the radio, Capitol made a volte-face. Late December back in 1963 saw the rush release of 'I Want to Hold Your Hand'. Within days, it had moved a million. Told you.

*

How and where did Bronx-born BBC broadcaster Paul Gambaccini, then just fourteen years old, first hear the Beatles?

'On WINS, the New York radio station. I was on the porch of our family house in Connecticut, tuned in. And the DJ said, at approximately one-forty in the afternoon, "I'm now going to play a dedication to the British shipping workers on the West Side of Manhattan. They're in town, and they would like to hear their country's Number One record, 'I Want to Hold Your Hand' by the Beatles." He played this record, and I heard the dog whistle. That's all I can say: I heard it.

'Now, you have to understand: President Kennedy had been assassinated on 22 November, a little over two months earlier. We went into profound national mourning, the deepest mourning of my lifetime. For several days after it happened, the nation was useless. And although she had been climbing the chart before his assassination, the Singing Nun suddenly got to Number One. As if it was national penance.[4]

'And then it was Bobby Vinton, with a revival of the 1940s song by Vaughn Monroe, "There! I've Said It Again". That too went to Number One.' And, as it turned out, was the final Number One song on the US Hot 100 before the Beatles.

'So,' Paul recalls, 'it was as if *everybody* was in mourning, including the pop charts. And then suddenly it was five weeks later, and out of nowhere we had this totally new sound, obliterating everything that had gone before. It happened that quickly, it was like social media today. My generation, who were all listening to stations similar to

WINS across America, heard "I Wanna Hold Your Hand", and we wanted more of it, immediately.

'I once said to Paul McCartney, "Psychologists say that a great sadness can only be replaced by a great happiness. The intensity of the Beatles' success in America during those first four months was an escape from the mourning over President Kennedy." "I never thought of that!" he replied. He had never even considered it! Seriously, it just hadn't occurred to him. Because he was living through it and it was happening to him on a day-by-day basis, he didn't give a second thought to President Kennedy.'

As 'Gambo' describes it, the Beatles 'reaped the advantage of having failed': 'Because the British successes had not been hits in America. And Capitol had licensed previous tracks to other labels. Once they'd decided that "I Want to Hold Your Hand" would be the one they would give the big push to, all the other songs came out again, on those other labels, at the *same time*. Everybody wanted a piece of the action. They weren't going to *wait*. And so you had "Love Me Do" on Tollie Records, "Please Please Me" was on Vee-Jay, "She Loves You" was on Swan; and there was that famous week, on the chart dated 4 April, 1964 when the Beatles had the Top 5 in America: "Can't Buy Me Love", "Twist and Shout", "She Loves You", "I Want to Hold Your Hand" and "Please Please Me". No one else has ever done that, before or since. Including with streaming. And of course, in those days, you had to have a physical single. So these babies were *selling*. And *they* had the Top 5. And the Beatles had twenty-five Hot 100 hits in that year. We literally couldn't get enough.'

What exactly was it about them that captured America's imagination?

'At the outset, it was just a strictly positive message: "I *want* to do something." And what was that something? "Hold your hand." "She loves you, yeah yeah yeah." They didn't say, "*No no no*." And the experience was such an uplifting one, after this terrible tragedy, that it made the Kennedy assassination instant history. We were now into a new happy time. That was surely proved by their appearance on *The Ed Sullivan Show*, when the largest audience *ever* tuned in. Imagine today, seventy-three million people watching the same show at the same time. It's the reason why so many rock stars have stated that watching that performance was a vocation moment for them. Bruce Springsteen, Billy Joel, Tom Petty and the rest, all saying that seeing the Beatles on *Ed Sullivan* made them think, "Oh, I've got to *do* this!"

But hold on. Other British groups had tried, and had got nowhere. The Beatles were forewarned by the failure of their predecessors. They knew that they had one crack. They therefore imposed an insurance policy, declining to board a Boeing 707-331 Jet Clipper Defiance and go looking for America until they had a Number One there. Then it happened, and the Beatles were coming. With their not-just-pretty faces all over *Time*, *Life* and *Newsweek*, it was panic and pandemonium at 1.20 p.m. EST on Friday, 7 February 1964, when Pan American World Airways Flight 101 disgorged them at JFK. They were greeted by four thousand hysterical fans and more than two hundred just-about-holding-it-together-journalists. They hit the ground running. 'I Want to Hold Your Hand' held the top slot for seven weeks, giving way to 'She Loves You', followed in April by 'Can't Buy Me Love'. Beatles singles reigned for more than three months, to be kicked aside in May by 'Hello Dolly'. With hindsight, the Beatles and Louis Armstrong is an intoxicating juxtaposition. Undeterred, the boys answered back with 'Love Me Do'. They released 'A Hard Day's Night' that July. Both its American and British singles, and 'I Feel Fine', followed. Six US Number Ones within a single year wrecked Elvis's record of the late 1950s. No one could touch them. The careers of many a fifties American idol, Neil Sedaka among them, seemed sunk. Beside the Beatles, everything that had preceded them paled into boring. Their cool so-what-ness, deadpan humour and cheek, all that disintegrating at their own jokes, nonchalant smoking and clowning during press conferences, their inability to take themselves or anything seriously, gobsmacked America.

On Sunday, 9 February, they were limo'd to CBS Studio 50, where even their soundcheck was filmed. Just after 8 p.m., it was, 'Ladies and Gentleman … The Beatles!' They warmed up with 'All My Loving' and 'Till There Was You', before ripping into 'She Loves You'. Their second set took 'I Saw Her Standing There' and 'I Want to Hold Your Hand' to orgasmic heights. They could barely hear themselves. It had begun. Ratings went skyscraper: seventy-three million, almost forty per cent of America's population.

'So seventy-three million people tune and it's just Beatles, Beatles, Beatles,' remembers Gambaccini.

You watched it?

'Of course! I have since thought, if you were to ask anyone of my generation, what was the origin of the phrase, "Sorry girls, he's married," it was that night. It was John. And it was amazing. They all made a phenomenal impact, but John above all. Everyone saw it, everyone remembers it. The lasting memory of that performance is that it is a visual, tangible representation of our generation.

'There's four of them. They're different from each other. So there's all aspects of young men, represented. And then, as we very quickly learned, because we couldn't get enough of them and everyone wanted to know more-more-*more*, Ringo was the door *in*. Because Paul, John and George already seemed like gods. They were untouchable. How could you be like them? You couldn't. But Ringo was what Americans would call an ordinary guy, what the British would call an ordinary bloke. So he was our representative in the Beatles. Now, that's me speaking from the male point of view. Of course, from the female point of view, it was completely different. I remember Bill Wyman talking, in reference to all those contemporaneous Rolling Stones gigs, about the smell of the urine. Women would literally piss themselves. Bill said the stench was unbearable. It's the result of a complete loss of muscle control, caused by hysteria. You only have to look at those early TV shows. The girls are going nuts. The boys are watching, and you know that they like it, but they're not screaming their heads off and passing out. Their hands are not in the air. They're relatively calm, given what's going on all around them.'

Some of the press bitched pointlessly about knowing what happens to 'fads'. The world, they yawned, had seen it all before: Franz Liszt, Frank Sinatra, Elvis Presley. *Next.* Ken Russell would in 1975 cast Who frontman Roger Daltrey as the nineteenth-century Hungarian composer and concert pianist in his sex-crazed flick *Lisztomania*, thus directing one of the world's biggest rock stars playing history's *first-ever* rock star. It featured a score by Rick Wakeman and a role for Ringo Starr. Liszt Fever was regarded as a medical condition, first recognised during the Paris concert season when women became hysterical to the point of attacking each other. Their behaviour was declared contagious. A hundred years later, Frank Sinatra's forties bobby-soxers went similarly berserk. Then came Presley in the fifties and the Beatles in the sixties, who would themselves hand the baton to Bolan a decade on. His glittering brand of fan worship would be dubbed 'T. Rextasy'.

'But in none of those earlier eras was urination reported!' says Gambaccini.

'Girls losing control to that extent, which in my lifetime is related to Elvis and the Beatles – you can't even imagine it now. No wonder people thought, this is only going to last a couple of years. Because after all, these girls are going to grow up. They are not going to scream forever. And you can't have the Top 5 hits on the chart every single week, so it's going to have to die down, or die off.

'But you hear the Beatles during that first year of extraordinary fame, taking seriously and trying to answer seriously the question, "What are you going to do when this is all over?" The assumption being that it *will* end. Of course, that's like asking Beethoven or Mozart, "What are you planning on doing when this is done?" It *doesn't end*. Not for the greatest classical composers, and not for the Beatles.'

Paul reminds me of something he's been saying for twenty years: that there have been two periods in music history when you were either there or you missed it. The first was Vienna during the eighteenth century, when the lives of Ludwig van Beethoven, Wolfgang Amadeus Mozart and Franz Schubert overlapped. Imagine the excitement of being one of the privileged, mostly aristocratic few who attended their first performances and got to mingle with them in the salons. Even though we weren't there, we are fortunate enough to be able to enjoy the music. But the thrill of being there must have been incredible. Then, suddenly, he says, it's the 1960s, it's Beatlemania, and either you were there or you were not.

'And it was *so* exciting,' he enthuses, almost a teenager again. 'The Beatles were cultural Mission Control. People grew their hair longer because the Beatles did. Then, they stopped wearing suits and ties because the Beatles stopped wearing suits and ties. And then they got psychedelic because the Beatles got psychedelic. It was really like a preview of what it would be like on a smaller scale with David Bowie, when fans would turn up at the concerts dressed and made-up in last year's Bowie image.

'It's still incredible to me that they both represented and led their generation. That hadn't happened before, and it set a precedent. Because remember, the Beatles wrote their own songs. Sinatra and Presley did not. One thing that the Beatles were great at, and which allowed them to generate so much material, was that they wrote what was on their minds *while* it was on their minds. They didn't censor themselves. It was a completely natural process. And it changed everything.'

Looking back, Paul describes his entire career as having been a reaction to the Beatles.

'I've always thought, if you're going to be alive in your time, you have to be involved in what there is in your time. There I was, going off to university while the Beatles were dominating music and popular entertainment, so I had to be involved in that somehow. The transmission of music via both radio and the press, by which I mean *Rolling Stone* magazine, was my obvious next move.'

*

Two days after *Ed Sullivan*, the three Untouchables and Ringo trained it to Washington, DC, for their debut American live gig at the Coliseum. Wherever they went, derangement – even at a

British Embassy reception in their honour after the show, at which a guest who should have known better sliced into the back of Ringo's hair and escaped with a souvenir lock. Starr stormed out in disgust. The fan needn't have bothered: cheap Beatles merchandise was everywhere. Let's not dwell on Eppy's disastrous deals, nor on the heights to which they were ripped-off. Following a brace of appearances back in New York at Carnegie Hall ('Remind me how you get there?' 'Practise!') they were conveyed to Miami to perform again for *Ed Sullivan*. The producers knew which side their bagel was Philly'd: on 16 February, some seventy million tuned in a second time. There followed a sun-soaking interlude. This was interrupted by a now celebrated photo op with Cassius Clay before he swaggered off to batter Sonny Liston, in a controversial fight since hailed as the fourth greatest sporting moment of the twentieth century. Legends, meet Legend: the future Greatest, Muhammad Ali.

Back to London days later. They returned to a heroes' welcome. Ten thousand schoolgirls, students, secretaries and shop girls desperate to catch a glimpse of their idols stood bobbing up and down in the dawn.

CHAPTER 10

ALMA

'The most surprising thing that I came to know about John,' said Keith Altham, 'was that he was desperately looking for love. He was married by the time I met him, remember, so he shouldn't have been looking for it at all. But he *was* looking. The trouble with John, whenever he found it, he grew terrified of losing it. So he would react against it, and push it away. As if to say, "I'm getting rid of you before you can get rid of me."'

He never got to get rid of his first love.

Cynthia Lennon told me that John believed that 'One' was Alma Cogan: a popular but fading female singing star eight years his senior. He was also convinced, bizarrely, that Alma was the reincarnation of his beloved mother Julia – despite the fact that the two women co-existed. Their lives overlapped by some twenty-six years. Cynthia insisted that it was Cogan's death, coupled with John's desperate need for a replacement mother figure, that threw him into the arms of Yoko Ono.

'John thought I didn't know anything about him and Alma, and I never let on,' Cyn confided. 'Now that I think about it, with all the emotion gone out of it, I can absolutely see the attraction. Alma was older than John, and very much the auntie figure.'

John obviously had a soft spot for the older woman.

'Don't forget that Yoko was also older than him, by about seven years. Like Yoko, in so many ways, Alma was a very compelling woman. Both were driven by self-worth. You couldn't really say that either of them was beautiful, could you, not in the conventional sense. But it was as if they truly believed that they were special. If you can convince yourself of that, other people tend to think you are too. They were very alike in that sense. No, the idea of John and Alma together doesn't surprise me in the least. She was sexy, vivacious and fun. A woman of the world. Why *wouldn't* John be drawn to her?'

When Alma died from ovarian cancer in 1966, aged only thirty-four, John was 'inconsolable', Cynthia said. 'It was tragic, and I felt sorry for them all: Alma, her mother and sister, and yes, even for John. At the same time, from a selfish point of view, I couldn't help feeling relieved. The woman that my husband perhaps earmarked to replace his beloved Mimi in his affections was now lost to him. My marriage was no longer under threat.'

Alma, 'the girl with the laugh in her voice' and the UK's first female pop star, was the highest-paid British woman entertainer of the 1950s. At the advent of television, she became a household name. Born Alma Angela Cohen in Whitechapel on 19 May 1932 into a Jewish family of Russian-Romanian descent, she started competing in talent contests as a little girl. She graduated to singing at tea dances to earn her keep while studying dress design, and performed in musicals and revues. She was then appointed the resident band singer at London's Cumberland Hotel. Snapped up by the HMV label, her first single release, which she recorded on her twentieth birthday, launched her on BBC radio. She achieved her first Top 5 hit, 'Bell Bottom Blues', in April 1954, four years before the death of John's mother. Come the sixties and the televisual age, she was hosting her own show. Her image was quintessential fifties ballroom: multi-layered petticoats of tulle and lace, all swingy and marabou-trimmed; sphinx-like eye make-up fringed with long false lashes; heavily lacquered, bouffed-up hair, red lips and diamanté galore. While her speaking voice veered between pouting child and come-on husky, she sang with bell-like clarity and a knowing wink.

'She was this typical East End Jewish glamour girl with a heart of gold, a beehive and these amazing sticky-out frocks,' remembered Cynthia. 'Which was not the sort of thing I'd ever have been seen dead in myself. She was a bit *passé*. Her songs were all fifties-America froth, like "Dreamboat" and "Sugartime". When John and I were at college, Alma Cogan was a huge star. John couldn't stand her, he used to take the mickey out of her all the time. He'd do this wicked impersonation of her singing "Sugar in the Morning, Sugar in the Evening, Sugar at Suppertime" that had us all falling about laughing. At the time, I would never in a million years have thought that he could have fallen for a woman so much older than himself, whose music he couldn't bear and who he ridiculed mercilessly. Because John did have this incredibly cruel streak. He just couldn't help himself.'

The Beatles first met Alma on 12 January 1964, sharing the bill with on her on ATV's hugely popular variety show *Sunday Night at the London Palladium*. The boys had made their debut on the programme the previous October.

'John was potty about her,' George Harrison later said. 'He thought her really sexy, and was gutted when she died.'

It was perhaps inevitable that they would be invited to her legendary all-night parties at 44 Stafford Court, the bijou Kensington High Street flat in a blue plaque-d building that she shared with her widowed mother Fay and sister Sandra. It was there that Alma welcomed some of the biggest names in show business: Sir Noël Coward, Sammy Davis Jr, Audrey Hepburn, Cary Grant. She was close to Brian Epstein. He was one of her regular 'walkers' along with *Oliver!* creator and composer Lionel Bart, who cast her in his musical as 'Nancy'. Insider gossip had it that Brian was planning to propose to his glamorous friend. He took her to Liverpool to meet his parents, and they were said to have adored her. The fly in the ointment was Bart, who also expressed a wish to marry her, despite his obvious soft spot for Judy Garland. That both men were homosexual didn't help. By then into her thirties, Alma was destined never to marry. It was even rumoured that she was a lesbian, and that she was linked to the Moors murderer Myra Hindley.

'I never got invited to Alma's parties, I was kept under wraps,' said Cynthia.

'John was a famous pop star, and it was all about keeping the legions of female fans happy. It wasn't good for his image to have a wife and baby trailing on his coattails. Brian insisted on that. John had to be perceived to be single, and I just had to lump it. Everyone who was anyone used to go to those parties: Roger Moore, Ethel Merman, Michael Caine, even Princess Margaret. I never went,' she told me. But she contradicted that statement in her memoir, published some fifteen years after our interview.

'We were frequently invited to parties in her opulent apartment on Kensington High Street,' Cyn claimed, describing Alma's home as being decorated 'like a swish nightclub with dark, richly coloured silken fabrics and brocades everywhere'. She wrote about the 'hedonistic luxury' therein, of how she was plied with champagne, that she was made to feel 'acutely conscious of her imperfections' in that environment and among such glamorous people, and that she felt 'out of my league'. Time had done wonders for her memory.[1]

'I only heard years later that John and Paul used to spend a lot of time round Alma's,' she told me. 'John's nickname for her mother was "Ma McCogie", and he used to call her sister "Sara Sequin". It was on Alma's piano, with her sister Sandra sitting beside him, that Paul composed "Yesterday". Paul was supposed to be having a thing with Sandra, too, but I don't know whether that's true. The working title of the song was "Scrambled Eggs", because that was what Fay had just cooked them for tea. "Scrambled eggs, oh my baby how I love your legs …"' Alma would become the first female to record 'Yesterday'.

She and John were soon enjoying a full-blown affair, which they conducted in London hotel rooms. They would arrive in disguise, and would sign the register as 'Mr and Mrs Winston'. The clue was John's middle name. With the Beatles so often away on tour, their trysts grew less frequent. Alma's star began to descend, thanks to the rise of younger, popsier chanteuses the likes of Dusty Springfield, Sandie Shaw and Lulu. She did everything she could think of to hang on to her audience, even recording Beatles hits such as 'Help!' and 'I Feel Fine', as well as 'Yesterday', and also a strings-heavy, melancholic 'Eight Days a Week' with a big, brassy, zapped-up finish that defied the mood of the song. Although they were worthy, honest renditions, they couldn't keep her bulb from blowing.

Alma experienced dramatic weight loss, which her friends explained away as the result of the slimming injections she'd become hooked on – perhaps in an attempt to stoke the ardour of her world-famous young lover. Ovarian cancer was diagnosed in 1966, but it's possible that this was never broken to her. Whether or not she knew, she declined to stop working and focus on her health. She began writing material for a new album, and continued to travel and perform. It was during her concert tour of Sweden that she collapsed. The severity of her illness was soon discovered. She was flown directly to the Middlesex Hospital in London, where she died on 26 October, aged thirty-four. She and John were denied the chance to say goodbye. He was in Spain with Cynthia at the time of her death, where he had been filming for Richard Lester's *How I Won the War*. He had also celebrated his twenty-sixth birthday there, a little over two weeks earlier.

There might have been a more sensitive way of announcing her death on the radio than playing her haunting cover of Irving Berlin's 'Heaven, I'm in Heaven'. So it goes. Her funeral was a celebrity mobfest – everyone who was anyone. Brian Morris, the manager of the Ad Lib club who was rumoured to be passionately in love with her, freaked out and attempted to hurl himself into her grave. She was buried at the Jewish Cemetery in Bushey Hertfordshire.

Cynthia was adamant that, had Alma lived, John would never have abandoned his wife and child for her. Their affair, Cyn believed, would have fizzled out naturally – 'like all his other flings,' she said ruefully – and John would have come home again with his tail between his legs, 'as he had always done'.

Did Cynthia really believe that Alma was John's true love?

'We can convince ourselves of almost anything in grief,' she said quietly.

'Because she was dead, it was safe for John to convince himself of that. It didn't threaten anything else. It certainly didn't threaten us.'

That was to come.

CHAPTER 11

LIVING YEARS

Always keep the door and your heart open, no matter what. Don't hold grudges. Ask the questions 'What happened?', 'Where were you?' and brace yourself for alternative truth. It's the kind of approach that the mature, more amenable, bigger-picture John might have taken in years to come, when faced with the ghost of his infancy. In his brittle, defiant twenties, he was of no mind to do any such thing. As far as he was concerned, his dad had abandoned him and his mother for a carefree life on the ocean wave. John was angry about that. He had a right to be. Nothing, at that point, could have convinced him otherwise.

Tales of Freddie Lennon turning up like a bad penny after discovering that his child was now world-famous, taking jobs as a dishwasher and as a kitchen porter in pubs and hotels not a throw from Kenwood, finding out where John and Cyn lived and showing up on their doorstep, dressed down like a tramp and seeking charity; of Cyn cutting his hair for him and grilling him Welsh rarebit while they waited for John to come home, which he didn't; of him barging into the NEMS office in April 1964, armed with a salivating journalist, demanding to see his long-lost son, the invasion prompting a panic attack in Epstein and a furious reaction from John, have perhaps been embellished with every re-telling. Did John come as summoned to an office showdown? Did he really snarl at his father, 'Where have you been for the last twenty years?' Would anyone say that, other than in a script? Then again, what was he supposed to say? How *would* you react? I have tried to imagine the moment when Lennons Snr and Jr came face to face for what may have been only the third time ever in their lives; the two men the absolute spit of each other, give or take the wrinkles, chins and greasy grey; the elder staring in wonder at his point-blank youthful self, as the younger confronted a glimpse of a careworn future. At such moments, faces become mirrors. Time travel exists.

Freddie was only fifty-three, but dear God … life had not favoured him. He might have looked more at home in a shredded sleeping bag under the arches at Waterloo, clutching a bottle of Bell's in brown paper. He protested that Julia had left *him*, not the other way around; that his own family and friends had turned their back on him, that his luck, meagre enough to begin with, had run out, and that he was of course skint. It looks as though John took pity, dipped his hand in his pocket and despatched his hitherto estranged parent whence he came. But simple, gullible Freddie was ripe for exploitation. Shame on those who seized the opportunity to bundle him into a studio to record 'That's My Life (My Love and My Home)', a song written by artist manager Tony Cartwright, who at the time was looking after Tom Jones. The single was released on the Pye label on 31 December 1965.

'Freddie was a born entertainer, and had a rich, emotional singing voice with which he regaled the whole pub,' Tony Cartwright imparted about his 'best mate' to the *Daily Mail* in 2012. 'He didn't want to hitch a ride on the Beatles' bandwagon, but I sensed that he could be a star in his own right. News gets around, and the next day, I had the Beatles' manager Brian Epstein on the phone. "Tell me it's not true, Tony," he pleaded. "Is John's dad really a kitchen porter? What are the papers going to make of *that?*"'

The single generated publicity. That the drummer and bassist on the recording were none other than Mitch Mitchell and Noel Redding was neither here nor there at the time. It emerged only later that Lennon Snr's single happened to be the first known recording of those soon-to-be revered members of the Jimi Hendrix Experience.

Freddie's record might have surprised the charts. It had seemed on course to. Why wouldn't it get airplay, given its Beatles connection? They recorded for Dutch TV in Amsterdam. Morris Levy of Roulette Records called Tony from the US, enthusing, 'You gotta bring Papa Lennon over here. He's sold one hundred and eighty thousand singles already, it's a hit in nine states!' Success was predicted, but then the single vanished. John and Brian would later stand accused of having sabotaged it. Did they actually? Underhand dealings were certainly suspected, causing Freddie and Tony to set off for Kenwood to confront John, asking him why he would do such a thing, and pleading with him to give Freddie a break. John allegedly had nothing to say. He refused to invite them in, and slammed the door in their faces. Did he? If so, it begs the question, how did they get through the gates and the girls in the first place? John or Cyn must have seen them coming.

'Freddie was heartbroken, and immediately gave up the music business,' Tony insisted. '"It's brought me nothing but unhappiness,"' he reported his charge as having said. '"I'd rather go back to washing pots." And so he did.'

But this was conveniently overlooking all the parading around London of Freddie Lennon as the latest hot-shot celebrity. There was a lot of that kind of thing back then. On 6 January 1966, for example, he loomed large at the launch party for David Bowie with the Lower Third's debut Pye single 'Can't Help Thinking About Me' at the Gaiety Bar in Bayswater, where he is remembered as having been off his face and falling over himself to impress guests with his illustrious identity. Cartwright also neglected to mention in his piece the three further Freddie Lennon singles, recorded with a group called Loving Kind. Not that any of those releases did anything either, though they fetch a tidy collector's sum today.

If not for that ill-advised first record, which served only to humiliate and infuriate John and drive him and Freddie further apart, could things have been different? Could bygones have been bygones, and might a relationship have been forged? Whatever else had evaporated, there was DNA. But love is thicker than blood, all right. We can't do much about that. The killer has always been betrayal.

*

John did relent. Freddie found himself another woman in 1966, or should one say 'girl'. He met teenager Pauline Jones, an undergraduate of Exeter University born in July 1948 and thirty-five years his junior, during the Christmas/New Year 1966-67 period, when both were working in the Toby Jug Hotel's kitchen.[1] Pauline begged her mother for permission to marry him. Jean Jones refused. Freddie continued to grace the pages of the newspapers, to John's mounting annoyance. During the summer of 1967, John's paternal Uncle Charlie wrote to him, imploring him to ignore the tabloids and pleading with him to see his dad. Softened by the teachings of Transcendental Meditation (TM) guru Maharishi Mahesh Yogi, John agreed. Maybe it suited him to have his own parent around, to dilute the caustic influence of Cyn's mother Lillian – who made no secret of her disdain for John while happy to spend his money. John invited his father to move in with him and Cyn. The novelty soon wore off: John was rarely there, and Freddie was lonely. He asked John to find him accommodation nearby. A Kew flat and an allowance were provided. Freddie and Pauline were invited to the Magical Mystery Tour premiere fancy-dress party at London's Royal Lancaster Hotel on 21 December 1967 – at which fifties-rocker John, three sheets gone, flirted outrageously with George Harrison's wife Pattie. Freddie and Pauline spent Christmas at Kenwood. Cyn then employed Pauline as a live-in nanny/fan-club secretary, giving her Freddie's old attic quarters. Pauline soon moved out to live with Freddie, and was pregnant before she turned twenty. Her mother tried to have her daughter made a ward of court. John paid their legal fees to challenge her. Pauline, over-stressed, miscarried. The judge allowed the relationship, but forbade them to marry before Pauline turned twenty-one. By June

1968, she was pregnant again. John helped them elope to Scotland, where they could legally marry. They did so at Gretna Green, on what may have been Pauline's twentieth birthday. John provided a one-bedroom flat in Brighton. He later bought them a house there, retaining the deeds. After David Henry, the first of John's two half-brothers, was born in February 1969, (Robin Francis arrived in October 1973), John severed contact. They would not see each other again for nearly two years.

John and Freddie were to meet again, just the once, shortly before John left England for New York, never to return. John and Cyn had divorced. John was now married to Yoko. The couple had relocated to Tittenhurst Park, their Georgian mansion near Ascot, and had just arrived home from a life-changing trip to Los Angeles, during which they submitted to personality-changing primal therapy at the hands of psychotherapist Dr Arthur Janov. The doctor helped patients to re-experience and process childhood pain by screaming it all out. He also instructed them to confront those perceived to have inflicted the pain in order to eradicate it. Thus, John invited his father to Kenwood on the occasion of his thirtieth birthday, 9 October 1970. Anticipating a celebration, Freddie arrived suited and booted with a befrocked Pauline, their little son David and a birthday present. But instead of welcoming him into a champagne-fuelled knees-up, John ripped the rug from under his father by saying that he had brought him there to inform him that he was cutting him off.

'I came out of the therapy and told him to get the hell out, and he did get the hell out, and I wish I hadn't really because everyone has their problems – including wayward fathers,' admitted John in 1976, during an interview revisited in *Anthology*. 'I'm a bit older now and I understand the pressure of having children or divorces and reasons why people can't cope with their responsibility.'

Not only was he taking their house away from them, but Freddie's and Pauline's allowance would no longer be paid. This was John getting his own back. We can understand him wanting to. But, however angry he felt with his father, however deeply he wanted to punish him for having deserted him, John went too far. He unleashed rage so vitriolic that chemically induced paranoia must have played its part. Clearly convinced that Freddie was the cause of his every last hang-up and dysfunction, he even threatened to murder his father if Freddie wrote a kiss-and-tell. Freddie would never get over the brutal attack. He and John never saw each other again.

'Janov had a lot to answer for,' sighs consultant psychiatrist Dr Cosmo Hallström.

'Many people feel they need something more. We are all seeking some form of explanation. It's natural and human to want one. Some, like John, have a route to work on it, others are less obsessed, and many more are too busy simply existing. Up pop these wacky people with "answers" – remember, these are the times of acid and Explore Your Inner Self – who provide a formula to work towards. To take advantage, and to make a living for themselves.

'Arthur Janov? Mumbo Jumbo. People seemed to enjoy that kind of therapy in those days, but it didn't stand the test of time. I don't think anyone seriously believed it. Having said that, what Lennon did with Janov may have had some effect on him. In the forties, fifties and sixties, the prevailing psychiatric view was that messed-up minds were the result of "inner conflict". The idea that you needed five years of therapy five days a week to let your conflict come out and let your ideas reformulate was very Freudian. Then along came LSD, to give you an explosion of unchannelled emotion. It was a fast track to enlightenment.'

Dr Hallström, who happens to have been a medical student in Liverpool, tried it himself.

'I don't deny it. It's no secret. It alters the way you see things, and it gives you different perception. If you're young and curious, you like to explore different ways of seeing things. It was psychedelic, different colours, different styles. And it was OK if you could take it. But, of course, a lot of people fell by the wayside because of it. LSD had a far greater effect on John than primal therapy. Especially with his kind of mind. It's a very powerful drug. It scrambles the brain. Lots of people took it, and they had trips. Disturbing trips. Fun trips. Some of it was a great experience. Much of it not. It's important to remember that in those days, taking it was something spiritual. It was about opening a new pathway. They thought it was part of the mission, to turn other people onto it – which was why John wound up giving it to his wife and so on. And, of course, LSD was undoubtedly the single most significant thing that changed the Beatles' songwriting.'

*

Freddie did write his autobiography, though it was not intended for publication. He wrote it for John, for the record, to give his side of the story of John's abandonment; to let him know once and for all that it was Julia, not he, who had trashed the marriage, and who had rendered John the victim of a broken home. In an eerie premonition of the lifestyle that John would adopt in New York during the mid-seventies, Freddie became a house husband and stayed home minding the babies. He lavished his little sons with the time and attention that he hadn't been able to give John, while his wife, just like Yoko, went out to work.

Five years after John excommunicated him, Freddie was felled by stomach cancer. It was 1976. Pauline had no way of contacting John and Yoko in New York, other than by going through the Apple Corps offices. She did John the courtesy of letting him know that his father was dying. What did John do? He sent flowers. He called the hospital, and got Dad on the line. He rabbited on, and he apologised. We can hope that his remorse was sincere, and that their telephonic reconciliation brought peace.[2]

John confessed to his father that he regretted the primal therapy. He took the blame for the fall-out. He said he was desperate for his little boy Sean, born five months previously, to come and meet his grandad. It never happened. It was as though Freddie allowed his disease the last laugh. On April Fool's Day 1976, aged sixty-three, he let go. John told his stepmother that he would pay for the funeral. The widow declined, and John was condemned to mourn remotely. All the lonely people. Only she and Freddie's old chum Tony Cartwright, who wrote Freddie's first single, turned up.[3]

CHAPTER 12

REDEEMER

It is sometimes easier to understand something when we examine what it wasn't or isn't, rather than what it was or is. We know that the Beatles 'changed the world', that they initiated a cultural cataclysm, that they were the progenitors of the modern music industry. What this was not, for them personally, was a dream come true. That which history has recorded as a success story beyond wildest imagining was, behind the curtain, a different scene. It came to deprive them of their liberty, vandalise their personalities, challenge their sanity, and stopped just short of sucking out their souls. It must have been like winning the lottery. Lucky them, it'll change their lives, what we wouldn't do with all that dosh! But then we remember how often such fortune spells the end: of marriages, families, friendships, even purpose and self-worth. When money becomes the focus, people can lose sight of what counts. Yes, the Beatles' ships had come in heaving with untold treasure, and that was well and good. The interminable slog and deprivation had reaped rewards. The tens of thousands of hours' relentless graft had paid off, generating filthy wealth and fame for these minimally educated backstreet boys who might otherwise have ended up … where? They 'got lucky'. The harder they worked, the luckier they got.[1] Yet it was obvious to those on the inside what a trap success was; what a charade the debilitating single-album-tour routine had so rapidly become; that they were now slaves to obligation: live appearances, press conferences, radio, television, interview after interview. 'Be careful what you wish for' is the maxim. For a while there, they weren't in any kind of mood to take heed. Each of them, however – with the possible exception of Paul – was soon experiencing the nag, that being a Beatle wasn't all it was cracked up to be; that it was taking too big a toll, and that they were paying too great a price. Bored with the screaming, the vain struggle to be heard, the wall-to-wall sex – oh, yes, they indulged; with the bringing of the blind, the crippled, the disabled to be touched by them, as though the mystical Beatles walked on water and were blessed with healing powers; and, so would we be, bored with confinement to hotel rooms, effectively imprisoned, seeing little more of the many countries they landed in than the airport, the venue and their accommodation. Their independence had vanished in the haze. They couldn't even eat out, because restaurants would be besieged. Room service on a tray was what it had come to. What was the point? 'Give me money (that's what I want),' went the song. There comes a time when a bank statement loses its charm and when the guy having the last laugh is the taxman – as banged home in George's song of that name on their new album *Revolver*, in which he blasts Harold Wilson's government for the 95% tax levy.

Something had to give. What? You're on a merry-go-round, it's whirling so fast it's getting out of control, and suddenly it's too dangerous to jump …

On Sunday, 15 August 1965, they gave the opening show of their second proper US tour. They were dropped by chopper into the World Fair site, Flushing Meadows-Corona Park (which would become the home of the US Open tennis tournament), and conveyed in a Wells-Fargo Bank truck to Shea Stadium, the new home park of the New York Mets. This was not only their largest concert to date but the first stadium rock concert in history. Its sell-out audience of 55,600 was unprecedented.[2] The warm-up acts included Brenda Holloway and Sounds Incorporated. Mick Jagger, Keith Richards and Marvin Gaye were there – as were seventeen-year-old Barbara

Bach and twenty-four-year-old Linda Eastman, both New York natives and future Beatle wives. 'It was John who interested me at the start,' said Linda. 'He was my Beatle hero. But when I met him, the fascination faded fast, and I found it was Paul I liked.'[3]

Footage of this gig is terrifying to behold. If you haven't, I urge you. The roaring and screaming deafened them as they ran from their baseball-locker dressing room onto the field, where they were blinded by what must have seemed like a million bulbs. Ed Sullivan introduced them: 'Honoured by their country, decorated by their Queen, and loved here in America ...' The sight of so many women and girls beside themselves, losing control, collapsing and being carried out is unnerving. Even cops and security guards clamped their palms to their heads and jammed their fingers into their ears as the boys appeared. The crowd was so loud, there was no hope of hearing music. The band couldn't hear themselves. Kicking off with 'Twist and Shout', they hollered their best, strummed and drummed their wildest, gave it welly through the dozen requisite songs for only about half an hour – imagine getting away with that, today – and let themselves go. Deafened Ringo, unable to hear the others, which he needed to in order to maintain the beat, would later admit that he'd had to resort to eyeballing the three guitarists' swaying bottoms to pick up the rhythm.

Paul, George and Ringo would all comment in years to come that they felt John cracking up during the Shea gig. Hovering on the edge at the best of times, the most eccentric Beatle gave in to the pervading air of surreality. It's worth watching the footage to witness him chortling like a crazed inventor, while the others catch each other's eyes as if to say, 'What the fuck's goin' on?' while zapping nervous stares at the audience. What to make of John flinging his arms skywards and chanting into the clouds, as if at the behest of some invisible deity? Of his horrible spastic clawings and off-beat stampings? It was one thing to inflict such crassness on a forgiving home-grown throng; another thing entirely to showcase such appalling behaviour in front of a tried but not altogether tested American crowd, as infamous events the following year would testify. As Paul launches into the concluding song, 'I'm Down', John surrenders to the madness. He takes to the electric organ and starts playing it with his elbow, laughing insanely. It's contagious. Paul whirls on stage as if about to take off, while George cracks his trademark poker face and dissolves into uncontrollable gales.

After their ordeal, there was a tangible sense of the Beatles having reached a pinnacle. When asked by a journalist whether it bothered them that they couldn't hear a note they played or sang, John deadpanned, 'No, we don't mind. We've got the records at home.'

He would later remark to Sid Bernstein, the concert promoter who had booked them for Carnegie Hall in 1964 without ever having heard them – 'At Shea Stadium, I saw the top of the mountain.'

It doesn't get better than this, was the apparent inference. Was that true? Could the musing have been made tongue-in-cheek? Knowing John.

Getting better all the time? As in, can't get no worse?[4]

*

It was a different story when they returned to Flushing Meadows a year later, on their fourth visit and final American tour. Not that they would recall, in decades to come, having played Shea a second time. They could be forgiven their vagueness, too many miles having been covered in the interim. Too many drugs having gone down. That they were living double lives didn't help. Out there on the global stage, they were everybody's Beatles, the darlings of the world. Back home, it was a balancing act, living up (and down) to the expectations of partners, friends, offspring and hangers-on, trying hopelessly to toe the domestic line. Paul was still with his strawberry-blonde sweetheart, actress Jane Asher, though their schedules and Paul's extra-curriculars were driving them apart. He eventually proposed marriage, and their engagement would be announced on Christmas Day 1967. But Paul would continue to play away, in every sense. Jane would confirm wistfully to BBC television host Simon Dee in July 1968 that it was all over. Only nine months later, he would marry single mother Linda Eastman, and they would spawn three of their own. Ringo had married hairdresser Maureen, aka Mo (born Mary Cox, whom he'd met at a gig in the Cavern Club) in February 1965. Their first of three was born that September. His (by his own blunt admission) relentless womanising, drinking, wife-beating and 'absentee-fatherism' would lead to their divorce ten years on. George tied the knot with Pattie Boyd, the pretty model they'd all worked with on the set of 1964's *A Hard Day's Night* (she had a one-word line) in January 1966. But they would not be blessed with babies. Enthusiastic adulterer George would sensationally bequeath his wife to his friend Eric Clapton, divorcing her in 1977 and marrying record company employee Olivia Arias in 1978. They would have one son, born the same year. John, meanwhile, was still wallowing in marital misery with Cynthia, and failing spectacularly at being a father to bewildered little Julian.[5]

Because what chance did the dysfunctional man-child at odds with life, who became even more screwed up by the madness of the Beatle years, have of being a good husband and dad? Slim at best. Make that none. This was, as anyone could see, an expectation too far of an immature, dysfunctional guy whose head had been turned by the worship of millions, and who hadn't had much of a handle in the first place on who he really was.

John was twenty-five when he invited journalist friend Maureen Cleave down to the large, wood-panelled 'Hansel and Gretel house' ('I'll get my real house when I know what I want') in fragrantly wooded Weybridge, a gaggle of fans there to greet her at the gates, to show her around his plushly carpeted castle. He impressed her with his purple dining room, his books – leather-bound classics, *Just Williams*, shelf upon shelf of obscure titles – wine cellar, posh cars, zany possessions – gorilla costume and suits of armour, anyone? – a giant Bible, a huge crucifix bearing the inscription 'IHS' (a Christogram for 'Jesus Christ') and a moggy named Mimi, after guess who. He gave her a rare glimpse into his enviable (for which, read 'on hold') private life. The astute interviewer observed in her impressive piece that his many chattels now appeared to own *him*. What was he doing these days, since the most recent tour had ended? Watching television, reading – books on world religions, including but not restricted to 'acid queen' Timothy Leary's study of *The Tibetan Book of the Dead*, and the best-selling *The Passover Plot* by Hugh J. Schonfield, with its contentious premise that Jesus Christ was a mere mortal who used his disciples to help him fake miracles – and playing records, records, more records. Listening to George's beloved Indian music, which was evidently having a profound effect on him. Sleeping. Ingesting hallucinogens (he didn't say that bit); and paying scant attention to his three-year-old. He and his driver spun Maureen back to London, dropped in on Epstein, did more shopping – because what else does a multi-millionaire superstar do when he's off the road, bored brainless and within coughing distance of Bond Street? – and nattering nineteen to the dozen about domestic bliss, the second coming of his father Freddie Lennon, and airing his off-the-cuff, slightly slanted views about this, that and nothing in particular, for the fun of it.

In the context of a casual chat between two young movers and shakers, who were also rumoured to be having/have had an affair – of *course* they were; a young, female journalist couldn't possibly have bagged such an exclusive because she was any good at her job – John's remarks were nothing to get hung about. Cleave's interview ran in the London *Evening Standard* on 4 March 1966, headlined, How DOES A BEATLE LIVE? JOHN LENNON LIVES LIKE THIS, and subheadlined, ON A HILL IN SURREY … A YOUNG MAN, FAMOUS, LOADED, AND WAITING FOR SOMETHING. The layout sub got that right.

Not an eyebrow was raised. Not a note of complaint was stamped and addressed to the editor. It was only when an innocuous seven-line quotation was lifted from the newspaper and was quoted out of context in the 29 July edition of *DATEbook* – a radical, bigger-picture American magazine familiar to the Beatles and their management/publicity team which, unusually, juxtaposed socio-political stories with showbiz puff – that things began to go awry; when Bible-Belt America in particular saw red, accusing John of blasphemy and effectively yelling for his head. This was just days before the kick-off of their major US tour. Picture the mayhem:

dozens of radio stations across a two-thousand-odd-mile stretch from New York to Utah banning their records. Public bonfires of their vinyl, books and merchandise, into which some stores dumped their whole Beatles stock. Disc jockeys and other influencers of the young, blinkered and impressionable inciting revolt against these fallen-from-grace losers who were clearly *not* what they appeared to be. Build 'em up, knock 'em down. The backlash looked to be far-reaching, furious and out of all proportion to the 'crime': Ban the Beatles!; Beatles Go Home!; Jesus Died For You, John Lennon! – aggression towards them and 'what they represented' was reported as mounting at a sickening rate. Onto the bandwagon leaped the Ku Klux Klan, of all white supremacist haters, threatening the usual violence and death. Even Cyn was being intimidated by hundreds of letters back home. Who wouldn't fear for their life in the face of such hostility and revulsion?

The all-pervading offending remark?

'Christianity will go. It will vanish and shrink. I needn't argue about that; I'm right and I will be proved right. We're more popular than Jesus now. I don't know which will go first, rock'n'roll or Christianity. Jesus was all right but his disciples were thick and ordinary. It's them twisting it that ruins it for me.'

In the UK, no big deal. The *Standard* hadn't found it sufficiently startling to project John's words as a pull-out quote. The rest of Fleet Street ignored the comment. It came and went. It was not, in itself, an unreasonable observation. While the majority of British citizens still married in and were buried by Anglican churches, and while most would give their religion as 'C of E' (Church of England) when form-filling, Britain was not, by then, a nation of fervent churchgoers. Plenty of high-profilers were poking fun at clergy, including Peter Sellers, whom John admired. The church seemed at best an anachronism, with nothing to offer the younger generation.

But in America, it was a different story. John was genuinely baffled by the reaction there. Although defiant in the face of accusation, he was terrified that someone was going to 'take a pop' at him the moment they landed back in the US. Even then, he refused to bow to

Brian Epstein's flu-ridden, damage-limiting command to apologise profusely, in an attempt to defuse the furore. It fell to the ailing manager to arrange a press conference at New York's American Hotel, to which he invited the world's media and at which he read aloud a statement half-heartedly approved by John.

From the moment the Beatles touched down, insiders observed a frightened anger exuding from him that he was clearly struggling to contain. This caused his responses to questions about It All to appear backhanded and grudging. For example, in Chicago, where they were set to open the tour on 12 August with two shows at the old International Amphitheatre, it was a restless: 'My views are only from what I've read or observed of Christianity and what it was, and what it has been, or what it could be. It just seems to me to be shrinking. I'm not knocking it or saying it's bad. I'm just saying it seems to be shrinking and losing contact.'

They weren't going to let him get away with it. No matter where the questions might stray, there was always a rogue reporter ready to jump in and drag it back to scandal. The dogs with bones would cross-examine him on the subject again and again, as if trying to trip him up, to get him to say something vile to compound the fracture. Lennon-baiting, what sport! To John's credit, he clung to his temper. Still, the storm in a teacup (as Epstein referred to it in the *NME*) brewed on. Because despite the fact that a minority were responsible for the protest, irresponsible media reporting augmented it into an affront of the majority and made it look much worse than it was. All the while, grown-up America was peering down its nose at 'The Kids', going, sneer, sneer, we told you. And in the end, John did say that he was sorry. He uttered the words. The waters parted. The rage subsided. The show would go on.

While it was reported that their Shea Stadium return on 23 August 1966 was a 'failure' and that 11,000 seats went un-sat-in, they still shifted more than 45,000 tickets. Big disappointment. Along with some other come-gone acts, they were supported by the Ronettes. John had long wanted hot lead singer Ronnie[6] to be his baby, and as she later confessed, she was sorely tempted. Not that Cyn knew jack. They got through eleven songs, including 'Day Tripper', 'I Feel Fine', 'Nowhere Man', 'Paperback Writer' and 'Long Tall Sally'. The boys skipped to it, they looked lively enough, they oooh-ed and cooed, smashed the tunes, delighted the weepers and went through all the other motions. Or rather, got through them. Because the damage was done. From that moment on, their days as a touring band were blatantly numbered. All who were in on it knew things would never be the same again.

The thing is, John was right. As he pointed out after the Take Your Life in Your Hands tour had wrapped, when he was in a position to balance common sense with the wisdom of hindsight, 'I said we were more popular than Jesus, which is a fact. I believe Jesus was right, Buddha was right, and all of those people like that are right. They're all saying the same thing, and I believe it. I believe what Jesus actually said – the basic things he laid down about love and goodness – and not what people *say* he said.'

'I was probably too young to be aware of the impact at the time of John's "Beatles more popular than Jesus" declaration,' says the Reverend Canon Doctor Alison Joyce, Rector of St Bride's, the Journalists' Church on London's Fleet Street.

'Thinking about it now, the Beatles did indeed have unprecedented global reach, and he was describing this in deliberately provocative terms (such is the audacity of youth!), but how could Christians be offended by such a statement? The Christian faith is far more robust than any disparaging remarks we can throw at it – and, as to it being blasphemous? Man had nailed God to a tree to die a criminal's death. There is nothing more offensive than that. Mere words and opinions are utterly irrelevant, by comparison.

'I don't believe, nor have I ever believed, that John Lennon was trying to compete with God. In common with most people, he was searching for a meaning to his existence. Because he was so famous, he was having to do his searching in the public eye. Millions of people around the world worshipped John as a kind of god, perhaps assuming, from his songwriting, that he had all the answers. But the opposite was the truth. He was looking for them like everybody else.'

CHAPTER 13

YOKO

Scientists call it 'cavitation': when a collapsing bubble releases a shock wave. This sudden blast of energy makes a noise. Under the sea, the many millions of miniscule bubbles that collect around a ship's propeller create a deafening knock as they implode. Blow after blow over time eventually paralyse the propeller. We may never have heard such a thing ourselves, but we are accustomed to the acoustic of bubbles: the bang of a bursting balloon, the hiss of Coke in an ice-clinked glass, the ejaculation of champagne. We recognise resonance. But when a child blows detergent through a hoop to send globes of iridescence into the air, what do we hear when those bubbles pop?

You've never heard the cry of the drowning man. There isn't one. There is a hushed collapse, a slow, inaudible sinking into oblivion. A giving up. A giving out. The sound of silence.

Ringo, generally the most equable of the four, was along for the ride, wherever it might take them. He'd had his wobbles, his crises of confidence. He will soon stalk off, telling the others that he's 'left'. He'll be back. Paul would have stayed on the road forever – which, looking back over the decades since, he pretty much has. George made no bones, he'd had his fill, yet he was waiting it out. But the Beatles phenomenon was killing John. It was a parasite. It had crept under his hypodermis and wormed into his myocytes. It was squatting in his heart.

The final live concert on 29 August 1966 at Candlestick Park, in those days home to the San Francisco Giants, was neither billed nor announced as the last show they'd ever do.[1] It just turned out that way. As their wagon train rolled across America, there seemed to be problems and challenges, bombs and belligerence wherever they went. Their energy flagged as their enthusiasm subsided. In more than a few destinations, they feared for their lives. It was no longer 'the same'. How could it be? In fabled Gold Rush Central, the city by the bay, they found less than a glittering reception. Though the stadium could accommodate a capacity crowd of 42,500, it was only just over half-full. The supporting cast again featured effervescent Ronnie and her '-ettes'. The wind was up, the fog was down, and a sinister chill hung in the air. The boys partied backstage with the has-beens, the wannabes and Joan Baez, as though reluctant to go out there and get on with it. They emerged to deliver their parting shot at almost nine-thirty that night. Resigned, relieved that this would be the last time, they took a camera, to capture the crowds and themselves against the backdrop, for posterity. The bubble had burst, not with a bang but with a whimper.[2] Ten years. Enough. Man overboard! John caught the lifebelt. He choked to the surface. He paddled his way to shore.

'The Beatles' had consumed what dear, disingenuous Paul has always loved to call 'a good little rock'n'roll band', while quietly gloating over the glory of it all (as well he may). Because 'The Beatles' were not four separate people. They were a concept, a creation, an ideal. Never of the real world, they could not have endured as a touring entity. They were incapable of becoming the Rolling Stones, still roaming the globe like rusty tanks without a war to go to, thrashing the same old tunes (because nobody wants the new ones). Jumping, jacking, flashing, posturing, these septuagenarian caricatures with faces that might have been microwaved but coming on like eternal thirty-year-olds, have but one role: to feed how-come-you-dance-so-good nostalgia to the mellow masses addicted to the reliving of their youth. The Beatles were all about fresh and new and endless reinvention.

Sentimentality had its place, as evident in so many of their most cherished songs. But only in context of continuous improvement and as an adjunct to unflagging, breathtaking creativity. They were about pushing boundaries and outdoing themselves. About never remaining the same. Hence, disintegration. Retiring their live-touring incarnation was vital to their survival, both as musicians and as individuals. For John, it was crucial, a matter of life and death. Just as the group subsumed maverick rocker Lennon, Beatlemania suffocated the Beatle. Last one out, turn off the lights. Don't forget to lock the door.

What now?

What else? Back to the studio to focus on making music. Specifically, the kind that could be sat down and listened to, pored over, marvelled at, enlightened by. That could not easily, in those days, be reproduced live.

*

Consultant psychiatrist Dr Cosmo Hallström, who experienced the Beatles phenomenon as a young medical student in Liverpool, thinks about John at this significant crossroads.

'Here he is, burned-out, angry, confused. He is also a rather important person, still in a bubble despite the fact that the bubble appears to have burst, and no one will stand up to him. Then along comes a person who is immune to his arrogance. Who has different ideas. Who is from another culture, and who therefore sees the world in a different way. And *she* is the one he falls in love with. She is the one person who stands out, who he can relate to. She is almost the polar opposite of his wife Cynthia, and she is a woman of her time.

'John and Yoko's connection was immediate, and their message was very simple. It was the hippie concept of *love*. Peace, love, nice, two-dimensional. Beautiful colours, pretty, happy – as opposed to the intense, confounding, debilitating relationships that he'd had with others, that he wrote songs about but couldn't understand.

'I suspect that they really did have a deep, powerful, all-consuming connection that was always going to last,' Dr Hallström asserts. 'It was not simply lust or passion. The concept of love – becoming entwined for all time with one other person, which is the foundation of so much music, art and literature – is biologically programmed. It is a characteristic of human beings to seek a life partner. Swans mate for life, and suddenly that's a higher power, something mystical. Because most animals don't, we value those that do. Being drawn to a long-term partner is an innate human need.'

Of all the mysteries of life, Cosmo is frank: love and attraction are the 'Big Ones'.

'Society also likes conformity,' he points out. 'There is cultural pressure to couple, as well as the whole eyes-meeting-across-the-room thing: finding The One. John Lennon was a highly sexed man, who, because of his position, had the ability to pull birds all over the world. Get it while you can, is what drives the male – even if your wife is at the party. People get up to all manner of nonsense, testing the boundaries of relationships. Lennon was a self-centred egotist who met his match. When that happened to him, it was like a bomb going off. His world fell off its axis. Everything changed.'

*

The newspapers said she'd gone to his head. Fans and scholars would quibble for decades over dates, times and locations, about whether she was oblivious of his Beatleness, or whether she targeted him because of it. Did she really invite him to pay for the privilege of hammering in a nail, as it were, at an exhibition of her own art and installations at London's Indica Gallery on 9 November 1966? Did he retort that he'd bang an imaginary nail without putting his hand in his pocket (see what she did there?)? Details. This happened once before, millions of times: two married people, married to other people, coming face to face and falling. Hook, line. The split-second suspicion that it's all over. It is now. Nowadays, they might meet, be hit by the bolt, find themselves scanning the room whenever the other vanishes, dash off loaded tweets or texts on the way home: 'Just to let you know that I haven't thought about you for several seconds.'

Which would be leaked to the rags, be slapped on the bench in evidence, and would maybe even lead to recrimination and divorce. Which, minus the tech (they wrote letters and phoned each other in those days) is kind of what happened.

Oh, Yoko. In the middle of a dream. Except that John's was a nightmare. For which read, loveless marriage, hopeless detachment, too much pressure, too many people, jets, sweats, blondes, brunettes, regrets, Tourette's, death threats. You know, he needs someone. Help! Home life? *What* home life? It wasn't doing it for him. He was going under. Listen, the drowning man again. Yoko plunged for him.

The twice-married mother was not, as they make her out to have been, a nowhere-woman in search of a meal ticket. Japanese-born, tertiary-educated in New York, with stark memories of the Second World War and the decimation of Tokyo, her eyes were widened by both horror and hope. She was a connected, respected avant-garde conceptual artist with a reputation and a following: if not in the Beatles league, financially speaking, then at least at a level impressive enough in her own professional sphere. She was an active member of Fluxus, an international sixties movement embracing artists from all corners and of all disciplines. She was striking, exotic, cultured, original. She leaned towards radical pacifism and politicised feminism. She spoke quietly and intelligently. Even shuffling across a room, she oozed mystique. On every level, to a woman like Cynthia, she was a threat. Cyn's take was fatally blinkered:

'John met Yoko when he needed to, just a fortnight into his grief over Alma Cogan. She was this obsessive fan who'd turn up and follow him around. She irritated the life out of John to begin with. But Alma died, and something odd happened to him. Things turned. Yoko must have seen her opportunity, and seized it. She wore the trousers, and would control and dominate John for the rest of his life.

'So, Yoko became John's new Aunt Mimi', Cyn told me. 'She worked out what John needed in a woman, right under my nose, and she reinvented herself.'

About that.

Yoko was thirty-three to John's twenty-six. Not exactly one *geta* in the grave.[3] Though, back then, for a woman to be even a year or two older than her man raised eyebrows. John, undeterred, was intrigued. His appetite was whetted. A guy who could have any woman he fancied wants this one? *Sheesh*. To be fair, Keith Altham was right: few photographs do her justice. But some of the footage is surprising. Silent Yoko exudes a coy and mesmerising charm. The close-ups, through curtains of thick black hair, reveal her clear skin, perfect features and timid smile. Her style is precise and minimal. Her eyes are deep, and only for John. The public was sold a witch, the bitch who went after the Beatle, who trashed his marriage, smashed Cyn's heart, deprived Julian of his father and destroyed the world's greatest group. Guess what, the Beatles were broken already. As Ringo reflected in the *Anthology* series, a marriage never collapses just like that. It takes years of misery to bring things to a head. He meant the band.

When she was a little girl, Yoko wrote wishes on pieces of paper, went to the temple and tied them to branches of trees. Many people did so during Japan's annual Star Festival. The trees of temple courtyards would be filled with wish knots, which from a distance resembled a great blossoming of white flowers. The ancient Shinto tradition was to recur in and influence her art throughout her life. As she would one day say, 'All my works are a form of wishing.'

Did she ever share with John her memories of American heiress Peggy Guggenheim, the 'mistress of modern art'? While it is known that Yoko met the thirty-five-years-older, sexually voracious multi-millionaire and bohemian socialite born Marguerite Guggenheim during the sixties and that they remained friends until Peggy's death in 1979, I wonder whether Yoko ever 'fessed up about the night that her daughter Kyoko was conceived.

Guggenheim, who befriended and bankrolled Pablo Picasso, Man Ray and Salvador Dalí and discovered Jackson Pollock, travelled to Japan with her friend the avant-garde composer and music theorist John Cage in 1956.

'He [Cage] was invited by the Master of Flowers to give concerts in different cities,' recalled Peggy in her autobiography *Out of this Century: Confessions of an Art Addict*. 'I followed him everywhere. I can't say I like his music, but I went to every concert. Yoko Ono (at the time twenty-three) was our guide and translator, and also took part in one of the performances. She was terribly efficient and nice, and we became great friends. She was followed everywhere by an American boy called Tony Cox who had come to Japan to find her, never having met her. He came on all our trips, even though her husband, a fine composer, was also with us.'

This was Toshi Ichiyanagi, who had studied with John Cage. So where was he?

'We were a large party, and had our own private photographer,' said Peggy. 'I allowed this Tony to come and sleep in the room I shared with Yoko. The result was a beautiful half-Japanese, half-American baby whom Tony later stole ...'

*

Life is short, art is long. Nine years later, it was John Lennon, not Peggy Guggenheim, who became Yoko Ono's patron, when he agreed to fund her new solo exhibition at London's Lisson Gallery. Did Cynthia question the intrusions of this curious interloper? She sure did. Would John plead ignorance and explain her away as some 'weirdo' looking for money? He would. What was Cyn supposed to do? Her sixth sense nagged. Never loudly enough.

*

I have sometimes thought of Yoko as the guru who got through. On an endless quest for answers and perennially in need of a saviour, John prized a guru above all. He was a sucker for the next big thing, the latest cause, for any mortal who presented with superlative ability and confidence. For a man who thought of himself as a been-there cynic, he could be remarkably gullible. Witness the way in which he fell for 'Magic Alex' Mardas, the young Greek techno-wizard who seduced him with blinking gadgets and promised to build the Beatles a futuristic recording studio, but failed spectacularly. Primal therapist Arthur Janov would soon see him coming, and would do more harm than good. For Maharishi Mahesh Yogi, leader of the Spiritual Regeneration Movement, his conduit to the Beatles was George's doe-eyed bride Pattie. Beyond Candlestick Park, the Harrisons had retreated to Bombay for six weeks, guests of Indian sitar hero Ravi Shankar, who was teaching George to play. They wafted on to Kashmir, making radical changes to their diet and exercise regime, becoming vegetarians and devotees of yoga. Back in London, Pattie tried to teach herself to meditate, couldn't, and joined Maharishi's movement in search of the secret. When Maharishi landed in London to promote his Transcendental Meditation retreat in Bangor, North Wales, with a press conference at the Hilton Hotel, Pattie and George persuaded Paul, Jane and Ringo to attend ... the latter without Maureen, who had just given birth and was still in hospital. Cyn also stayed at home, minding Julian. She did make the trip to Wales, missing the train and having to be driven all the way by Neil Aspinall, an occurrence that she would later consider as having signposted the collapse of her marriage. Why did John leave her struggling with suitcases and board the train without her? Exactly. Mick Jagger and Marianne Faithfull came too. It was in Bangor that the Beatles received an overexcited press to make a public declaration of their rejection of drugs ... only weeks after having campaigned for the legalisation of marijuana.

And Brian Epstein was the original guru, conjuring a world-class, planet-conquering act out of a rough rock'n'roll quartet without any previous experience or track record. So completely did John defer to the authority and the superiority of 'the Prince of Pop' that he allowed him to rub the rocker out of him. Brian had run the Beatles' and their families' lives for six years. John and Cyn's wedding, their first home, their relocation from Liverpool to London; breaking America, making them the biggest band in the world, defusing the Jesus crisis, keeping them alive: Brian had stage-managed it all. For the other three Beatle families, too. No one could have served them more diligently nor have championed them more relentlessly. He had nurtured, nursed, protected, projected, packaged and promoted his precious boys with devotion bordering on worship. He had adored them unconditionally, as if they were his own sons, even though he was not many years their senior. But he tended to keep his distance from the recording studio. He was in the habit of leaving them and their producer George Martin to the music, acutely aware that he had nothing to offer them there. Now that they were off the road, now that the Beatles were no longer a touring band but 'only' about the records, what was the point of him?

CHAPTER 14

QUICKSAND

Goethe said, 'It is a great error to take oneself for more than one is, or for less than one is worth.'[1]

John was guilty of both. On the one hand so infused with a sense of his creative superiority, he feared on the other that he was a fraud, and that he would be found out. That old devil imposter syndrome, it gets to the best of them. A dominant force on stage, John's was a demanding voice in the studio, even though he often complained that he hated the way he sang. He would get their producer to double-track what was already widely considered to be one of rock's greatest voices, and bring all manner of technical wizardry to bear to 'make it sound better'. 'Can't you smother it with tomato ketchup or something?' he once said to George Martin. The mild gentleman, who may have been tempted, managed to hold back.[2]

What producer ever went further to capture magic, interpret genius and distil essential brilliance? With endless patience, George poked into their crevices, winkled out gems, and polished and perfected them to sonic gleam. He revelled quietly in their fertility and productivity. Perhaps no one but he could have translated, enhanced and lifted the Beatles' songs to unprecedented levels of recording excellence. No one else held a key to their creative core. For this, he earned little more than grudging respect and half-hearted acknowledgement from John, whose feelings, post-Beatles, festered into resentment. John would begin to play down and then insult George's contribution. He would stoop to ruining a nice evening by spitting venom into the dinner, as he once did in New York, crushing his companion with the taunt that, if he had his way, he'd go back and re-record every last Beatles song. '*What*, even "Strawberry Fields"?' exclaimed George, instinctively protective of John's superlative creation. '*Especially* "Strawberry Fields",' snarled John. He couldn't help himself.

George shrugged it off. As he explained, none of the Beatles was ever overly concerned with dishing out praise where it was due.

'But then,' he pointed out in his memoir, *All You Need is Ears*, 'I never expected that of them. They had an independent, cussed streak about them, not giving a damn for anybody, which was one of the things I liked about them in the first place, and one of the factors which made me decide to sign them.'

*

Though their early songs were basic and unrefined, Paul and John learned quickly. They learned on the job. By 1963, a sensitivity and sophistication was already creeping in, particularly in their harmonies. As their life experience expanded and as they grew more attuned to their emotions, they found the confidence to reflect and express their feelings in their songwriting. Modest Martin was adamant that almost any producer could have extracted credible, market-worthy recordings from their material in those early days. Come the *Help!* album in 1965, things began to change. The pivotal composition was 'Yesterday'. He didn't realise it at the time, but George could see clearly with hindsight that the song was the point from which, 'I started to leave my hallmark on the music, when a style started to emerge which was partly of my making.'[3]

It was on 'Yesterday', he said, that they first experimented; when he began to score the Beatles' music; when they became amenable to the inclusion of other musicians and instruments. Until then, only the four of them backed by George himself on piano where required had been the routine. 'Yesterday', George thought, could sound all the more heart-rending with the addition of a plaintive string quartet. He put it to them, and it got one. Still hindered by the elementary recording techniques of the day, they nevertheless managed to bend and break pop music's 'rules' to come up with often surprising and provocative takes. Galvanised by seemingly endless possibilities, the boys embraced their producer's and engineers' skills, and allowed themselves to be guided onwards. The brilliant ideas were John's and Paul's. Wise George deferred. He laboured to bring out the best in them.

George would later describe the Beatles as the Cole Porters and George Gershwins of their day. When one commentator dared to liken them to Franz Schubert, the Austrian classical composer of an enormous oeuvre in an all-too-brief life, naysayers scoffed at the pretension. George defended the comparison, pointing out that the Beatles' prolific output encapsulated and embodied their own era, just as Schubert's had. Their music was of its time, resonated with their generation and became its abiding soundtrack. Its subsequent ascension may have rendered it everlasting. Is it? Tomorrow never knows.

*

Leaps and bounds. *Revolver*, recorded throughout April and June 1966 and released early that August, was their final album before they came off the road. They took full advantage of the latest technology, and of new techniques including close-mic'd drums and backwards recording, to flaunt songs as diverse as 'Eleanor Rigby', 'And Your Bird Can Sing', the drugged-to-the-eyeballs 'Doctor Robert', 'Here, There and Everywhere' – inspired by 'God Only Knows', which, sweet irony, Brian Wilson had been prompted to write when listening to Rubber Soul – and the hypnotic, menacing, multi-layered, seagulls-in-an-Indian-restaurant swirl of 'Tomorrow Never Knows'. One raving critic picked up on a 'filter that made John Lennon sound like God singing through a foghorn'. George establishes his songwriting credentials with 'Taxman', 'Love You To' and 'I Want to Tell You'.

The album is complicated, psychedelic, multicultural. Sitars rule. Stepping back from the love theme, its subject matter roams. It is spirited and substance-driven, notably by John and George, who were experimenting enthusiastically with LSD, while Paul confined himself, for the moment at least, to dope and arty pals. Many and diverse are its influences, from Bob Dylan and Ravi Shankar to the aforementioned Beach Boys. The project equalised the two chief songwriters, but also exposed dissent. Was *Revolver* revolutionary? Well, you know, we all want to change the world. Did it burst the banks of pop and overturn the methods by which records were made? We can say that. Did it spawn the prog rock movement of the seventies? This and more must be true. Their old Hamburg mucker Klaus Voormann designed the striking sleeve. He won a Grammy for it. He has never stopped answering questions about it.

*

Twelve consecutive Number Ones were the breeding ground of a hitherto unimaginable run of albums that crystallised for all time the Beatles' prominence in the pantheon. The paradox being that, throughout the creation of *Sgt. Pepper's Lonely Hearts Club Band*, the *Magical Mystery Tour* soundtrack, the 'White Album', *Yellow Submarine*, *Abbey Road* and *Let It Be*, the band itself was disintegrating. Not that there was anything sinister about it. It was not as if hell was breaking loose via the dissolution of inter-band marriages or relationships as in the case of, say, Fleetwood Mac or ABBA. Yes, there were women involved, but not in any threatening sense. No female could have forced her way into that impregnable set-up and convinced any of them to pull the plug and walk away unless the Beatle in question *wanted* her to. The most passive observer can see what arrogant, chauvinist show-offs they were. They called the shots. No Yoko, nary a Linda, could have exerted the level of influence required to detonate them. Not unless such a thing were expressly desired. Much was scribbled and gossiped about this at the time. Much of the abundant abuse hurled at Yoko was gratuitously sexist and racist. But the situation was more complicated than boy meets girl, boy falls in love, boy stands aside while girl tramples all over boy's sandcastle. Isn't it more likely that John, who was desperately seeking a get-out, used Yoko as his scapegoat in order to extract himself from the band? Maybe she was in on it. Perhaps they contrived it together. It is entirely possible that she was content to take the blame, if that's what it took to ease John's passage. Especially when you consider that he himself, the greatest rock star, was to be her reward. Far-fetched? She's not going to tell us. But, stranger things.

There is also the obvious. The boys had grown up. They were always going to have to. They were maturing outwards and naturally away from each other, shrugging off their dependence on boyhood buddies. They had families, other priorities, conflicting interests. It couldn't be *Boys' Own* and sod the world for the rest of time, much though they might secretly have wished that it could. In the concluding episode of the *Anthology* series, Paul compared their predicament to that of army buddies going their separate ways after demobilisation, referencing the old song 'Wedding Bells': 'Those wedding bells are breaking up that old gang of mine.'[4] Watching it again all these years later reminded me of his namesake, the apostle, who reflected nearly two thousand years before, 'When I was a child, I spoke as a child, I understood as a child, I thought as a child: but when I became a man, I put away childish things.'[5]

John wanted out. He was bored. He craved freedom. He was desperate to work with others. Even with Yoko – who, unbeknown to the others, had been working and experimenting with musicians since before their own Hamburg days. In 1960, for example, she had appointed composer La Monte Young, enfant terrible of the avant-garde, as musical director of the concerts she hosted in her New York loft. Young, who was strongly influenced by Japanese Gagaku, the centuries-old Imperial Court classical music, and who scored works as brief haiku-esque texts, would often be described as 'the most influential composer living today'. He and Yoko took each other seriously. She was not the musically ignorant interloper that both Beatles fans and a sniping press presumed her to be.

'Their breakdown was happening before Yoko and Linda came along,' assert Klaus Voormann. 'If there was a defining moment, that came when they decided not to play live together again. From that moment on, it seemed quite unnatural to be together anymore. After that, things deteriorated much more quickly. The truth is that you cannot be a community living together forever. They had all moved on. George had become interested in mysticism. Paul and John had separate lives. Yoko was really just the catalyst that made things happen. She could see that John wasn't happy and that he'd had enough.

'Was Yoko a manipulator? Well, she knew what John wanted, so she made it happen. So, in some ways, she was. But if she hadn't come along, it would have still happened. It might just have taken a couple of weeks longer.

'By the end, things were very unpleasant. I remember being with them in the studio, and Linda and Yoko were there, and everyone was whispering behind one another's backs. It was a poisonous atmosphere.'

*

Rolling Stone magazine sized Sgt. Pepper's Lonely Hearts Club Band as 'the best album of all time'. Recorded between December 1966 and April 1967, it emerged on the verge of the hot Summer of Love, when a hundred thousand hippies descended on San Francisco's Haight-Ashbury. Hallucinogens, race riots, sexual freedom, violence, take your pick. This astonishing work was both the accompaniment and the antidote. Its 'band within a band' concept was Paul's reaction to the suffocation of fame, a device designed to distance the Beatles from the moptop madness. Its what-to-make-of-it blend of Indian music, Motown, music hall, blues, pop, classical, rock'n'roll and more floored the competition – such as The Doors, Jimi Hendrix's Are You Experienced, The Velvet Underground and Nico and the Stones' Their Satanic Majesties Request, all released that year. Paul wrote more than half the songs on Pepper, played a chamber orchestra of instruments, and overtook John as the commanding force in the band. Not that

John's contribution on this work is insignificant. 'Being for the Benefit of Mr. Kite!', inspired by a Victorian circus poster picked up in a Sevenoaks, Kent antiques shop while the band were filming in Knole Park, is the song that he would one day single out as his personal favourite (or was that John just being contrary, having trashed it earlier?). 'Lucy in the Sky with Diamonds', prompted by a drawing that his son Julian brought home from school, is *Alice in Wonderland*-lite. 'A Day in the Life' is the track of tracks. Why no 'Strawberry Fields Forever' or 'Penny Lane', both recorded for it? Because EMI in its wisdom demanded a holding single, and got a double A-side. The Beatles had a policy of never re-releasing on an album any tracks that had gone to market as singles. George Martin described the faux pas as 'his greatest regret'.

'It is perhaps hard for younger generations to understand the phenomenal significance of *Sgt. Pepper* when it was released that summer,' reflects Jonathan Morrish, former CBS and Sony Music executive, Michael Jackson's publicist and subsequently Director of Communications at PPL.[6] 'Whatever you think of it musically – and it is astonishing, although by no means the most popular Beatles album – it is, arguably, their most important. It was the first album they made after they stopped touring, so it was no longer a case of hastily stringing an album together to push up ticket sales. This was them now saying, "We're going to spend all our time on the album and focus our attention on what you can do in the studio. That's the real art, the real craft. And we are the real artists." Record companies at that time did not spend a huge amount of time or money on making albums. Suddenly, the album as a concept became more important than the single. It changed everything and was truly a landmark moment. It also had beautiful packaging, a front cover you could pore over, and was pretty much the first album to have the song lyrics included, which we could peruse as we listened. You couldn't pick out a particular track, either, and just play that. There were no obvious grooves on the vinyl between tracks. So the commitment was to sit there for forty minutes and listen to the whole thing. Like a classical recording, it was all in one piece. This raised the perception of pop and rock music as art.'

The Beatles were also addressing the broader themes of life and the universe from the higher state of consciousness reached through drugs. Paul too was now experimenting with LSD. They invited their fans on the journey of a lifetime, back to their Liverpool childhood and through the landscape of their dreams and fears. They showcased their philosophy. They did things that had never before been done. From the broader viewpoint, the album stands as a monument to the moment when and why the music industry changed.

'Pop music was now important for its own sake,' says Jonathan, 'and not just as an also-ran to classical.'

Publicist Keith Altham was disappointed by it. '*Sgt. Pepper* was the end of the Beatles,' he laments. 'It wasn't really them. It was their *Pet Sounds*. It had very little to do with the group we knew and loved.'

Patrick Humphries points the finger: 'My feeling is that when Yoko appeared, she convinced John that whatever he did was art, which covers a multitude of sins,' says the music journalist and author. 'She distracted him from the day job: even with all the squabbles and testiness in the Beatle camp after Brian Epstein died, they were a *band*, with George and Ringo happy to defer to Paul and John. But once Yoko comes on the scene, Lennon loses interest in being in a pop group. It is left to Paul to shoulder the burden, which he does magnificently. I offer the following as proof: *Sgt. Pepper* – entirely Paul's concept. *Magical Mystery Tour*, ditto: a rotten film, but great songs (the title song, "The Fool on the Hill", "I am the Walrus", "Hello, Goodbye"). *Abbey Road*: Paul again, insisting that they get back to making an LP like they used to. While John loathed "Maxwell's Silver Hammer", I would contend that "I Want You (She's so Heavy)" is self-indulgence prodded by Yoko. *Let It Be*: Paul's conviction that by playing gigs again, as Ricky and the Red Streaks rather than as the Beatles, they could make it work. But Yoko was pouring poison into John's ear that he didn't *need* the group.'

Keith concurs.

'John got himself badly torn up with Yoko,' he says. 'I always thought she was bad news. She evidently had a reasonably good head for business, and a huge appetite for fame and fortune. Her arrival certainly upset the other three, however much they have all tried to play that down over the years. But I watched it happen. John lost perspective in the Beatles. Once she came on the scene, he wanted to cut himself off completely. True, he had got fed up with the whole teenage-idol thing, and the fact that they couldn't get any respect as a live act. It made him even more unstable than he was to start with. He never found stability in his life, of course, not even with Yoko. She was an extremely disruptive influence. She was a schemer and a control freak. She photographed badly. In pictures, she looked like an old witch. In the flesh, she was rather attractive: bosomy, with beautiful hair, lovely eyes, perfect skin. She did come in for some terrible flak from the media, most of which was unfair. Whether she was or she wasn't all the things that they said about her, she was the great love of his life. If she was a bad influence, it's because John allowed her to be. He wasn't stupid. He *was* a chauvinist. This was a man who believed that a woman's place is in the home. Which could never be said of Yoko. She had her own spirit, her own life. If she was responsible for breaking up the Beatles, it wasn't the worst thing she ever did. What was? Turning him on to heroin. Why did she *need* that crutch? I suppose it was just the arty thing to do at that time, but it didn't do John any favours. He was paranoid enough as it was.'

John, concludes Patrick Humphries, was a 'good, possibly great rock'n'roller. He was not an artist. In mitigation, during the dog days of the group, when he did get off his arse – as on the 'White Album' (largely written in Rishikesh), the old magic was there. And Yoko did sand off the edges to make a more rounded human being. But there was a lot of redeeming to do.

'There is no denying that he was the motivating force behind the Quarry Men and the Beatles. He was quick-witted and acerbic, but the overwhelming cynicism and low attention span too often made him take his eye off the ball. For a long time – 1957 to 1965 – you could argue that he was the motivating force. From then on, the Beatles were Paul's band, and much of the Beatles' greatness was built on those last few substantial years.'

*

Sgt. Pepper was by no means the only Beatles phenomenon that summer. They also found themselves chosen by the BBC to represent the UK in *Our World*, the first live, satellite-enabled television linking of some twenty-six countries to be broadcast on 25 June. The band appeared in a psychedelic EMI Studios, Abbey Road performance of John's simple, slogan-driven 'All You Need Is Love'. They delivered their peace-and-love, flower-power anthem to a pre-recorded backing track, with an orchestra and many other high-profile British artists and hangers-on in the studio: Mick and Keith, some Small Faces, Eric Clapton, Graham Nash, Keith Moon, Pattie Boyd, Jane Asher and Marianne Faithfull among them. The live black-and-white telecast attracted the then biggest television audience in history, estimated at between 350 and 400 million. On the song's release as a single the following month, it zapped to Number One and sat there for three weeks. By August, it was a chart-topper in the US and many other territories, and had become the anthem of the Summer of Love – though it would later be scrutinised and ridiculed for its naïvety.[7]

Far from diminished by their renunciation of moptop-ism and live touring, the Beatles and their musical influence had never been greater. Making it up as they went along, they found themselves perfectly in step and in tune, musically, culturally and socially. Boosted by the positive response the non-materialistic and altruistic ideals they were now espousing, they swanned off to the Aegean to snap up a Greek island, heaven-bent on setting up their own hippie commune. The idea, like so many with their name on, came and went.

*

For Brian Epstein, 'All You Need Is Love' was his boys' 'finest moment'. It must have meant all the more to him because their public highs were now concealing his private lows. Within weeks, it was all over. A string of regrets – the recent death of his father, major gambling losses, a spell in rehab where he tried desperately to kick his drug addiction, and having sunk into the sordid underworld of rent boys – caused Eppy to torment himself. Up to his neck in booze and barbiturates, he died on 27 August. Suicide was suspected. Accidental overdose was ruled. He was thirty-two, with everything to live for. But money couldn't buy the one thing he craved, the thing that had always eluded him. The lack of romantic love had induced depression at a level too great to bear.

He heard the news today, oh boy. Nothing much stopped John in his tracks, but this floored him. Did they march through his mind as one, the dear departed? His mother, Julia. His Uncle George. Tragic Stuart Sutcliffe. Now Brian, dear God. How come every time he opened himself up to someone, they went and died on him?

John would later observe that Brian's death signalled the beginning of the band's end.

'I knew that we were in trouble then,' he said, '… I thought, "We've fucking had it now.[8]"'

*

Brian's boys did not attend his funeral in Liverpool. Not, as has been suggested, because they couldn't be bothered, but because Brian's mother Queenie couldn't bear the idea of an intensely private family occasion being reduced to a media circus by the presence of the most famous band in the world. So they missed the presiding rabbi's denunciation of Brian as 'a symbol of the malaise of our generation'. Which was just as well. Imagine John, hearing that. The Beatles and their partners made the memorial instead, gathering that October alongside their NEMS stablemates Billy J. Kramer, Cilla Black, the Fourmost and Gerry and the Pacemakers at the New London Synagogue on Abbey Road. Where Brian was honoured in peace and with love, and remembered with kinder words.

CHAPTER 15

REVELATION

Where to now, Johnny?

Look: four rich, famous, rudderless young Beatles, ripe for the taking. Maharishi Mahesh Yogi was on hand. He counselled them in Bangor to think positively about Brian's departure. Reassuring them that his spirit remained among them, he encouraged them to feel joyful about their manager's death in order to help ease his passage into the next world. Negativity, warned Maharishi, would hinder the journey. This shred of sacred Hindu teaching did seem to comfort them. It also primed them for the giggling guru's subsequent exhortation: that they should travel forthwith to India and join him at his ashram in Rishikesh, in the foothills of the Himalayas.[1]

While Epstein would doubtless have counselled caution at the idea of such an intrepid expedition, he was no longer around to ask. The boys had dipped into the ancient texts and had elemental awareness of the fourth level of consciousness: 'pure', transcendental consciousness. They knew enough to know that they couldn't reach it without 'the mantra'. Maharishi had the mantra. Perhaps he also held the secrets of the Buddhas with the half-closed eyes …

To the eastern bank of the Ganges they went, in February 1968. Their WAGS, PAs and the press trolled along too. The latter were kept at bay by barbed wire, but some found their way up trees to decent vantage points. There was a sizeable contingent of TM trainees, among them the children of Tarzan's Jane: Prudence Farrow, twenty, her brother John and their luminous elder sister, twenty-three-year-old actress Mia Farrow, who was going through a harrowing divorce from three-decades-older Frank Sinatra.[2] Jenny Boyd was with her sister and brother-in-law Pattie and George, and Magic Alex. The Beach Boys' Mike Love was there, as were saxophonist and flautist Paul Horn and Scottish folk singer Donovan. The expedition attracted worldwide media attention, some good, some less so. The hundreds of 'Beatles Guru' and 'Year of the Guru' headlines were offset by *Private Eye*'s hilariously derisive VERIRICHILOTSAMONEY YOGI BEAR.

The sun was up, the sky was blue. The younger Miss Farrow ignored plea after plea to come out and hang out, inspiring one of John's best-loved songs. The aptly named sister was undeterred. Said John, 'She wouldn't come out of the little hut we were living in ... We got her out of the house – she'd been locked in for three weeks and wouldn't come out. She was trying to find God quicker than anyone else. That was the competition in Maharishi's camp: who was going to get cosmic first.'

John, said Prudence Farrow, was 'very brilliant and extremely funny. He was very astute in terms of sizing people up. So how do I know what he would write? I didn't know. He could have written anything. What was nice was my privacy – he respected it to a great extent.'

What does she think of the song 'Dear Prudence' today?

'It epitomized what the sixties were about in many ways. What it's saying is very beautiful; it's very positive. I think it's an important song. I thought it was one of their least popular and more obscure songs. I feel that it does capture that essence of the course, that slightly exotic part of being in India where we went through that silence and meditation.'

Prudence continued to meditate hard regardless, would complete the course, and would work as a TM teacher for many years.[3]

On went John, deeply inspired. He wrote prolifically in Rishikesh, as did Paul and George. They produced a string of songs for what would become the double 'White Album', including one of John's most exquisite compositions, 'Julia'. Ostensibly an homage to his late mother, he snuck in a love note to the woman who had turned his heart: 'Ocean child calls me' – 'Ocean child' being one translation of Yoko's Japanese name; the other being 'Positive'.

*

Jenny Boyd recalled with fondness those Rishikesh days and nights when I interviewed her and DJ 'Whispering Bob' Harris before a live audience at London's Gibson Guitar studios. The former fashion model, who threw aside that 'flimsy' career for TM and a more meaningful lifestyle, described her two months in India as 'joyful, challenging and inspiring'. She spoke of abundant flora and fragrant mountain air; the freedom of dressing in little more than a sari; vegetarian Indian food, which she and her sister relished, but which John couldn't stand and Ringo couldn't eat; long mornings spent lazing in the sun on the roof of their bungalow; lectures, lessons and endless meditations; hanging out with Pattie and Cynthia, having their palms painted with henna as they listened in on George, Paul and John strumming their guitars and working out songs. She was still laughing over Ringo, who described the retreat as a 'spiritual Butlin's' and who, allergy-prone and unwilling to partake of local fare, had arrived with an extra suitcase filled with tins of baked beans. The only other thing he consumed during his stay was eggs. For his diet, the others could only pity Maureen Starkey. Beautiful Jenny, not yet twenty-one, became the object of Donovan's affections, to the point that what he wrote about her there would become a famous song. Born Helen Mary and nicknamed Jenny by her sister after one of her favourite childhood dolls, she would be 'Jennifer Juniper' for evermore. The idyll soured when Jenny fell ill with dysentery, which was misdiagnosed, bizarrely, as tonsillitis. John was sick too, she remembered. He struggled to overcome his jet lag, and was plagued by insomnia most nights. How much of his sleeplessness was down to his longing for Yoko?[4]

Cynthia had left Julian at home with her mother for the duration. A proposed three-month stay was an awfully long time to leave such a little child. At that age, a week can feel like forever. A parent's prolonged absence can seem as though they are never coming back. John himself knew this only too well. Perhaps Julian had grown accustomed to his father going missing when the Beatles were on the road. The disappearance of his mother, however, would have alarmed him. The trip also meant that his mum and dad were going to miss his all-important fifth birthday. Cynthia was a good mother. When we discussed it, she admitted that she must have been desperate to neglect him to such an extent. Cyn hoped that Rishikesh would afford seclusion, privacy and an opportunity for her and John to rediscover each other and to revive their marriage.

'Impossible hopes,' she said sadly. 'John said to me just before we went to India that he wanted us to have more children. Well that came out of the blue, I can tell you. I was really surprised, as he'd never said a word about that before. Then again, why not? I wasn't averse to the idea. It wasn't as if we too old to have any more. I was not yet twenty-nine, after all, while John would turn twenty-eight that October. We still had more than enough time. I suppose what concerned me was Julian. A five- or six-year gap between siblings is quite wide, isn't it? I would have loved to have three or four children, actually, and to have had them all close together. It just hadn't happened. But maybe ...'

Alas, a fortnight in, '... I was apparently distracting his meditation,' Cyn sighed. 'It was all my fault, and John was a bear about it. He started grumping all over the place, snapping at me, insisting that we sort our "useless" accommodation out and that we were going to have to sleep in separate rooms from now on, before he went round the bend. It was humiliating and hurtful. I'm sure the others all knew what was going on, not that anyone ever said anything to me. Even then I was convinced that I could bring him back to me, if you know what I mean. How stupid and blinkered I was. I know now that this was John up to his old tricks again, saying one thing but meaning another. Just like when he was on the road and he'd write to me all the time, telling me how deeply he loved me and how desperately he missed me. Just the way he used to when we were at art school. But when he was at home and actually with me, under the same roof, he was either asleep, ignoring me or picking pointless fights. He'd rather look at a television set than at me. He'd much rather read a book than talk to me. He always wanted what he couldn't have, did John. Never what was under his nose. When he had me, he didn't want me. God help me, I was clutching at straws. It got me wondering whether I always had been, and whether I had never been enough for him. I searched my soul in the ashram, and it was the only conclusion I could come to.'

What she didn't know at the time was that John used the excuse of separate sleeping quarters so that his wife would not notice him getting up early each morning to walk to the compound's post office, where he would collect the copious telegrams sent by Yoko. The reason behind his moods was that he was missing her.

As the Lennon union dragged towards its conclusion, Cyn's energy flagged, while John's soared. For the Beatles, this proved to be the most productive songwriting period of their career. All told, they generated between thirty and fifty songs during their stay in India and just beyond. They wrote most of the 'White Album' there. Some songs made it onto *Abbey Road*. Others would land on various solo LPs, such as 'Child of Nature', a song that John would rework as the introspective 'Jealous Guy' for his *Imagine* album. More still would eventually find a home in the *Anthology* collections. 'Back in the USSR', 'Blackbird', 'Dear Prudence', 'Julia', 'Revolution', 'Mean Mr. Mustard' and 'Polythene Pam' were India-inspired, as was George's sublime 'While My Guitar Gently Weeps': within its subtle layers an unmitigated message, that Harrison was already mourning the Beatles.

That folky Donovan chap would later claim credit, in a nice way, for at least some of their inspiration while in the ashram. He recalled that John had become fascinated by his guitar-picking techniques, which John and Paul would soon acquire, and which would change the shape of their songwriting.

'I used to play acoustic guitar all the time. In fact, Ringo used to say, "Don, you never stop playing guitar!" In that non-stop playing, after we meditated, after we ate our health food, after we chased the monkeys off the table, we would play. And as I picked one day, John said, "How do you *do* that?"'

Donovan promised John that he would teach him, but warned that it would take a few days.

'"I've got time, Don, here in the jungle," John said.

'We sat down, and John learned it in two days.

'Songwriting changes when you have a new style, and a completely new style opened up to John. It was really cool to watch this ... Paul was so smart, he's a genius of course. He picked it up by ear, and his particular picking was completely different. Out of that, Paul got "Blackbird" and "Mother Nature's Son". John got "Dear Prudence" and "Julia".'

Recalling the 'distinctive acoustic feel' of the 'White Album', Donovan adds, 'Also, there were the chord structures that I'd learned from flamenco, classical, early New Orleans blues and folk. Chord structures that these three guys in the Beatles hadn't really experienced much. They also entered the new songwriting. It was really cool to pass these techniques on, not just for the 'White Album' but for the millions of their fans who would pick up a guitar ...'[5]

*

Ringo and Maureen made themselves scarce after only ten days, tormented by insects, loathing the food and missing the kids. Paul and Jane managed five weeks before throwing in the *tauliyā*. John and Cynthia, George, Pattie and party would have sat it out for the full three months, but for a blow-up, after Maharishi was accused of making sexual advances towards some of the girls, including Mia Farrow. Magic Alex may have had something to do with the allegation. Mia herself has never said much, beyond a fleeting, non-committal mention in her 1997 memoir *What Falls Away*.

Scales fell from Beatle eyes. The rest of them flounced out on 12 April. It was left to John, as resident mouthy git, to inform their guru that they were off: 'If you're so fucking cosmic, you'll know why,' was his parting shot.[6]

Typical John, he then dashed off an angry little ditty about him, which he was forced to tone down and retitle from 'Maharishi' to 'Sexie Sadie' to ensure its place on the 'White Album'. Tossing the guru and his teachings aside, they returned to London, went public with a statement that their association with him was over and that it had all been a mistake, and turned instead to the business of taking control of their troubled empire. They conveniently forgot that Maharishi had done them a massive favour by weaning them off LSD. Although less than a year later, John was on heroin.

The guru's reputation was damaged by the scandal, for which no evidence was ever brought. Nearly thirty years later, George and Paul apologised unreservedly to him, and all were reconciled. Transcendental Meditation continued to thrive throughout the world, attracting millions of converts, and is practised to this day. Mahesh moved to the Netherlands, where Paul and his daughter Stella visited him in 2007. The following year, aged ninety, the old guru called it a day. Magic Alex, his alleged accuser, died ten years after.

*

Back in London, the Beatles remained adrift. Brian Epstein's PA Peter Brown had assumed the day-to-day running of the management office, but the boys were headless chickens. They had launched their own company, Apple Corps, the previous January, and would announce it to the world in May. Under its banner they intended to continue their recording career, consolidate other interests and develop new ideas including Apple Films, Electronics, Publishing, Retail and more, plus their own label to record and promote other artists as well as release their own music on. All of which seemed like a good idea at the time. New premises were acquired at 3 Savile Row, Mayfair that June. The elegant Georgian former Hylton House, which set them back £500,000, was restyled the 'Apple Building'. The Apple Studio was in the basement. Each Beatle had a personal office. John would launch his and Yoko's Bag Productions world peace initiative from his. There was a bouncer on the door to manage the fans, known as the 'Apple Scruffs'. Loyal friends such as Pete Shotton and Neil Aspinall were rewarded. John's childhood chum Pete was dubbed manager of the Apple Boutique. The psychedelic store flogging hippie garb dominated the corner of London's Baker Street and Paddington Street, in the building that had formerly housed Apple Music. The shop was short-lived. Their faithful road manager, personal Mr Fix-It and trusted confidant, affable Neil, was gifted head of the corporation in 1970, and would eventually be made CEO. He was to remain at the helm for nearly forty years.

On paper, all fabulous. Sort of. It was the best of times, it was the worst of times, it was the age of wisdom, it was the age of foolishness …[7] In truth, this period was one of resistance of the inevitable, of tearings-apart, point-scoring, interloping and meltdown; of personal crises, scarcely credible profligacy and shocking waste. Apple HQ, with its wall-to-wall gold discs and plush Granny Smith-green carpets, was one of the most palatial and extravagant destinations in the capital. Mod-conned to the roof, it was staffed by a barmy army with scant grasp of their point to proceedings. It would be observed not a few times that Brian must be turning in his grave. The band's management was still up for grabs. Indecision, disagreement and mayhem were hardly avoidable.

The band convened at Twickenham Film Studios to commence work on an idealistic project of Paul's called *Get Back*, which would feature them filmed around the clock by American director Michael Lindsay-Hogg as they rehearsed for what was supposed to be a back-to-basics, gimmick-free album and live-gig comeback. Harmonious this was not. George was the first to stomp out, agreeing to return only on condition that they would dump drafty, hostile Twickenham in favour of their own Apple Studio at Savile Row. The only live expression of this doomed experiment would take place, not on the *QE2*, in an amphitheatre in Tunisia, at the London Palladium, before the pyramids at Giza nor in the Sahara desert, all of which, no joke, were proposed, but up on the roof of their own building in the bleak mid-winter, on an ordinary Thursday lunchtime, 30 January. The music caused crowds to gather in the street below. Traffic stopped. Constables from the West End Central police station down the road pricked up and rushed in. What's goin' on around here, then? They played for forty-two minutes – only half of which would make it into the eventual film. Nine takes. Five songs.

'I was at the Apple Corps offices the day of the gig on the roof,' remembers composer and musician Mike Batt. 'I just happened to be, I used their studios a lot. It was amazing timing for me, being a massive Beatles fan. I was nineteen years old, and the Head of A&R for Liberty Records. As soon as they started up, publisher Wayne Bardell and I went over and stood in the street. We could have gone in and up, but we were better off outside. It was loud. There was a crowd. There was a sense of being caught in an important and defining moment. If you're around at a time when something so significant happens, you feel part of it. I still do. It makes me feel lucky.'

Mike wasn't the only notable name present at the rooftop gig. 'The last word I heard from John Lennon was the last time they played together live as the Beatles, on the rooftop of their Apple HQ in Savile Row,' said Keith Altham. 'It was a freezing morning. We had been tipped off by our colleague Alan Smith via his wife Mavis, who worked in the NEMS press office, that the boys were filming and that we could go and watch. Neglecting to grab my jacket, I rushed out of the NME and jumped in a cab. I soon stood shivering on the roof with a gang of photographers while the Beatles played and sang "Get Back" twice. When the police broke it all up because crowds were gathering in the street below, John brushed past me in his fur jacket and noticed that I was trembling with cold. "It's Fabs Keith!" he sneered, by way of a friendly greeting, referring to our earlier skirmishes when I was a cub reporter on a teen mag. "You cold, lad?" I nodded. "Would you like my fur?" "Yes, please," I said. "Tough," he responded, and was hustled away by the roadies. I never saw him again.'

That's your lot, pop-pickers. This spur-of-the-moment performance, accompanied by the exceptional American session keyboard player Billy Preston, was probably John's idea. George didn't want to do it. Red-mac'd Ringo (it was Maureen's coat) couldn't see the point. John borrowed Yoko's fur for what was to be their last-ever turn. He broke with tradition to take centre-stage, George standing to his left. The last word was, who else's, John's:

'I'd like to say thank you on behalf of the group and ourselves, and I hope we passed the audition.'

Though a single, 'Get Back', would be released that April, the remaining tracks for a possible album, and all the film footage, were put aside.

*

Beyond the boundaries of the music business, countless figures from Beatles history are now consigned to the annals and are mostly forgotten. Even on the inside, few remain who are old enough or interested enough to recall. Fewer care. But there was a time when the whole world knew the name Allen Klein.

It would boil down to a toss-up. In the blue corner, this gruff, predatory New York rock manager and contract rottweiler who had steered the Rolling Stones to gainful glory, and who had been hovering like a raptor since 1964, hell-bent on sinking his talons into the Beatles. In the red corner, a dynamic father-and-son duo, lawyers Lee and John Eastman, who also hailed from the Big Apple and had a significant female on their side. When Lennon went public with his fear that, the way things were going, the Beatles would be broke in six months, Klein seized the day. Reach out, he'll be there. He and John got together in January 1969. John took him on there and then to take care of his financial affairs. The following day, Klein sat down with the others. Paul explained that his preference was for his future in-laws, given that he would be married to Lee's daughter and John's sister Linda within a matter of weeks. Ringo and George, deferring to Lennon, plumped for Klein. Meeting, anger, meeting, acrimony, fall-out, you bastard, get stuffed. So far, all the usual. Klein won, and was appointed their provisional manager during April, while the Eastmans signed on as their lawyers. Like that was gonna work. The in-laws were kissed goodbye. All except Paul signed Klein's three-year management contract.

Big Al's first move was to blast through Apple, juicing the useless. He got shot of the costliest employees and even tried to banish Neil Aspinall. The boys weren't having that. Matters grew mangled when news dropped that Brian Epstein's brother Clive had sold NEMS to British investment group Triumph, who now owned twenty-five per cent of the Beatles' earnings. Further frantic negotiations ensued. In such dealings, Klein's true colours surfaced, and they were all red. What were they going to do about the publishing company – Northern Songs Ltd, managed by Dick James – who had clearly hoodwinked Brian during their original bargaining? As soon as he heard Klein coming, DJ hot-footed it round to Lew Grade's television company ATV to flog the mogul his share, rather than let John and Paul get their own songs back. Klein tied himself in knots to trump Grade with a superior offer. Oh, no, then John and Paul go and out-Klein Klein, who swooped on EMI, firmly resolved to sort the Beatles' pathetic deal there. If timing is everything, John's was atrocious: he chose that precise moment to inform the band and Klein that he was quitting. While EMI were reluctant to renegotiate terms, their US subsidiary Capitol were leaping up and down over the *Abbey Road* album, recorded between February and August and released on 26 September. Lo, the magnum opus, la pièce de résistance. It couldn't help but up the ante. A new deal was agreed. Oblivious of the sinking ship, the band played on. The music reverberated. There was nothing else for it. McCartney got his Biro out.

*

'When I first heard *Let It Be* in 1981, at the age of about nine, and saw that it had been released in 1970, I assumed that the Beatles had just had enough,' remembers James Irving, a founder member of the Vinyl Vaults (South London branch) evenings we held regularly over the river during the early 2000s.

'This was a tired-sounding, uneven collection of warm-ups with a couple of classics thrown in. While Paul sounds as though he's desperately trying to hold things together, John is preoccupied and lazy, and makes several mistakes, generally on the bass, throughout McCartney's songs. I'd previously heard the 'White Album' and *Abbey Road*, their other two late-period releases, and assumed that *Let It Be* had been subsequently and reluctantly recorded and released to satisfy a record deal. I then saw the *Let It Be* film on BBC television (I don't think it's been shown since), and this further seemed to enforce the bleak, detached state of the music.'

Then, over the years, James reports, he became aware of a number of facts that encouraged him to reappraise the work.

'Firstly, I discovered that the rawness of the songs was due to the fact that they had been recorded live, rather than overdubbed, which made the music feel rather fresh and honest. Secondly, in an attempt to make the record sound more like a polished Beatles album, the subsequent production lavished by Phil Spector – soupy choirs and strings – was an act of vandalism which ruined songs such as "The Long and Winding Road". When, eventually, the *Let It Be Naked* album was released in 2003, we could finally hear what the songs were intended to sound like. The Beatles were, of course, able to reconvene after the recording of *Let It Be*, and make *Abbey Road*, which stands as a suitable finale, thereby ensuring that *Let It Be* can be viewed as a quirky experiment with an alternative producer, rather than as a sad farewell.'[8]

*

All the while, a love affair was ripening. No sooner had they returned from India that spring than John was urging his wife to join Magic Alex, Jenny and Donovan on a holiday to Greece, excusing himself because he had too much work to do. Having just been away from him for two months, how odd it now seems that packing Julian off to their housekeeper's and swanning off again didn't bother Cynthia. On her return, a rude awakening: another woman, sitting on the floor of *her* conservatory, wearing *her* dressing gown, gazing into the eyes of *her* husband. Unbeknown to Cyn, John had invited Yoko to the matrimonial home. You know how it goes. 'Do you want to hear some stuff I've been recording?' – the musical equivalent of: 'Come up and see my etchings.' They had spent the night experimenting with a tape machine, recording sound effects, funny voices and other weirdness for what would become *Unfinished Music No. 1: Two Virgins*, their debut album together. The sleeve depicts the pair in their naked glory, full-frontal and full-backal. Bushy genitals and pendulous breasts are on display. At the time considered offensive and obscene, it was released on the Apple label. EMI declined to distribute it. That task fell to Track, owned by the Who's managers Kit Lambert and Chris Stamp, who offered it in a brown paper bag. It still caused an outrage, and failed to chart in the UK. Tetragrammaton put it out in America, where it didn't make the Top 100. Of the three 'diary of a relationship' albums created by John and Yoko while the Beatles were still a band, this must be the worst.

They sealed the deal that night back at Kenwood by having sex in Cyn's bed. Instead of doing the decent thing and sitting down with his wife to explain that the marriage was over because he had fallen for someone else, he contrived for her to walk in on them. Was it arrogance, cowardice or just carelessness that caused him to hurt her so savagely? Whatever. John's callous behaviour still beggars belief.

*

For John, there was a sense of relief, of liberation. That was all that business taken care of. He was now free to get on with his life in the arms of the woman who made him feel alive. Who effectively had saved him.

For Cyn, there was only emptiness. A silent desperation. Why didn't she march straight round to Dot the housekeeper's, retrieve Julian, and immerse herself in him? Why did Cyn keep her distance from her son for several more days?

'I can't explain that,' she said, cringing. 'I couldn't think straight, I was out of control, I didn't want my child to see me in that state.

I was destroyed by the thought of them together, how close they looked, how in tune with each other, and what they must have been getting up to in my home, behind my back. I was sick to the stomach. Any woman would be. I have asked myself so many times down the years, why did I feel that *I* was the one who had to walk out? Why did I feel uncomfortable sticking around? It was my house, not hers! I should have kicked them both out, there and then. But I know that I wouldn't have had it in me to do that – even though, when I saw her there, I was so angry and humiliated, I wanted to kill her. I went back with Alex and Jenny, to the place they shared. Jenny was shattered, and went straight to bed. Alex loitered, got me drunk, and made a pass at me. I was horrified. I ran to the bathroom and threw up. It wasn't until a few days later that I went home to face the music, terrified of what I would find there.'

Cyn remembered trying desperately to drag up all kinds of badness about John, to fortify herself for the confrontation:

'Things like, the time he slapped me across the face when we were still at college. The time he told me that the *sound* of me putting on my mascara really irritated him. There was a time when he used to love watching me put on my make-up. When we were courting. It was the sexiest thing, he said. But then, of course, there was Yoko, with her make-up-free face ... I had to find ways of making myself hate him, and to help me feel stronger, more ready for him, for whatever else he was going to throw at me. But you wouldn't believe it: when I got there, it was as if nothing had happened. Julian was already at home, everything was shipshape, and John acted like he was pleased to see me. Was I hallucinating? Nothing made sense. I really did start to doubt my own sanity.

'Once Julian was in bed and John and I were able to talk, he sat there dismissing Yoko as just another of the meaningless women he had previously confessed to having gone with. I mustn't let them bother me, he said. God help me, what kind of a wimp was I? I wouldn't take that lying down now! He insisted that he loved me and only me. I was in turmoil. But, once again, I found myself forgiving him. We went to bed, and we made love. I didn't know what to think. None of this was normal. Was it the drugs? Even then, I dared to believe that everything was OK between us. It was about as far from the truth as you could get.'

There was further ugliness to come. Divorce is never fair. John played dirty. The lawyers did their worst. Cyn was accused of adultery, and threatened with losing Julian. They settled out of court. She was paid off with a pittance. Heartbroken, blindsided and bewildered, she never stood a chance.

On 26 August, the debut single release by the Beatles on their new Apple label was the song of comfort that Paul had penned for Julian: 'Hey Jude'. It topped charts all over the world.[9]

'I knew it was not going to be easy for him,' commented Paul in 1997. 'I always feel sorry for kids in divorces.'[10]

When Paul presented the song to John, he misunderstood its meaning and assumed that it was about him. Don't you, don't you. 'You were made to go out and get her' was the lyric line John took as his clue, thinking that this was Paul telling him to dump Cyn for Yoko. 'I always heard it as a song to me,' said the narcissist.

During his early twenties, by now a rock star in his own right with two albums to his name, the acclaimed *Valotte* and the less well-received *The Secret Value of Daydreaming*, Julian bumped into Paul in New York. Their meeting afforded Julian the opportunity to hear, from the horse's mouth, the true story behind the creation of 'Hey Jude'.

'I've never really wanted to know the truth of how Dad was and how he was with me,' confessed Julian. 'There was some very negative stuff – like when he said that I'd come out of a whisky bottle on a Saturday night. That's tough to deal with. You think, where's the love in that? It surprises me whenever I hear the song. It's strange to think someone has written a song about you. It still touches me.'[11]

The following month, in 1968, John recorded 'Happiness is a Warm Gun', in which he sang explicitly about his new lover. On 8 November, his divorce from Cyn was declared Absolute. A fortnight later, Yoko miscarried John's second son.

*

Christ, you know it ain't easy. Nothing is. Cyn, who'd had it all, had now lost everything. She would be reduced to exploiting his name and trashing him in public. She would rewrite history in her first memoir *A Twist of Lennon* – dashed off, she would admit, out of 'economic necessity': 'I was broke,' she said candidly. 'I had no alternative but to debase myself by doing such things, in order to pay the bills.' John would eventually address her alleged deviations from the truth in a withering letter to his former wife, written on 15 November 1976, which came up for auction in 2017 in New York.

'As you and I well know, our marriage was over long before the advent of L.S.D. or Yoko,' he snarked, '… and that's reality! Your memory is impaired to say the least.'

John had his reasons to berate his ex-wife. Had he compensated her adequately for all the years and the child that she gave him, she would not have been forced to kiss, tell or marry three more times. Yet her connection to John outlived her. Once a Beatle wife, always a Beatle wife.[12]

*

Cynthia and Julian were not the only victims. Yoko's second husband, Tony Cox, took betrayal badly. She divorced him on 2 February 1969. Six and a half weeks later, on 20 March, she and John were married in Gibraltar, as the song goes, at the British Consulate Office. Their honeymoon was a week-long Bed-In for Peace, which they staged to global attention at the Amsterdam Hilton.[13]

CHAPTER 16

METAMORPHOSIS

Try to see it his way. John had known Cyn since his teens. He probably did love her at one point, in his impetuous, self-centred way. In normal circumstances, their relationship might have fizzled out naturally, before they got within kissing distance of a register office. They were calcite and camembert from the off, finding little in common as they progressed. John was unfaithful. He was abusive of and had been known to be violent towards her. In time, Cyn would most likely have plodded her way through the blind-love stage and out the other side, to the stark awakening that he wasn't the one she was looking for after all. But many factors contrived to complicate their romance and perpetuate their attachment. Cyn's pregnancy backed John into a corner. He tried to do the right thing, but felt trapped. Can we blame him? He was a kid for whom the struggle was at last coming good, for whom priorities were nowhere near domestic. He wasn't ready for the responsibility of a wife and child. That his family were made to lay low and were kept a secret forced him to live a double life. While not exactly a hardship for John – who, according to Bill Harry, editor of *Mersey Beat*, carried on having affairs 'as if Cynthia or Julian didn't exist' – it was a ridiculous idea, doomed to backfire. He was distracted by all that was to come. Had their unwanted pregnancy occurred today, it may never have resulted in marriage – nor even, let's be honest, in Julian. I seek not to offend the poor man by saying so. It must have crossed his mind.

The global superstar's life expanded outwards while the shop girl's stood still. She made no attempt to keep pace with her husband, content as she was to run the big house, enjoy the chauffeurs, the housekeepers, the holidays, the designer gear and live the charmed life. Cossetted mum, celebrity wife: what's not to like? She made no attempt to develop a career. The 'way things were' in those days? Ain't necessarily so. Not for a woman with her advantages. The point being that Cyn was not someone to rush home to. She was not fascinating. She was supposed to be an artist, but had let her talent go. She had done little more than work in Woolworths. She stagnated, was bored and resentful, and moaned constantly that he'd rather laze around watching telly, listening to music, reading and sleeping, all the usual, than talk to her. But what was there to talk about? She tried LSD reluctantly, because John as good as made her. She admitted to thinking that it might sex her up a bit, make her more exciting to him. But she loathed the trips and the after-effects and disapproved of him for persisting. He was contemptuous of her because contempt was his default setting. Life had moulded him that way. Yet still, half-heartedly, quixotically, he clung to her. What Cynthia represented was home. Liverpool. Their shared if distant past. It was inevitable that both John and Paul, having voyaged and conquered, would become nostalgic for their childhood and would start to reach back into it for inspiration, summoning 'Strawberry Fields Forever', 'Penny Lane', 'In My Life' and the rest. This was not gratuitous sentimentality. It was a primal need.

The psychotherapist and counsellor Richard Hughes likens John to Homer's Odysseus. Come again? I was slow at first to comprehend the comparison. But as he talked, it began to dawn. Hughes describes the Greek hero of the epic poem *The Odyssey* trying to return home to the island of Ithaca after the Trojan War.

'Odysseus is a very human character – flawed but with good

intentions – and we now see his eventful voyage as an archetypal story which reflects the experience of self-discovery,' explains Hughes.

'Let's not forget, the search is just as important as the destination. Perhaps even more so. When I first read *The Odyssey*, I questioned whether Odysseus even wanted to return home. As Homer writes, "A man who has been through bitter experiences and travelled far, enjoys even his sufferings after a time." Odysseus yearns for a life free of war and suffering, and for the love of his wife Penelope. He has no idea if and when he'll get home or what he will find when he gets there. As the story develops, "home" begins to take on a mythological status. The idea of "home" – a secure base or safe haven – is a powerful one. It's also a fundamental "need". It doesn't just have to be a physical place. Often, that's not even possible. It's more a sense of belonging.'[1]

To John, Cyn was 'home'. She was a tangible connection to everything he thought he missed. They clung to reminders of childhood and home because none of the Beatles could ever have returned full-time to Liverpool. Those places, those times, those folk no longer existed. Only real in our minds and memories? Those days when I was young enough to know the truth … Gerry, Carole, wherefore art thou? Long to your hearts' content, go on, do it. The past is still the past.[2]

While the others still had parents in the north, for John there was not even Mimi to go back to. Concerned by the constant pestering of hordes of fans outside Mendips, John had heeded his aunt's pleas to relocate her before she was driven mad. Thus did Mimi swap one 'pool' for another. In 1965, John paid the then vast sum of £25,000 for Harbour's Edge, a six-bedroom bungalow on the Sandbanks peninsula in Poole, Dorset, with a view of Brownsea Island – where Robert Baden-Powell created the Boy Scout movement in 1907, and which is a nature reserve today. It was the best part of a five-hour, three hundred-mile drive from home. Mimi would live there blissfully for twenty-six years, until her death in 1991. John visited frequently. He had his own bedroom, reminiscent of his single room over the porch at Mendips, with gold discs instead of posters on the wall. John relished the tranquillity. In his mind, he revisited long summers spent on remote Scottish beaches at Sango Bay, Durness. He called similarly dune-y Sandbanks 'the most beautiful place I know'.

'He'd nip down weekends,' said Mimi. 'It was usually if the pressure got a bit much. He'd come down here and do cartwheels on the beach. By himself, there was nobody else there.' But he did sometimes take Cynthia and Julian with him too. He also took to sailing up the river Frome to Wareham, in a boat borrowed from a neighbour. Was the lyric 'Picture yourself in a boat on a river' from 'Lucy in the Sky with Diamonds' inspired by those trips? It is not so far-fetched.

*

Mimi would say that she first met Yoko in London. John subsequently took her to see his aunt in July 1968, on a weekend break from recording sessions for the 'White Album'.

'That was in the early days, when he brought her,' said Mimi. 'Well, I didn't know what it was all about. I wondered who it was. I said, "Who's this?" He said, "It's Yoko." But I didn't think anything of it, you know? I did say to her, "What do you do for a living?" And she said, "I'm an artist." I said, "That's funny, I've never heard of you!" Mimi was never inclined to be impressed.[3]

Where have you gone, John? Our nation turns its lonely eyes to you. Nobody got why he wore Yoko Ono like a weapon. Whatever else would go down between them, he was never contemptuous of her. She was the Alpha female he needed, the partner he felt he deserved. He didn't want someone who could merely keep pace with him, but with whom he would have to make an effort to keep up. She was already the artist. She intimidated both men and women, which he loved about her. He looked up to and deferred to her. Of the two, she was by far the better-educated. She had moved among the wealthy, the well-bred, the supremely artistic and the gifted all her life. She felt comfortable and could hold her own in sophisticated company. John tended to feel inhibited among those whom he considered to be his superiors. He would behave in an offhand, snarky and supercilious manner in order to disguise his inherent nervousness and feelings of inadequacy. This was his armour. He met Yoko, and his cynicism began to melt away. He was at long last able to evolve. He would henceforth look to her for guidance and approval in most things, as a child looks to his mother. You want your mother to be strong, and to be there for you, don't you. To never show weakness. To be the backbone of the family. To be someone to come home to.

He called Yoko 'Mother'. It wasn't just 'the Northern thing'.

'John was adrift when he met Yoko,' reflects Richard Hughes. 'He was not alone. Many of us have felt that sense of being adrift at one time or another, for all the reasons, both internal and external. His personal struggle was compounded by the fact that he was living his life on the world stage, his every utterance, move and blink subjected to public scrutiny. Not just in the UK, but all over the world. It's virtually impossible for most of us to imagine the immense pressure of such an existence. As the song said, "Nothing is real." He must have felt, most of the time, as though he were having an out-of-body experience; that it was someone else living that mad, extraordinary life at breakneck pace, and that "John Lennon, rock superstar" was not really him. He had success, wealth and ongoing opportunity beyond most people's wildest dreams. So what on earth did he have to worry about, we could be forgiven for thinking. Well, of course, he had the same problems as everybody else. Despite his fantastic achievements, he was still looking for the one thing we all long for and strive for.'

'There's no place like home' is Dorothy's refrain in *The Wizard of Oz*. She pined for Kansas, for Uncle Henry's and Aunty Em's farm. But home is where the heart is. 'Home' is 'love'. Poor Cyn, love didn't live there anymore.

*

There prevails an impression that, in exploding his marriage and riding off into the sunset with Yoko, John hit the red button on the Beatles. It is said so often, but is hardly true. Not one of them was without fault on the romance and relationship front. Paul had done with Jane Asher and was now married to Linda. Ringo had, he admitted, womanised for England, and had driven his distraught wife Maureen into the arms of another lover … who happened to be George Harrison, whom John accused of 'virtual incest'. You can see where he was coming from. George's wife Pattie spilled to Ringo, who demanded divorce, which Mo resisted; she almost wiped herself out on a motorbike, and had to have her face rewired. But, in the end, it was Starr's affair with an American model that destroyed their marriage anyway. Pattie Harrison moonlighted with Ronnie Wood while Harrison had an affair with Wood's first wife Krissie Findlay, whom Wood had nicked from Eric Clapton. Pattie closed the Clapton circle, marrying Eric and inspiring yet more love songs. You see? All's fair in love and war and Rock Land.[4]

*

The killings came rapidly.

Beatle John was annihilated. Yoko replaced Paul as Lennon's primary creative collaborator.

'When he met Yoko, it was the start of a new life,' their old Hamburg faithful Klaus Voormann told me. 'He put the Beatles right behind him. The fans don't want to hear that, but it is true. The band, that music, those years belonged to his past. He wasn't John anymore, he was JohnandYoko: one half of a whole. He stopped trying to be a tough rock'n'roller, which he never really was, and he became himself. I was so proud of him for that, and of course I was happy for him.'

'It was exactly what he needed,' insists Richard Hughes. 'He had outgrown the Beatles once and for all. His energy was really powerful at that point, and it remained so throughout the seventies. That's the John we respond to and respect nowadays, I think – rather than sixties Beatle John, who after all wasn't really 'him'. That version of John was a motif, a fake. Historians love to impose upon us otherwise, but they are wrong. What Lennon represents to us in the twenty-first century is hope. Because weirdly, after all that we have been through, we are still so hung up on certainty and truth. He is representative of something more meta.'

Yet it was one of his simpler songs, a sixties Beatles number, that conveyed the greatest message: 'All You Need is Love'. Is that true?

'Absolutely,' states Hughes. 'At the same time, there's nothing more uncertain than love. We all need to be loved and held and validated. John knew that. He got it, from self-exploration. He may have been dysfunctional and misguided on so many fronts, but he got that right. How did love become the be-all and end-all for him? Because he was deprived of it as a child. He knew its worth.

'What is certain is that John Lennon truly loved Yoko Ono. It was a grand love affair. The real thing. The yardstick. His salvation was that he recognised it when it came.'

Pete Shotton, who knew John better than anybody, believed that Yoko was the best thing that ever happened to him.

'His attitude to all kinds of things changed considerably,' he said. 'He became less selfish and more concerned. He started communicating with a lot of people, just to say "thank you" and so on. Pre-Yoko, he was very blasé about everybody, his attitude towards his fans and all that. He really started to appreciate others. Maybe it's because he felt that what he was doing now was important.'

Not only did John become a prolific writer of notes, postcards and letters, post-Beatles, but he acquired an entirely different set of fans.

'Exactly,' says Shotton. 'A lot more *intelligent* people became interested in him, if I may say. I think that people of *importance* were taking more notice of him. They realised that this wasn't just a cuddly, long-haired, moptop Beatle. This was an intelligent man who was thinking, doing and acting, and in a way was a yardstick to a lot of people, even if they didn't exactly go along with all that he did. He became a figure against which people could measure themselves. They started relating to him on a very personal level. It wasn't at all like it was when he was a Beatle. He was a pop star, he was famous and he was rich. But there was something more to him now. Fans felt that they had contact with him personally. He achieved that while still keeping his feet firmly on the ground, and not letting any of the crap get to him.'[5]

Like Shotton, Klaus Voormann had watched the boy become a man; had witnessed anger born of frustration, and had marvelled at the way he blossomed in the arms of his new love.

'As soon as Yoko came up, they were never apart,' he says. 'She'd be in the studio, sitting in his lap. She'd go to the bathroom with him, even – because he wanted her to, not because she was forcing herself on him and wouldn't let him out of her sight. It was strange at first, but I soon got used to it. For the first time in his life, I could see that he was himself, and that he was happy. It was like a miracle.

'Yoko saved him. The fans don't want to believe that. They see only the bad in her. But she's a great person. They were funny together. John often stopped her to say something, or she would stop him, or they would finish each other's sentences, just like that. They completed each other. Whether you liked the music they made together or not, they really inspired each other. I can tell you this first-hand. What people don't realise is that she's hilarious. I came to think of them as like Siamese twins, who had been separated at birth.'

*

Roger Scott, a passionate Beatles fan who would become one of Britain's best-loved and most respected radio hosts, was a fledgling twenty-five year-old DJ working for Canadian AM station CFOX Montreal when a crucifix-wearing John and Yoko came to town on 26 May 1969, with five-year-old Kyoko in tow. This was the latest leg of their international peace mission, during which they staged their infamous Bed-In for Peace inside room 1742 of the Queen Elizabeth Hotel, in Montreal, packed in with pink and white carnations, overflowing film and recording equipment and books.

'I'd got an afternoon show by this time,' Roger told me. 'It was organised with their people for me to broadcast my show from their very bedside for the duration. Imagine that: it still gives me goose bumps. I had no previous experience of anything on this scale. I was unprepared for the fact that the world's media would descend on their bedroom, and that I would have to keep a cool head and focus on presenting my radio show regardless. There we all were, the pair of them in the bed holding court, members of the local Hare Krishna chapter, the Beatles publicist Derek Taylor. Tommy Smothers, half of the musical comedy duo the Smothers Brothers. This went on for an entire week, towards the end of which it emerged that John and Yoko intended to make a record in that very bedroom on the Saturday night. The record turned out to be "Give Peace a Chance", and it featured every Tom, Dick and Harry who was hanging about in there. There must have been at least fifty of us, Tommy on guitar, me banging on the coffee table, singer Petula Clark and beat poet Allen Ginsberg, singing the words which had been scrawled hastily by John on giant bits of card. What a shambles the whole thing was. And yet, it worked.'

So far, so good. But then, a moment of humiliation that was to haunt Roger for the rest of his life.

'For whatever reason, John suddenly refused to be interviewed by me, and insisted that he wanted this sixteen-year-old girl who happened to be there to do it instead. What on earth had I done wrong? Probably nothing, it was just John being capricious. I wracked and wracked my brains, and I could never think of any other reason. It kind of did break my heart.'[6]

As for John, his message to the media was clear.

'The whole effect of our bed-ins has made people talk about peace,' he stated. 'We're trying to interest young people into doing something for peace. But it must be done by non-violent means – otherwise there can only be chaos. We're saying to the young people ... and they have always been the hippest ones ... we're telling them to get the message across to the squares.' Something like that.

*

The recording of the iconic *Abbey Road* album was a long, drawn-out affair under the one-last-go guidance of George Martin – coaxed back into the fold on the promise that they would make this record according to the old rules, just as they used to make them, with the producer resolutely in charge. From the end of February until until late mid-to-late August, they worked sporadically at Olympic and Trident studios as well as at EMI – which, come the end of the recording of this momentous LP, would be renamed Abbey Road Studios in its honour. Perfecting perfection took time. Dissent and animosity clouded the mood. But out of adversity and complication would rise what many consider to be their absolute, all-encompassing and most spectacular work. Although no decision had been taken that this would be their last album together, a sense of finality prevailed. John would later trash the work, particularly Paul's contributions, dismissing the songs as 'granny music' and finding fault with the album's construction. Already long over the Beatles and keen to get on with the rest of his life, his own music and his marriage, John was obviously resentful of the confinement his commitment to it imposed. The car accident (of which, more later) can't have helped. Nor could the installation of Yoko's bed in the studio, where she lay during recording sessions, ridiculously, after doctors had ordered her to rest as much as possible. Why not just stay home?

But who can argue with *Abbey Road*'s immensity? With 'Come Together', John's opener; his cloying, passionate 'I Want You (She's So Heavy)'; his wistful, otherworldly 'Because', inspired by Yoko playing Beethoven's 'Moonlight Sonata' on the piano and John getting her to re-play the chords backwards, and hallmarked by George Martin's squirling harpsichord. With George's 'Something' and 'Here Comes the Sun', and Paul's doo-woppy 'Oh! Darling', which John resented because he thought it would have been better sung in *his* voice. Macca's 'You Never Give Me Your Money', reflecting the band's unholy financial mess and impending collapse. The complicated, multi-layered 'The End': distinguished by Ringo's sole Beatles drum solo, and the central message, 'And in the end, the love you take is equal to the love you make.' It marked the last time that all four Beatles ever recorded together. What about the sleeve? This was their only original UK LP to feature neither their name nor the title. Who needs? The world knew who they were and what it was! Six days before its release on 26 September 1969, John told the others he was quitting. The fact that it shifted four million copies during its first two months of release did fuck-all to change his mind. *Abbey Road* debuted at Number One on the UK chart, and hung there for eleven weeks. It gave way briefly to the Stones, but soon reclaimed its rightful place. In America, it became the best-selling album of 1969. In Japan, it stayed in the Top 100 chart for nearly three hundred weeks, and was the album of the seventies.

'Apart from being the final Beatles album to be recorded, *Abbey Road* was also their first since *Help!* in 1965 to feature an opening track written and sung by John, namely the Jabberwocky-influenced, anthemic "Come Together",' comments *SongLink* publisher and musician David Stark. 'The Fab Four, pop music and the world had changed an awful lot during those four short years. But it was totally appropriate that the group's founder and leader should reclaim his position at the helm of what would turn out to be a wave goodbye, to Beatles admirers and fans the world over. Of course this was not officially known at the time, though suspected by many, while the patchy *Let It Be* album was kept on hold for eventual release the following year.'

Amazingly, Stark says, initial reaction to *Abbey Road* was lukewarm: 'Reviewers were not getting the fact that, together with the invaluable contributions and demands of George Martin, the Beatles had managed to record an album of sheer technical brilliance in the last year of the 1960s. It still stands, over fifty years later, as a masterpiece – and one which George's son Giles Martin found almost impossible to improve on when he was remixing it for the anniversary release in 2019. Along with its iconic cover – which will surely continue to attract Beatles fans to "come together" at the world's most famous recording studio and zebra crossing long after "the end" has passed, whenever that may be – *Abbey Road* remains unsurpassed, to my ears at least, and is pop's absolute zenith. As a sixteen-year-old schoolboy, I was lucky enough to receive an advance copy from Apple around a week before release. I can recall to this day being mesmerised by its combination of musical and vocal brilliance, the startling contrast between its lyrical humour and genuine pathos, and Martin's beautiful arrangements and superb production. I remain mesmerised to this day.'

*

A fortnight before *Abbey Road* emerged, 13 September 1969 saw John, Yoko, Klaus, Eric Clapton and others taking part, as Plastic Ono Band, in rock'n'roll revival concert 'Live Peace in Toronto' at Varsity Stadium. Almost every artist taking part was a hero of John's: Little Richard, Gene Vincent, Jerry Lee Lewis, Fats Domino. John and his crew's set included 'Give Peace a Chance', 'Blue Suede Shoes', 'Cold Turkey' and Yoko's 'Don't Worry Kyoko (Mummy's Only Looking for Her Hand in the Snow)', about her little daughter. Unsurprisingly, Yoko's screams, sobs and howls left the audience unshaken. Wasn't it John they'd come to see? What's *she* all about? Klaus explains.

'The first time that Yoko's artistic talent was really apparent to me was during that concert,' he says. 'She was in her bag, on the floor. She came out and started to do noises, and then began screaming. She was trying to say something important to the audience. I felt this huge urge that she had. It was quite overpowering. She screamed herself hoarse, she was croaking in the end. I was standing right behind her. I get goose bumps even now, thinking about it. You immediately thought about war, tanks, bombs, destruction. She was using herself to express the full horror of war, in a very shocking way. That's what she was feeling, and that was what she was trying to get across. Me, right behind her, I felt it with her. But the audience didn't feel it. They were too far from the stage to pick up on her energy. Also, an unrehearsed band at a rock'n'roll concert with Yoko coming out of a bag and screaming at people – at that time, it was too much for people. Yoko was ridiculed. All they wanted was John, playing music. They didn't exactly throw tomatoes, but their reaction was humiliating. She learned. She soon knew how to handle an audience. She said, "When I'm here on stage and I'm singing to you, it's like I'm in a tunnel. And I want you to go with me into the tunnel."

'The thing is, John was on the same wavelength as her. He supported her and stood up for her. To him, what she was doing was perfectly appropriate, and he marvelled at her. Do you see? He was so happy with her. There was genuine solidarity between them. Whether you agreed with the method or not, you could not fault the message. John was way ahead of everybody else.'

Timing: still everything. John and Yoko were right there, right place, at the vanguard of the global peace movement. A month later, on 15 October, millions of Americans staged the largest demo in US history, a Moratorium to End the War in Vietnam. The new Republican president, Richard Nixon, unmoved, gave his infamous 'silent majority' speech. The anti-war movement, now galvanised by the awful revelation of the My Lai massacre, was undeterred, and went again. That November, half a million protestors marched on the White House, Washington, DC. During the peaceful rally, joined by Peter, Paul and Mary, Leonard Bernstein, Arlo Guthrie, John Denver and the Cleveland String Quartet, as well as touring companies of the avant-garde musical *Hair*, folk singer and activist Pete Seeger led the vast crowd in a ten-minute rendition of 'Give Peace a Chance'. Are you listening, Nixon? Agnew? Pentagon? The president followed proceedings on television, then attempted, pointlessly, to count the exact number of demonstrators from his window in the White House. He heard the song. Lennon had crossed his radar. The former Beatle would pay for this. Of which John, at the time, was oblivious. All he was saying was what millions of others were thinking. He described the mass live performance of his song as 'one of the biggest moments of my life'. Abbey Road? Where's that?

CHAPTER 17

KYOKO

H ell hath no fury like a man scorned. Tony Cox would have his revenge. He was to punish his ex-wife in the worst way imaginable. A significant part of the story of how he did so has until now never been told.

The world assumed that John and Yoko upped sticks, abandoned Britain and moved to the States to save the world. But the world was wrong. The real reason for their relocation to New York was more personal, and heartbreaking. Yoko's eight-year-old daughter Kyoko had vanished. They believed her to be with her father, and went looking for her in America. It had never been their intention to remain there permanently. Circumstances contrived to make it impossible to leave. When eventually they were free to do so, it was all but too late. As for her child, Yoko would pay the ultimate price.

The run-up to their departure was a whirlwind. From the moment they came together, media interest in the comings and goings of the brash head Beatle and his oriental muse, their scandalous double marriage-wrecking, their bi-racial relationship and their apparent abandonment of their respective offspring, had gone berserk. All too eager to identify as peace-seeking, good-doing activists harnessing their art for the common good, but carried away by media attention and their global worth, they made mistakes. Aligning themselves with off-colour causes and questionable campaigns, they got it wrong as often as right. Their fame, status and wealth were exploited endlessly. It's almost impossible to comprehend, today, how intense and all-consuming this was. Everything they did – freaky recordings, art exhibitions, excruciating films, sculpture, 'Acorn Events', a stage dramatisation of John's pair of strange little books *In His Own Write* and *A Spaniard in the Works*, all the wearing of white and black, the miscarriages, the jealous obsessions with themselves and with each other, the sugar-free self-reinvention, the macrobiotic brown-rice-and-veg evangelism, John's refusal to relinquish smoking, Yoko taking up the habit, madly, according to the pledge they had made to be equal and joined in all things, their self-satisfied 'chemistry' and sexual appetite for each other; everything they did, didn't, good, bad, ugly, beautiful, boring, fascinating, indifferent, ill-advised, cock-eyed or just plain daft, was a multilingual headline and happening. Imagine living like that. I know I couldn't. They endured it together, building a relationship of equals, perfectly in tune, that would see John happily slaughter his inborn misogynist to embrace and even start promoting feminism. *What?* It's what Yoko wanted. It was what she demanded of him. She gave him no alternative, and calmly informed him that she would leave him otherwise. Said John, on the subject of female liberation and his increasing enlightenment about sexual equality: 'It's so subtle, the way you're taught male superiority. It took me quite a long time to realise that my maleness was cutting off certain areas for Yoko. She's a red-hot liberationist, and was quick to show me where I was going wrong, even though it seemed to me that I was just acting naturally. That's why I'm always interested to know how people who claim to be radical treat women.'

Yoko's take was more succinct.

'You can't love someone unless you are in an equal position with them. A lot of women have to cling to men out of fear or insecurity, and that's not love – basically that's why women hate men …'

'… and vice versa,' chipped in John.

As he would later explain,

'She changed my life completely. Not just physically … the only way I can describe it is that Yoko was like an acid trip or the first time you got drunk. It was that big a change, and that's just about it. I can't really describe it to this day."[1]

It was another nail in the coffin of the John of yore.

*

They had gone to live in Ringo's old London flat, at 34 Montagu Square. It was no secret that the situation with Yoko's ex-husband Tony Cox was a miserable one, not least because Yoko had deserted Cox and Kyoko to be with John. Next up, a police raid on the apartment. Yet another media circus, and all for the merest twitch of cannabis, for which they were charged with possession. John pleaded guilty, charges against Yoko were dropped, and John, if only he'd known, signed his own death warrant. Albeit in invisible ink.

The other side of divorce, Cynthia retained custody of Julian while Yoko and Tony would share Kyoko. Now, thanks to the drugs bust, the whole world knew their address. John and Yoko were obliged to get the hell out. Another Ringo residence, this time back in Weybridge, we're going round in circles here, would do for the moment. There, they planned to receive both Julian and Kyoko, who were as good as the same age, for cosy family weekends. By making this domestic commitment, John astonished all who had witnessed his hitherto paternal hands-offness. Yoko had awoken his inner parent. It was she who helped him to value children as a blessing. Caring for, cooking for, playing, reading and making music with Julian and Kyoko, immersing themselves in simple family life, would attune them to and prepare them for the brood they planned to create. So enthused by this opportunity to redeem himself as a father was John, so eager to surrender to it, that he decided to drive the four of them back through his own childhood, to Liverpool and his beloved Scottish Highlands. It was time.

Redemption. Suddenly, there *was* a way back, and a significant new other with whom to relive it. This was June 1969, midway through the *Abbey Road* sessions. He was excited by the thought of Yoko meeting his other aunts, Nanny and Harrie in Liverpool and Mater in Durness. They would kip with family and do the whole thing low-key, keen to avoid as much press attention as possible. In his excitement, John overlooked his obligations to Cynthia. As Julian's mother, she ought at least to have been informed that the child, still only six years old, was being taken on such a long journey, and with John at the wheel of the vehicle – always a risk. As it was, his mother had no inkling of their departure or whereabouts. Remember, of course, back then, no mobile phones.

Once they had reached his hometown, John conceded that the Mini Cooper was too small to convey them much farther. He had his chauffeur fetch him a more accommodating Austin Maxi. The combination of an unfamiliar ride, John's lack of driving experience, poor eyesight and general inability to concentrate on such mundane things as roads for extended periods caused him to crash the car into a ditch near Golspie, a Highland village en route to Mater's. Only Julian escaped unscathed. Hospital, stitches, treatment for shock. John's face would forever bear the scar. Julian was whisked off into the care of Mater, where Cynthia soon found him, but her efforts to communicate with John in order to find out what had happened were in vain. He refused point-blank to see her, which was cruel. Simple injuries, compound fractures.

Kyoko's little face required negligible embroidery to restore its utter perfection. It was a face upon which John loved to gaze. How beautiful was this child? Her fringed black hair, obsidian eyes and angelic smile were all it took to melt him. He adored her because she was an extension of Yoko, but also for her own sake, as if she were his own. A black-and-white photograph of this little clan on their jollies in the Highlands depicts the two bonny bairns in kilts, tartan waistcoats and sporrans, smiling shyly from beneath peaked plaid caps. They are clutching each other's hands between Daddy and Mummy, walking along in the open air, she in head-to-toe black, with white plimsolls, he heavily bearded and sporting a thick Arran knit. They look thrilled to be alive, and are tightly together.

But a switch had flicked. While Cynthia had little choice but to put up with John's selfishness and impetuosity, Tony Cox was no longer inclined to be amiable or reasonable. Vexed by what he must have perceived as their neglect of his daughter, he would now prohibit Kyoko from spending time with her mother and John without him. He would also make access increasingly difficult. Their acquisition of Tittenhurst Park, a majestic mansion on a vast estate close to Ascot in Berkshire, the one that is on full gauzy, ethereal show in the 'Imagine' video with Yoko drawing the curtains, must have inflamed him – being beyond grand, just to rub salt in, and an inconvenient schlep down the M4. Anyone who has ever shared a child with an ex-partner and who has felt ground down by all the to-ing, fro-ing and endless, exhausting confrontation with a dismissed spouse will empathise, on both sides. At least John and Yoko had plenty in the bank. Can't buy me love? Sure helps. It was at Tittenhurst that both John and Yoko, faithful to their pact to do everything together, pledged their troth to junk. *Why?* One more arty trend to get off on? Not only was it not all it had been smacked up to be, but the fact that they were users of heroin must have filtered down to Cox. Or possibly he simply witnessed with his own eyes its glaring effects: the slurring of speech, staring eyes and ghostly pallor, the nausea, the confusion. Who in their right mind would leave a little child in the care of druggies under the influence? Cox himself had been an acidhead, back in the Swinging Sixties. He knew the score, and how to.

'I took a lot of acid thinking this was going to improve my mind, and it took me years to discover the opposite was true,' he said. 'All drugs are a very bad scene.'[2] He resolved to put more distance between them, and to protect his daughter from their precarious, self-centred lifestyle.

Yoko would later stress that their experimentation with the euphoric opioid was fleeting. They turned their back on it for family reasons, she insisted. They were anxious to conceive again as quickly as possible, and did not want to risk damage to the foetus or giving birth to an infant addict. Unable to put themselves through rehab for fear of media exposure, they had to help each other kick the habit behind closed doors. John made a Plastic Ono Band single of their experience, 'Cold Turkey'. That's the one on the other side, Kyoko, about Mummy looking for her hand in the snow.

*

John and Yoko wended their way to northern Denmark, where Cox was now living with his daughter and his American girlfriend Melinda Kendall and where they were involved in the first of several cults. The Lennons spent January 1970 there, catching up with Kyoko, kissing the sixties goodbye, relinquishing their smoking habit via hypnosis with one of the Harbinger cult's leaders, and cropping their long hair to launch Year One for Peace. They lugged their shearings home and gifted them to Michael X, Britain's Trinidadian-born answer to Malcolm X, to be sold to raise funds for Black Power. Misguided benevolence, as it turned out: at the end of the year, Michael X was charged with robbery and extortion, and had vanished back to Trinidad ahead of his trial. The primal therapy to which they committed with Arthur Janov both in London and Los Angeles – 'This therapy forced me to have done with all the God shit' – broke the dam, shaking John free of the last remaining shackles of Beatledom and released his true musical personality. Never before had he been able to make such honest, genuine *John* music, singing his own songs by himself, fully vocal and confident, unreliant on studio tricks and techniques, independent of sophisticated harmonies to disguise what he perceived as shortcomings and make him *sound* better. Henceforth, it would be the real, raw, unapologetic John Lennon. Just himself and his songs. Himself and his life. There would be no separation. While he had tackled personal pain and insecurity in earlier songs during the Beatle years, his pain was invariably camouflaged. Dark lyrics would be dressed up in jolly tunes – 'Help!' and 'I'm a Loser' being perfect examples. No one thought too deeply about the 'messages' in those songs, because the music was so upbeat. I think I always assumed that he was writing abstractly, about someone other than himself. I now believe that his songs were mostly about him, John. He threw himself right into them. 'Jealous Guy', to come, on the 1971 album *Imagine*, was a similar cry for help. McCartney's writing, by comparison, can feel controlled and even detached.

But no more of that. What John wanted to sound like now was his real, stripped-back self. His debut solo album, *John Lennon/Plastic Ono Band*, which he co-produced with Yoko and Phil Spector and which features Klaus Voormann on bass, Ringo on drums and Billy Preston here and there on keys, is as real as contractions.

'McCartney may still be regarded as a greater musician, composer and melodist. But he wasn't like John: a provocateur,' observes former *Melody Maker* writer Michael Watts, the publication's US editor during the seventies.

'John expressed his feelings about the world in ways that were so unexpected. That made him a fantastic interviewee. He would say things that opened and stretched your own mind, and which made you consider things in new ways. That's what made him so popular among journalists. I think McCartney always felt a bit out of his depth in interviews with the press, because John was so brilliant at expressing himself in lively and amusing ways. Paul was every bit as literate, but he didn't have that gift for animating issues that John had. He was naked and outspoken to a fault. *John Lennon/Plastic Ono Band*, which has on it tracks like "Mother", "God" and "My Mummy's Dead", is extraordinary. The songs are so naked. They reveal him as so vulnerable. The album stands as *the* best expression of what he was. He clearly strove to tell things in a completely open-hearted way. It is confessional to the hilt. I thought, and I still think, that it is a great album.'

Reminding us that John embarked on one of the greatest journeys of self-discovery ever undertaken by a rock star, Watts points out that John was more courageous than most. He set out to find himself. What he found was that he didn't like the person he really was.

'Thus began his campaign to become someone different. Imagine most rock stars attempting such a thing. It wouldn't happen. What he was saying was that the guy they had all fallen for was fake, no good, and now he was going to offer them a different version of himself: a John Lennon whom he himself could love and respect. What a risk that was, because it could have gone completely the other way. He could have lost all credibility. Look at the admissions he made, the confessions: "I used to be violent, now I'm no longer violent," and so on. In doing so, he achieved something remarkable. He knew about himself. He wanted to be someone better. He wished to transcend, and to become a more worthwhile human being. People tend to think that much of what he said was dopey nonsense. Because we journalists are a cynical lot, part of me agrees. But what is in no doubt is that he genuinely believed what he was preaching. He really did want to change the world.'

Much of his desire to pursue that was down to Yoko, agrees Watts: 'She *was* his true love, his genuine soulmate. There's no doubt. He found, in her, someone who was completely on his wavelength. Because of all the daft things they did, she was so often dismissed as having led him astray. But the two of them together, and she on her own, did very interesting artistic things.'

What were the bed-ins but pre-emptive of Tracey Emin's unmade bed? What was Yoko's music but the shape of Björk to come?

'Exactly. The world wasn't ready for Yoko. She was a true avant-garde artist. Those bed-ins, the bagism, the hiding in bags, being interviewed in bags, John said, were sort of Dadaist events, and the public hadn't cottoned on to that. His fans couldn't reconcile John the pop star with this figure who had begun increasingly to absorb influences from the art world, and was expressing himself in more complex, less conventional ways. What he and Yoko were doing was quite extraordinary, really. Because they were getting audiences of a million times more people than you would get in the art world. Because they were so famous already, before they lifted a finger and actually did anything. He was really enthused by that. He realised and harnessed his power. It charged his batteries beyond his imagining.'

Still, everyone wanted more of the Beatles. More like before. Supplements of same. What they didn't want was four Beatles and Yoko.

'John's problem was that he was not subtle in the way that Paul managed to be,' Michael concludes. 'John was always on it, always rushing towards a gap, to fill a vacuum. The fact that he had no filter is what made him such an exciting figure. With a little more tact and pragmatism, the Beatles could have progressed to other things, and still have developed their solo careers on the side. But it was all or nothing with John. He was hell-bent on a new career with Yoko, and that is what he went out to get. With him, it was always "on to the next thing".'

*

Seven-year-old Julian's weekend visits to his father and step-mother made him confused. For a start, Cynthia didn't take him there herself, as she should have; nor did John make the journey to London to fetch him. The return trip was tasked to a chauffeur, who conveyed the little boy to and fro in John's huge Rolls-Royce. Divorce is hard enough on a child. The damage wrought by separation from a parent, the removal from home and relocation to unfamiliar surroundings, and the insecurity caused by exposure to the inevitable extreme emotion and anger, all take their toll. One of the most important means by which parents can limit the impact and fall-out of divorce on their children is to take responsibility for the hand-overs, however uncomfortable, until they are old enough to travel independently. While John and Julian were at last at liberty to avail themselves of full, unthwarted father-and-son time, taking advantage of all the pursuits – biking, rowing, tearing about – that the vast, wonderful Tittenhurst estate had to offer, Julian's relationship with Yoko was less than ideal. Neither warmed to the other. His stepmother would later admit that she had no idea how to bond with little boys. But she could have found out. She did what she could, she believed, but it was not enough. The elephant in the room was that Julian's presence made her obsess about the baby son that she and John had lost, and reminded her of her miscarriages. She was frankly resentful of the fact that John was getting to enjoy all this unfettered time with his child while she was deprived of her own. In all things, equality. Only not in this. Not quite yet.

Their relationship with Tony and Melinda had been pretty cool until this point. It has been said that the two couples were up for doing creative work together. The idea of another group featuring the four of them was even mooted, and Cox had already filmed John and Yoko for a planned documentary. As Pete Shotton recalled, 'One of the oddest features of John's life at Tittenhurst Park – for a period of several weeks, anyway – was the constant presence of Yoko's previous husband, Tony Cox, whom the Lennons now used as an errand boy.'

But relations soon soured. Whether it was John's blatant adoration of Kyoko that got up Cox's nose, making him jealous, or John's suspicious nature stirring fear that Cox was wielding the fact that he was the custodian parent to exert control over Yoko and him, the two men reached breaking point. A seemingly innocent invitation to Kyoko's seventh birthday party at Cox's London flat drove John into a rage. Interpreting it as a trap, he refused to attend. Worse, he barred her mother from attending too. Yoko was distraught. There was then what appeared to be a blatant taunt of Lennon by Cox, when the latter became a devotee of Maharishi Mahesh Yogi and Transcendental Meditation. Without a by your leave he vacated his London apartment, and disappeared with Melinda and Kyoko. Neither John nor Yoko had any idea where they had gone. A tip-off led them eventually to Majorca, where Maharishi now happened to live. Possibly spooked by the moonlit flit and terrified that they would never see Kyoko again, the Lennons made the requisite enquiries and then steamed in heavy-handed, accompanied by a lawyer and an assistant. It was then that they made their fatal mistake, snatching Kyoko from her new nursery school and rushing her back to their hotel, whence they would return to England by private plane. Cox, however, had been informed, and was ahead of them. John and Yoko were intercepted by police, arrested and incarcerated. An emergency overnight court hearing ensued. Come the dawn, the judge was calling for Kyoko to decide with whom she wanted to live. Comparisons have been drawn between this unbearable scenario and the apparent plight of little John Lennon, forced as a boy to choose between his father

Freddie and his mother Julia, and waving goodbye to his dad for the next twenty years. It didn't happen. Kyoko's nightmare did, however, and it was not over yet.

Despite the fact that poor, pushed-and-pulled Kyoko had elected to remain with her father, John and Yoko were permitted to take her home with them – provided they gave a solemn undertaking to re-present to the Majorcan judiciary a few weeks later, for further formalities. But commitments at the Cannes Film Festival, with Michael X in Trinidad, here, there and everywhere contrived to keep them away. By the time they were ready to turn their attention to the ongoing issue of Kyoko, Cox, Kendall and the child had done another bunk. Intelligence indicated that Cox and co. had hot-footed it home to the US, which made sense. Cox and Kyoko were American nationals. Yoko did not have citizenship. John and Yoko sped to New York. But their leads went dead.

Back at Tittenhurst that February, John threw himself into his new recording facility, Ascot Sound Studios, and buried his anger and frustration in what would become his finest solo hour: the *Imagine* album. Co-producing with Yoko and Phil Spector, leaning on the talents of George Harrison, Klaus Voormann on bass, Jim Keltner and Alan White on drums and Nicky Hopkins on keys, and continuing the good work at both Abbey Road Studios and at Record Plant NYC, John created a multi-layered flight of fantasy that would soar to Number One on both the UK album chart and the US *Billboard* 200. On its release in September, it became a gigantic commercial success. The album is a self-portrait, a tapestry, weaving experiences of primal therapy with sex and love, malevolence and grudgery, pomposity and humility. It presents the whole human being in all his light and shade, in all his warped and contradictory glory. Criticised at the time for being more uptight and less meticulous than its predecessor, for its hubris and self-indulgence and even for technical sloppiness, it shook off negative reviews to cement itself for all time as John's most popular and defining solo album. Of its ten tracks, the title song reverberates. Disingenuous, a little plodding, it got under our skin and it stayed there. 'How?' is irresistibly fluid, plaintively orchestral, as deep as a mountain lake. Its lyrics are excruciating: was there ever a more telling line than 'How can I give love when love is something I ain't never had'? 'Oh My Love' is charming, bell-like, innocent, with an almost Elizabethan quality. For the first time in his life, eyes and mind are wide open. 'Oh Yoko!' is loved-up. 'How Do You Sleep?', John's outlandishly cruel, vindictive yet addictive denunciation of Paul, can still shock. 'Jealous Guy' is harrowing and needy. 'Gimme Some Truth' is one of his best protest songs, heaving with invective. John was never afraid to go outside in the nude. He does so figuratively here, with explosive candour.

*

The Lennons' lawyers pressed Yoko to apply for full custody of her daughter in the American Virgin Islands, which was where she obtained her divorce. The court there granted her wish, on the condition that Kyoko be raised in America. Yoko had already resolved to remain for as long as it took, anyway, so that she would be on hand to deal with Cox and receive Kyoko when eventually her former husband put his head above the parapet and returned her baby to her.

Which proved just the impetus that John needed. He was bored, worn out by relentless media attention and obligation, and was losing faith in the homeland. He was revolted by his country's failure to accept his new wife, and disgusted by the racism and abuse of her. One might say, today, that Prince Harry, 'is-he-or-isn't-he Duke of Sussex?', knows precisely how John felt. He saw political and social upheaval coming that he wanted no part of. He was sick and tired of being asked, everywhere he went, by every kinda people, 'So when are the Beatles getting back together, then?' and 'Do you think you'll ever tour again as a group?' He had not formed any plan in his mind to emigrate permanently. He simply wanted to step outside the frame for a bit. To breathe different air. Stretch out in a new space. He wanted to be with his beloved wife, upon whom he relied solely, and to support her desperate endeavours to be reunited with her child. Little did he realise, as he set about applying for a further visitor's visa to the US, that the more energy he would pour into the quest to find Kyoko, the less time he would have for his own son. Little did he know that he would see neither his step-daughter nor his Aunt Mimi again.

*

Cox's explanation, given decades later and long after John's death, was that he had been terrified that Yoko would at some point hang on to their daughter, refuse to part with her and never let him see her. With Lennon's might and money they could never compete. So they legged it, not to New York but to Houston, Texas, where his second wife Melinda was from. It was there that they pledged themselves to the evangelical Christian church. By bizarre, couldn't-make-it-up coincidence, seventeen-year-old Meredith Hamp, the daughter of Granada TV boss Johnnie Hamp, the guy who had given the Beatles their earliest television exposure back in the early sixties, had also just been indoctrinated.

There are few sadder stories, and this one has never been told.

'Merry', as only Johnnie is allowed to call her, remembers in minute detail the many times that she accompanied her father to Granada Studios and met the stars. She enjoyed Cliff Richard and the Shadows and the Hollies, but it was the Beatles who made the biggest impact.

'John Lennon looked to me like the Prince in *Snow White*,' says Meredith, echoing her father's recollection. 'Until I met them face to face, I'd never seen them in colour, only on television in black-and-white, so I wasn't prepared for the sight of John's hair, which was a gorgeous strawberry blond. Almost towards red, but not quite red itself. He had a chiselled face and a very strong profile. I was enchanted. I was about ten years old at the time, and of course I didn't realise how big the Beatles actually were. They were performing a song, and they were miming. Then we all went into a viewing room to watch it back. Only George went out of his way to talk to me. The others didn't take any notice, they were intent on watching themselves on screen. But it was John that I couldn't take my eyes off. The impression that he made on me was incredible. He stood out like sore thumb. He was so beautiful.'

But then Meredith suffered a terrible accident, after which everyone took notice of her. All through childhood, she'd had 20:20 vision. A fortnight before her twelfth birthday, in her first year of her brand-new secondary school, a science experiment exploded in her face. Doctors at the local hospital had not seen burns like hers since the Second World War, she says: '... and never on a child. I was unrecognisable. I was later flown to Barcelona and then Houston for surgery. Between the ages of thirteen and sixteen, I had forty operations. As each operation came and went, my vision would come back, then fade again. Eventually, it faded completely. I had what was left of my eyes removed for cosmetic reasons.'

'After that, I got loads of stuff from pop people. The Hollies sent me a huge stuffed toy. I got a signed photo from the Walker Brothers. Lulu came to see me in hospital, as did Jimmy Savile, and Peter Noone – but my mother kicked him out, because he was smoking Russian cigarettes. There was nothing from the Fabs, but that was at the height of it all, so I was not surprised. They were busy. Although George did phone me once, on my birthday. I continued to follow their music all the same, and I loved John just as much.'

How did she come to be in a church in Houston at the same time as Tony and Melinda Cox?

'Life does things,' nods the BACP counselling psychotherapist now in her sixties as she, her father and I reminisce over dinner in Stockport. 'Connections appear. Weird and extraordinary things have always happened to me. When we moved up here' – she means to the north of England from London, for Johnnie's job – 'we stayed in Milverton Lodge, which at the time was a private hotel. Wolf Mankowitz the writer and playwright was staying there at the time. There was also an unusual couple: a white American man and a Japanese woman. Husband and wife. They had a baby in a pram, and I used to play with her. She was adorable. But then I had the accident.'

She never went back to school. Her personal injury damages were set at £88,284, the highest sum ever awarded to a female. Since that time, she has lived in total darkness.

'At seventeen, I was back in Houston, Texas, receiving treatment and attending an evangelical Christian church. It was all quite hippie. I played the guitar there, and became very friendly with the wife of one of the musicians. It was she who introduced me to this really nice couple, Tony and Melinda Cox. They were on a spiritual path, looking for answers, and they were in Houston because Melinda's parents lived there.

"I'm looking for a church home," Tony said to me.

"It's nice to meet you," I said.

'They had a little girl of about seven, called Rosemary. I became very fond of her. They invited me to their house to eat, where I had my first truly vegan meal. I got to know Rosemary very well, though of course I had no idea what she looked like. She suddenly decided that she wanted to be baptised. "I've got this really lovely godmother in England," I told her. Which prompted them to ask me to be Rosemary's godmother. "We don't have them in the evangelical church," I said. But they insisted, so I agreed. I attended the ceremony the following week. It was a full immersion. As a present, I gave Rosemary the enamel and silver heart that my own godmother had given me.'

A couple of weeks later, Tony called her out of the blue one day. 'We've got to go away for a while,' he said. 'Can we leave Rosemary with you?'

'I told him of course. She was no trouble, so sweet, and she loved everybody. She had a beautiful nature, and thick, soft hair. She'd sit in my lap and snuggle up for a cuddle. A friend of mine took us to see the Disney film *Bedknobs and Broomsticks*, though I could only listen to it. After that, Rosemary came back with me to my apartment, and eventually Tony and Melinda returned to get her. I never had reason to suspect that Melinda was not Rosemary's real mother. They certainly related to each other as mother and daughter, and Rosemary was very affectionate towards her. But shortly afterwards, they just disappeared into the night. They did not tell me that they were leaving, and I didn't get a chance to say goodbye. I never heard from them again.'

'Rosemary', of course, was Yoko's daughter Kyoko. That Cox parked their small child with a poor seventeen-year-old blind girl, albeit a kind, loving and willing one, is a measure of his desperation that Kyoko must not be found. Meredith did not know, when she took her goddaughter in, that the Coxes were on the run from the authorities and the police, or that the most famous couple in the world were hunting them down. John and Yoko never discovered that Cox had left Kyoko in the care of a disabled teenager. Cox must have thought it would be the last place that anyone would look. Late in 1971, when a Houston judge ordered him to let Yoko visit her daughter, they did not stick around for it to happen, but fled yet again. 'I was not getting a fair shake at all,' he later commented, confoundingly.

Meredith had no reason to suspect anything untoward. She had no idea that there could be any connection to John Lennon. She didn't really follow the news at that age, she says. Few teens do. She didn't even know that Rosemary was oriental in appearance, because of course she could not see her. But the weirdest thing was that Meredith *had* seen her. Years earlier, when this cute little girl was a baby, in a private hotel in Manchester ... in the arms of her real mother, Yoko Ono ... who was in town to visit the Granada Television studios, where she would try to sell a film to Meredith's father, Johnnie Hamp. In his words, 'a film about bums'.[3]

The Coxes made a run for it to the home of a friend in Los Angeles, who was a member of another sect-y set-up: the Church of the Living Word, aka The Walk, practising a 'religious blend' of Pentecostalism, Eastern mysticism and the occult. Melinda and Tony signed up, and the family dwelled among the disciples in California and Iowa. Cox rose to become one of their elders and quasi-prophets. Eventually, he saw the light. He would later claim that the cult's founder, John Robert Stevens, believed himself to be the 'earthly incarnation of Jesus Christ', and that he practised hypnotism and 'forehead bonding', a type of mind control. He also accused Stevens of praying for the deaths of political leaders such as Jimmy Carter and Robert F. Kennedy. When the leader died in 1983, Cox said that they kept his body for eight months, in readiness for his resurrection. He lost faith in the sect and its teachings, divorced Melinda and left in 1977. His former second wife went on to marry another follower.

But there were kidnap nightmares for Kyoko yet to come. By this time known as Ruth Holman – what havoc these identity changes must have wreaked on the child – she was by now a pupil at a North Hollywood junior high school. Cox said that when word reached the leader that he was planning to leave, cult members were assigned to walk his daughter to and from school. So fearful was he that they would abduct her to prevent him from withdrawing from the sect, he turned up at the school early and took his daughter away himself. They fled town there and then, in what they stood up in, and never went back. The Walk would later refute his accusations.

Kyoko became herself again. Cox declared, as he would, that she 'came out of the experience smelling like a rose'. But, despite the fact that Yoko had been granted custody in March 1972, with the proviso that Kyoko must be raised in the US, it wasn't worth the paper it was written on. She never got Kyoko back. Cox also said that the Lennons 'nearly destroyed him'. That, too. He did eventually concede that Yoko must have suffered dreadfully. Too little, too late. She was not the only one. Because Yoko's appalling loss of her daughter rendered her incapable of being around children, John effectively lost Julian, too. Although there would be the odd reunion here and there, their relationship was never restored to what it had once almost been. It was not allowed to develop as it should have. After John and Yoko left England for New York, father and son would not see each other again for three years. There came the all too tragic time when Julian was effectively cut from his father's existence. Kyoko never saw her stepfather again. She was only reunited with her mother when she herself became one.

Cox remained an evangelical Christian, and made a film about his sect experiences, which he released in 1986. It was the first time that Yoko had received word of him or their daughter since the telegram of condolence they sent her in December 1980, after John died. She was prompted to publish a heart-wrenching open letter to the daughter whose childhood had been stolen from her.

'Dear Kyoko,' she wrote,

'All these years there has not been one day I have not missed you. You are always in my heart. However, I will not make any attempt to find you now as I wish to respect your privacy. I wish you all the best in the world. If you ever wish to get in touch with me, know that I love you deeply and would be very happy to hear from you. But you should not feel guilty if you choose not to reach me. You have my respect, love and support forever. Love, Mommy.'

*

'I have a strong feeling that she'd remember me,' says Meredith Plumb, née Hamp, of the now fifty-seven-year-old Kyoko Chan Cox. 'I have never tried to make contact with her. People who go to live in such sects are delicate. If I ever had the chance to meet her again, I would love to tell her, because I think she would be amazed, that she was the child I played with all those years ago in Milverton Lodge, and that I saw her in those days with my own eyes.'

*

Thirty years after she had last set eyes on her daughter, two decades on from John's murder, Yoko Ono Lennon was spotted one bitter New York day in her late husband's Strawberry Fields memorial garden in Central Park, opposite the Dakota building. Yoko sat bouncing a little girl with Japanese looks in her lap. Had time miraculously rewound? What she wouldn't have given. The adorable three-year-old was the spit of her mother, who was hovering nearby. The toddler's name was Emi and she was Yoko's granddaughter – the firstborn of Kyoko Chan Cox.[4]

Thirty years. For most of that time, Yoko had no idea whether

her child was even alive. How awful that she should have had to endure such loss.

Then, in November 1997, a few weeks after she had given birth, a breakthrough. Kyoko at last reached out to the woman she had been raised to regard as evil. What prompted her to call?

'I didn't feel it right for me to become a mother without at least letting my mother know that I'm alive and well,' explained charity worker Kyoko, who had made a new life with her devout Christian husband in Denver, Colorado. A year on, she accepted her mother's invitation to meet in person. Kyoko and Emi eventually made their way to see Mommy and Grandma in New York.

It is said that half of Mrs Lennon's billion-dollar fortune resides in a trust fund for her granddaughter. The other half is reckoned to be due to Yoko's and John's son Sean. What about Julian? Was he forced to sue the Lennon estate for a share of his father's fortune? It has been claimed, but he has denied it. He ought to have received a bequest as his birthright, without having to resort to legal action. If not, why didn't he?

CHAPTER 18

MAY

Why didn't the Lennons return to England, to their beloved Tittenhurst Park and the life they had built here? Because it was their firm belief that Kyoko was still in the States. They never gave up hope, who would, of getting her back. To have headed home would have been to relinquish the fight. Don't worry, Kyoko, Mummy's only looking … we are right here, waiting for you. They never wanted their little girl to think that they had abandoned all hope, and that they no longer cared. They needed to be right there for her when she turned up.

But they couldn't leave, even if they'd wanted to. Immersed in controversy thanks to overhanging drug offences, and having gained a reputation as aggravators and agitators as a result of having thrown their impactful, media-worthy weight behind dubious causes and extremist campaigns, they were all too aware that the Nixon administration wanted rid of John. As a subversive, law-breaking rock star, he was among the least desirable of all. The fact that his fans numbered in the tens of millions made him dangerously influential. His battle against deportation and his quest for the vital Green Card that would grant him permanent residence would be bitter and long. The spectre of the President and his henchmen loomed large. Unable to face leaving his wife there alone, and terrified to travel home for fear that US immigration authorities would prevent his re-entry, John stayed put. He would contradict himself about this in future interviews, declaring one minute that he had got the hell out because he was sick of Britain and the way we were treating Yoko; the next, that their New York sojourn was never intended to be permanent. We all change our minds. But when your global profile causes your every utterance to be recorded for posterity, to be pored over to eternity, discrepancies can confuse. There can be few greater human miseries than to be torn. In striving to do the right thing, we are so often driven to do the opposite. Yoko's personal grief and torment over her daughter compromised John's relationship with his son. Before judging him for his perceived coldness and indifference towards Julian, we should pause to consider that there were no winners here. Every individual involved was damaged. All souls, if only partly, were destroyed.

*

Little did John know that 31 August 1971 would be the last day he would ever spend on English soil. Their first home in New York was the uptown St Regis Hotel on East 55th and 5th Avenue. The Lennons set up home there in a pair of interconnected, gilded, glorious, full-on-butler-service suites. It was hardly John's style, but hey. From there, they would continue to run their empire, manage their campaign for world peace, record, film and mount art exhibitions. Within weeks, they had swapped the Astor-style glamour of the residence where the Bloody Mary was invented for a modest, borrowed semi-basement apartment in a townhouse at 105 Bank Street off Bleecker in the West Village. The street on which Sex Pistol Sid Vicious was to die of a drug overdose in 1979; where Mark Knopfler would own a grand house in the late 1980s. Their neighbours were John Cage – that once penniless, now prosperous composer pal of Peggy Guggenheim – and his male lover and collaborator, the dancer and choreographer Merce Cunningham. Cage, you'll recall, had travelled to Japan with Guggenheim in 1956, where twenty-three-year-old Yoko had worked as their guide and translator, and where Yoko had cheated on first husband Toshi Ichiyanagi to conceive Kyoko with Tony Cox in Guggenheim's bedroom … of which Peggy was all too aware, being present at the time. Paranoid that the FBI were on their case and had taken to tapping their phone, John and Yoko were soon taking the precaution of using Cage's.

This cobbled, multicultural end of town with its clash of ethnic cultures, cuisines and languages was a revelation. In so many ways, it felt like home. John recognised Liverpool at every ragged row and on every warehoused corner. He heard in the brash banter and drawl of Noo Yawkers the Scouse twang and slang of the city of his birth. He would soon be extolling wildly, to journalists and whoever else would listen, the virtues of the city and of the American lifestyle, its laidback-ness, the infinite choice, the effortlessness, the unencumbered freedom to be able to just walk and cycle about as if he were no one special. To do exactly as he pleased.

When John's and Yoko's visitors' visas expired in February 1972, they expected and planned to follow the usual renewal routine. They received notification from the INS,[1] however, that both visas had been cancelled, together with a warning that they must depart within two weeks. They could no longer fight their corner without lawyers, and they got lucky with Leon Wildes: a smart, measured legal eagle champing to take on the federal might and challenge their deportation order. Endless hearings and postponements ensued. Until that point, it had never been John's intention to make himself at home in America. He simply wanted permission to come and go, and to work there whenever he wished. It was only when Wildes floated the idea that they should seek inclusion in the category of 'persons of special artistic merit whose presence enhanced American cultural life', and guided them to tone down all the political jumping about, shut up about Nixon and focus on their anti-war, peace-promoting pursuits, that an idea began to dawn. John, Yoko and their entourage knew that they were under surveillance; their phone lines were tapped. They had known for some time that they were being followed. The UK's secret service MI5 now joined in, sharing evidence of John's support of the

Provisional IRA and of 'revolutionary' publications such as Tariq Ali's *Red Mole*, to which he had gifted funds and would share dialogue. John backed down only so much. He continued to thumb his nose and to voice strident opinions in interviews that attracted audiences into the millions. He and Yoko persisted in the making of music designed to provoke, as with 'Sunday Bloody Sunday', 'The Luck of the Irish' and the feminist single that arose out of a so-Yoko slogan, 'Woman Is the Nigger of the World' – which was banned, no shit, throughout the US.

At the epicentre, two mere human beings under intense public scrutiny and private pressure, striving valiantly to do the best they could. Separated from their offspring, no longer certain as to whom they could trust, they had now spent the best part of half a decade keeping themselves only unto each other. This was so alien to John, so at odds with his experience as a Beatle. He had never in his life, until then, had a woman at his neck around the clock. As a married father, he had enjoyed the full freedom of the unattached and fancy-free bachelor. The old-faithful pals upon whom he had long relied, Pete Shotton and Neil Aspinall, were three and a half thousand miles away, no longer on hand night and day to do his bidding. His Aunt Mimi, to whose bungalow on Sandbanks in Dorset he had been in the habit of popping down to hide out and recharge, immersing himself in the single-bed-egg-and-chipness of childhood, was now but a weekly voice at the end of a phone.

Perhaps most significantly of all, he was missing the zipless fuck[2]. During the Cynthia years, he had indulged his feverish sex drive whenever the urge kicked, with the kind of girls who didn't need him to love them. Now, he had 'only' Yoko to satisfy his lustful needs. By his wife's own assessment, she could never have been termed sexually adventurous. In their bed, John was bored. The crux came during the evening of Richard Nixon's re-election to the White House. John and Yoko attended a party, to which John rocked up exceedingly worse for wear. No sooner had he shrugged off his coat than he spied a woman sitting minding her own business. He made a beeline for her. He yanked her to her feet and led her into an adjoining room where a pile of guests' coats had grown. The next thing, the entire party became uneasily aware of what John and the woman were doing in there. Yoko, paralysed, clay-faced with passive indignance, just stood there. No one was going in to get their coat. Although she protested indifference, the humiliating experience proved a turning point, sowing seeds of doubt that would provoke an unexpected next move.

But first, a routine one. Anxious to make themselves less accessible and more secure, the Lennons had been looking for an apartment of their own. The spookily Gothic Dakota building on the Upper West Side of Central Park came to their attention. The fortress-like refuge of the rich and famous had a residents' board to vet potential purchasers. There were bound to be objections to this pair. Against the odds they were approved, their initial acquisition a seventh-floor, four-bed fantasy home with gorgeous views over the park, to which they would soon add a further four grand apartments. They engaged a medium to hold a séance for previous inhabitants. Who wouldn't? They had the interior stripped back, whited-out and installed with comforts and cats. A bit premature? John was not yet out of the woods with regard to his status. The INS were still on his case. But there was hope.

Less so for their short marriage. Yoko confronted the problem head-on. Their age gap must have felt significant at this point. John was only thirty-three, while Yoko was on the downslide to forty: a fragile age for any woman. However confident, we all fear loss of allure and impending menopause. We all doubt our hold on our man, no matter how proudly we project our feminine invincibility. She was vehemently opposed to them remaining a couple out of habit, just for the sake of it, only because they were married. Better that they should part than suffer the humiliation of the living death that a sexless, motion-going marriage tends to be. John clearly needed space. He craved passion. A whole lot more of it. Instead of going out and pulling birds behind her back, as he had always done behind Cyn's, husband and wife agreed together that he must not be bone idle, and was now free to heat-seek extramarital bed partners.

Unusual? Millions of couples apparently live this way. They simply tend not to share the ins and outs with family and friends, never mind the population of planet Earth. Just as John was now making music independently of Yoko – his next album, *Mind Games*, would not be a typical JohnandYoko production, would bear not a whiff of Spector, and would, while offering songs honouring his relationship with his wife, be a completely solo effort – he would have an independent sex life, too. For the nagging ache, a remedy was found – guess what, by Yoko. John must spend time in Los Angeles, she decreed, where he could lark to a prick's content without embarrassing She Who Must Be Obeyed. He would need a companion to keep an eye, hold his hand, whatever else. For this, Mrs Lennon selected May Pang.

*

To this day, May maintains that she and John were deeply in love. He had never occurred to her as a potential love interest during her earliest days as part of their team, she says, before the Lennons had even relocated to the US. She had worked diligently in a Girl Friday capacity, assisting on film shoots, recordings and in the mounting of art exhibitions, cheerfully receiving whatever tasks they assigned to her. She was the twenty-two-year-old good Catholic daughter of Chinese immigrants. She was pretty, sweet, kind, inventive and smart. She had hip-length glossy black hair, and kept her head down. The suggestion that she should become John's concubine shocked her. Particularly as it came from his apparently possessive and adhesive wife.

Everybody loved May. She listened to her mother; would always extend a helping hand. Her better judgement was late to work the day she boarded a flight to Los Angeles with John, the latter insisting to the many media reps who quizzed him that there was nothing remotely wrong with his marriage and that he and Yoko were very much together. May moved into a borrowed West Hollywood apartment with him, and then migrated with him from place to place, patiently packing his belongings and seeing to the necessary. She put up with his endless phone conversations with

Yoko, whom he needed more than ever; with his interminable pleadings with Mother to be allowed to come home. At times, there would be more than twenty calls a day. May gritted her teeth, grinned, bore it, soldiered on as his lover, his muse, his collaborator, his dogsbody, his nursemaid, his excuse. He declared undying love to her, she said. If he did, he probably meant it in the moment, though one has to wonder whether sobriety ever uttered those hollow words. Because he also dumped her, time and again, leaving her sobbing as she gathered up her pieces. She humoured his mad cavortings with fellow hellraisers Ringo, Harry Nilsson, Klaus Voormann and Keith Moon. She accompanied him on benders. She dealt with the fall-out, that infamous night when he fell into the Troubadour club with a sanitary towel stuck to his forehead and made headlines wherever you cared to look. She turned a blind one when he got spiteful, absorbed his abuse, wiped his ass, cleaned up his puke. Crucially, with Yoko out of the way, she encouraged him to restore his relationship with Julian, whom he had not seen for three years, to whom he had spoken only once or twice in the interim and who was now, where did *that* go, eleven. It was she who fixed it for them to greet Julian and his mother off the ship that conveyed them to New York, and who sorted it for them to extend their visit to spend more time with John in LA. She fussed and cooed over Julian. She befriended Cynthia. She said and did all the right things. She could tell the difference between want, need and desire. She provided uncomplainingly.

May convinced herself that John was The One. She remembered their fourteen, some say eighteen, months together as mostly blissful. She told me that they'd planned to buy a house on Long Island. She said that John returned to her again and again, long after he and Yoko were reunited, but by then behind Yoko's back. She would publish a book, *Loving John*, about what he had termed his 'Lost Weekend', and the part that she had played in it. She was lamenting the book's tone and content by the time we got together in 2019, revealing how it had been souped-up by the publishers for 'impact' and that it had not presented her quite as she had wished to be perceived. She would do it differently now. It does read as though theirs was the be-all, end-all love affair. My gut tells me that May was used. To many who were there and who witnessed it, she was no more than a PA with benefits. An on-off shag. She was not paid for the duration of the relationship; was left without a roof over her head, and was ultimately dumped, unemployed and surplus to requirements. No provision was made to compensate her for her time and dedication. I really liked her. To think of the way she'd be treated left me distressed.

May is knocking seventy. Divorced from record producer Tony Visconti, she is the mother of two of his adult children. She struggles financially. She heaves with regret.

'What on earth made you agree to Yoko's proposition in the first place?' I asked her at lunch. She shrugged.

'I couldn't say no to him.' She smiled thinly. 'Nobody could. Plus, he needed me. A hundred per cent.'

*

He needed Yoko. Prodigal son needed Mother. Calm down, Johnny, wait a minute. Not yet. Back we go to New York anyway, and crikey, he's only still with that May. On rumbled John's case against the INS, Leon Wildes whipping up the pace to the point that he started fantasising about calling Nixon himself as a witness. As if. But then came Watergate, in the nick of time, its result the shaming and toppling of Lennon's nemesis – the same month, August 1974, that John's case went to the US Court of Appeals.

John and May had relocated from the posh Pierre Hotel to a small penthouse, 'the Tower', in the 'Southgate' apartment building at 434 East 52nd Street on Sutton Place. It was in this perfectly-formed apartment, in which the kitchen window gave them access to the entire roof, where they would famously claim to have seen a UFO. John referenced the moment in the liner notes of his next album, *Walls and Bridges* and in the song 'Nobody Told Me': 'There's UFOs over New York /And I ain't too surprised.' May reckoned that some four hundred sightings of the same saucer were reported, and that all independent descriptions matched. Contrary to claims that John had shouted at the was-it-wasn't-it a spacecraft in the hope that it might take him away, May explained: 'He didn't call out to it. He later said he wished it had taken us with it.' They holed up cosily in the cute penthouse, hanging with close friends Mick and Bianca Jagger, and also with 'PaulandLinda'. So much for all those 'exclusives' that Paul and John had fallen out terminally. No time for fussing and fighting, my friend. Sure, they had done their share of trading musical snipes, and had left the fans wincing. Paul's mournful 'Dear Friend' on *Wild Life* is hard to listen to. His '3 Legs' on *Ram* pointedly attacks the other Beatles, while 'Too Many People' from the same album goes for the 'JohnandYoko' jugular with the line: 'That was your first mistake/You took your lucky break and broke it in two.' John's efforts were more brutal. In the stark, poignant 'God' on *John Lennon/Plastic Ono Band*, he not only turns his back on the Beatles but forsakes all religion and idols, making clear that nothing else matters now, only him and Yoko. The *Imagine* album's 'How Do You Sleep?' is his most vicious assault of all on Paul: 'The only thing you done was *Yesterday*/And since you've gone you're just *another day*'. Even worse: 'Those freaks were right when they said you was dead' – referring to the 'Paul is dead' rumours that started to circulate in 1969, after he traversed the Abbey Road zebra without his shoes. According to some media reports, they now regarded each other with such disgust that John and Paul could no longer be in the same room. Funny, that: they'd only just jammed together in a recording studio in LA. Julian came to stay with Dad again, this time without Mum. They all cramped together in the little apartment, where May lovingly fed and took care of him, basking in the glow. At last, John and Julian had something in common: guitars. Back home, Julian was having lessons. Come on, now, try *this* chord.

*

On 14 September 1974, a Saturday, the *Melody Maker*'s Chris Charlesworth took himself to the Commodore Hotel[4] near Grand Central Station for Beatlefest: the first Fabs fan event of its kind.

'False rumours suggested that John was there, wearing heavy disguise,' said Charlesworth. 'May attended alone, armed with a wad of cash to acquire interesting memorabilia. She clocked me and asked for advice on what to buy. I suggested she spend John's money on some bootleg LPs, a bit of merchandise and some old pictures of the Beatles in Hamburg, taken in 1960.' Among them was the portrait shot by Jürgen Vollmer that wound up gracing the sleeve of a contentious covers album.

'In my mind, it was John's masterpiece,' declares Leo Sayer. 'It's a stunning album that I make sure to play once a month, just to remind myself how pop music should be played and how it should sound.'

Sick to the molars with the many production and legal shenanigans over an innocuous collection of much-loved songs that he had recorded in LA and that would eventually be released in 1975 as *Rock'n'Roll*, John had begun to write for *Walls and Bridges*. Its theme took shape as a hymn to his wife. Its most arresting track was '#9 Dream', sounding a thousand times better today than ever it did back then. Magic in the air, was there magic? Listen. I never tire of it, though sometimes it's too painful to hear. That's May's voice whispering his name there, not because John 'convinced' her to record the bits that Yoko would normally have voiced, but because the booked female vocalist didn't show up on the day. Ever-willing May took to the mic. This is according to David Thoener, an engineer at the recording sessions. 'Surprise Surprise (Sweet Bird of Paradox)' and 'Whatever Gets You Thru the Night' blared their pal Elton John on vocals and piano. It's all right, it's all right. The latter became John's first solo Number One in the US. Its success, striking dead the statistic that John remained the only ex-Beatle never to have scored a solo chart-topper, obliged John to honour a handshake deal that if it hit the top, he would join the Rocketman on stage at Madison Square Garden and deliver it live.[5]

'I only ever met John once,' says Paul Gambaccini, recalling a night when they could have been killed together.

'It was 1974. He came up to see Elton in the Boston Garden so that he could get a grasp of the set before they did the show in New

York. After Elton's gig, we all got on a private plane. There was a storm, maybe an early-season snowstorm. The flight was horribly bumpy. We were going up and down, up and down, and a few on board, Kiki Dee included, were terrified. Connie Pappas, who was Elton's manager John Reid's American representative, was sitting next to me, and she was not taking this well. I said, "Connie, *relax*. There's never been a plane crash this famous. This would make the Buddy Holly crash look second-division. John Lennon and Elton John, on the same flight: it ain't gonna happen.'"

That Thanksgiving night of the gig, 28 November, while John was getting Elton's guitarist Davey Johnstone to tune his black Fender Telecaster backstage, Elton mysteriously said to Paul, 'The third song.'

'*Huh?* What does he mean by this? I go sit in the audience – I have my backstage pass so that I can go back and forth – and Elton makes his introduction to John Lennon. You hear it, it's on the record. Well, if the top of the building could be levitated simply by the force of energy coming from an audience, Madison Square Garden would have been topless. The minute he said, "*John Lennon!*" … *WHOOSSSSHHHHH!* I've NEVER felt anything like it in my life. The absolute enthusiasm and love for John was unbelievable. No one knew it was coming.

'We did a half-hour radio programme on this, which is on the BBC Listen Again, from the series *One Night Only*, called *When John Met John*. It included a line we were supposed to pass by a higher-up at Radio 4. Davey Johnstone recalled that John Lennon was quite nervous – as everyone agrees. And John said, "It was at this point that I would usually get some fanny." Erm – meaning, *sex* – just before a show. The executive said, "Under the circumstances, 'fanny' can be broadcast on BBC Radio 4."'

As a recording payback, John appeared on Elton's cover of 'Lucy in the Sky with Diamonds', recorded at Colorado's Caribou Studios high up in the Rocky Mountains.

'Elton wanted to do a cover, a one-off non-album single, and he had narrowed it down to a choice of two: "Lucy" and "Rockin' Roll Baby" by the Stylistics,' recalls Gambaccini. 'But there's a line in "Rockin' Roll Baby" about an orthopaedic shoe. Elton didn't feel comfortable singing about an orthopaedic shoe! So, it was "Lucy". John does his Winston O'Boogie guitars on that. That and "Whatever Gets You" are the two songs that they are going to play, both of which are Number One singles. And then, *the third song* that Elton had flagged up to me. Which was "I Saw Her Standing There."'

Lennon's famous intro to the song that night went like this: 'We tried to think of a number to finish off with, so I can get out of here and be sick, and we thought we'd do a number of an old, estranged fiancé of mine called Paul. This is one I never sang. It's an old Beatle number, and we just about know it.'

John would later insist he had no idea that his wife was in the crowd. The disingenuity is baffling. It was he who had sorted the tickets; she who had sent a lackey back to the dressing room with good-luck notes and the white gardenias worn by Elton and John onstage.

'She was backstage afterwards,' said John, 'and there was just that moment when we saw each other and like, it's like in the movies, you know, when time stands still. And there was silence. Everything went silent, y'know, and we were just sort of lookin' at each other.'

Were they? Despite his words, the idea that they got back together after the concert that night could be little more than romantic wishful thinking with hindsight. John scurried off to the after-show party at the Pierre Hotel with May, telling lurking journalists, 'It was good fun, but I wouldn't like to do it for a living.'[6] Yoko sloped off home. She and John would not be reunited for almost three more months.

There was John, as they so often say, tragically unaware of the fact that he had just played his last-ever gig. For what was that if not Beatlemania revisited, a re-enactment of the bad old days? Get on, give 'em twenty minutes max, wow them, thrill them, drill them, leave them pissing for more. In those enervating few moments with Elton on stage at the Garden, he had tasted again the love of a live audience, the joy of doing what he did best, the fruition of ten thousand penurious hours spent slaving and groaning in Hamburg. Imagine it all rewinding at breakneck speed through his pent-up mind. He'd had half an eye on McCartney out there all this time, trawling the world, clocking up huge hits, doing and getting what *he'd* wanted, being the Big I Am ex-Beatle as a grown-up solo artist with his own band, back on the road, unconfined and uncompromised by Fabness. Being a rocker, a proper musician. Now, thanks to Elton, John had been given the chance to relive it a little. His ears were still ringing from it, they would throb for weeks. All my loving, Johnny baby. All my loving. It was still *there*! Maybe it would always be there. Shouldn't we give it another go, just to make sure?

Amid sensational babble of a comeback, a world tour, a Beatles reunion, of sailing triumphantly home to England on the *QE2* to tour again, to start over – which was what the masses were hoping for, baying for, they'd been begging for it for years – John knew that he was done. The Lost Weekend had taken its toll. That last hurrah of hellraising had drained him. This was the moment when he turned his back on the madness, the drugs, the floozing, the boozing. This was John, waking up to what mattered, to whom he truly loved. This was John, the bereaved, abandoned nipper, the callow groove cat, the fuckless spouse, the surly Beatle, the snidey cunt, the knackered activist, the muso with nothing left to prove. So why keep proving? He may as well prove *bread*. May? Forget *her*, this was never about her.

Not long now. John would soon be kidding the world that he'd turned his back on music, that he'd gone and buried himself in the pillows. The world would wait with bated breath. So when's he coming out?

Above: A new-look Beatles seated outside Brian Epstein's house in Belgravia.

© *Getty Images/Jan Olofsson*

Below: The Beatles perform their last ever live concert, on the roof of the Apple Corps building, Savile Row. © *Getty Images/Express*

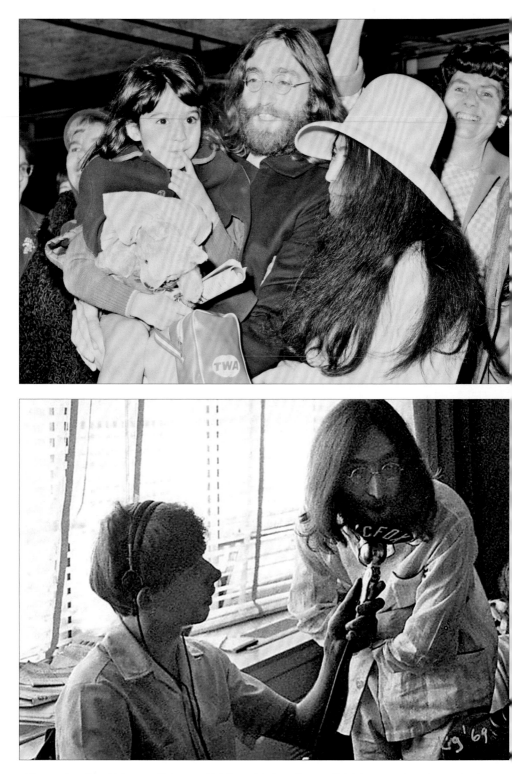

Above: Apple of his eye: John and Yoko with her first child, his step-daughter, Kyoko.
© *Getty Images/Stroud*

Below: The definitive DJ: Roger Scott interviews John during the Montreal bed-in, 1969.
Collection Lesley-Ann Jones

Above: Sweet nothings on the infamous 'Lost Weekend' with May Pang.

© Getty Images/Art Zelin

Below: 'Once I had a secret love … and then there was Bowie': John and David at the 17th annual Grammy Awards. Uris Theatre, NYC. © Getty Images/Ron Galella

Left: Yoko clings to John as they leave court in London following charges of marijuana possession and obstructing police.

© Getty Images/Bettmann

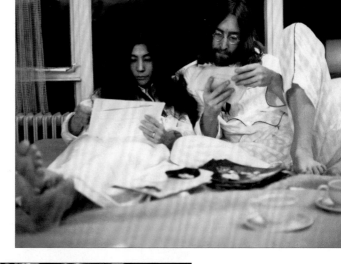

Right: During the 'Bed-In for Peace' at the Amsterdam Hilton.

© Getty Images/Mark and Colleen Hayward

Left: The Dirty Mac (comprising Eric Clapton, Mitch Mitchell, John Lennon, Keith Richards and Yoko Ono) play their one-time special in London, in 1968.

© Getty Images/Mark and Colleen Hayward

Above: 'Didn't we have a lovely time the day we went to Bangor . . .': the Beatles join Maharishi Mahesh Yogi in North Wales, ahead of their sojourn in Rishikesh.

© Getty Images/Archive Photos

Below: With love from me to you: Julian Lennon at the Golden Rose/Montreux Rock Festival, Switzerland, 1986, where the author interviewed him. *Collection Lesley-Ann Jones*

Above: Starr turn with an Ox who was no ass: Ringo, Barbara Bach, the author and John Entwistle at Fulham Town Hall, London, March 1985, for the filming of the video for Willie & the Poor Boys (Ronnie Lane ARMS appeal). *Collection Lesley-Ann Jones*

Below left: The author with May Pang. London, September 2019. *Collection Lesley-Ann Jones*

Below right: . . . and with Sir Paul McCartney at the LIPA graduation ceremony, 26 July 2019. *© David Stark*

Above left: Andy Peebles with John and Yoko at the Hit Factory NYC, 6 December 1980.

Above right: Andy and Sean Lennon on the train from Tokyo to Karuizawa, 1983.

Middle: Andy with Sean and Yoko at the Mampei Hotel, Karuizawa. Note Sean on the left, getting ready to throw a snowball. © *Andy Peebles Collection (and above)*

Below left: An evening with Earl Slick in St. Leonard's-on-Sea, Hastings, 2019. The man himself stands in front of a photo of him performing with Yoko. © *Lesley-Ann Jones*

Below right: The author with Slicky at Balthazar restaurant, London, 2019. © *Martin Barden*

Above: 'Imagine . . .' John's mosaic memorial in the Strawberry Fields garden, Central Park, NYC, opposite the Dakota building. © *Lesley-Ann Jones*

Below: John Winston Lennon. Beatle, father, husband. 9 October 1940 – 8 December 1980. © *Getty Images/Allan Tannenbaum*

CHAPTER 19

RESURRECTION

As to whether John's house-husband years were genuinely that, or a psychological lapse concealed, we can keep wondering. My guess is that what he was going through was a combination of the two, with other pressures and disturbances thrown in. For the millions who fell for his puzzling reincarnation as reformed partner, parent and homemaker, there are as many who see through the artifice to a sclerotic, incapacitated creature who had renounced the struggle for much-needed time out. There would come the day when the sycophants and flunkeys spilled their beans about his life behind closed doors; some to agents of 'assassin' Albert Goldman, others in tomes of their own design. We can choose what we want to believe, always mindful. There are three sides to every story: his, hers and the truth. The deeper we delve into the black, the nearer we get to the white. Nothing, no one, nowhere is ever cut and dried.

May swears to this day that the 'black widow' Yoko reeled in her catch of the day with the promise that she could cure him of his nicotine addiction, using magic that had worked on her. She was putting spells on John now? Reducing him to catalepsy? Yoko has stated for the record that it was John who was desperate to return to *her*, that it was he who was putting the pressure on. He chased her and chased her until she caught him … and in the end, both gave in. Sayonara, Miss Mayfly.[1]

The Lennons went public with their marriage-mending at the seventeenth annual Grammy Awards, staged at New York's Uris Theater on 1 March 1975. What a bizarre occasion that was. Not that John was on the receiving end, he was presenting. His walk-on part with Paul Simon to read out the nominees and announce the winner for Record of the Year descended into farce when Simon's former partner turned adversary Art Garfunkel came forward to accept the trophy on behalf of Olivia Newton-John and her producer John Farrar, for 'I Honestly Love You'. Art for Art's sake? Nobody's knees went, but the froideur was tangible. Unable to resist a gag at the expense of the five-years-estranged creators of the album of the seventies, *Bridge Over Troubled Water*, John quizzed the golden-haloed one: 'Are you guys getting back together again?' Quick as a rattlesnake came the crack at the former Beatle: 'Are *you* guys getting back together again?'

How odd yet how right John and Yoko looked together. She in a skinny marabou-trimmed white gown, her thick hair flowing to her hips, just like May's, her face serene and glowing; he a fancy-dressed cross between a Dickensian bookkeeper and a French librarian, in black velvet frock coat, beret, white silk scarf and battered tan biker boots, a glittering 'Elvis' brooch and a white gardenia on his lapel. Mingling afterwards with winners and guests – Marvin Hamlisch, Stevie Wonder, Roberta Flack, 'PaulandLinda' – the latter there to accept a gong for McCartney and Wings' masterpiece 'Band on the Run', which took Best Pop Vocal, and their old Beatles engineer Geoff Emerick, who claimed Best Engineered Recording for the same album – they had eyes only for each other.

Or did they? A few red-carpet shots reveal John flirting with a delicious specimen right over Yoko's head. The handbag-clutching object of John's fascination was fashionably androgynous, ashen and gaunt, dressed in white tie and Fedora, sporting cheekbones that could have cut coal. Good guess, David Bowie.

*

Come together. John and Yoko buried their differences and renewed their marriage vows in a private candlelit ceremony in their own home. They also honeymooned at the Dakota. In a beat, forty-two-year-old Mother was with child. The father, thirty-four, was ecstatic. Given her advanced age – relatively normal nowadays for child-bearing, still chancing it back then – together with her sad history of miscarriage, Yoko was forced to slow down, rest up, and let John take charge and run around after her. He did so tenderly, with patience and love, in ways that might have made Cynthia and Julian squirm. So much, too much, was riding on this pregnancy: not only all the poor little Ono Lennon babies who didn't make it, but the children they no longer had. For John's reconciliation with Yoko damaged paternal rebuilding with Julian. There would be, after that, only a couple of visits more. Julian would see his father for the last time in Florida, when he was turning sixteen. Of Kyoko, there was still no sign.

*

Let the music play on. So it did, before John retired to the kitchen and the bed chamber and gave in to those fabled house-husband years. The troubled *Rock'n'Roll* album made its at-long-last appearance, as did the single he had helped Bowie with that January, 'Fame': a happy accident, this, a studio interruption that turned into a jam; a bit of why-not improv that acquired a life of its own and crystallised into a song, much as 'Under Pressure' would emerge from Swiss mountain air for David and Queen a few years later. 'Fame' occurred during David's recording of a cover of the Beatles' 'Across the Universe' for his new album *Young Americans*. It featured Carlos Alomar, and a mean young guitarist by the name of Earl Slick.

That Bowie worshipped Lennon was no secret. He'd banged on about it often enough. The ex-Beatle had gone to his hedonism. They'd met in Los Angeles, he told me, during John's Lost Weekend. I lunched from time to time with David in New York while working there as a music journalist, before he married Iman. He lent me his house on Mustique, to write the first draft of my first biography of Freddie Mercury. The crazy pair went out to play, according to David, when John was on yet another break from May and far away from Yoko. They gender-bender-ed about, John indulging again that 'inner fag' of his. What larks. They later 'hooked up': 'There was a whore in the middle, and it wasn't either of us,' David smirked. 'At some point in proceedings, she left. I think it was a she. Not that we minded.' By the time they made it back to New York, the ambisextrous pair were 'lifelong friends'.

It was the seventies. Rock'n'roll, ya know? Bowie had Jagger, too, remember? No big surprise. But 'Fame' was. The single gifted David his first US Number One. It irked him, truth be told, that he couldn't have had it to himself, but that it took the connection with Lennon to get it up there.

John finally won his case against the INS that October. His four-year fight for the right to remain was won. No more endless applications for temporary permission, no more avoiding flights that might stray beyond US airspace and scupper his re-entry. Yet, when VJ day came, there was no time for glory. The Lennons were in hospital, on John's thirty-fifth birthday, to bring their new baby into the world. A tortuous, precarious C-section later, a son: Sean Taro Lennon. Sean being Irish Gaelic for John, and the Japanese Taro denoting 'firstborn son'. Did it even cross their minds what such a statement might do to Julian? That simple routine act, the naming of his half-brother, told John's actual firstborn son exactly where he stood.

*

Much has been made of the fact that John's recording contract with EMI and Capitol at last expired in February 1976; that no longer having a label home was the real reason for his retiring from music and retreating into domesticity. But the decision, even if subconscious, had been made fourteen months earlier, post-Elton, in November 1974. Now, with his precious newborn in his arms, as far as the outside world was concerned at least, he'd downed tools. He'd lost interest in the music business. He couldn't be bothered to listen to anything, beyond the sound of a helpless baby breathing and gurgling. Even Sean's squalling wee-small-hours cries were heard as melodies. He surrendered himself to fatherhood, becoming the devoted, hands-on dad he'd never had, the parent he ought to have been to Julian. He hadn't been ready, then, not in his early twenties, but he was ready now. Everything he did for Sean completed John: in singing to his child, he felt sung-to; in reading to him, read-to; in bathing him, cleansed; in giving, gifted; in caring, cared-for; in loving unconditionally, he finally got the point of love. The baggage of his own pitiful childhood fell away. John felt reborn. Though it is true that he baked bread, and derived enormous pleasure from creating food for others to enjoy, it was not as if he became a full-time cook. The part about not making music anymore? A bit hit and myth. He never really stopped writing songs, because that had long been a primary form of communication. He captured them, together with his monologues, quirky-voice pieces and experimental all-kinds on cassette after cassette, always meaning to get around to setting up his own studio so that he could record things properly. If only he could figure out how to make stuff work. If only he could be bothered.

'I don't buy this idea that he gave up completely and turned himself into a house husband. It doesn't ring true,' reflects Michael Watts, who knew the Lennons well enough in New York during the seventies.

'I'm sure he did some of it – baking bread and changing nappies and whatever. But I think the truth is that he'd lost some sort of impetus. Maybe he was too happy and contented. Maybe he needed, the way most artists need, to be unsettled and troubled in order to be able to create. He didn't have the same kind of drive that he'd had as a Beatle, that's for sure. To his complete chagrin, I'd wager. He saw McCartney going out on world tours and being this tremendously celebrated figure, representing the Beatles without John being involved, and that must have been a source of huge irritation to him. At the very least. So their great rivalry continued.'

Looking back in 1980, during his interview with *Playboy*, John was still flogging his house-husband years. 'I've been baking bread and looking after the baby,' he repeated. The interviewer appeared doubtful, suggesting that John surely must have been working on secret projects all this time, down in the dungeons of the Dakota.

'Are you kidding?' scoffed John. 'Because bread and babies, as every housewife knows, is a full-time job. After I made the loaves, I felt like I had conquered something. But as I watched the bread being eaten, I thought, well, Jesus, don't I get a gold record or knighted or nothing?'

Why did he make that choice? 'There were many reasons,' John explained. 'I had been under obligation or contract from the time I was twenty-two until well into my thirties. After all those years, it was all I knew. I wasn't free. I was boxed-in. My contract was the physical manifestation of being in prison. It was more important to face myself and face that reality than to continue a life of rock'n'roll … and to go up and down with the whims of either your own performance or the public's opinion of you. Rock'n'roll was not fun anymore. I chose not to take the standard options in my business... going to Vegas and singing your great hits, if you're lucky, or going to hell, which is where Elvis went.'

John fostered the impression of reclusiveness because he fancied the idea. He read up on Howard Hughes, the eccentric OCD-afflicted tycoon. He warmed to the theme of Greta Garbo, demanding to be alone. He loved the mystery, the enigma. He kept diaries. He kept in regular touch with his Aunt Mimi, via calls, long letters and copious cards, and got her to send him his school uniform, books, her china, anything and everything that reminded him of home and childhood. He kept saying that, sooner or later, he'd go back to England, his England. He never made it. Or did he? His aunt would insist to her dying day that John undertook the voyage from New York by sea, and that they'd had one last private moment at Sandbanks together, just the two of them. Nobody else knew that he had been.

Delusion? Wishful thinking? *SongLink* owner and publisher David Stark wanted to find out. He drove to Sandbanks to see Mimi not long after John died. He went shopping for her, she cooked him egg and chips, and they spent the afternoon and evening examining

John's drawing books, his *Daily Howl*, and raking through drawersful of his belongings. What the fans wouldn't give.

'She was a lovely old lady,' said David. 'Not at all the old witch she's so often been made out to be. Would John have made a point of keeping in such touch with her, had she been that bad? Surely, he'd have brushed her off and forgotten about her. She told me he'd come from America to visit her, incognito. In her mind, she was convinced that he came. In fact, she was adamant, and kept saying that she wasn't mistaken. She had all her marbles, so I had no reason to doubt her. He did travel extensively towards the end of his life. We know that he went to Japan a few times, to Grand Cayman, Hong Kong, Egypt, South Africa. Why not England? He could have come by boat, which would have docked at Southampton, only just down the road from Mimi's. Immigration records are a legal requirement, of course, and what would he have done about his passport? But just supposing someone else was in on it, and that they crossed somebody's palm to turn a blind eye. Anything's possible, especially when you're that rich. I like to think that it was true, and that he really did see her one last time, after ten long years of separation. A moment to cherish for Mimi, if he did. Who knows?'

*

A baby and a Green Card changed John's life. Once he was at liberty to leave America without fear, the first trip he wanted to make was to Yoko's homeland. He even committed to learning Japanese before travelling to Tokyo with his wife and toddler. They would remain in Japan for most of summer 1977. On that first visit, they entertained the wider Ono family in style at a party in Karuizawa, the Nagano Prefecture resort in the shadow of active volcano Mount Asama. Yoko had been taken there for holidays as a child. They stayed in the traditional Mampei Hotel, a significant destination in the Lennon story. Both town and hotel make much of their connection to John and Yoko. John enjoyed anonymity there. He and Yoko indulged in a programme of clean eating and exercise that would leave them rejuvenated. September saw them in full tourist mode in Kyoto, once the seat of the Emperor and now the cultural capital, before heading back to Tokyo and on home. There would be two further holidays in Japan, deepening John's love of the country and his appreciation of its culture.

All the while, Yoko took care of business – which included the interminable, hair-tearing unravelling of old Beatle business – while John (and the nanny) took care of Sean. His astute wife swelled their fortune with acquisitions of fine art, real estate, farms, cattle, a bunch of bulls, even (presumably plundered) treasures from ancient Egypt. They created an Egyptian room in one of their apartments at the Dakota, to make an actual mummy in a sarcophagus feel at home. They bought a waterfront mansion in Palm Beach, Florida, where John adored sitting quietly by himself, just staring out to sea. The ocean was luring him. Perhaps he was winding himself back to a long-ago moment in Rishikesh, when he consulted folky Donovan over a song about his mother, and about the childhood he'd never had.

'He asked me to help him with the images that he could use in lyrics for a song about this subject,' Donovan recalled. So I said, "Well, when you think of the song, where do you imagine yourself?" And John said, "I'm at a beach and I'm holding hands with my mother, and we're walking together." I helped him with a couple of lines – "Seashell eyes/windy smile" – for the Lewis Carroll, *Alice in Wonderland* feel that John loved so much.'

The song being 'Julia'.

The Lennons would soon add to their formidable portfolio a Cold Spring Harbor, Long Island, retreat. Imagine no possessions … It was during escapes to the have-yachts hamlet on the island's wealthy North Shore that John rediscovered sailing, picturing himself in a boat on a river, rowing his cares away at Sandbanks. He had succeeded in teaching Sean to swim. Father and son would now learn the ropes and take to the briny.

Meanwhile, for Yoko, it was all about alchemy and auras, angels and spirit guides. She seemed obsessed with numerology, astrology, Tarot, clairvoyants and psychics. Esotericism ruled, to the point that the family could barely move without it having been predicted by a seer or written in the numbers, the cards or the stars. So astute in business, yet so confoundingly dependent on divination. We mustn't judge, but come on, such insecurity. By the age of forty-seven, when Sean was only five, his mother was using heroin again. She concealed it from John. So much for togetherness.

*

Forty is forty. Some accept and soldier on. Some slide into denial, and keep on kidding themselves. Some rebel, and fall about fornicating, or making idiots of themselves in other ways. Others still, those with the wherewithal, commit to grand gestures or journeys by which they will forever be changed. This was John, on the threshold of what became a life-threatening odyssey. So profound was the experience, it shocked him into shape. It would cause him to kill phoney homemaker John. To resurrect the greatest rock star one last time.

CHAPTER 20

REPLAY

Spring 1980 saw John restless for further adventure. While his wife was busy getting herself off smack, he was planning a little excursion. Though he had fantasised as a child about running away to sea, and had tried to imagine what life on the ocean wave had been like for his father and grandfather, he had never yet ventured farther than Long Island Sound. Now it was time.

Yoko's trusted numerologist having issued warnings about adverse compass points, and having prescribed the most beneficial direction in which to head, John would sail the wild North Atlantic from Newport, Rhode Island to Hamilton, Bermuda, a jaunt of some seven hundred miles. A small crew was assembled by his sailing coach Tyler Coneys, and a suitable boat was chosen: the forty-three-foot Hinckley sloop *Megan Jaye*.[1] The team set sail in fine weather on the morning of Thursday, 5 June, at the start of the hurricane season. Conditions looked favourable. Then out of the Bermuda Triangle, a storm arose. In a region infamous for tropical cyclones, this at first appeared routine. But the storm soon swelled into a tempest. All were terrified. One by one, the crew fell sick. Only the skipper managed to hold tight, but after two days was passing out. Although petrified at the walls of waves and by the prospect that the *Megan Jaye* could sink, John sent Captain Hank down to rest and took the wheel himself. With precipitous waves constantly smashing him as he shook, lashed to the helm, it's a miracle that his glasses stayed on his face. He could barely see out of his brine-stung eyes. He could give in and they'd all go down, or he could confront the elements and try to save them. Twenty minutes into his shift, the relentless swell still coming at him, John remembered his balls. He fought back. He howled and yelled like a banshee. With no idea where his courage was coming from, he hurled sea-dog ditties and crusty ballads from the top of his lungs, and cackled madly in the face of near-certain death. So now he knew, *this* was what it was like! He would later describe it as the most fantastic experience he'd ever had. He had exorcised his ghosts, was newly empowered and felt invincible.

'Once I accepted the reality of the situation, something greater than me took over and all of a sudden I lost my fear,' he recounted in his *Playboy* interview. 'I actually began to enjoy the experience, and I started to shout out old sea shanties in the face of the storm, screaming at the thundering sky.'

After the storm, a calm. They made Bermuda in six days. On 11 June, John wrote in the sloop's logbook: 'Dear Megan there is no place like nowhere.' He scribbled a note for the captain; sketched a self-portrait and one of the boat. He drew it sailing off into the sunset.

For John, who had not been in England for nearly a decade, this British Overseas Territory was as home as home got. Although the setting was lushly tropical, Bermuda's colonial culture felt wonderfully familiar. He took a house called Undercliff a couple of miles outside the capital, Hamilton, in a neighbourhood known as Fairylands. He was enchanted to find red pillar boxes and telephone kiosks, and that cars were driven on the left. He sent for four year-old Sean, who flew down with his nanny and one of their assistants. Yoko would come later, for the briefest of visits. The plan was to stay for a couple of months. Father and son soon established a beach routine, swimming in the sea, building sandcastles and sailing in a borrowed dinghy. Hey, Julian, remember when we did all this? Of course you don't. They found the street markets and Hamilton's quaint Front Street. Among its pastel pillars lurked island musicians. John immersed himself in their sounds. The locals, accustomed to rich, famous types invading their island on holiday, were unruffled by the global icon moving among them, and let him be. The extraordinary beauty of the thirty-six-acre hilltop Botanical Gardens with its giant weeping figs and palms drew them back and back. It was here that they stumbled upon the exquisite yellow freesia called 'Double Fantasy' that would spark an idea for an album. It was here, for the first time in five long years, that John realised he had it in him to record again.

Bermuda was a kind of homecoming. This would have dawned when he and Sean went poking around in St George's. Where, in the oldest-inhabited English town in the New World, they could not help but happen upon St Peter's Church ...

The simple limestone edifice, four hundred years old, dazzles white against unbroken blue. It stands atop a flight of some twenty-odd wide steps. Twenty flight rock ... would John pause to pay homage to his old hero Eddie Cochran, or would he bound straight up, amazed, to peer inside? The coincidence is uncanny. Not that this, the oldest-surviving Anglican church in continuous use outside the British Isles, has much in common with St Peter's Church in Woolton. Not much, that is, beyond the name. But imagine his face, the moment he finds it. John is right back there, before the imposing red sandstone church of his childhood with its buttresses, parapets and gargoyles. He sees himself in naughty-boy mode in the Sunday school, and giving less than his best in the choir; he clocks teenaged John playing guitar on the back of a truck in a garden-fête field in July 1957, almost twenty-three years earlier to the day; wanders purposefully through the graveyard, past the headstone of Eleanor Rigby, unaware that his beloved Uncle George will soon lie there, too. Through the big timber lychgate, down the slope and over the road, to the small church hall for a Quarry Men rehearsal ahead of their big show that night. Then in strolls Ive Vaughan with a baby-faced scrapper in tow. A wet-behind-the-ears fifteen-year-old called Paul, who can tune a guitar and who plays him 'Twenty Flight Rock' ...

John flew home to his wife towards the end of July, refreshed and ready for anything. What might he have done differently, at this point, had he known that he had only four months left to live?

*

'John was always my favourite Beatle, because he was dark and he told the truth. He spoke up. He was visible outside of music as well, which I liked. But I didn't have any preconceived ideas about what he was going to be like. I tend not to do that.'

Earl Slick, a precocious Brooklyn-born axeman who started life as Frank Madeloni, earned his chops in the shoes of Mick Ronson on Bowie's 1974 US Diamond Dogs tour. He also supplied lead guitar on David's *Young Americans* and *Station to Station* albums, and worked with Mott the Hoople's Ian Hunter, in his own solo band, and in the duo Slick Diamond, with my dear late buddy Jim. He was now hired to contribute his talent to John and Yoko's comeback offering, *Double Fantasy*.

'I was the only guy in that room who couldn't read music, who wasn't a bona-fide session player. John wanted a street guy. In the producer Jack Douglas's words, I was "the wild card".'

Does he remember his first-ever studio encounter with John?

'I totally remember it. I got there early. I don't normally get nervous, but, you know? When you get a call out of the blue to play on a Beatle's record – especially your favourite Beatle – I got a little nervous. I thought, "OK, ya know what? Let me get to the Hit Factory early." I knew the place because I'd already recorded there, I was one of the first artists to do so.

'So, I got there and, dammit, he was there already. He was sitting in a chair in the middle of the room. And he said to me, "Nice to see you again!" I go, "Huh? Have we met before?" Like you're gonna forget meeting a Beatle! But of course, we *had* met, in Electric Lady Studios in the Village, the day we recorded "Fame" for David. John Lennon remembers meeting me and I don't remember meeting him: *imagine?*'

Slicky was nervous but not intimidated.

'This was just two musicians getting together. We were twelve years apart, but that meant nothing. In the music world, age gaps don't exist. But him having been a Beatle wasn't nothing. I'd been a fan, growing up, hell yeah. It was bigger than huge. John was right, it was bigger than Jesus Christ. Let's be real, man. You couldn't say that kind of thing back then, obviously, and John took some heat. He apologised, but it was pretty half-hearted. Which I loved. He completely understood what he'd done. He was a lot smarter than they were. The thing about that scenario, he was right, but he wasn't right *yet*. His thinking was way beyond their ability to comprehend. So, yeah, I was a Beatles fan. Their attitude was so irreverent. If you took them exactly as they were and fast-forwarded it to now, they would be extremely tame. Right? But that tame, back then, oh, God. They were *so* not tame. The way they looked. The way they played. They were funny. They were great musicians, they'd done their time in Hamburg, they'd tightened themselves up as a band. It didn't get better.'

Now here was John, the outspoken one, the dirty one, the one who wasn't afraid to speak his mind, poised in a chair centre-studio, staring down this twenty-eight-year-old 'wild card' just as they were about to begin working together.

'He lived up to all of it,' Slick says. 'Everything that I saw was everything that he was. He didn't turn into this major asshole when I met him, as so many of them do, so that you're left thinking, "Oh, God: there goes *that* myth down the drain." And from the outset, I'm identifying with him. As successful as he was, he hadn't turned into a pseudo intellectual or a pseudo socialite. He had maintained the core of himself. He wasn't doing the working-class-kid-hobknobs-with-princes-and-queens-and-politicians and all *that* bullshit, or wearing tuxedos and make-up every time he went out for dinner or a coffee and it's like, *please*. That wasn't John, not at all. He was real. He did things his way, it was very downplayed. He was still being the John Lennon that he was before the Beatles. He was just a humble working guy.

'I remember one of the last conversations I had with him – the *last* one I had with him, actually. He was in New York, I was in LA. I called the studio about something, and he happened to be there. He got on the phone and we talked for a little while. About the tour for 1981 that he had planned. And he was like, "Are they liking the record out on the West Coast?" Another planet, right? I goes, "Yeah!" I say, "You know it's charting?" He goes, "Yeah, but do they really *like* it? The record, I mean. I really hope they like the record."

'That was his insecurity coming out. That little kid was *still in there*. Which is great. It shows that he was still of a mind to grow. 'Cos when you think that everything you do is gold-plated and perfect, you can't *grow* anymore, and you gotta grow. Even right 'til the end, he was insecure.'

Slicky and I were speaking ahead of his tour of 'Evening with …' shows around the UK, during which I interviewed him on stage a couple of times. Talk turned to what John was like in the studio. Was he one of the band or was he the boss, the leader? Did he alone call the shots, or did he take direction and run with suggestions?

'He was perfect at it. I'll tell ya why. He *was* the boss. It was *his* career. It was *his* record. He hired guys he liked to play on the record, but that was never shoved down anybody's throat. We were left to our own devices. We were treated with respect, we knew what he wanted and we just did it. We enjoyed the hell out of it, because we weren't being pushed around. There was no attitude or hierarchy in the studio with John. You could totally tell he just wanted to be the singer in the band. You know, he wrote these songs, he knew that he'd picked the right guys to work on them with him, so he didn't have to sit on top of everybody and constantly bark out orders. He treated people the way he wanted to be treated. At the same time, you didn't tell John Lennon what to do.'

Did they ever get the chance to sit down and compare notes about their lives?

'We didn't have to. We were from similar backgrounds. It was there. We knew it. I think that was one of the reasons why we understood each other and got along as well as we did. We genuinely liked each other. It's always the unspoken stuff. Not a lot needs to be said. Not nearly as much as people do say. It's the difference between a song and a book. The song says it succinctly, in few words. The book goes on and on about it.

'Obviously, with or without the Beatles, he's one of the best songwriters ever. He knew how to say it, whatever "it" was. He knew how to express things. It made you cry, the way he could encapsulate something in so few words that would generate such huge emotion. That ability comes from dysfunction, pain, difficulty in one's childhood, and is about finding a way of resolving issues. Of making things stable. Whether he got all that in the end, I don't know. But I think he must have.'

When the band had finished recording *Double Fantasy*, Slick was getting ready to catch a flight back to LA when he received a last-minute call informing him that his schedule had changed.

'I said, "Whaddya mean, you moved my flight?" "Um, John wants you to come by the studio, 'cos there's a solo he wants you to do." OK, great. I get down there. We end up doing the "solo" together, and we have a conversation. He really didn't call me to do the solo, he called me for something else. I didn't put it together until years later. He said, "By the way, you remember we talked about me going and doing concerts and stuff?" I said, "Yeah." He said, "You wanna go, right?" I said, "Yeah … but I just signed with Columbia Records, I have to get this album in, and then they're gonna want me to go on tour." He said again, "You wanna go, right?" I said, "*Yeah!*" He said, "OK, this is what I'm gonna do. I'm gonna call them directly, on your behalf. I'm gonna get them to push back your tour so you can come on the road with *me*." And he did it! His tour never happened, of course, but, yeah, he made the call personally. He was a man of his word. He was determined to bring that particular group of people out on the road with him because he knew we knew the stuff. We recorded it. Who could do it better than the guys who made the record? That was John, going, "This is *my band*. This is cool, and this is how I wanna keep it."'

It had been a long time since John had been out on the road.

The odd concert here and there, but that was it. Did he still have what it takes?

'He was excited about it, I know that much,' says Slick. 'That's what he loved, being in a rock'n'roll band. He'd had to tone down that side of himself to be a Beatle. Going back to it, and not having a fake image, that's what turned him on. He'd got himself back. He showed us. It is so fucking tragic that he didn't get to show the world.'

CHAPTER 21

FINALE

'When we got to the Dakota, I saw a pudgy-faced twenty-something hovering outside. I did look twice, because there was definitely something odd about him. He was often there, I was later to learn. He was getting John to sign copies of *Double Fantasy*, which he was probably selling on. John was always too nice to say no. He was tolerant and polite with the fans who came to see him. Yoko was definitely aware of that young man. She didn't know his name, but she knew him by sight as one of the regulars who hung around waiting to meet and speak to John.'

Andy Peebles pinches at his thumbs and sips flat Coke slowly as he relives, forty years on, the crowning moment of his long, distinguished career. He bagged the interview every broadcaster had been desperate to secure. For the then BBC Radio 1 presenter, the first exclusive audience with John in ten years was a remarkable coup. Andy was, in those days, a big name in his own right. A respected DJ and music authority who spent thirteen years at Radio 1, he created the long-running 'My Top Ten', interviewing A-list artists about their favourite records. Millions heard his extraordinary Lennon interview early in 1981, made all the more compelling by his horrific death only two days after its recording, before its producers had a chance to take it to air. The episode would prove to be a turning point, not only in the history of popular music but also in Andy's personal life. It cast a shadow that has haunted him for four decades.

Bound by professional obligations to the BBC, as well by his own natural sense of dignity and discretion, Peebles has always been reluctant to reveal details of his unlikely friendship with Yoko after John's demise. When he agreed to discuss it with me, he raised some disturbing questions.

'Why did Yoko seem so much happier after John's death?' he wondered. 'Why did she start parading her new lover Sam Havadtoy around New York so soon? And why did she exploit John's memory and legacy, as she appeared to me to be doing, for personal fame and gain? I have a horrible feeling that I was manipulated for the sake of commercial profit. It wouldn't be the first time that such a thing has happened. It's part of the game. You make an album, it goes out – in this case on David Geffen's record label – and you are duty-bound to promote and sell it by whatever means available to you. Everybody knows how it works. Nonetheless, there are boundaries of honesty and decency over which, no matter who you are, you do not step. When I think back to the things that happened forty years ago, it still upsets and disturbs me. Mainly because I now feel that John and Yoko's "Starting Over" period in December 1980 was a sham promotional exercise, designed to restore John's profile after his five-year absence from the UK. I am also saddened by and extremely angry with the BBC for having kept my most famous interview locked away, inaccessible to the public, instead of treating it as the public document it should have been.'

Andy had never met John and Yoko before he flew to New York with his team: Executive Producer Doreen Davies, his producer Paul Williams and Bill Fowler, Head of Promotion at Warner Bros. Having realised that the key to *Double Fantasy*'s success was to re-establish themselves back home, they decided to gift their exclusive to the national broadcaster that John held so dear. A controversial album that featured an equal number of songs by both husband and wife, they risked ridicule if they made the wrong choice. The

BBC it had to be. It reminded John of all that he cherished about long-distance home.

Andy admits how excited he was by the thought of finally meeting his boyhood idol. But, first, he had to get through Yoko.

'We had agreed to meet her at the Dakota at midday on Friday, 5 December,' he remembers. 'Even though everything was arranged before we left the UK, we still had to be interviewed by her in person, to ensure that she wanted to proceed.

'Their apartment was palatial, gorgeous. We were asked to remove our shoes, and were shown into Yoko's enormous office. She was seated behind a huge antique Egyptian desk. I sat cross-legged on a sofa, and barely got a word in edgeways. Yoko was opinionated and emphatic. She told us she'd had better offers than the BBC's, from Radio Luxembourg and Capital, among others. "So, why exactly, should we do the interview with you?" she asked. She was being deliberately provocative. Doreen said, "You need to understand that Capital Radio, wonderful though it is, broadcasts only in London. Radio Luxembourg is a historic and important station, granted, but its signal keeps fading. BBC Radio 1 is national, and is reliable." It was obvious that Yoko wanted us to beg for it.'

He was struck by her appearance in the flesh. At forty-seven, Yoko was 'small and hard, with a slim figure but also very busty. What was going through my mind as I sat there looking at her? I was thinking, frankly, "So, this is the woman who broke up the Beatles."

'"Right, if we are going to do this," she said, "I need to make very clear to you that this interview will be fifty per cent about John, and fifty per cent about me." I felt like saying, "Who on earth are *you*? You're the woman who has done for singing what Wayne Sleep has done for Rugby League."'

Despite the shaky start, the interview the next evening at the Hit Factory, world-famous for having generated albums by the Stones, Stevie Wonder, Paul Simon and Bruce Springsteen as well as *Double Fantasy*, was a triumph. Andy and the production team were already in place and ready to roll when the Lennons arrived, late, at around 6 p.m. They greeted their visitors warmly, especially John, who said, 'Mother and I have been up all night mixing her new single "Walking on Thin Ice", come and listen to it!'

'The minute John set eyes on me,' said Andy, 'he fell on me like a long-lost friend. He was clearly dreadfully homesick, having not been back for almost a decade. Once the tape was rolling, we talked candidly for hours. No subject was taboo. Yoko said afterwards that she was amazed by much of it, that she'd learned things she had never known before. John openly admitted that the Beatles circus had done his head in. The band had stopped touring because they could no longer be heard above all the screaming. He said he was changing lyrics, just for the hell of it. He said he sang "Pissed with Gout" instead of "Twist and Shout", because nobody could hear them, anyway. He told me that by 1969, the four Beatles were barely speaking, and relived the moment in April 1970 when Paul announced that he was quitting and effectively stole John's thunder ... because he had already decided to leave. As far as John was concerned, it was his band. He should have been the one to decide when it came to an end.'

John and Yoko also talked candidly about how they met, about Yoko's effect on the Beatles, about the BBC World Service, about homosexuality, feminism, bagism and bed-ins; about Kyoko and the custody fight, about their wedding and their drugs bust; about his behaviour during the Lost Weekend, about performing with Elton John, his break as a house husband and baking bread; about Bowie's brilliance on Broadway as 'The Elephant Man', about new wave and punk, and, significantly, about John having taken credit for 'Imagine' when the inspiration was Yoko's.[1]

'... Actually that should be credited as a Lennon–Ono song, a lot of it – the lyric and the concept – came from Yoko,' John told Andy. 'But those days, I was a bit more selfish, a bit more macho, and I sort of omitted to mention her contribution. But it was right out of *Grapefruit*, her book, there's a whole pile of pieces about imagine this and imagine that and I have given her credit now, long overdue... if it had been Bowie, I would have put "Lennon–Bowie". If it had been a male, you know.' He also referred to work he recorded with Harry Nilsson as credited to 'Lennon–Nilsson'.

'But when *we* did it, I just put "Lennon", because, you know, she's just "the wife", and, you know, you don't put her name on, right?'

'It was the most devastating, most moving, most powerful interview that John had ever given to the British media,' Andy remembers. 'It went so well that, the moment it was finished, he was demanding to do it again. He said that he'd be back in England in the New Year, and promised to appear live on my show.'

Although the interview later became as much millstone around his neck as defining moment, it remains to this day the one that Andy cherishes the most. John and Yoko were obviously pleased, too, because it concluded, at their invitation, in a celebratory dinner at their favourite New York haunt, Mr Chow: a glamorous old midtown restaurant with a sunken dining room and wall-to-wall mirrors. A place in which to preen and to be seen.

Andy and his team spent the next day Christmas shopping, and boarded their return Pan Am flight on the evening of 8 December. For the first time in a career that had gifted him the opportunity to travel the world, he experienced the fear of flying. It hit him unexpectedly mid-flight, and caused him acute distress. He couldn't fathom why he felt so unsettled.

'Then I heard that one of the doors halfway down the plane wasn't sealed properly,' he recalls. 'There was a good deal of faffing about, and it really upset me. I wasn't convinced that we were safe. I'm not at all the nervous type. I'd flown tens of thousands of miles without tension or upset. But, this time, a stewardess had to come and reassure me, I was in such a state.' He remained too stressed to read, listen to music or watch the film, let alone sleep. Three hours and forty-five minutes into the flight, roughly halfway across the Atlantic, he jumped up out of his seat.

'I went for a wander down the aisle, and suddenly heard someone calling out my name. It was the great sportswriter Hugh McIlvanney, your father's [this author's] closest friend of sixty-odd years. He asked if I was OK – I obviously didn't look it – and invited me to sit down beside him. He asked what I'd been doing in New York. I told him about John, about how much time I'd spent with him, and he was amazed. As it turned out, I'd got up out of my seat and gone down the plane at the precise moment that Mark Chapman pulled the trigger on John. I don't want to imagine how I would have felt and behaved, had I known what was going on at that very moment back at the Dakota.'

News of John's murder was broken to Andy only after the plane had landed at Heathrow. He was escorted by officials to the BBC's airport studio, where he had to talk about the killing live on BBC Radio 4's *Today* programme without being given a moment to collect his thoughts.

One of the aspects of the tragedy that puzzled him the most was the absence of the Lennons' minders the night John died. Despite John's insistence that he loved living in New York because he could move around freely, visiting cinemas, restaurants and galleries and walking in Central Park without being bothered by fans, they never went anywhere without their bodyguards.

'They had their own two uniformed security guards who accompanied them at all times,' he says. 'They wore blue blazers, plain slacks, and were built like brick outhouses. I didn't get to learn their names. They were definitely armed: I saw their gun holsters under their unbuttoned jackets. On the night that John was murdered, they were nowhere to be seen. I have so often wondered: where were they? They were with John and Yoko round the clock, but not that night. Why not? For forty years, there have been more questions than answers.'

Back at Broadcasting House a couple of hours after sharing his thoughts on the *Today* programme, Andy and fellow DJ John Peel hosted a live tribute. Andy was later conveyed to the west London television studios to appear on BBC2's *The Old Grey Whistle Test* with Anne Nightingale, Paul Gambaccini and *Melody Maker*'s Michael Watts. Five years earlier, the show's former presenter 'Whispering Bob' Harris had flown to New York for an upbeat interview with John to promote his *Rock'n'Roll* album, at the end of which John addressed the camera directly. He seized the moment to send all his loving to his elder son Julian, his Aunt Mimi and the rest of the clan back home. 'Helloo, England,' he chirped, like an end-of-pier variety host. 'Keep sending those chocolate Olivers! Keep yer chin up!' He then broke into the morale-boosting song: 'We'll meet again, don't know where, don't know ... *when* ...' – the late Dame Vera Lynn's most celebrated wartime recording. Aunt Mimi would have approved.

But there was nothing cheery about the *Whistle Test* studio that day. 'Long faces, few words,' Andy said. 'I sat there in shock. It hadn't dawned on me yet. The greatest rock star who ever lived was dead – and I had been one of the last people on earth to talk to him. Annie cued the video of "Imagine", the one with John at the white piano. The next thing, the red light on the desk started flashing with an incoming call. It was Paul McCartney. "Linda and I are watching," Paul said. "Tell the gang, they're doing a great job."

'Hearing John's boyhood friend and fellow Beatle on the line was the moment when it sank in. But still I didn't cry. I bottled it all up when I should have wept it all out. I know now that the experience damaged me profoundly for years.'

A few days later, Andy took a phone call at Radio 1 from Beatles producer George Martin, inviting him to pop along to AIR Studios at Oxford Circus, a short walk away. When he arrived, he found Paul McCartney waiting for him.

'We both became incredibly emotional and had to console each other. I felt awful for upsetting him, but he kept saying, "No, honestly, don't apologise." What Paul desperately needed was for me to reassure him that John still loved him. I told him I was convinced that he truly did. "He talks about you in the interview," I said. "He is sarcastic, funny and irreverent, as only John can be. But there is no doubting his fondness for you. It was as if he couldn't help wishing you were right there in the room with us." I have never forgotten the encounter. It cut me to the bone. Paul, more than anyone, now had to face a bitter reality: that the greatest songwriting partnership in the history of pop music was finished for good.'

*

Perhaps the last thing Andy could ever have expected was that he and Yoko would become close friends. But soon after his historic interview was finally broadcast in January 1981, he began receiving calls from New York. Drawn together, so it seemed, by their common love for John, they grew intimate. Each time a Lennon anniversary approached, it was to Andy that Yoko turned, insisting that only he would be allowed to interview her. He spent many hours with her on three continents over several years, and came to love her son Sean. Each time he travelled to New York, whether for pleasure or on business – such as when Elton John flew him by Concorde to attend his Madison Square Garden concerts – Andy and Yoko would get together. Whenever she came to London, the first thing she did was make contact with him. In between, they talked endlessly on the phone, always at her instigation. She would even suggest that there was a psychic dimension to their relationship, usually commenting, 'You knew I was going to call you at that exact moment, didn't you? You knew that it was me.' It would not be long, however, before the scales fell from Andy's eyes. He was at first surprised, then bemused, by the extent to which Yoko's energy and enthusiasm increased. The merry widow started mounting exhibitions around the world, and expanding her own profile as a musician. She became more creatively active than ever before.

'It became obvious to me that John's murder was working to her advantage,' Andy says. 'I started to feel embarrassed, and ashamed of some of the decisions she was making. She used his death to hype her own new record, for example, and rushed to record a sentimental B-side compilation of bits of John talking, as a souvenir. She openly compared his killing to the assassination of John F. Kennedy, and likened herself to Jackie Onassis. She declared their influence to be greater than the Kennedys'. Out of nowhere, we suddenly had "Brand Lennon", which I knew John would have loathed. I just knew he wouldn't have been at all comfortable with the mass merchandising and so on. It wasn't him. He'd have laughed it off, most likely, but he would have seethed with anger inside.'

A year after John's murder, the BBC decided to organise a tribute.

It was decreed that Martin Bell, the then Washington correspondent, or presenter Sue Lawley, should interview Yoko. Mrs Lennon kicked up, and insisted on talking to Andy. Although he had been growing increasingly uneasy about her behaviour, he was pleased to receive the commission. Back to the Big Apple.

'She used her own film crew, which was fine,' Andy said. I sat her at the white piano in the living room of the Dakota, and she was very good. She cried, and said how much she missed John, and how stunned she still was by what had happened. All was proceeding perfectly until I referred to Mark Chapman. At which point she went utterly berserk. She had never wanted his name mentioned in her presence.

'But I found it hard to take her tears seriously. I knew she was already in a new relationship with Sam Havadtoy, a former Lennon aide twenty years her junior. It was quite scandalous.'

John was said to have been well aware that his wife was attracted to Havadtoy – a London-born Hungarian watchmaker's son and former waiter and butler who had worked his way up in interior design in New York, had befriended Warhol, Baechler and other artists, and had schemed the interiors of one of the Lennons' Dakota apartments and a couple of their country abodes. One of the tracks on *Double Fantasy* is entitled 'I'm Losing You'. John composed it in a two-hour frenzy, fearful that their spell was broken and that Mother had lugged her heart elsewhere.

On the very night of John's murder, it is alleged, Sam moved into the Dakota. For twenty years, he barely left Yoko's side. He soon acquired a new image: the widow had her Havadtoy-boy dress up in what looked like her late husband's clothes and wear his hair long, just like John's. The impersonation shocked and embarrassed some of their neighbours, including ballet star Rudolph Nureyev, who commented on it.

Yoko and Sam lasted way longer than Yoko and John. They separated in 2000. Having launched his own art gallery in Budapest in 1992, he returned to live there permanently. 'I was never her husband,' he has stated. 'We never got married.' He also said that they had promised each other never to discuss their association publicly. In return for his silence, a hefty settlement is reported to have been paid.

Says Andy, 'I started asking myself whether Yoko and Sam had been having a relationship for quite some time before John's death. I began to wonder whether Yoko had encouraged John to go off and have his fling with May Pang so that she could explore her attraction to Havadtoy. My blood ran cold. Had the whole "Starting Over" episode, the culmination of which was my interview with them, been nothing but a charade? Was their "happy couple back together and making their marriage work" stance all about the "product" – the album – ensuring that they got a hit out of *Double Fantasy*? I felt sick. If indeed I had been duped, they were the finest actors on earth, she and John. It was Oscar-winning. It convinced me.'

Two years on, Andy agreed with Yoko to make another programme with her in New York. The venue then changed to Los Angeles, and ultimately to Tokyo.

'The production team and I switched our flights, arrived in Japan, and there was Yoko with her son Sean and Sam Havadtoy, waiting for us. We all travelled together to the Mampei Hotel in Karuizawa, deep in the forest in the southern Japanese Alps. This was where John and Yoko had spent several long holidays. Yoko had known the Mampei since childhood, and was clearly terribly fond of the place. It was utterly magical, and such a privilege for me to stay there. The only uncomfortable aspect was that Yoko was now openly sharing her bed with Havadtoy.

'We were there out of season, so the hotel was closed to the public. Yoko had had it opened up specially. Staff were brought in, and fires were lit all over the hotel, just for us. She also had local restaurants opened, in which we were the only guests. Why? Because she could! To try and impress me, I suppose. I have to say, she seemed genuinely happy during that period. She probably *was* happier. No longer living in John's shadow; no longer part of that relentless Lennon–Beatles circus. Or should I say, she had been able to turn the circus into something that suited *her*. The bottom line, to me, was that she was just an average Japanese artist who got lucky, and wrecked the greatest band Britain has ever produced.'

Sean would talk to Andy about his father during their long, private evenings together.

'That little boy had very happy memories of his dad, and I was glad about that,' he says. 'I have cried more over Sean in recent years than about anything else, especially as I get older. I lost my own father when I was eleven. A child never gets over the loss of a parent. I knew exactly how he felt. For that reason, I so wanted Sean to be happy. I wanted him to feel loved. He reminded me of myself in so many ways. I really identified with him. Perhaps spending time with him allowed me to face certain aspects of the loss of my father that I hadn't been able to confront. We'd sit on the sofa together, watching *Inspector Gadget*, his favourite TV show, and we'd talk and talk. Like the song on *Double Fantasy* that is dedicated to him, he really was a very beautiful boy. It's hard to think of him as a forty-four-year-old musician now. How I wish I'd been allowed to keep in touch with him.'

But Andy was pretty angry with Yoko, who in his eyes was 'very misguided': 'By her own ego. By her need to remain important in the context of John Lennon. But she isn't. She is no more than his widow. What I find uncomfortable is that she has made a career out of that. I got no real buzz from Yoko's efforts to impress me, nor from the fact that she persistently stayed in touch. I knew it wouldn't last, and it didn't. The minute she heard that I'd left the BBC to go elsewhere, I never heard from her again.'

*

In the aftermath comes disbelief, so often followed by fury. We seek reasons for the inexplicable. For someone to blame. But it has always been too easy to judge Yoko Ono. We are not world famous. We were not once married to someone who influenced hundreds of millions of human lives for the better. We are not sitting on a cushion of unimaginable wealth. We have no idea what that feels like, neither the privilege nor the burden of it. We never will. All of that must make a person do what ordinary mortals might regard as peculiar things. We cannot argue with the fact that Yoko's star has since risen. Her art is now rated to be of significant worth. She is an acknowledged pioneer. At long last, and with good reason, her work is appreciated.

'Examine the dynamic between Yoko and John,' says Michael Watts. 'There must have been one. He was a very conflicted, tormented guy, and she wanted to be an art-world star. He was completely suffused by this idea. He was so new to her. Somebody who was doing things that he thought were amusing, in ways that a low-rent Liverpudlian was allowed to think were amusing. All those crazy little things she did like making films about bottoms, and the one featuring John's penis: what was a basic bloke to make of all that? What was he supposed to do about such things at first, other than laugh and make fun of them? Which we tend to do when confronted with things we don't understand. Yoko got him to appreciate the more intelligent and aesthetic approach. She raised his game. She was undoubtedly manipulative. She found a willing person with whom to collude. Yes, we could say that she went for the richest and most famous benefactor. The question is, did John feel that he was manipulated, or did he go willingly? The defining point is that he left her and then he went back to her. He had a get-out. He didn't want it. He wanted *her*.'

*

When was the last time that Klaus Voormann saw John?

'In the Dakota building, September 1979. I went with my son Otto, who was about the same age as Sean. The two little kids had a good time together. John was baking bread and cooking rice, and he was very happy. Very domestic. While we were talking, he said to me, "This is the first time I'm not obliged to do something for a record company. I'm free. I can do whatever I want." I could tell that this was a great weight lifted from his shoulders. People like to assume that he must have missed touring and recording in the studio, because that's what *they* wanted from him. But he didn't miss it. He told me how much he loved his life. He didn't want to be on stage. He had done all that. He definitely didn't need an audience.'

Publicity about a possible Beatles benefit reunion for the Vietnamese 'boat people', refugees who had started fleeing their country in 1975 at the end of the Vietnam War, had recently revved into overdrive. The *Washington Post* reported it (like it was really going to happen) as 'the most long-awaited concert in rock and roll history'. Former Beatles promoter Sid Bernstein took a huge ad in the *New York Times*, practically pleading with the four of them to agree to it. The then United Nations Secretary-General Kurt Waldheim committed to sponsoring the event. A grand concert featuring Elton John as MC and Leonard Bernstein conducting the Vienna Philharmonic was floated. 'All four Beatles except John have said yes.' Hello, goodbye, they lied.

'Leonard Bernstein called John while I was there,' recalls Klaus. 'I witnessed the call. I heard John say to him, "*No!* I don't!" John got very pissed off, and he told him straight: "I don't have to do anything for anyone! I do what I like!" It made me so happy to hear it. The truth is, only Ringo would have been happy to do that gig. The rest of them had ripped one another apart. For years, Beatles fans all over the world had been dreaming about the four of them getting back together. But we who had remained close to them the entire time knew that it would never happen. The truth is that "The Beatles" mattered more to the fans than it did to the four members of the band. For them, the Beatles were dead.'

All hope of any kind of reunion ever in the future was all too soon blown to pieces.

'I was in Germany when it happened,' says Klaus. 'Living in my brother's place. I got a call from a German magazine, asking me what I felt about the "John Lennon situation". *What* situation? I didn't know. His death took quite a long time to sink in. To this day, I think about it.

'When Sean was still a baby, I went round to see John one day and we decided to go over to the park for a walk. We left the apartment, went down into the basement, through the cars and out into the sunshine. John had Sean strapped to his body in a backpack. We walked a little, sat down, had a cup of coffee. He was hanging out in the park like anybody else. Nobody was bothering him. I wasn't so often in New York, so I wasn't used to it the way he was. I saw crazy people running around, and I was afraid. Wow, I thought, this place is dangerous. So when I heard that he had been killed, my first thought was that it could so easily have happened much earlier.

'At first, I felt sorry for Mark Chapman. For what he had done to my friend, and for what he had done to the world. But as time went on, he showed no remorse, and I changed my mind. John's death did not affect my ability to make music. But it did make me decide to move back to Germany and live a more simple life. I'd done my time in rock'n'roll. So I left Carly Simon, B.B. King, Randy Newman, Manfred Mann, Jerry Lee Lewis, Lou Reed, all these great people it had been my pleasure to work with. I left it all behind, and I went home.'

For Michael Watts, a strikingly similar life change: 'I had a great deal of time for John Lennon,' he reflects. 'He died, and I stopped writing about popular music. His death affected me profoundly. I lost heart, somehow. I felt that a light had gone out.'

If there is one consolation about his death, Klaus observes, it is that it came at a time when John had reached a resolution.

'He was living the way he wanted. He was no longer a puppet of circumstance or fame. No one was telling him what to do. He had recaptured his life. He had found his freedom.'

Pete Shotton was still in bed when the early call came: 'I immediately called George [Harrison]. He was still asleep, he didn't know anything about it. I drove up there to his place, Friar Park in Henley-on-Thames, to see him. We all sat round the table, and we talked. Ringo phoned from the States. George had a studio in his house, and he'd arranged a session. All the musicians started arriving, ready for work. 'Are you going to carry on?' I asked him. 'Yeah,' George said, 'we've got to get on with it. What else are you gonna do?' He was calm about it. His inner feelings must have been in turmoil, but he was philosophical. George being a very spiritual person. Ya know.'

Paul Gambaccini's phone rang at around 5:50 a.m.: 'Here in London. It was my brother who lives in New York. "I have some bad news," he said. "I thought you'd want to hear this from me." The tone in his voice, the intimacy, I thought, "Oh, God, this must be family." "John Lennon has been killed," he said. "Four blocks away. People are standing around singing. Everybody's horrified and in shock. I thought you'd want to know before your phone starts ringing." Of course, he was right. I had my shower, my phone started ringing, and there started the longest day of my life. In which, pre-Internet, no Skyping, I and a handful of others criss-crossed London to various studios, ending the night at *The Old Grey Whistle Test*. This was all indicative that this was much more than just a pop star dying. This was an entire *era* murdered. The love for John was off the scale, as everybody tried to express what he'd meant to them. It wasn't like Elvis dying, because Elvis, God bless him, had peaked. With the release of *Double Fantasy* – although it was not going to be as big as it became, it was nonetheless an album with some strong songs – John was clearly a major functioning artist. There was, in America, an element of spookiness that was lost on Britain. Because the killer, who, in the tradition of the prime minister of New Zealand, I will not name, had actually considered killing other people. Johnny Carson. David Bowie. So it was John's bad luck to be chosen as the avatar of – no pun intended, considering the collaboration with Bowie – fame.'

*

Yoko was not the only Japanese wife to be 'deprived' of a younger husband the night of 8 December 1980. Nearly five thousand miles west of New York in Kailua, north-east of Honolulu on the Hawaiian island of Oahu, Gloria Hiroko Chapman caught the newsflash on television. She knew, even before they said his name, that her Mark was responsible. It didn't even shock her that much. Not until thirty-eight years later, in August 2018, when Chapman was gearing up for his tenth parole bid, did she confess that she'd been aware of his plans to assassinate John. Pewter-haired, scrawned-down, now sixty-nine, the fervently religious former travel agent who first met her psychologically fragile groom when he approached her for assistance with a round-the-world trip, has stood by him. She told the media that Mark had shared with her two months earlier his intention to kill John. He said this, she claimed, on his return from an excursion east. She swears that he promised he'd changed his mind, that he'd tossed his gun into the sea. She had, she said, no reason to suspect otherwise. No reason at all, other than the violence to which he had subjected her during their brief, terse marriage, demonstrating that he was more than capable of inflicting injury on others. But killing them? She said she had no idea, when he left her to fly back to New York some eight weeks later, that he was going to go through with it.

'The only reason I was OK with Mark making another trip was because I had believed him when he said he needed to grow up as an adult and husband, and needed time to think about his life,' she said. 'He wanted me to sacrifice being alone for a short time so that we could have a long, happy marriage together.'

Gloria and I conversed by email. She wasn't keen on me coming to Hawaii, nor did she warm to the idea of me visiting her husband in prison. Not all publicity is good publicity. In their case, there is always a parole appeal to harm. Well. It hasn't been all bad for the Chapmans. Despite her life having 'changed dramatically', despite her global infamy as a notorious killer's wife, Gloria still has Mark. They wallow in the luxury of forty-four hours a year together, free to make love and pizza in an un-camera'd caravan in the grounds of New York's Wende Correctional Facility. Between conjugal visits, isolated and unknowable, Chapman ekes out his days trapped in his troubled mind, his life a prairie of emptiness. It's all relative. It's a tiny amount of time, less than two days a year. It's still more than John gets with Yoko. Regardless of whether Chapman walks free, he is imprisoned for all time in his heart.

Which brings us to the core of what the world regards as a pointless tragedy, but which John, for all we know, given the way John was, may have considered to be a fitting end. We can dwell on the hideous: that this man who enhanced the lives of countless millions was deprived of his own full life; that he never got to see his sons into adulthood, or his stepdaughter ever again; that he was robbed of the right to grow old with his wife; that just as he was returning to the field, he was snuffed out, with so much music still inside him, music we will never get to hear. Or we can console ourselves with the fact that he was in a good place. He was at peace. He personally had killed every version of himself that was no longer valid or real. At forty years of age, he had his answers. He was complete.

At the heart of a glade on Central Park West lies the Imagine Circle within Strawberry Fields. What happens here day and night has been happening for forty years. It has been described as 'the longest-running church service in Christendom'. Its congregants speak many languages. They are of all ages and from all walks of life. They flock here in blizzard or balm, gale or swelter. They arrange loose flowers in intricate patterns across the mosaic, stretch out across the marble, pose for pictures, eat sandwiches, swig beer, huddle together on the benches, take naps, nurse infants, blow harmonicas, light candles, play guitars. All human life, humming, strumming, singing, clinging, to each other as well as to John's memory. They do not mourn. They come so that he will not go. People are there. People will always be there.

'Just pray for him,' said George Harrison, cradling John's crushed best friend Pete in his arms, that long-ago day to change all days. 'Think about him. He's just been blasted out of his body, right? But *he's* still there. He's OK, he's just moved on. We're only passing through here. This has nothing to do with what we really are. This is just a bit of material we have to move around in for a while. Then we move on to other things.

'Life does go on. So don't dwell on his death. We've got to remember his life. That's the important bit.'[2]

CODA

DAYS IN THE LIVES

A SELECTIVE TIMELINE

24 April 1906
John's 'Aunt Mimi' Smith born Mary Elizabeth Stanley in Toxteth, south Liverpool, the eldest of five daughters, to former Merchant Navy seaman George Ernest Stanley and his wife Annie Jane.

14 December 1912
John's father Alfred Lennon, later known as, variously, 'Alf', 'Fred' or 'Freddie', born in Liverpool. He will become a ship's steward, merchant seaman, jailbird, hotel porter, dishwasher and occasional singer.

12th March 1914
John's mother Julia 'Judy' Stanley born in Toxteth, south Liverpool, fourth of the five Stanley sisters.

28 July 1914–11 November 1918
The Great War (First World War)

3 January 1924
Alice Mona Shaw, who will become club promoter and 'Mother of the Beatles' Mona 'Mo' Best born in Delhi, British Raj India.

3 January 1926
George Martin, future record producer, 'Fifth Beatle' and knight of the realm, born in Highbury, London.

19 May 1932
Alma Angela Cohen, who will become singer Alma Cogan, 'the girl with the giggle in her voice' and secret lover of John, born in Whitechapel, London's East End.

18 February 1933
John's second wife Yoko Ono born in Tokyo, Japan, into a conservative aristocratic family. Her parents Isoko and Eisuke Ono are a wealthy banker and a classical pianist. The name Yoko means 'Ocean Child'. Her father is working in San Francisco at the time of her birth, so Yoko does not meet him until she is two years old. The family live for a while in California. Yoko studies piano from age four. They return to Japan, then move to New York in 1940. The following year, during the Second World War, they again return to Japan.

19 September 1934
Future Beatles manager Brian Epstein born at 4 Rodney Street, Liverpool.

8 January 1935
Elvis Aron Presley born in Tupelo, Mississippi.

3 December 1938
Julia Stanley marries Alfred Lennon, Bolton Street Register Office.

1 September 1939–2 September 1945
Second World War

10 September 1939
Cynthia Lillian Powell born in Blackpool, Lancashire, the youngest of three children. Her father Charles works for GEC (General Electric Company). The family are from Liverpool, but pregnant women are evacuated to Blackpool to give birth once the Second World War is declared. The family

relocate to the middle-class Wirral Peninsula. Charles dies from lung cancer when his daughter is seventeen years old.

15 September 1939
Mimi marries George Toogood Smith, dairy farmer/shopkeeper.

7 July 1940
Richard 'Ritchie' Starkey, the future Ringo Starr, born at home in Madryn Street, Dingle, inner-city Liverpool, the only child of 'confectioners' Richard and Elsie.

9 October 1940, at approximately 6.30 p.m.
John Winston Lennon is born to Julia Lennon at Liverpool Maternity Hospital, during the Second World War. His father Freddie is away at sea. His aunt Mimi Smith runs all the way to the hospital to see him. Freddie as good as deserts Julia – who soon releases John into the care of her sister Mimi and Mimi's husband George.

1942
Julia and Alfred Lennon are legally separated.

18 June 1942
James Paul McCartney born at Walton Hospital, Liverpool (where his mother qualified as a nursing sister) to nurse/midwife/family breadwinner Mary, and Jim, a volunteer fire-fighter and musician.

25 February 1943
George Harrison born at 12 Arnold Grove, Wavertree, Liverpool, the youngest of four, to bus conductor Harold and shop assistant Louise.

9 March 1945
During the Second World War great fire-bombing of Tokyo, 'the single most destructive bombing raid in human history', Yoko Ono shelters with family in Azabu district, and is relocated to the Karuizawa mountain resort that she and John will eventually visit numerous times. Her missing father is thought to be in French Indochina, in a Saigon, Vietnam, concentration camp.

19 June 1945

As a consequence of her affair with a Welsh soldier, Julia gives birth to John's half-sister Victoria Elizabeth. The baby is given up for adoption, and her name is later changed to Ingrid Pedersen. John never learns of her existence. Ingrid and Yoko will meet after his death.

November 1945

John starts school at Mosspits, Mosspits Lane, Wavertree. Julia moves in with John 'Bobby' Dykins. Mimi reports them to Social Services upon learning that John has to sleep in the same bed as his mother and her boyfriend. Julia yields John into the permanent care of Aunt Mimi and Uncle George at their home, Mendips, 251 Menlove Avenue, Woolton, Liverpool.

1946

John is enrolled at Dovedale Primary School, off Penny Lane, where he meets his lifelong friend Pete Shotton. One day, his father Freddie turns up at Mimi's, to 'take him out for the day to Blackpool'. But Freddie plans to emigrate with his son to New Zealand, and start a new life. His mother Julia hears of the plan and goes to Blackpool to bring John back to Liverpool. Disputed legend has it that John is made to choose which parent to live with, chooses his father, cannot bear watching his mother walk away, and races to be with her instead. This was the last time that Freddie heard of or saw his son until he became a Beatle. John believes that he will now live with his mother again. Julia promptly hands her son over to Mimi. John grows close to Uncle George, who teaches him to read, write and draw. At George's encouragement, John devours books and newspapers. Favourite books include *Alice's Adventures in Wonderland* and the *Just William* stories. By the age of seven, he has created his own magazine, *Sport, Speed & Illustrated*, featuring cartoons, drawings and jokes.

Julia and John's other aunts, Anne, Elizabeth and Harriet, visit John at Mimi's house, Mendips. John's childhood is happy, secure and stable. But at school, he is at odds with other kids, perhaps in reaction to his parents' perceived neglect. Frustrated, angry and bored, his artistic talent shines through, but he is mischievous, spiteful and prone to fighting. He tells dirty jokes, is sexually precocious and is disliked as a bad influence by the parents of other kids. Despite Mimi's strenuous efforts to keep him smart and decent, he cultivates a dishevelled look as a badge of rebellion. He scrapes through his 11-Plus exam. Uncle George gifts him a brand-new emerald-green Raleigh Lenton Mk II bicycle as a reward.

5 March 1947
John's second half-sister Julia Dykins (later Baird) born in Liverpool.

5 July 1948
National Health Service (NHS) launched in Britain by the post-war Atlee Labour government, revolutionising the provision of medical services.

26 October 1949
John's third half-sister Jacqueline Dykins born in Liverpool.

6 February 1952
Princess Elizabeth accedes to the British throne as Queen Elizabeth II, following the death of her father King George VI.

September 1952
John and Pete Shotton begin secondary school at Quarry Bank Grammar, selected because it is closer to home and more convenient than the more prestigious Liverpool Institute (later attended by Paul McCartney and George Harrison). John makes himself the centre of attention, class hero and leader of the pack. He and Shotton break every rule, and are often caned by their headmaster. John fights, writes, makes up rude poems, smokes and swears. His school reports feature frequent misdemeanours: truancy, backchatting teachers, hurling blackboard rubbers out of windows. John is spirited and non-conformist, disrespecting teachers and deriding subjects and teaching methods. Some teachers notice his finely tuned sense of humour, wit and intelligence. John and Pete continue to torment teachers and fail to submit homework. John drops to bottom of the class. He already recognises his own 'genius', and believes himself to be the cleverest in the school: 'I was different. I was always different. Why didn't anybody notice me?' His magnetic personality renders him 'the cool one'. The kids all want to hang with John.

During his mid-teens, he begins to develop an intense relationship with his mother, who is more like a big sister to him, and who lives less than two miles away. John starts spending weekends at her home in Allerton, where she lives with her boyfriend John 'Twitchy' Dykins.

2 June 1953

The Coronation of Her Majesty Queen Elizabeth II at London's Westminster Abbey sees 1.5 million people gather in town halls, hospitals and churches, which have been granted collective licences to watch television. In London's Royal Festival Hall, 3,000 ticket-holders witness the transmission. As many again clog the Odeon Leicester Square. Butlin's holiday campers in resorts from Filey to Clacton also watch en masse on giant screens. In all, some 20.4 million watch at least thirty minutes of the service, almost double the radio audience, with nearly as many watching the live processions. There being only 2.7 million TV sets in the land, every set was watch by approximately 7.5 people, not including children.

20 May 1954

Bill Haley and His Comets release 'Rock Around the Clock' on the American Decca label. John is unmoved by the Bill Haley era, but will always associate his mother with that music, to which she loves to dance. Julia is the opposite of Mimi. John feels more at home in her company. She is eccentric, bohemian, unusual, a practical joker. Her son begins to feel like a chip off the old block. Still disruptive at school, he begins writing his own periodical, the *Daily Howl*. The paper is crammed with caricatures, cartoons and nonsense rhymes. His talent for wordplay and double entendre emerge.

5 June 1955

John's Uncle George Smith dies suddenly of liver haemorrhage, aged fifty-two. Fourteen-year-old John is devastated. He withdraws to his bedroom to suffer in silence. When his cousin Liela arrives to console him, the pair collapse helplessly in hysterics. John feels guilty afterwards. His offhand reaction to a traumatic situation will often be repeated. Uncle George is buried in St Peter's Church graveyard, Woolton. Liela Hafez later became Dr. Liela Harvey. She died in 2012, aged 75.

22 September 1955
Commercial television launches in UK with the first ITV broadcast, challenging the monopoly of the BBC.

Also in 1955
Oscar Preuss retires from Parlophone/EMI. George Martin, aged twenty-nine, is made head of the Parlophone label.

Influential American movies *Rebel Without a Cause* starring James Dean and *Blackboard Jungle* with Sydney Poitier are released.

1956

Twenty-three-year-old Yoko Ono elopes with and marries Japanese composer and pianist Toshi Ichiyanagi.

11 May 1956
'Heartbreak Hotel' by twenty-one-year-old Elvis Presley from Memphis, Tennessee, enters early UK singles chart. John hears it on Radio Luxembourg late one night. The song about loneliness, in language that any teenager can understand, awakens sixteen-year-old John. He later says, 'Nothing really affected me until Elvis.' Film characters had exerted their influence, but Elvis is real. John adopts his look, drainpipe trousers, crepe-soled shoes, quiff and sideburns, and affects a brooding stance. In Mimi's eyes, 'He became a man overnight, and all because of Elvis Presley.' Up goes the Elvis poster in John's bedroom. He becomes even more unruly and untidy around the house. Mimi despairs.

John is soon addicted to other artists of the era: Chuck Berry, Carl Perkins, Little Richard, Jerry Lee Lewis and Lonnie Donegan – a Brit who scores a 1956 hit with a cover of the American 'Rock Island Line'. The skiffle craze of DIY rock'n'roll begins. John acquires his first guitar, which Mimi later claims to have bought him. Having taught her son to play chords on the banjo – the first song he learned was 'Ain't That a Shame' by Fats Domino – Julia buys John a Gallotone Champion acoustic guitar 'guaranteed not to split'. She has it delivered to her home, because Mimi disapproves. His aunt forces him forces him into the front porch of her house to practise. John masters 'Rock Island Line' and is soon seeking other boys to form a band.

31 October 1956
Paul McCartney's midwife mother Mary dies from an embolism following surgery for breast cancer, when Paul is fourteen and his younger brother Michael twelve. A year after John and Paul meet, John will lose Julia. The pair will bond over the loss of their respective mothers.

November 1956
John and friend Eric Griffiths form a skiffle group, with Pete Shotton on washboard and another school chum, Bill Smith, on tea chest bass. They call themselves the Blackjacks, soon changing the name to the Quarry Men, after their school. John is both leader and lead singer, makes all the decisions and chooses the songs. Smith leaves, and is replaced by Nigel Whalley, Ivan Vaughan, then Len Garry. Colin Hanton and Rod Davis join. Lennon, Griffiths, Shotton, Garry, Hanton and Davis become the 'official line-up', and they seek local gigs. They will play Liverpool's Cavern Club, although their repertoire will be deemed 'too rock'n'roll'.

1957

4 April 1957
End of conscription. Until now, healthy males aged eighteen-plus were obliged to serve in the armed forces for eighteen months; from 1950, after the outbreak of the Korean War, for two years. National Service in the UK was at last abolished, although the programme would not conclude until 1963. John would not be called up.

22 June 1957
Having rehearsed at Julia's three-bedroom council house, 1 Blomfield Road, on the Springwood estate, Allerton, the Quarry Men make their debut public performance on the back of a coal truck at a carnival in Rosebery Street, Liverpool. Further bookings come in. Julia tunes John's guitar like a banjo, so that John plays banjo chords on it using only the top four strings.

6 July 1957
Fifteen-year-old Paul McCartney is introduced to John by mutual friend Ivan Vaughan in the church hall of St Peter's Church, Woolton, after a

garden fête where the Quarry Men had played a gig in a field. Paul is fascinated by John's odd guitar-playing style, and by the way he peers at the audience: John is extremely short-sighted, and not keen on wearing his glasses. Paul picks up a guitar, starts playing Eddie Cochran's 'Twenty Flight Rock' and Gene Vincent's 'Be-Bop-A-Lula'. Paul then tunes both John's and Eric's guitars, and writes down the correct lyrics to the songs. John later asks Pete Shotton what he thinks of asking Paul to join the band. Shotton approves. John: 'That was the day, the day that I met Paul, that it started moving.'

September 1957

John, almost seventeen, enrols at Liverpool College of Art.

He is a misfit at the college from day one in his Teddy Boy garb, among the fogeyish, jazz-loving art students. Bill Harry, another misfit a year older than him, finds John a breath of fresh air. Bill is already contributing to music magazines. The pair take to drinking at Ye Cracke, a tiny pub round the corner from the college, and hanging together at other students' houses.

John is exasperated by the college, which is too structured for his liking. He finds lessons reminiscent of school, and resumes his disruptive behaviour. He soon acquires a reputation as the college bad boy.

The Quarry Men continue to play locally, in small clubs around Liverpool, through the end of 1957 into 1958. Bookings begin to drop off. They perform at private parties. Some of the band members lose interest and drift away. Fifteen-year-old George Harrison, a fellow pupil of Paul's at Liverpool Institute next door to the art college, joins. John dismisses him as just a kid, but his musical ability is impressive. George's mother lets the group practise at her house. John, Paul and George are able to rehearse in Room 21 of the canteen of the college, playing covers to entertain other students. Mimi still disapproves. Julia continues to encourage.

1958

15 July 1958

Forty-four-year-old Julia leaves Mimi's house after a visit, goes to cross the road to get her bus home, and is knocked down by a car driven by off-duty police constable PC Eric Clague. She dies instantly. John is thankfully not at Mendips at the time, but is awaiting his mother's return to her own home. A policeman arrives to inform John and Bobby Dykins.

Having lost his own mother when he was fourteen, Paul bonds with John over the loss.

Summer 1958

John becomes more of a rebellious misfit than ever. He hits the bottle to ease the pain. His sense of humour becomes bitter and cruel. He never recovers from the loss of his mother. He turns for comfort to fellow art student Cynthia Powell. Opposites attract. 'Cyn' changes her appearance to mirror the image of John's fantasy woman, French actress Brigitte Bardot.

Putting all his time and energy into music, John fails miserably at his studies. His stance infects Paul McCartney, who also begins playing truant for rehearsal sessions during lunch breaks at the art college. John and Paul go to the latter's home, 20 Forthlin Road, Allerton, where the McCartney family had lived since moving from Speke in 1955. John writes 'Please Please Me' in his bedroom at Mendips, but John and Paul write 'I Saw Her Standing There', 'Love Me Do', 'From Me to You', parts of 'She Loves You' and Paul writes 'When I'm Sixty-Four', at Forthlin Road. They talk about girls.

McCartney is the superior musician/all-rounder, and plays several instruments. Much of his output is imitative. John is an original, a one-off. He has the perfect rock'n'roll voice. He borrows from Buddy Holly, but sings in an English accent. He doesn't try to copy others, being confident as himself. He emerges as the more inventive lyricist. Paul is better at melody. A unique songwriting partnership is forged between the pair. They agree to share credit on every song. Where Paul excels at stories, John learns to express his own emotions, in the first person. While Paul is upbeat and positive, John is often cynical, always questioning, and demands answers. Paul, the younger, looks up to the more mature and dangerous John – who is at times condescending to his angelic, goody-two-shoes partner, but acknowledges how good he is for the group.

John befriends Stuart Sutcliffe, a slight, Scottish, immensely talented art student. Again, opposites attract: 'Stu' is modest, quiet and intelligent. Both are babe magnets. Stu lives the bohemian life in a rented room in a dilapidated Georgian house. They become fascinated by the Beat generation. John Stu, Bill Harry and Rod Murray hang around drinking into the small hours, discussing the new literature and poetry.

John quits Mendips to live with Stu at Gambier Terrace, near the college. Mimi gives him his college grant, and kisses her beatnik goodbye. Within a month, the allowance is spent, the place a disgrace. Come the winter, they can't afford to heat it.

1959

29 August 1959
Mona Best opens the Casbah Coffee Club, 8 Hayman's Green, West Derby, Liverpool.

1960

1960–1973
The dawning of sixties counterculture, which begins as a reaction to US military intervention in Vietnam. It will affect recording artists and their songwriting for years to come.

Meanwhile, in Liverpool, Stu joins the Quarry Men. Local businessman Allan Williams becomes their promoter, books them to perform at his Jacaranda club, and lands them gigs including a tour of Scotland as the backing band for singer Johnny Gentle. Stu sells a painting. John encourages him to buy a bass guitar, which Stu does not know how to play. Stu proposes renaming the group 'the Beatals', in homage to the Beat movement.

August 1960
Having changed their name from Beatals to Silver Beats to Silver Beetles to Silver Beatles, the band at last become the Beatles. Pete Best, son of Mona, joins as drummer.

17 August–30 November 1960
The first of their five West German sojourns: John, Paul, George, Stu Sutcliffe and Pete Best arrive in Hamburg for a two-month stint at the new Indra Club. John has now finished art college, having failed his lettering exams. The Beatles are lodged at the Bambi Kino, a small cinema,

and perform on the Grosse Freiheit at the heart of the city's red light district. Club owner Bruno Koschmider closes the Indra due to poor ticket sales and complaints from local residents. The Beatles move to the nearby Kaiserkeller, a popular venue, which is packed nightly. They perform there for the first time on 4 October. Koschmider urges them to '*Mach schau!*' ('Make a show!') They do their 10,000 hours and grow from boys to men.

John and Stu grow closer. The band are befriended by Klaus Voormann and Astrid Kirchherr. Astrid and Stu fall in love. The trip ends in disaster when the band break their deal with Koschmider and the Kaiserkeller to perform at rival club the Top Ten. George Harrison is exposed as under-age, and is deported – as are Paul and Pete. Stu remains in Hamburg with Astrid, leaving the Beatles.

10 December 1960
John makes his way home to England alone.

27 December 1960
The Beatles perform at the Town Hall Ballroom, Litherland, Liverpool, taking the place by storm. John is now convinced they can go all the way. They will play twenty shows at this venue, their last on 9 November 1961.

1961
January to March, back-to-back gigs in and around Liverpool.
Bill Harry launches music paper *Mersey Beat*, covering the North of England's pop scene. Bill asks John to contribute a feature. John submits a piece on how the group was formed, entitled: 'Being a Short Diversion on the Dubious Origins of Beatles'. He will submit further poems, stories, drawings and cartoons.

February 1961
Beatles begin performing regularly at the Cavern Club, Mathew Street.

27 March–2 July 1961
Beatles' second trip to Hamburg. They play ninety-two nights from 1 April at the Top Ten Club and make their first professional recordings. Produced by Bert Kaempfert, they back singer Tony Sheridan on three songs; record a Lennon–Harrison instrumental, 'Cry for a Shadow'; and

perform their own rocked-up version of the Tin Pan Alley standard 'Ain't She Sweet'. John, now twenty, sings the lead vocal distinctively.

July–December 1961
Endless gigs all over Merseyside, with a few trips down south.

September 1961
Two weeks before his twenty-first birthday, John's Aunt Elizabeth in Scotland gives him £100 cash. John takes Paul to Paris on it, for a fortnight. They frequent clubs, cafés and bars, and rendezvous with Jürgen Vollmer. Egged on by 'Jürg', John and Paul copy his haircut.

Back at the Cavern, John develops a strong stage persona. He stands with his legs apart, head up, holds his guitar high on his chest. His extreme myopia prevents him from seeing their audience. His banter and wit offsets the dismal performing conditions, with dangerous electrical wiring, amps crashing and regular power cuts. John frequently falls onto the piano and carries on, wielding sick humour. He appears more mature than his bandmates.

9 November 1961
Brian Epstein's first experience of the Beatles live, at a Cavern lunchtime session. The manager of a large Liverpool music shop is drawn instantly to John, his polar opposite: Brian, the Jewish homosexual, groomed, besuited and debonair; John, the rough, foul-mouthed, chain-smoking, womanising rocker. Brian, a thwarted thesp, is instantly charmed by all four Beatles. He offers to manage them. Their leather look is replaced with suits and ties. Epstein rakes in bookings. John is sold on 'Eppy''s obvious business acumen, but still can't resist dressing himself slightly 'off', to wind Brian up.

1962
Mounting refusals from record companies. Brian supports the boys and coaches them to believe in themselves.

19 March 1962
Bob Dylan releases his first, eponymous album. Initiates civil-rights/anti-war stance, predicting the route that contemporary popular music will take.

11 April 1962

Beatles arrive back in Hamburg, are met at the airport by Astrid, who tells them that twenty-one-year-old Stu has died the day before, from a blood clot on the brain. Stu and John had corresponded regularly, and had maintained their close friendship despite John's cruel behaviour. John, no stranger to tragedy, shows little emotion.

13 April 1962

They are the opening act of the new Star-Club, performing there for seven weeks until 31 May.

9 May 1962

Brian returns to Liverpool from London with news that he has landed them a recording contract with Parlophone/EMI. The Beatles being still in Hamburg, he cables them with the news: 'Congratulations, boys. EMI request recording session. Please rehearse new material.'

6 June 1962

Beatles meet producer George Martin for the first time.

Martin soon decides that Pete Best is not the right drummer for the band. Pete is sacked – by Brian on the boys' behalf, as they cannot face telling him. Ringo Starr, whom the Beatles know from Hamburg as the drummer in Rory Storm and the Hurricanes, is invited to replace Best. Pete, always close to John, is deeply hurt.

23 August 1962

John marries his pregnant girlfriend Cynthia Powell at 64 Mount Pleasant register office. Disgusted Aunt Mimi boycotts the wedding. Marriage vows are said against infernal pneumatic drilling in the road outside. Chicken-and-trifle wedding reception at Reece's Café. John and Cyn move into a flat near the art college owned by Brian, who insists that both marriage and baby are kept secret so as not to deter female fans.

5 October 1962

Debut single 'Love Me Do'/'PS I Love You', released in the UK. Burning slowly, it reaches Number 17 by December. Written by Paul pre-Beatles, in

1958, it is credited to 'Lennon–McCartney'. Released in the US in 1964, it reaches Number One.

1 November–14 November 1962
Beatles return to Hamburg for the fourth time, to perform once again at the Star-Club.

28 November 1962
Yoko Ono marries American jazz musician/film producer/art promoter Anthony Cox. The marriage is soon annulled, because Yoko has not finalised her divorce from Ichiyanagi. Ono and Cox will remarry on 6 June 1963.

18 December–31 December 1962
Their fifth and final Hamburg stint, at the Star-Club. They have outgrown the experience, but Brian Epstein insists that they honour the contract.

1963

22 March 1963
Beatles' first album *Please Please Me* is rapidly produced to cash in on their success. Band are promoted as squeaky-clean cheeky chappies. John is uneasy about the image, but goes along with it. He smiles, waves and bites his lip … and every now and then, lets slip a glimpse of his true nature.

8 April 1963
John Charles Julian Lennon born to Cynthia in Liverpool. Brian Epstein is his godfather.

18 April 1963
Beatles play London's Royal Albert Hall as part of their spring UK tour.

28 April 1963
Less than three weeks after his son's birth, John leaves for Spain with Brian Epstein, sparking rumours of a homosexual relationship.

27 May 1963
Bob Dylan releases his LP *Freewheelin' Bob Dylan*, featuring 'Blowin' in the Wind'.

18 June 1963
Paul's twenty-first-birthday party, in a garden marquee at his Auntie Gin's house, Huyton, Liverpool. The Fourmost band entertain. The Shadows and Billy J. Kramer attend. Paul is with his actress girlfriend Jane Asher. Cavern Club Bob Wooler teases John about his 'honeymoon' in Spain with Epstein. Drunken John attacks Bob and puts him in hospital. John later sends Wooler a telegram of apology, which is leaked to the *Daily Mirror*.

8 August 1963
Four months after Julian Lennon is born, Yoko Ono gives birth to daughter Kyoko Chan Cox. Tony Cox cares for their baby while Yoko concentrates on her art.

22 November 1963
US President John F. Kennedy is assassinated in Dallas, Texas. Marxist Lee Harvey Oswald is arrested, but is himself shot dead by nightclub boss Jack Ruby two days later. That same day, the Beatles release their second album *With the Beatles*, eight months after their debut.

24 December 1963–11 January 1964
The Beatles' 1963 Christmas variety shows, London's Finsbury Park Astoria.

1964

12 January 1964
The Beatles meet Alma Cogan when they appear on *Sunday Night at the London Palladium*. Alma issues the first of many invitations to her famous parties, held at the Kensington apartment she shares with her mother and sister.

15 January–4 February 1964
They play their winter '64 France shows, one gig in Versailles and twenty at the Paris Olympia.

7 February 1964

The Beatles arrive in New York for their historic appearance on CBS TV's *The Ed Sullivan Show*. It will be watched by half the population of America. Beatlemania is now in full swing. On their winter US tour, they make their live-gig debut in Washington. They also perform at New York's Carnegie Hall, and again at Miami's Deauville Hotel for Ed Sullivan.

23 March 1964

John's first book *John Lennon in His Own Write* published by Jonathan Cape in UK and Simon & Schuster in US. A collection of nonsense rhymes and drawings, it is a critical success.

April and May 1964

They play their spring '64 shows, including London's Prince of Wales Theatre on 31 May.

23 April 1964

Foyle's literary luncheon in John's honour at London's Dorchester Hotel, at which the badly hungover author disappoints both hosts and audience by failing to deliver a witty speech.

4 June–16 August 1964

World tour, twenty-six concerts, Denmark, Netherlands, Hong Kong, Australia, New Zealand, UK and Sweden. Aunt Mimi accompanies John to Australia, elegant in her floral hat, taking the opportunity to get together with relatives including cousin Jim Mathews living in Eketahuna, New Zealand.

6 July 1964 (11 August in US)

Beatles musical comedy feature film *A Hard Day's Night* is released in the UK. A huge commercial success, it is still ranked as one of the most influential and inspirational musical films of all time. The royal world premiere is held at the London Palladium, attended by HRH Princess Margaret and Lord Snowdon; 12,000 fans cram Piccadilly Circus.

10 July 1964

A Hard Day's Night album is released.

19 August–20 September 1964

Summer '64 US and Canada tour, beginning in San Francisco, ending in New York, and taking in the Hollywood Bowl Los Angeles, Red Rocks Amphitheatre, Morrison (Denver), Chicago International Amphitheatre, the Boston Garden and the Dallas Memorial Auditorium.

28 August 1964

They meet Bob Dylan for the first time, in a room at the Delmonico Hotel, New York City. Dylan has become a recluse, using bodyguards and drugs to distance himself from the outside world. He introduces the Beatles to cannabis.

John is becoming increasingly frustrated by the Beatles' image and global fame. He finds solace in his art, and in expressing his personal emotions. Fresh courage begins to infuse his songwriting, which soars to a new level. The band's relentless touring/recording/promotional schedule is taking its toll on them all. John and George especially are exasperated by performing live to hundreds of thousands of fans unable to hear them for the screaming. They can't hear themselves play. Frustration is compounded by inadequate sound equipment. Extreme security conditions prevent them from enjoying their travels. Their lives are an unmerry-go-round of planes, hotel rooms and concert venues.

Autumn 1964 UK tour

Twenty-seven dates around Scotland, England, Ireland and Wales, beginning in Bradford and concluding in Bristol.

4 December 1964

Beatles for Sale album released.

24 December 1964–16 January 1965

Beatles Christmas variety shows at London's Hammersmith Odeon.

1965

12 June 1965
Beatles announced as recipients of the MBE in Queen's Birthday
Honours.

24 June 1965
John's second book *A Spaniard in the Works* published. More nonsense tales
and drawings.

Cynthia and his son are now public knowledge. The family is frequently
the subject of newspaper and magazine articles. John plays along, but his
unhappiness and unease are on the rise. As a husband and father he is
distant and detached. He neglects to engage with his wife and son. Guilt
gets the better of him while away on tour, causing him to write long letters
home. He keeps from Cyn his increasing obsessions with groupies and
narcotics. He writes his private life obscurely into his songs.

29 July 1965 UK (11 August in US)
Second Beatles film *Help!*, a musical comedy/adventure piece, released in
the UK. Royal world premiere at London Pavilion Theatre in presence of
HRH the Princess Margaret, Countess of Snowdon. The film becomes a
blueprint for future rock and pop videos.

John is deeply unhappy, drinking and overeating, going through what he
will later describe as his 'Fat Elvis' period.

John's long-lost father Freddie Lennon, now a washer-upper in an hotel
not far from John's Weybridge home, arrives seeking financial support.
It is the first time that father and son have set eyes on each other for
twenty years.

6 August 1965 UK (13 August in US)
Help! album released in the UK.

15–31 August 1965
Sixteen-show US tour, opening at Shea Stadium, New York – 55,600 fans
attend this show, the largest Beatles concert to date. On 29 and 30 August,
they perform at the Hollywood Bowl, Los Angeles.

26 October 1965

The Beatles receive their MBEs (Members of the Most Excellent Order of the British Empire) – announced in this June's Queen's Birthday Honours – by Her Majesty the Queen at Buckingham Palace, sparking public delight and outrage. Some previous recipients return their own medals in protest.

3 December 1965 (6 December in US)

Rubber Soul album released in the UK.

3–12 December 1965

UK tour, beginning in Glasgow and ending in Cardiff.

31 December 1965

John's father Freddie releases single 'That's My Life (My Love and My Home)'. It achieves considerable press coverage, begins to climb the charts, then falls away suddenly. Co-writer Tony Cartwright suspects sabotage by John. The record is the earliest known recorded performance by bassist Noel Redding and drummer Mitch Mitchell, future members of the Jimi Hendrix Experience. Freddie's vampiric attempt to capitalise on his own child's fame will later be compared to the efforts of Mitch Winehouse, father of late songstress Amy Winehouse.

1966

The Beatles' increasingly sophisticated recording work leaps ahead of what they can achieve as live performers. The widening gulf frustrates them. On stage, they go through the motions.

4 March 1966

John's interview with friend-of-the-band Maureen Cleave appears in the London *Evening Standard*, in which he discusses his home life, art, books, money, politics – and religion. In context, his remarks about Christianity and Jesus are not inflammatory. Picked up and quoted out of context by US teen magazine *DATEbook*, John stands accused of declaring the Beatles to be bigger than Jesus. Conservative America turns on the 'blasphemous'

Beatles. Twenty-two US radio stations ban their recordings. Beatle bonfires are held, at which records, books, and merchandise are destroyed. John receives assassination threats. The Ku Klux Klan promise to cause upheaval throughout the band's pending US tour.

24 June–4 July 1966
Tour of Germany, Japan and the Philippines.

Their first concerts in Germany since December 1962, when a New Year's Eve gig is their final performance at Hamburg's Star-Club.

Their homecoming to Hamburg affords a reunion with Astrid Kirchherr and Bert Kaempfert. A return visit to the Grosse Freiheit is deemed too dangerous, due to overwhelming fan and police activity. John and Paul sneak there later by themselves.

In Japan, they play the Budokan, sacred martial arts stadium and shrine to Japanese war dead, and face angry opposition from many opposed to the venue being used for mere rock concerts. As a result, 35,000 police and fire officers are deployed. During their press conference on 30 June, John condemns the Vietnam War.

While performing in Manila, the Beatles unintentionally snub an invitation from the First Lady Imelda Marcos to an audience with her at the Malacañang Palace. They are forced to flee the country, running for their lives.

30 July 1966
Before an almost 97,000-strong crowd at London's Wembley stadium, England beat West Germany 4-2 to win the FIFA World Cup Final for the first and (so far) only time.

5 August 1966
Revolver album released.

6 August 1966
Brian Epstein arrives in New York to give a press conference addressing the bigger-than-Jesus backlash. But his efforts fuel the flames.

11 August 1966
Beatles give a follow-up press conference at Chicago Astor Towers Hotel,

ahead of their two concerts in the Windy City next day. John weeps privately in his room before facing the media. He apologises publicly for his 'mistake'.

12–29 August 1966
Summer '66 US tour, from Chicago through Cleveland, Washington, Memphis, New York, Los Angeles and San Francisco.

23 August 1966
The Beatles return to Shea Stadium. In the wake of John's 'Bigger than Jesus' 'faux-pas', they sell 'only' 45,000 tickets, 11,000 seats remaining empty.

This US tour has not been an unmitigated success. The exhausted Beatles, worn down by controversy and by having to present a false public image around the clock, agree to call time on touring. All of them have been experimenting with drugs. John in particular is taking a new musical direction. Their *Revolver* album marks a turning point in the band's creativity, both lyrically and melodically. Their psychedelic era begins.

29 August 1966
Their last-ever concert as a touring band, Candlestick Park, San Francisco.

September 1966
John begins filming for Richard Lester's *How I Won the War*, his only non-musical film role, shot in Germany and Spain. He begins to wear the round granny specs that become his trademark for the rest of his life. He awakens to the possibilities of a post-Beatles career, and becomes introspective. Rumours of impending Beatles break-up are rife.

26 October 1966
Alma Cogan dies from cancer, Middlesex Hospital, London.

9 November 1966
Two days after returning home from the *How I Won the War* shoot, John attends a London exhibition by Japanese-American avant-garde artist Yoko Ono at London's Indica Gallery. Attracted at first sight, they will meet on a string of occasions over the coming year.

Paul proposes that the Beatles record an album as a fictitious band performing, allowing them to experiment and expand musically, away from the Beatles framework. Inspired by the Beach Boys' *Pet Sounds* LP, which in turn was inspired by the Beatles' *Rubber Soul* album, they fly 'a band within a band'.

24 November 1966
After a two-month break, work begins on *Sgt. Pepper's Lonely Hearts Club Band* in Studio 2, EMI Studios, Abbey Road. The broad remit is an album that cannot be performed live. Recording lasts five months.

1967

Abortion and homosexuality are legalised in the UK. Changing attitudes result in various Acts of Parliament. The 1967 Sexual Offences Act, decriminalising homosexuality between consenting males over twenty-one, and the 1967 Abortion Act, legalising abortion in certain circumstances, will be followed by the 1969 Divorce Reform Act and the 1970 Equal Pay Act.

26 May 1967 (2 June in US)
Sgt. Pepper's Lonely Hearts Club Band album released in the UK. Heavily influenced by their increasing use of drugs, and received enthusiastically as 'the soundtrack to the Summer of Love', it out-sells all previous Beatles albums and changes the face of LP recording. It features John's self-declared favourite of all his own songs, 'Being for the Benefit of Mr. Kite!' and his masterpiece 'A Day in The Life'.

June–July 1967
Monterey International Pop Music Festival, the world's first official rockfest, takes place over three days in California. It features performances by Jimi Hendrix, the Who, Ravi Shankar, Janis Joplin and Otis Redding. During the Summer of Love, 100,000 hippies descend on San Francisco's Haight-Ashbury district. The hippie revolution is born.

25 June 1967

At the EMI recording studios, Abbey Road, the Beatles perform the first of their final three live performances: their anthem 'All You Need is Love' for the *Our World* satellite broadcast, to an audience of 400 million on five continents. The song's slogan encapsulates the ideology of the sixties. They turn to face the world with a completely new image.

John has his Rolls-Royce repainted in a psychedelic design.

27 July 1967

Male homosexuality partially decriminalised in the UK. The British Number One this week is 'All You Need is Love'. Subsequently, 1967 is referred to as 'the year pop came out'.

8 August 1967

London premiere of Yoko Ono's and Tony Cox's 1966 *Film No. 4. 1966–67* (aka *Bottoms*), featuring 365 close-ups of famous derrières, and which Yoko claimed to have made to encourage dialogue for world peace.

24 August 1967

John and Cyn, George and Pattie (Boyd) Harrison, and Paul McCartney and Jane Asher attend a lecture in Transcendental Meditation (TM) given by Maharishi Mahesh Yogi at London's Hilton Hotel.

25 August 1967

All the Beatles travel from London's Euston Station to Bangor, north Wales, to take part in Maharishi's weekend seminar. John boards the train, but Cyn is caught in the crush and misses it. She is forced to make the journey by car. Already aware that her marriage is disintegrating, Cyn regards the mishap as a bad omen.

27 August 1967

Brian Epstein dies in London from barbiturate overdose. None of his obituaries refers to his homosexuality. John reads the tragedy as prophetic of the Beatles' demise.

The band conceive the idea for BBC TV film *Magical Mystery Tour* as a means to perform as a group, now that they are no longer touring.

11–25 September 1967

Magical Mystery Tour shoot takes place: much of it in West Malling, Kent, the tour itself through Devon and Cornwall (most of the footage of which was not used), and in London's Soho and the South of France. Without Epstein there to guide them, they go off the rails.

27 November 1967

Magical Mystery Tour soundtrack released as an LP in the US. In the UK, songs from the film would later be released as a double EP on 8 December 1967.

26 December 1967

Magical Mystery Tour broadcast on TV in the UK on BBC1 on Boxing Day. Ridiculed as dense and self-indulgent, it is their 'first failure'. Its saving grace is the music, the jewel in its crown John's 'I Am the Walrus'. John is undisturbed by criticism of the film. Music writers perceive that he is allowing Paul to move forward as leader of the Beatles.

1968

January 1968

Apple Corps launched, to replace the band's existing company Beatles Ltd. They will henceforth have complete control over their artistic and commercial affairs. That's the idea, at least.

4 February 1968

Beatles record Paul's 'Lady Madonna' and John's 'Across the Universe' at EMI Abbey Road. The latter's wordplay, poetry and breathtakingly beautiful melody singles it out as one of John's finest creations. But it is shelved, becoming the beginning of the *Let It Be* project, and 'Lady Madonna' is released as a single 'to be going on with' during their forthcoming absence.

Later in the month, they travel to Rishikesh, India, in the foothills of the Himalayas, with various friends, to further study TM with Maharishi. The spell is broken when Maharishi is accused of making advances towards actress Mia Farrow. John is disillusioned.

May 1968

While Cyn holidays with friends in Greece, John invites Yoko Ono to the Lennon's Weybridge home. They record music and make love for the first time. John decides immediately to leave Cyn and live with Yoko, who is the soulmate he has been waiting for all his life. Despite a brutal press, those closest to John say that Yoko is the best thing ever to happen to him. Cyn returns from holiday to find that another woman has commandeered both her home and her husband. Cyn flees. John and Yoko are so close that he describes her as 'me in drag'. The British public turn against John for abandoning his wife, child and 'the Beatles ideal'.

30 May 1968

Work commences on *The Beatles* – the otherwise-known 'White Album' – until 14 October 1968.

15 June 1968

John and Yoko's first public happening together, when they plant a pair of acorns in the land surrounding Coventry Cathedral. One faces east, the other west, in a gesture symbolising both their love for each other and the blending of their respective cultures.

18 June 1968

John and Yoko attend London Old Vic theatre production of the stage adaptation of John's book *In His Own Write*. Huge press coverage the next day.

1 July 1968

John's first major art exhibition *'You Are Here'* opens at Robert Fraser Gallery, Duke Street, London, largely inspired by Yoko's art. The 365 helium-filled balloons, cut and sent bobbing into the London sky, lead their finders to return the labels to John urging him to go home to his wife. John is confused and disheartened. Racial abuse of Yoko is rife. Undeterred, John brings Yoko into Beatles recording sessions for the 'White Album', breaking an unspoken rule that Beatle WAGS stay away from their work. But John does not want to be apart from his soulmate. Yoko irritates the others by attempting to sing along, and even offers them musical advice.

22 August 1968
Cynthia Lennon sues John for divorce, on the grounds of his adultery with
Yoko. He does not contest.

4 September 1968
At Twickenham Film Studios, they film the second of their final three
live performances: promo clips for 'Hey Jude' and 'Revolution', directed
by Michael Lindsay-Hogg with a thirty-six-piece orchestra in white tie.
Three hundred extras, many of whom were gathered locally, and fans from
the bunch who routinely hung around EMI Studios were also employed
for the shoot. Also present was TV presenter David Frost, who would
premiere the sequence on his show *Frost on Sunday* four days later.

18 October 1968
John and Yoko are arrested at Ringo's apartment, Montagu Square,
London, for possession of cannabis and obstruction of police.

8 November 1968
Cynthia's and John's divorce made absolute.

21 November 1968
Thirty-five-year-old Yoko miscarries John's baby at five-plus months
in Queen Charlotte's Hospital, London. John doesn't leave her side
throughout, in stark contrast to the way he treated Cynthia during her
pregnancy and the birth of their son Julian. It is the first of Yoko's three
miscarriages with John. Yoko's baby boy was due in February 1970. Just
before they lose him, they record his heartbeat, and later feature it on their
1969 album *Life with the Lions*, followed by a two-minute silence. The baby
is given the name John Ono Lennon II, and is buried in a secret location.

22 November 1968
The Beatles, popularised as the 'White Album', is released, on the group's
own Apple label. The album heralds the start of the Beatles' demise. While
Apple Music forges ahead, the company's various other enterprises swallow
their fortune. The accountants protest. In-fighting among band members
begins. Ringo is soon bored with the negativity, George is frustrated that
Paul and John don't take his songwriting and musicianship seriously,

John is fed up with Paul throwing his weight around, and with his self-obsession. Paul can't take much more of John's increasing eccentricity and his flaunting of Yoko. John and Paul are no longer on the same songwriting wavelength. There is writing on the wall.

29 November 1968

John and Yoko release *Unfinished Music No. 1: Two Virgins*, recorded on their first night together at John's and Cynthia's home. The front cover is them, full-frontal naked, the back cover same, from behind. The 'music' is a concoction of unintelligible squawks, twittering and sound effects.

1969

The turning-point year for the Beatles.

The *Let It Be* project continues. It will become the Beatles' twelfth and final studio album, although it is recorded before *Abbey Road*. Recording is marred by fighting among the band members. They are also losing money at a terrifying rate. John insists on appointing notorious rock manager Allen Klein to sort things out. Paul wants John Eastman, his future brother-in-law (Paul is now engaged to photographer Linda Eastman). Ringo and George back John. Altercation continues. The creation of *Let It Be* halts, and begins again March–April 1970.

13 January 1969

'Yellow Submarine' soundtrack released.

20 January 1969

Richard Nixon sworn in as 37th President of USA.

30 January 1969

The Beatles' last-ever live public performance together takes place on the roof of the Apple Corps headquarters at 3 Savile Row, London. Keyboard player Billy Preston accompanies them. Footage of the performance will feature in the film *Let It Be*.

2 February 1969
Yoko Ono's and Tony Cox's divorce is finalised. Yoko is granted custody of their daughter Kyoko.

3 February 1969
Allen Klein is appointed business manager, after a hearing in London's High Court to dissolve the Beatles' partnership. Paul's refusal to accept Klein intensifies problems within the group.

22 February 1969–20 August 1969
The recording of the *Abbey Road* album, at EMI Abbey Road, Olympic and Trident Studios.

John is now increasingly engaged in solo projects. He prefers working and experimenting with Yoko to working with the other Beatles. He has moved on. Despite this, he makes extraordinary contributions to this album in the shape of 'Because', 'Come Together' and 'I Want You (She's So Heavy)'.

There are no immediate plans to disband. The Beatles remain friends, and plan to record together going forward.

20 March 1969
John and Yoko marry in Gibraltar, and spend their seven-day honeymoon on a Bed-In for Peace in the Netherlands, in Room 902 of the Amsterdam Hilton. This is followed by a bagism press conference at the Hotel Sacher in Vienna, at which the slogan 'All we're saying is give peace a chance' is coined. The couple also promote their avant-garde film *Rape*. Other film collaborations between 1968 and 1972 include: *Smile*; *Self-Portrait*, a fifteen-minute close-up of John's penis; *Erection*, focusing on the building of the London Intercontinental Hotel; *Up Your Legs*, featuring the pins of 331 people; and also, *Apotheosis* and *Fly*, featuring, respectively, a short balloon flight into the clouds, with John and Yoko in hoods and cloaks, and an insect on a naked female body.

May 1969
John is refused a US visitor's visa. The Ono Lennons resolve to take their message to Canada instead.

26 May–2 June 1969

John and Yoko stage their second Bed-In for Peace, this time at the Queen Elizabeth Hotel, Montreal, Quebec. John composes and records 'Give Peace a Chance' during proceedings. The song is credited to Lennon–McCartney, but is actually the debut single release of the Plastic Ono Band.

8 June 1969

US President Nixon and South Vietnamese President Nguyễn Văn Thiệu meet at Midway Island, an atoll in the North Pacific Ocean equidistant between Asia and North America. Nixon declares that 25,000 US troops will be withdrawn from Vietnam by September.

28 June 1969

The Stonewall Riots in New York City denote the beginning of the modern gay-rights movement.

1 July 1969

While on holiday in the Scottish Highlands, John crashes the car in which he is driving pregnant Yoko and their children Julian and Kyoko. All are treated for shock at Golspie's Lawson Memorial Hospital, and John, Yoko and Kyoko receive stitches for substantial face and head injuries.

3 July 1969

Rolling Stone Brian Jones (twenty-seven) is found drowned in his pool at home in Sussex, England.

20 July 1969

Apollo 11 conveys astronauts Neil Armstrong, Buzz Aldrin and Michael Collins to the Moon, lands Armstrong and Aldrin on its surface, and returns them safely to Earth.

8 August 1969, 11.30 a.m.

The Beatles are captured by photographer Iain Macmillan on a zebra crossing on Abbey Road, near the recording studios. The image will be used on the cover of their swansong album, which will become one of the most recognisable and beloved album covers of all time.

9 August 1969
Charles Manson's 'Family' cult murder pregnant actress Sharon Tate and friends at Roman Polanski's LA mansion.

15–18 August 1969
Woodstock Festival, White Lake, New York State, featuring Jimi Hendrix, Sly and the Family Stone, Ravi Shankar, Joan Baez, Janis Joplin, the Who, Jefferson Airplane. Shankar is unhappy with conditions at the festival, and will distance himself from the hippie movement during the 1970s. Bob Dylan boycotts Woodstock, and travels to the UK to star at the Isle of Wight Festival, (30–31 August) before an estimated crowd of 150,000. Other featured acts are the Band, the Pretty Things, the Nice, the Who, Bonzo Dog Doo-Dah Band and Joe Cocker. Among the many celebrity guests are John and Yoko, Ringo and wife Maureen, George with Pattie Boyd, actress and activist Jane Fonda and the Stones' Keith Richards.

13 September 1969
Plastic Ono Band appear at the Toronto Rock and Roll revival concert, which features popular artists from the 1950s and 1960s.

20 September 1969
A meeting is held at Apple HQ to discuss the next album. Ringo is absent, due to illness. A new single is also discussed. John proposes his own latest composition, 'Cold Turkey', which Paul and George reject. John records it anyway, with Plastic Ono Band, having said to the others, 'I'm leaving,' and 'It's over.' This marks the true end of the Beatles – not Paul's official press release on 10 April 1970. The break-up occurs when John, the creator of the band, leaves the others. He is twenty-nine years old.

26 September 1969 (1 October in US)
Abbey Road album is released in the UK to mixed reviews. It is today widely regarded as their finest.

15 October 1969
Hundreds of thousands take part in the Moratorium to End the War in Vietnam in demonstrations across the US.
   Yoko suffers another miscarriage.

13-15 November 1969
Between 250,000 and 500,000 protestors stage a peaceful demonstration in Washington, DC, with their 'March against Death'.

25 November 1969
John returns his MBE medal to Her Majesty the Queen.

6 December 1969
Altamont Free Concert in North California, hosted by the Rolling Stones as a 'Woodstock West', turns violent and goes down in history as marking 'the end of the sixties'.

John and Yoko continue to strive to keep themselves on the front pages with their campaigns and antics, to throw focus on both their political views and their art – which are rapidly morphing into the same thing. At the expense of their credibility, they are getting their message across.

Also in December, the Ono Lennons campaign to clear the name of James Hanratty, one of the last men to be hanged in Britain. They contrive to promote peace all over the world by erecting huge billboards in eleven cities: 'War is Over! If You Want It – Happy Christmas from John and Yoko'.

1970

January 1970
John and Yoko cut their hair, declaring 1970 as 'Year One for Peace'.

6 February 1970 (20 February in US)
The Ono Lennons release their single 'Instant Karma! (We All Shine On)' in the UK.

1 April 1970 (April Fool's Day)
They release a joke press statement, announcing their sex-change surgery.

Problems with Yoko's former husband Tony Cox regarding custody of their daughter Kyoko are ongoing. The Ono Lennons pursue them to Majorca. Cox flees with Kyoko to Houston, Texas, the home town of his new partner Melinda Kendall. Stress takes its toll on John and Yoko.

23 April 1970
The Ono Lennons fly to LA to submit to four months' psychiatric treatment with Dr Arthur Janov, the champion of Primal Therapy. John confronts his deepest insecurities – his father's abandonment of him, his mother's death and his own self-loathing. The couple return to England, and John deals with all three issues in songs for his first formal studio album as a solo artist.

18 September 1970
Jimi Hendrix (twenty-seven) is found dead in a London apartment hotel.

4 October 1970
Janis Joplin (twenty-seven) is found dead in the Los Angeles Landmark Motor Hotel.

26 September– 23 October 1970
John Lennon/Plastic Ono Band is recorded at Abbey Road Studios, and at Ascot Sound Studios at their home, Tittenhurst Park, Berkshire.

11 December 1970
John Lennon/Plastic Ono Band released. Its theme is 'face up to your problems'. Hugely acclaimed, it features the tracks 'Working Class Hero' and 'Mother'.

1971

11–12 February (and 24 May–5 July) 1971
Imagine album recorded at Ascot Sound Studios, Record Plant, New York City and Abbey Road Studios.

12 March 1971 (22 March in US)
'Power to the People' released in the UK. John and Yoko are clearly taking a more direct and rebellious stance.

3 July 1971

On the second anniversary of the death of Rolling Stone Brian Jones, the Doors' frontman, lyricist and poet Jim Morrison (twenty-seven) is found dead in his bath in Paris.

1 August 1971

George Harrison and Ravi Shankar front Concert for Bangladesh, Madison Square Garden, New York. The world's first international benefit concert, it is staged in aid of refugees following the 1970 cyclone and atrocities during the Bangladesh Liberation War. Ringo, Bob Dylan and Eric Clapton also perform.

3 September 1971 (some reports state 31 August)

John and Yoko leave England for New York, on a brief trip to locate Kyoko. John will never again live in the land of his birth.

They stay at the St Regis Hotel, then move to a two-room flat in the West Village, where they attract political activists intent on removing Richard Nixon from power. John and Yoko become immersed in protest rallies and benefit concerts, some dubious. They record another album, *Some Time in New York City*. The FBI become increasingly interested in their activities. After their protest song 'John Sinclair' helps secure the release of an individual convicted for marijuana possession, President Nixon steps up surveillance on the Ono Lennons.

9 September 1971

Imagine album released. It features the tracks 'Imagine', John's signature song; 'Crippled Inside'; 'Jealous Guy'; 'How Do You Sleep?' is his sarcastic, insulting message to Paul, a scathing response to Paul's apparent snipes at John on his *Ram* album.

28 and 31 October 1971

'Happy Xmas [note the "X"] (War is Over)' recorded at Record Plant East, New York City. The melody is from an old English folk song, 'Skewball'. This is John's seventh single release independent of the Beatles, and has since become a Vietnam protest ballad and a Christmas classic.

1 December 1971 (24 November 1972 in UK)

'Happy Xmas (War is Over)' released in the US. But its UK release is delayed until almost a year later, due to a rights dispute with the publisher, Northern Songs. John is the first ex-Beatle to release a Christmas song. George's 'Ding Dong, Ding Dong' came later in 1974, Paul's 'Wonderful Christmas Time' in 1979 and Ringo's album *I Wanna be Santa Claus* in 1999.

John talks of touring the US to protest against Nixon's 1972 re-election campaign. With the voting age about to be reduced to eighteen, Nixon panics, worried by Lennon's power to sway the younger electorate. The president is in no doubt, given John's attacks on him on the *Imagine* album, such as 'Gimme Some Truth', as to how John feels about him: 'No short-haired, yellow-bellied son of Tricky Dicky is gonna Mother Hubbard soft-soap me', sings John, over George Harrison's guitar. FBI agents are despatched to observe at Lennon's gigs. It is soon discovered that John has previous in England for marijuana possession. This should, technically, have prevented John from entering the US. John's tourist visa is due to expire. Nixon spots his chance. At first, John believes that he is imagining cars following him and his phone being tapped. He soon gets the message. A long legal battle commences.

1972

17 March 1972

Ringo releases single 'Back off Boogaloo', produced by George Harrison, naming his friend Marc Bolan as the inspiration for the lyrics. It is rumoured that Marc, flying high since the breakthrough of his second T. Rex album *Electric Warrior* (the biggest-selling album of 1971 in the UK, later voted Number 160 in *Rolling Stone*'s '500 Greatest Albums of All Time'), contributed to the recording. It reaches Number 9 on the US Hot 100. At Number 2 in the UK, it is Starr's biggest domestic hit. The next day, Bolan performs two shows at Wembley's Empire Pool, where fan madness eclipses Beatlemania. Ringo films the show for a proposed documentary for Apple Films. It extends to a full-length feature. Further scenes are shot at John and Yoko's home, Tittenhurst Park, Ascot, where Ringo is house-sitting; and at an Apple Studios jam session, featuring Elton John on piano and Ringo on drums. A few weeks later, Marc, his wife June, George Harrison and Ringo depart for Cannes on a sailing holiday. Ringo's film, *Born to Boogie*, is premiered at Oscar 1 Cinema, Brewer Street, in London's Soho. A box-office flop, it is ignored by US buyers and distributors. The following April, Marc records a demo at George Martin's AIR Studios for Ringo's eponymous album, which fails to make it onto the final LP.

18 April 1972

John and Yoko attend an immigration hearing, at which John is issued with a deportation order and given sixty days to leave the US.

May 1972

John backs down and confirms that he will not act to disrupt Nixon's re-election campaign. He seeks the support of many friends including Bob Dylan, Joseph Heller, Leonard Bernstein and Joan Baez, to support his appeal to remain in the US.

12 June 1972 (15 September in UK)

Some Time in New York City album with Greenwich Village band Elephant's Memory and Invisible Strings released to poor reception in the US. The later UK release is again due to a dispute with publisher Northern Songs. John and Yoko are accused of 'incipient artistic suicide' by *Rolling Stone* magazine, because of its focus on political and social issues, from the Northern Ireland crisis to the Attica State Prison shootings. John seems, for the first time, overwhelmed by his subject matter and out of his depth. In the UK, songs like 'The Luck of the Irish' and 'Sunday Bloody Sunday' cause offence, particularly as John has turned his back on these shores to reside in New York.

17 June 1972

The Watergate scandal in Washington, DC breaks. It emerges that the Committee to Re-elect the President is corrupt. Forty-eight Nixon administration officials are convicted.

30 August 1972

John and Yoko headline two One to One concerts at Madison Square Garden. John buys $59,000-worth of tickets and gives them away to fans, raising $1.5 million for mentally and physically handicapped people.

Although there will be a couple more stage appearances, these will prove to be John's last major shows.

7 November 1972
Richard Nixon re-elected in one of the biggest electoral landslides in US history.

23 December 1972
Imagine film released. Filmed primarily at Tittenhurst Park, it depicts a loving couple perfectly in tune. The reality is less agreeable. Immersed in legal problems and the continuing desperate search for kidnapped Kyoko, and disillusioned with political pursuits, their marriage is in trouble.

1973

April 1973
John and Yoko move into the exclusive Dakota Building on New York's Upper West Side.

July 1973
President Nixon is exposed as having a secret taping system. The White House connection to the Watergate burglaries breaks. Nixon is shown to have approved plans to prevent the investigation.

July–August 1973
Mind Games album recorded at Record Plant East, New York City. It is Lennon's first self-produced recording. Work on the album marks the beginning of his separation from Yoko. At her encouragement, production coordinator/assistant May Pang, who has worked with the Lennons since 1970, becomes John's companion and lover, during a spell that will become immortalised as Lennon's 'Lost Weekend' – after the 1945 film of that name, starring Ray Milland as an alcoholic writer.

29 October 1973 (16 November in UK)
Mind Games album released in the US.

October 1973

John and May go to LA to promote *Mind Games*, and stay on. Without Yoko around to manage him, John drinks heavily. He decides to record an album of inspirational rock'n'roll classics. He re-establishes a relationship with his son Julian, whom he has not seen for four years.

Also during the Lost Weekend, John has a Top 10 hit with '#9 Dream', a Top 20 with his cover of 'Stand By Me', works with David Bowie on 'Fame' and with Elton John on his cover of 'Lucy in the Sky with Diamonds'. He gifts Ringo 'Goodnight Vienna', gives 'Rock And Roll People' to Johnny Winter and 'Move over Mrs L.' to Keith Moon.

1974

March–May 1974

John produces Harry Nilsson's album *Pussy Cats*, its title a reference to all the bad press they have been getting for their drunken, disorderly behaviour in LA. Ringo, Klaus Voormann and Keith Moon are among the guest musicians on the album.

13 March 1974

John and Nilsson are ejected from LA's Troubadour Club for disruptive behaviour.

Also during March, Yoko contacts John and asks him to come to the Dakota to discuss a treatment programme for his nicotine addiction. The couple have been in touch daily throughout their separation. John pleads with Yoko to be allowed to return home, but she is not ready to take him back.

28 March 1974

During the *Pussy Cat* sessions, John enjoys an impromptu jam with Paul McCartney at LA's Burbank Studios. It is the last time they will ever play together in a recording studio. It is also the only known time that they ever do so between the break-up of the Beatles and John's murder in 1980. Future recordings are discussed.

July–August 1974
John records fifth solo studio album *Walls and Bridges* at Record Plant East, New York.

5 August 1974
President Nixon accepts blame for misleading America.

9 August 1974
Nixon resigns in disgrace, the only US president to resign office. Karma, though not quite instant, is good enough for John.

26 September 1974
Walls and Bridges album released. 'Whatever Gets You Thru the Night' and '#9 Dream' are the stand-outs. Elton John contributes. He has a bet with John that 'Whatever Gets You . . .' will be a Number One. Lennon being the only ex-Beatle who has never had a solo Number One, he agrees to perform with Elton at Madison Square Garden if it makes it. It does.

20 November 1974
John flies to Boston to watch Elton John's gig at the Boston Garden, prepare himself for the New York appearance and tackle his stage fright.

28 November 1974
John appears on stage with Elton John at Madison Square Garden. It will be John's last major concert appearance. He performs 'Whatever Gets You Thru the Night', 'Lucy in the Sky with Diamonds' and 'I Saw Her Standing There'. John has arranged tickets for Yoko. She and John reconnect backstage after the show. John leaves with May Pang. Soon afterwards, John and Yoko begin dating.

Christmas 1974
John spends Christmas in Florida with May Pang and his son Julian. They visit Disneyworld Orlando.

1975

Mid-January 1975 (May Pang remembers it as first week February 1975)
John and Yoko resume living together at the Dakota, deeming their
separation 'a failure'.

17 February 1975
Rock'n'Roll, John's sixth solo studio album, of late 1950s and early 1960s
songs, released. The sleeve features an old photo of John in a Hamburg
doorway, taken by Jürgen Vollmer in 1961. The album is critically acclaimed.

18 April 1975
John makes his last-ever stage appearance, in television special *A Salute to
Sir Lew Grade: The Master Showman*.

7 October 1975
John's deportation order is overturned by US judges at the New York State
Supreme Court.

9 October 1975
On John's thirty-fifth birthday, his son Sean Taro Ono Lennon is born to
Yoko (forty-two) by Caesarean section, at a New York hospital.

1976

26 January 1976
The Beatles' contract with EMI expires. John is now without contractual/
recording obligation.

1 April 1976
John's father Freddie Lennon dies of cancer in Brighton, Sussex, aged
sixty-three. He and John have been in constant contact during Lennon
Snr's final days.

27 July 1976
John is at last granted his US Green Card. For the first time in five years,
he is free to travel outside the US without the worry of being refused re-

entry. During the final four summers of John's life, the family spend long holidays in Japan, visiting Tokyo, Kyoto and Karuizawa. John becomes enamoured of Japanese culture, art and lifestyle, gets to know his in-laws, and travels extensively to other countries.

1977

20 January 1977
John and Yoko attend inaugural gala for Jimmy Carter, 39th president of the United States. John is officially *persona grata*.

John and Yoko fly via Geneva to Cairo, Egypt, and are photographed at the pyramids at Giza. It is later claimed that they take part in a covert archaeological dig and purchase Egyptian artefacts.

16 August 1977
Elvis Presley dies in Memphis, Tennessee, aged forty-two.

16 September 1977
Marc Bolan (twenty-nine) is killed in a car crash on London's Barnes Common.

September-October 1977
John, Yoko and Sean travel to Japan for a long holiday.

4 October 1977
John and Yoko give a press conference at the Hotel Okura, Tokyo, at which John announces an extended period of retirement from music. The media rechristen John the 'Howard Hughes of Rock'.

Turning his back on the music industry, he becomes a house husband and looks after the baby while Yoko takes care of business. Her job will involve unravelling John's Beatle-related legal/financial affairs, and to building the value of his estate, while John brings up their child, and teaches him to read, write and draw.

Caring for Sean rekindles John's interest in his own long-lost childhood. He asks his Aunt Mimi to send him his drawings, poems, paintings, school reports, uniform and other mementoes from home.

John still writes songs and records demos privately, but spends most of his time lying around daydreaming, watching TV and reading, drawing, sketching cartoons and writing poems. After his death, the best are collated and published as a book, *Skywriting by Word of Mouth*.

May-June 1978
The Ono Lennons are said to be in Paris.

1979

20 March 1979
John and Yoko celebrate their tenth wedding anniversary.

27 May 1979
John and Yoko run a full-page ad in the UK in the *Sunday Times*, entitled 'A Love Letter from John and Yoko, to People Who Ask Us What, When and Why', to let their fans know that they and Sean are well. Bringing the public up to date with their lives, they seem happy together. Having campaigned for years for world peace, John at last appears at peace with himself.

Already paranoid about deranged fans, John meets Paul Goresh, a fan who becomes his walking companion.

1980

20 March 1980
John and Yoko celebrate their eleventh wedding anniversary at their home in West Palm Beach, Florida. John gives Yoko five hundred fresh gardenias and a diamond heart. Yoko gives John a vintage Rolls-Royce.

Late spring, John is reported as having travelled alone to Cape Town, South Africa, where he stays at the exclusive Mount Nelson Hotel as 'Mr Greenwood'. It is claimed that he meditates on Table Mountain. On Memorial Day, 26 May 1980, he has his last conversation with May Pang, calling her from South Africa. John solo, and John and Yoko together, are also said to have visited Spain, Germany, Hong Kong and other destinations during this period, by private plane and by sea; and John's Aunt Mimi later claims that John visited her secretly, at home in Sandbanks, Dorset, shortly before his murder.

4 June 1980

John sails from Newport, Rhode Island, to Hamilton, Bermuda, on
the sloop *Megan Jaye*, on a two-month adventure, surviving a squalling
storm. Deeply affected and rejuvenated by it, John resumes songwriting
in earnest. He composes 'Watching the Wheels', 'Starting Over' and
'Woman', the first songs towards a new album after his long self-imposed
exile from the music industry. Four-year-old Sean joins him in Bermuda.
Yoko makes a brief visit.

28 July 1980

John returns to New York by air, to plan the recording of *Double Fantasy*.

4 August 1980

John and Yoko resume their recording career, signing a deal with David
Geffen. They resume media interaction.

7 August–19 October 1980

Double Fantasy recorded at the Hit Factory, New York City.

9 October 1980

John's fortieth birthday, and Sean's fifth. Yoko hires a plane to skywrite
'Happy Birthday John and Sean. Love Yoko' over New York.

17 November 1980

Double Fantasy album released. It is the fifth album by John and Yoko, the
seventh and final studio album released by John during his lifetime. It is
poorly received. After John's assassination, three weeks on from its release,
it becomes a global smash hit and wins 1981 Album of the Year at the
twenty-fourth annual Grammy Awards. It features seven tracks by John
and seven by Yoko, alternating. The album re-establishes John as one of
the great composers and lyrical communicators of the twentieth century
and showcases his brilliant rock'n'roll voice. Tracks include '(Just Like)
Starting Over', 'I'm Losing You', 'Woman', 'Watching the Wheels' and
'Beautiful Boy (Darling Boy)'. John and Yoko have also made a demo of
their next album, and are talking about a world tour.

John, at forty, is healthy, having relinquished hard drugs, meat and sugar
(though not strong cigarettes or black coffee).

6 December 1980

BBC Radio interview with Andy Peebles in New York. The theme of the piece is John looking forward to a bright future.

8 December 1980

John gives his last interview to RKO Radio at the Dakota.

That afternoon, he and Yoko are photographed by Annie Leibovitz at home, for the cover of *Rolling Stone*. John once again poses naked, while Yoko is fully clothed.

4.15 p.m. EST: John and Yoko depart for the recording studio (some reports say the Hit Factory, others that it was Record Plant), to mix Yoko's new song 'Walking on Thin Ice'. Outside their building, fan Paul Goresh shows them photos he has taken of them. Another apparent fan, Mark David Chapman, is hovering. John signs his copy of *Double Fantasy*. Goresh photographs John and Mark together.

10.50 p.m.: John and Yoko return home. Chapman is waiting. As John gets out of their car in front of the building – an unusual occurrence, their driver normally drops them off in the safety of the Dakota's private courtyard – Chapman fires five bullets at John. Four hit him. John is conveyed to hospital by police officers.

11.07 p.m.: John dies, at New York's Roosevelt Hospital (since renamed Mount Sinai West).

9/10/11 December 1980 (all dates given)

John's body is cremated at Ferncliff Cemetery, Hartsdale, New York State, twenty-five miles north of New York City. Yoko does not consult his family in England as to the fate of his remains. She has at times suggested that she retained his ashes in an urn 'under her bed', but has also stated that she scattered them in Central Park, at the site of what is now his Strawberry Fields memorial.

14 December 1980

At 2 p.m. EST, 400,000 people congregate in Central Park to observe, with millions of others around the world, ten minutes' silence in John's memory.

24 August 1981
Mark David Chapman is sentenced to twenty years to life in prison. This is five years less than the maximum twenty-five years to life because he has pleaded guilty to second-degree murder. A lengthy and costly trial is not required.

9 January 1984 (27 January in US)
Milk and Honey, John and Yoko's final album together, released in the UK – a fragment of the music John still had to give, and of how much the world has lost. The best tracks are 'Borrowed Time' and the demos 'Let Me Count the Ways' and 'Grow Old with Me'.

15 October 1984
Julian Lennon, at twenty-one, releases his debut album, *Valotte*, featuring the Top 10 (UK and US) single 'Too Late for Goodbyes'. The album, named for the French château in which he composed the songs, is Grammy-nominated. It is dedicated 'To my mother Cynthia and to my Father', and mixed at the Hit Factory New York, on the same console used by John and Yoko for *Double Fantasy*.

24 March 1986
Julian releases his second album, *The Secret Value of Daydreaming*.
On **1 April 1987**, he appears as The Baker in Mike Batt's musical *The Hunting of the Snark* at London's Royal Albert Hall. His next two albums are, respectively, *Mr Jordan* (**March 1989**) and *Help Yourself* (**August 1991**).
He withdraws from the music business to concentrate on other pursuits, including cookery, photography and philanthropy. In **May 1998**, he makes a comeback with his fifth album, *Photograph Smile*. In **2009**, he launches his White Feather Foundation, in support of environmental/ecological/humanitarian concerns. Having collected Beatles memorabilia since his father's death, he publishes a book about his collection in **2010**. The following year, in **October 2011**, he releases his sixth album *Everything Changes*.

9 October 1988
Mona Best dies, aged sixty-four, on what would have been John's forty-eighth birthday.

Also in **1988**, George Martin is awarded the CBE (Commander of the Most Excellent Order of the British Empire).

1991

Having created music with his mother Yoko from a very young age, sixteen-year-old Sean Ono Lennon begins his own career, co-writing 'All I Ever Wanted' with Lenny Kravitz for the latter's album *Mama Said*. He goes on to found/collaborate/perform with various bands, including Cibo Matto and the Claypool Lennon Delirium. He releases his debut solo album *Into the Sun* in **1998**. His follow-up *Friendly Fire* appears eight years later in **October 2006**.

6 December 1991

Aunt Mimi dies at home in Dorset, aged eighty-five.

22 April 1994

Richard Nixon dies.

1996

George Martin is made a Knight Bachelor, and becomes Sir George, in recognition of services to the music industry and popular culture.

11 March 1997

Paul McCartney is knighted, becoming Sir Paul.

7 December 2000

The day before the twentieth anniversary of John's death, an English Heritage Blue Plaque is unveiled at Mendips. In **March 2002**, Yoko purchases the house and donates it to the National Trust, who restore it to its original appearance.

Yoko and her daughter Kyoko are reunited after thirty years' estrangement. Kyoko was seven years old when her father disappeared with her. Yoko becomes grandmother of two. In **August 2020**, Kyoko turns fifty-seven.

29 November 2001
George Harrison dies at a friend's home in Los Angeles, aged fifty-eight. His ashes are scattered in a Hindu ceremony in the Ganges and Yamuna rivers, Veranasi, India. He leaves nearly £100 million in his will.

10 April 2006
Cynthia Lennon publishes her second memoir about her former husband, entitled *John*.

9 October 2007
On what would have been John's sixty-seventh birthday, Yoko unveils her outdoor work of art, the Imagine Peace Tower memorial, on Viðey Island, Reykjavik, Iceland.
   'Hold the light in your hearts and know that you are not alone.'

9 October 2010
On what would have been John's seventieth birthday, Julian and Cynthia unveil the John Lennon Peace Monument in Liverpool.

February 2012
Mendips and 20 Forthlin Road, John's and Paul's respective childhood homes, where they wrote songs both individually and together, are Grade II Listed by English Heritage.

15 November 2013–23 February 2014
Approaching her eighty-first birthday, Yoko opens *War is Over! (If You Want It)*, a major retrospective of her work at the Museum of Contemporary Art, Sydney, Australia.

1 April 2015
Cynthia Lennon dies of cancer at home in Majorca, Spain, aged seventy-five.

8 March 2016
Sir George Martin dies in Wiltshire, aged ninety.

24 March 2017
John's childhood friend Pete Shotton dies from a heart attack, in Cheshire, England, aged seventy-five.

20 March 2018
Ringo Starr becomes Sir Ringo, the last Beatle to be knighted, by the Duke of Cambridge, at Buckingham Palace. Because knighthoods are not awarded posthumously, neither George Harrison nor John will ever be referred to as 'Sir'.

May 2018
Yoko's *Double Fantasy* exhibition of her life and work with John, part of their ongoing Imagine Peace Campaign, opens at the Museum of Liverpool. Attracting more than 300,000 visitors to its first run, the exhibition, one of the museum's most successful ever, is extended. It is the first to explore the personal and creative chemistry between John and Yoko, and features many objects, artefacts and personal possessions and mementoes that have never been displayed before.

14 December 2018
Sean Lennon, Mark Ronson and Miley Cyrus record a cover of John and Yoko's 'Happy Xmas (War is Over)'. The trio perform the song on 15 December, on NBC TV's *Saturday Night Live*.

18 February 2020
Yoko Ono Lennon turns eighty-seven. She continues to maintain John's memory, in the name of world peace.
www.imaginepeace.com

CHAPTER NOTES

ECHOES

[1] The end was a long time coming. John informed Paul and Ringo privately on 20 September 1969 that he was quitting, during a meeting at the Apple HQ, 3 Savile Row, London W1. (George was with his mother in Cheshire.) Paul stated same on 9 April 1970 – but publicly, in a strange Q&A, as though interviewing himself – to herald his covertly home-recorded solo album, *McCartney* (Apple Records, 17 April 1970). Bare and simple, it was critically panned (but a US Number One/UK Number Two, held back by Simon & Garfunkel's *Bridge over Troubled Water*). Features the author's all-time favourite McCartney song, 'Maybe I'm Amazed'. Q: 'Do you foresee a time when Lennon–McCartney becomes an active songwriting partnership again?' PAUL: 'No.' This was interpreted by the press as the official announcement of the Beatles' demise, provoked global headlines, devastated George and Ringo and enraged John. Having been the first to say he was leaving, he was deprived of his 'right' to go public with the news. Thus is 10 April 1970 recognised as 'the day the Beatles broke up'.

[2] One of Lennon's most famous quotes, he was not the author of it. A 1957 *Reader's Digest* magazine article credits the saying to American journalist/cartoonist Allen Saunders, 1899–1986).

[3] Alan Weiss, a senior programme producer of WABC TV's Channel 7 *Eyewitness News*, later won an Emmy Award for his part in the coverage of John's death. 'All My Loving' was the Beatles' opener during their debut performance on *The Ed Sullivan Show*, 9 February 1964. It was

Paul's composition, credited to Lennon–McCartney. 'It's a damn good piece of work,' John acknowledged during his 1980 *Playboy* interview. '[…] I play a pretty mean guitar in back.'

[4] *The Tragedy of Hamlet, Prince of Denmark*, written between 1599 and 1602, Act 3, Scene 1. William Shakespeare's longest and most influential play.

[5] Justin Bieber became the first artist in the UK's Official Singles Chart history to hold concurrently the first, second and third positions, with 'Love Yourself', 'Sorry' and 'What Do You Mean?'.

[6] 'Broken light' and 'tumble blindly' are phrases that feature in 'Across the Universe' (on the charity album *No One's Gonna Change our World* [1969] and re-worked for the *Let It Be* album (1970). The song's Sanskrit words '*Jai Guru Deva Om*' are a mantra, translating as, 'I give thanks to Guru Dev', Maharishi Mahesh Yogi's teacher. The mantra is engraved on brass bracelets bought by John in Rishikesh, India, during the Beatles' sojourn there with Maharishi, now owned by his son Julian. 'One of the best lyrics I've written,' said John, in his 1971 *Rolling Stone* interview. 'In fact, it could be the best. It's good poetry, or whatever you call it, without chewin' it. See, the ones I like are the ones that stand as words, without melody. They don't have to have any melody, like a poem, you can read them.' On 4 February 2008, to mark NASA's fiftieth birthday, 'Across the Universe' was the first song to be beamed directly into space. Transmitted via NASA antennae towards Polaris, the North Star, 431 light-years from Earth, this also commemorated the fortieth anniversary of the song.

CHAPTER 1

[1] Sir Winston Leonard Spencer-Churchill, born 30 November 1874, UK Conservative Prime Minister, 1940–1945, led Britain to victory during the Second World War. Served again as PM 1951–1955. Died on 24 January 1965, aged ninety, and honoured with a state funeral.

CHAPTER 2

[1] Rita Hayworth, born Margarita Carmen Cansino on 17 October

1918, popular Hollywood leading lady in the 1940s. She starred in sixty-one films, including 1946 film noir *Gilda* with Glenn Ford. Top pin-up for American GIs during the Second World War. Fred Astaire's favourite dancing partner. Twirled with Gene Kelly in *Cover Girl*. First Hollywood actress to become a princess: her five husbands included Prince Aly Khan and Orson Welles. Her lips were once voted the best in the world. In later life, she became the first public face of Alzheimer's disease. Her 1980 diagnosis raised awareness and led to research and funding. She died in 1987, aged sixty-eight.

[2] One of the most surprising abortionists in recent history was the mother of an artist who had them screaming in the aisles long before Beatlemania. Natalina Maria Vittoria Garaventa, dubbed 'Dolly' because of her beautiful face, worked as a midwife and provided 'safe abortions' to Italian Catholic women from all over Hoboken, New Jersey between the wars. 'Hatpin Dolly' was arrested at least six times and convicted twice. She was Frank Sinatra's mother.

[3] While 'the prom' in American culture refers to the graduating dances and balls held by US high schools and universities, 'down the prom' is an old-fashioned British term for a stroll along a seaside or riverside promenade. We also enjoy 'The Proms', the summer concert series staged in parks around the country, and by the BBC at the Royal Albert Hall.

[4] ACE Study: Ref. Bellis, M.A., Hughes, K., Leckenby, N., Perkins, C., and Lowey, H., (2014), 'National Household Survey of adverse childhood experiences and their relationship with resilience to health-harming behaviours in England.' *BMC Medicine*, 12 (72).

[5] Hyacinth Bucket was a television sitcom character in the long-running 1990s BBC series *Keeping Up Appearances*. Patricia Routledge plays the snobbish, social-climbing, lower middle-class leading lady, who pronounces her own surname as 'Bouquet', and who chases relationships with her perceived superiors while striving to disguise her humble roots and family. It proved popular internationally, becoming BBC Worldwide's most exported TV programme.

[6] Blackpool, just under thirty miles north of Liverpool, was in those days a hugely popular Lancashire, NW England, resort on the Irish Sea, famous for its Eiffel-esque tower, the Blackpool Tower, its piers and

promenades, and all the candy-flossy, 'Kiss Me Quick'-hatted, donkey-riding fish-and-chip-ness of seaside culture.

[7] Beatles historian Mark Lewisohn gives a comprehensive account of Billy Hall's recollections in his work *All These Years Volume 1: Tune In* (Little, Brown, 2013).

[8] Scouse is short for 'lobscouse', a word of obscure origin, but which echoes similar terms in Scandinavian languages: 'lapskaus' (Norwegian), 'labskovs'(Danish) and 'lapskojs' (Swedish); Also, 'labskaus' in Low German, a Northern German/north-eastern Netherlands language. It refers to an eponymous stew, often eaten by sailors, made from lamb or beef and onion, carrots and potatoes, not dissimilar to Lancashire Hotpot or Irish Stew. During the nineteenth century, the poor folk of Liverpool and its provinces were routinely fed on scouse because it was cheap to make, and was a staple of the families of mariners. The lower-class working folk who ate scouse eventually became known as 'Scousers' … also referred to as 'Wackers' or 'Wack'. A dense Scouse dialect evolved down the years, which can be almost unintelligible to outsiders. Thus, you sag off work, give the scallies a swerve, pick your Judy up from the ozzy, bring her some clobber (or threads), and take her for some scran. In English, you leave work early without permission, avoid your cocky-lad mates, collect your girlfriend from the hospital, give her some clothes and take her out for a meal.

[9] *Alice in Wonderland* and *Alice Through the Looking-Glass* by Lewis Carroll, whose poem 'Jabberwocky' John adored. The *Just William* stories by Richmal Crompton, and *The Wind in the Willows* by Kenneth Graham. John also favoured Robert Louis Stevenson's *Treasure Island*, Edward Lear and Edgar Allan Poe. He told his childhood friend Pete Shotton that his ambition was to 'write an Alice' one day.

[10] As recounted in Pete Shotton's memoir *John Lennon in My Life* (Stein & Day, 1983), co-authored by Nicholas Schaffner.

[11] 'I Am the Walrus', John's best nonsense song, was a nod to his favourite song of the time, Procol Harum's 'A Whiter Shade of Pale'. 'Walrus' was inspired by Lewis Carroll's creature in his poem 'The Walrus and the Carpenter' from *Alice Through the Looking-Glass*. Released in November 1967, it featured in *Magical Mystery Tour*, the Beatles' TV film that was

aired the following month; on the eponymous UK double EP; and on the US LP. It was also the B-side of their Number 1 hit 'Hello, Goodbye'. This was their first studio recording after the death of manager Brian Epstein. The single and double EP claimed the Number 1 and Number 2 slots on the UK Singles Chart in December 1967. Pete Shotton supplied John with the words of a nursery rhyme the pair had once chanted in the school playground:

> 'Yellow matter custard, green slop pie/all mixed together with a dead dog's eye.
> Slap it on a butty, ten foot thick/Then wash it all down with a cup of cold sick.'

(A butty being a thick slice of white buttered bread, folded around its filling to make a single-slice sandwich. Thus, that rare delicacy, the chip butty.)

Shotton also advised John to change his lyric 'waiting for the man to come' to 'waiting for the van to come'. John would later confess to *Playboy* magazine (1980) that he wrote parts of the song while on acid trips, and that he had been 'trying to write obscurely, à la Dylan'.

The walrus was revisited in the 1968 song 'Glass Onion' ('the walrus was Paul'); in 'Come Together' ('walrus gumboot') and in John's solo track 'God' ('I was the walrus but now I'm John').

The recording incorporates a Shakespeare reading from *King Lear*, Act IV, Scene 6, lifted from a radio broadcast.

It was banned from broadcast by the BBC because of its line: 'You've been a naughty girl, you let your knickers down.'

'Eleanor Rigby', one of the Beatles' most legendary compositions, from the 1966 album *Revolver*, was also a double-A-side single with 'Yellow Submarine'. The album and double-A-side were released simultaneously. It topped the UK chart for four weeks (reached Number 11 in the US). 'Yellow Submarine' made it individually to Number Two in the US.

A ground-breaking, experimental song with a stark narrative about loneliness and the plight of the elderly, it was mainly McCartney's creation. Although Macca said that he borrowed the name 'Eleanor' from the actress Eleanor Bron who appeared in the Beatles film *Help!*, and that he'd taken 'Rigby' from the name of a Bristol shop, Rigby &

Evans Ltd (a wine merchant) when he was visiting that city to watch his then actor girlfriend Jane Asher in *The Happiest Days of Your Life*, there is an actual Eleanor Rigby buried in the graveyard of St Peter's Church, Woolton, John's childhood parish church. Paul subsequently agreed that he may have been subliminally reminded of Eleanor Rigby's name on the gravestone, which he is likely to have seen as he and John spent so much time there. There is also a gravestone bearing the name 'Mackenzie'.

All the Beatles and Pete Shotton suggested ideas for the lyrics. Pete said the name of the priest should be changed from Father McCartney to Father Mackenzie, in case people presumed Paul was writing about his own dad. Pete also came up with the idea of the two lonely old people getting together too late: the vicar presiding over Miss Rigby's funeral.

Although John claimed in 1971 to have penned 'a good half of the lyrics or more', and said in 1980 that he wrote everything but the first verse, Pete Shotton stated for the record that John's involvement was minimal. Said Macca: 'John helped me on a few words, but I'd put it down eighty-twenty to me, something like that.'

[12] Bill Harry quoted in the *Liverpool Echo*, 24 March 2017, following Shotton's death from a heart attack aged seventy-five.

[13] David Bowie's permanently enlarged pupil has always been attributed to a punch administered by George Underwood following an argument over a girl when the boys were still at school. During research for my book *Hero: David Bowie* (Hodder & Stoughton, 2016), I was told by a leading ophthalmic surgeon that trauma could not have caused the condition, and that it was most likely attributable to maternal congenital syphilis. Complications including neurosyphilis and meningovascular syphilis can lead to sight impairment and affect mental health.

[14] John's words about Christmas in a November 1969 interview by radio reporter Ken Zelig, recorded at the Lennon stately home Tittenhurst Park.

CHAPTER 3

[1] Corporal punishment: see also *Violence Against Children: Making Human Rights Real*, (Routledge, 2017), edited by Gertrud Lenzer. (Routledge, 2017)

² Interview by Jann S. Wenner for *Rolling Stone* magazine, published 4 February 1971.

³ Richard Hughes: www.richardhughestherapy.com

References:

Bowlby, J. (2005). *A Secure Base.*UK: Routledge Classics.

Jung, C.G. (2006). *The Archetypes and the Collective Unconscious* (R.F. C. Hull, Trans.). UK: Routledge.

Jung, C.G. (1989). *Memories, Dreams, Reflections* (A. Jaffe, ed.). US: Vintage Books.

Kohut, H. (1971). *The Analysis of the Self.* Madison, CT: International Universities Press.

Kohut, H. (1978). *The Search for Self: selected writings of Heinz Kohut: 1950–1978*, Vol. 2. (P.H. Ornstein, ed.). Madison, CT: International Universities Press.

Schaverien, J. (2015). *Boarding School Syndrome: the psychological trauma of the 'privileged' child*. Hove: Routledge.

Siegel, D.J. (1999). *The Developing Mind*. US: Guilford Press.

Winnicott, D.W. (1971). *Playing and Reality*. US: Basic Books.

Winnicott, D.W. (1990). *Home is Where We Start: essays by a psychoanalyst*. UK: Penguin.

⁴ *Imagine This: Growing up with my brother John Lennon* by Julia Baird, (Hodder & Stoughton, 2007).

⁵ The village of Durness boasts a small commemorative garden for John. The John Lennon Northern Lights Festival was staged there in 2007, a celebration of poetry, music, theatre and other arts dedicated to his memory. John would revisit in 1969 with Yoko, her daughter Kyoko and his son Julian, when they were involved in an accident at Loch Eriboll.

⁶ Speaking to writer Lorna Maclaren in 2002. Charles Stanley Parkes died of vascular dementia in January 2016. The Beatles' 'In My Life' and John's 'Imagine' were played at his funeral.

[7] Yes, DNA was 'around' by then. Deoxyribonucleic acid, the double-helix molecular structure that bears the genetic blueprint in all life forms, was identified in the late 1860s, and 'discovered' in 1952 by chemist and crystallographer Rosalind Franklin – a monumental achievement by a woman during an era when some university dining rooms were still men-only – and established by US biologist James Watson and British physicist Francis Crick in 1953. They would be credited in a share of the Nobel Prize. She would barely be remembered.

[8] Julia Dykins was born 5 March 1947. Her sister Jacqueline, known in the family as 'Jackie' (though sometimes written 'Jacqui') arrived 26 October 1949.

[9] In parts of the American South, the harmonica was known as a harp, mouth harp or French harp. This term for blues harmonica is now used all over the world. It may have been inspired by the Aeolian harp, an outdoor instrument that is 'played' by the wind – so named for Aeolus, in Greek mythology the god of the wind. John may have known his first instrument as a 'gob iron'.

[10] As recounted in Pete Shotton's 1983 memoir *John Lennon in My Life*, co-authored by Nicholas Schaffner.

[11] *Ibid.*

[12] Elizabeth Anderson is the author of the 2008 study 'The Powerful Bond between People and Pets: Our Boundless Connections to Companion Animals' (*Practical and Applied Psychology*), Prager Publishers, Inc., US.

[13] The hornpipe refers to various styles of folk dancing from around Britain dating back to the sixteenth century, and adopted by sailors during the mid-eighteenth century. The word also refers to the music danced to. The 'blanket hornpipe' is an old English euphemism for sexual intercourse.

[14] The Quarry Men were captured by one of the fête-goers, Bob Molyneux, on a portable Grundig reel-to-reel tape recorder. Molyneux stumbled across the tape again by chance in 1994. It sold at Sotheby's to EMI Records for £78,500. The label acquired the recording with the intention of including it in the Beatles' *Anthology*, but later decided

against it because the sound quality was so poor. It is now widely accessible on the Internet.

'Baby Let's Play House' was a 1955 release by Elvis Presley. John Lennon borrowed the song's line 'I'd rather see you dead, little girl, than to be with another man' for the Beatles' 'Run For Your Life' on their 1965 album *Rubber Soul*. 'Puttin' on the Style' was a 1957 hit for Lonnie Donegan. The song became an American standard after having been a hit for Marion Try Slaughter, better known as Vernon Dalhart, in 1926. Dalhart, an American country singer-songwriter, was the first country artist to sell a million records.

[15] Paul McCartney speaking to *Record Collector* magazine in 1995.

[16] 'Come Go with Me' was a 1957 hit for the doo-wop Del-Vikings. It was famously covered by the Beach Boys, on the albums *M.I.U. Album* (1978) and later on their compilation *Ten Years of Harmony* (1981), when it was released as a single.

[17] John speaking to the writer and Beatles biographer Hunter Davies in 1967.

[18] In a 1970 interview with *Rolling Stone* magazine's Jann Wenner.

[19] Peter Michael McCartney, born 7 January 1944, left school to work as a trainee tailor and then a hairdresser's apprentice before becoming part of music-and-comedy group the Scaffold alongside performance poet Roger McGough and comedian/singer John Gorman. For this purpose, he adopted the pseudonymous surname McGear, 'gear' being a Scouse term for 'fab'. They went on to have several hits between 1966 and 1974, including the 1968 Christmas Number One 'Lily the Pink'. Having always been a prolific photographer, he published several books, and is acclaimed for his unique images of the Beatles.

[20] 'When I'm Sixty-Four' was eventually a track on the Beatles' 1967 album *Sgt. Pepper's Lonely Hearts Club Band*. It is possible that Paul remembered the song he composed as a young teenager just as the band started recording the album in late December 1966, because his father had celebrated his sixty-fourth birthday earlier that same year: Jim McCartney was born on 7 July 1902.

[21] Widely claimed to be the first song that Paul ever wrote, 'I Lost My Little Girl' was composed using just three chords on Paul's very first guitar, a Framus Zenith (model 17) acoustic that he still owns. The song features on Macca's 1991 album *Unplugged (The Official Bootleg)*. A variation of it with John on lead vocals was performed by the Beatles during the 'Get Back' sessions.

[22] 'La Huchette' is probably a derivation of the ancient French word 'hutchet', meaning 'bugle'. The building at number 5 Rue de la Huchette was originally converted into a jazz club in 1949, and welcomed the greats, including Count Basie. It has appeared in numerous films, from 1958's *Les Tricheurs (Young Sinners)* to 2016's *La La Land*.

[23] As Alan Sytner told author, broadcaster and Merseybeat expert Spencer Leigh in 1998, and as Leigh recounted in his obituary of Sytner in January 2006.

[24] George Harrison's first performance at the Cavern took place during a lunchtime session on 9 February 1961.

[25] John would later explain that the Buddy Holly-esque 'Hello Little Girl' was inspired by a 'thirties or forties song' that his mother used to sing to him. That song was Cole Porter's 'It's De-Lovely'. It would be one of the songs the Beatles performed at their doomed Decca audition in 1962. Credited to Lennon–McCartney, it was recorded a year later by Merseybeat outfit the Fourmost, and was even produced by George Martin. Gerry and the Pacemakers had also recorded it, but their version was not chosen for release.

[26] *Imagine This: Growing up with my brother John Lennon* by Julia Baird (Hodder & Stoughton, 2007). In a terrible twist of a postscript, the girls' father Bobby Dykins was also to lose his life in a car crash at the bottom of Penny Lane, in December 1965.

[27] John talking to Beatles biographer Hunter Davies in 1968.

CHAPTER 4

[1] Charles Sargeant Jagger, (1885–1934), British sculptor, who also created the Hyde Park Corner, London, Royal Artillery Memorial.

[2] As recounted in Pete Shotton's 1983 memoir *John Lennon in My Life*, co-authored by Nicholas Schaffner.

[3] 'Hey Jude', written by Paul and credited to Lennon–McCartney, was a non-album single in August 1968. Often cited as one of the greatest songs of all time, it was the longest single ever to claim the British Number One slot (at seven minutes and eleven seconds) and was a Number One hit around the world. It was also that year's top seller in the UK, US, Canada and Australia. This was the Beatles' first single release on their own Apple label. Paul wrote it originally as 'Hey Jules', in sympathy for John's son Julian, after his father left his mother Cynthia for Yoko Ono. It was recorded during the band's sessions for the 'White Album' (aka *The Beatles*, November 1968), and was the first song they ever recorded on eight-track, at Trident Studios, Soho.

[4] *Rolling Stone* interview: 'John Lennon. Part Two: Life with the Lions', February 1971, by Jann S. Wenner.

[5] The John Moores Painting Prize remains the UK's best-known painting competition. It is named after Sir John Moores (1896–1993), the prize's sponsor. Launched in 1957, it feeds into an exhibition held at the Walker Art Gallery every two years, being a prominent feature of the Liverpool Biennial.

[6] Paul McCartney speaking in the Beatles' *Anthology*: a TV documentary, a three-volume set of double albums and a book recounting the history of the band. Paul, George and Ringo collaborated officially. There is also archive footage of John. The series was originally broadcast in November 1995. The book appeared in 2000. A video, LaserDisc and DVD followed, the latter in 2003. The three *Anthology* albums feature outtakes, unreleased material and two new songs based on demo tapes made by Lennon during his post-Beatle years, namely 'Free as a Bird' and 'Real Love'.

CHAPTER 5

[1] 'Peter-Panic paranoia' is referred to by Aldous Huxley in his 1962 novel *Island*. *The Peter Pan Syndrome: Men Who Have Never Grown Up* by psychoanalyst Dr Dan Kiley was originally published in 1983, and became an international best-seller.

[2] Sharon Osbourne, daughter of fearsome rock entrepreneur Don Arden, married Black Sabbath's frontman Ozzy Osbourne and managed him as a solo artist. Apollonia Kotero came to fame via Prince, starred in his film *Purple Rain*, and formed her own multimedia talent company to manage young artists. Tina Davis is a music business veteran who managed Chris Brown. Janet Billig Rich managed Smashing Pumpkins, Hole, Nirvana, the Lemonheads, Lisa Loeb and many more, and is a respected music supervisor. Dianna Hart de la Garza rose to prominence as the 'momanager' of her daughter Demi Lovato.

[3] Roag Best interviewed by David Leafe in the *Daily Mail*, December 2018.

CHAPTER 6

[1] 'Doing one's 10,000 hours' is the principle credited to pop-psych author Malcolm Gladwell, who propounded that 10,000 hours of 'deliberate practice' are required to become world-class in any discipline. His assertion that this pans out at around twenty hours per week of dedication over a period of ten years has been challenged. In his book *Outliers: The Story of Success*, Gladwell contends that their performing of relentless all-night Hamburg shows from a very young age equipped the Beatles to become the greatest band in history; and that Bill Gates was able to amass his vast fortune thanks to having been glued to a computer since his teens. A recent Princeton University study has torn into the theory, finding that the rule only really applies in fields of set rules and specific structure, such as chess, tennis and classical music. In the looser, more flair- and chance-driven 'disciplines' of rock'n'roll and entrepreneurship, where there are no rules, they demonstrated with extensive data that mastery is more than just a matter of practice. Talent is, and has always been, the great indefinable.

[2] John quoted in *Anthology*, 1995, which celebrates its twenty-fifth anniversary in 2020.

[3] Existentialism, as much literary as philosophical phenomenon, became identified with a cultural movement that flourished in Europe during the 1940s and 1950s. Various important philosophers identified as or

were considered to be existentialists, including Jean-Paul Sartre, Albert Camus, Simone de Beauvoir and Maurice Merleau-Ponty in France, and Karl Jaspers, Martin Heidegger and Martin Buber in Germany. The nineteenth-century philosophers Søren Kierkegaard and Friedrich Nietzsche came to be regarded as precursors of the movement. Sartre's own ideas were/are better-known through his fictional works (for example, *Nausea* and *No Exit*) than through his more philosophical offerings (such as, *Being and Nothingness, Critique of Dialectical Reason)*. The post-war years linked together a diverse array of writers and artists under the banner, including (retrospectively) Dostoevsky, Ibsen and Kafka, Jean Genet, André Gide, André Malraux and Samuel Beckett. Abstract Expressionist artists the likes of Jackson Pollock, Arshile Gorky and Willem de Kooning, and filmmakers Jean-Luc Godard and Ingmar Bergman, were evaluated in existential terms. By the mid-1970s, its cultural image had descended into cliché, and was parodied in books and films by Woody Allen.

[4] Astrid Kirchherr quoted in *The Beatles: The Biography* by Bob Spitz (Little, Brown & Co., 2005).

[5] In 1968, John met the real Brigitte Bardot. He was nervous, arrived stoned, and later remembered it as a 'fucking terrible evening – even worse than meeting Elvis'. Any fantasies he may still have cherished about his boyhood sex goddess melted away, and perhaps marked a turning point in his marriage to a woman who had become a peroxide blonde at his behest.

[6] Astrid Kirchherr interviewed on talk-radio show *Fresh Air*, produced by WHYY-FM, a public FM station in Philadelphia, and syndicated on National Public Radio (NPR) stations across the US in January 2008.

[7] Yoko One quoted on the official Stuart Sutcliffe Fan Club website: www.stuartsutcliffefanclub.com

[8] Pauline Sutcliffe interviewed by Gary James, (www.classicbands.com). Her book, *The Beatles' Shadow: Stuart Sutcliffe* and his *Lonely Hearts Club* (Sidgwick & Jackson, 2001), was co-written by the late journalist Douglas Thompson and published by Sidgwick & Jackson in 2001. Ms Sutcliffe died on 13 October 2019.

[9] From the song 'You Always Hurt the One You Love', written by Allan Roberts and Doris Fisher, a huge hit for the Mills Brothers in 1944, Connie Francis in 1958, Fats Domino in 1960, and many others, and recorded by Ringo Starr on his solo album *Sentimental Journey*. Released just as the Beatles were breaking up, the LP featured featured songs sung around the house by his mother Elsie Starkey when Ringo was growing up.

[10] Author interview with Frank Allen of the Searchers.

[11] Giant Ted 'Kingsize' Taylor fronted rock'n'roll band Kingsize Taylor and the Dominoes who emerged on the Liverpool scene in the late 1950s as rivals of the Beatles. They were briefly part of Brian Epstein's management stable, moving on from him in July 1963, having first performed at the Cavern in January 1961 with seventeen-year-old Cilla White as their guest singer – prior to the launch of her solo career as Cilla Black.

Adrian Barber became famous for having recorded the Beatles' *Live! At the Star-Club in Hamburg, Germany; 1962*. He became even more famous as a recording engineer and producer at Ahmet Ertegun's and Herb Abramson's legendary Atlantic Records, where he produced the Allman Brothers Band's debut album in 1969. He also produced the Velvet Underground's *Loaded*, released the following year.

When a court case erupted in the 1980s over the possible release of *The Hamburg Tapes* on CD, Frank Allen was asked to appear as a witness for the Beatles. Quite why, he had no idea. All that he was able to offer was that he had heard the recordings being played. 'Nothing more,' he admitted. 'But I did my bit and gave my puny evidence on the same day as George Harrison and Cliff Bennett.'

Live! At the Star-Club in Hamburg, Germany; 1962 was released as a double album in 1977, featuring some thirty songs performed by the Beatles. The low-fidelity recording had been made on a Grundig reel-to-reel home tape recorder with a single microphone, which had been set at the front of the stage. Taylor claimed that John agreed in person to the live recording in return for free beer for the duration. The recording date, oft-disputed, was likely 31 December 1962, the Beatles' final day in Hamburg, with possible additions recorded at other times. Taylor attempted to sell the tapes to Brian Epstein at the height of Beatlemania.

The manager was unimpressed by their quality and offered a paltry sum. Taylor retained them at home until 1973, when he decided to investigate their commercial value. Allan Williams, also involved, contradicted Taylor's story. The plan was to sell the tapes to Apple for around £100,000, but the proposed deal did not proceed.

Comprehensive audio enhancement improved the sound quality of the recordings to some extent, but this is no great sonic experience. The album has value primarily as a historic record of the group's live club performances pre-global fame. The Beatles lost their court case to block the album's release. It was issued in various formats until 1998, eighteen years after John's death, when at last they won the rights to their performances.

CHAPTER 7

[1] Royal Academy of Dramatic Art, London.

[2] Sexual activity between men in England and Wales was not decriminalised until the late 1960s, later in Scotland and Northern Ireland. The Sexual Offences Act was passed and received Royal Assent on 27 July 1967. During the 1950s, the law was actively enforced.

[3] 'Colonel Tom Parker' started life in the Netherlands as Andreas Cornelis van Kuijk. He absconded to the US at eighteen, possibly to escape prosecution for involvement in criminal activity, and jumped ship. He never had an American passport, meaning that he could never leave the States. Due to his own inability to travel, his protégé Elvis Presley was never able to tour outside America. Parker progressed from carnival work to music promotion, assumed the title 'Colonel' and discovered Elvis in 1955. He made himself indispensable to his artist, landing him a recording contract with RCA Victor, and capitalised on the success of his debut 'Heartbreak Hotel' to win big deals for merchandise, TV contracts and movie roles. Parker claimed fifty per cent of everything that Elvis earned. But he sold the rights to Presley's early recordings, which would have kept him comfortably into old age. The Beatles damaged his popularity. Presley's ill-advised relationship with underage Priscilla Beaulieu, and their brief marriage, scarred his image and took their toll. Elvis became addicted to prescription drugs,

and ate his way to obesity. He became a Las Vegas circus act, and also toured, but had lost the magic. Parker faded from his life and gambled away most of his fortune. Elvis died following a heart attack in August 1977, aged only forty-two. Parker lasted twenty more years and died in January 1997 aged eighty-seven.

[4] The Grades were a family of Russian Jewish immigrants by the name of Winogradsky, who rose to prominence during the 1940s as Britain's foremost entertainment moguls. Lovat/Lev/Louis Winogradsky became Lord Lew Grade, the Baron, media mogul, producer and impresario. His younger brothers were Boris/Boruch, who became Lord Bernard Delfont, a theatre impresario, and Laszlo, aka Leslie Grade, a talent agent and co-founder (with Lew) of the Grade Organisation.

[5] Frank Sinatra famously declared 'Something' to be the 'greatest love song of the past fifty years'. He would also introduce it during live performances as his 'favourite Lennon–McCartney song' … which might have been Frank's sardonic sense of humour. And in the middle eight, Francis Albert changes the word 'now' to 'Jack': 'You stick around, Jack, it might show …' George Harrison was tickled by this, and also sang 'Jack' when he performed his own song live in the US in 1974, and in Japan, 1991–2.

[6] Jeff Dexter interviewed by the author, London, 2012.

[7] Johnnie Hamp interviewed by the author, Stockport, 2019.

[8] Cynthia Lennon in conversation with the author, 1989.

[9] Brian's flat was on the ground floor of a house, 36 Falkner Street, since famous as a location for the popular Netflix series *Peaky Blinders* and, in 2017, the scene of a real-life murder. Neither John nor Cynthia could have known that John's mother Julia had married his father Alf at the same register office, twenty-four years previously, or that they had also celebrated over lunch at Reece's Café.

CHAPTER 8

[1] Pete Best remembering Hamburg days in *Beatle! The Pete Best Story*, (Plexus Publishing, 1985).

[2] John quoted in *All We Are Saying*, Last Interview (Sidgwick & Jackson, 2000), David Sheff's published-book version of his last-ever interviews with John and Yoko conducted at the Dakota building in December 1980. Once again, John's memory may have failed him: he stayed with Brian Epstein in Sitges on the Catalan Costa Dorada, on the north-east coast of Spain. Torremolinos is on the Costa del Sol, some five hundred miles south-south-west by air and a nine-hour drive.

[3] John quoted in *Lennon Remembers*, Jann S. Wenner.

[4] Sitges, thirty-five kilometres south-west of Barcelona, was an epicentre of the 1960s counterculture in Spain, and gained a reputation as a mini-Ibiza. It was effectively 'Barcelona's beach' and has both gay beaches and nudist beaches.

[5] Paul's paternal Auntie Gin had her moment in the spotlight on Wings' 1976 album *Wings at the Speed of Sound*, in the song 'Let 'Em In', which became a Number Two hit single in the UK, and Number Three in the US. As well as his adored aunt, Paul flagged up his brother Mike McCartney, his brother-in-law John Eastman, and 'Phil and Don': the Everlys. 'Uncle Ernie' refers to Who drummer Keith Moon, who played the part of Uncle Ernie in the film version of their rock opera *Tommy*. Ringo voiced the same role for the London Symphony Orchestra's recording of the piece. 'Sister Suzy' is Linda McCartney, who recorded the self-penned song 'Seaside Woman' as Suzy and the Red Stripes in 1977. 'Martin Luther' is neither the sixteenth-century German cleric nor Dr Martin Luther King, the twentieth-century American civil-rights activist, but John Lennon. Paul, Ringo and George used to call him 'John Martin Luther Lennon', perhaps making fun of the name he assumed after he married Yoko in 1969: John Winston Ono Lennon.

[6] *John Lennon: For The Record* by Peter McCabe and Robert D. Schonfeld (Bantam USA, 1984).

[7] John and Pete talking in *John Lennon In My Life* by Pete Shotton, co-authored by Nicholas Schaffner.

[8] In *Mick: The Wild Life and Mad Genius of Jagger*, author Christopher Andersen quotes Angie Bowie on the subject of her former husband and

Mick: 'They were writing "Angie" when I found them in bed together.' (Robson Press, 2012).

[9] John talking to Jann S. Wenner in *Lennon Remembers*. The published-book version of Wenner's long interview with Lennon conducted in December 1970 and serialised in *Rolling Stone* magazine.

[10] Speaking of novelty recordings, Andy White was married to artist Lyn Cornell, a former Vernon's Girl and one-time member of the Pearls, protégées of Phil 'the Collector' Swern. As a member of the Carefrees, she enjoyed the biggest-selling novelty Beatles single 'We Love You Beatles' (1964). The author's personal favourite in this category remains Dora Bryan's eccentric offering 'All I Want for Christmas is a Beatle' (1963, Number Twenty in the UK chart).

[11] Paul's widely published press statement, 9 March 2016.

CHAPTER 9

[1] As John said in the *Anthology* series.

[2] From sixteenth-century Spanish author Miguel de Cervantes's *Don Quixote*. To 'tilt at windmills' meaning to pursue an unrealistic, impractical or impossible goal, or to battle imaginary enemies.

[3] *All You Need is Ears*, George Martin with Jeremy Hornsby, 1979. (Macmillan, 1979).

[4] 'Soeur Sourire' and 'the Singing Nun' were stage names of Belgian singer-songwriter Jeanne-Paule Marie Deckers (17 October 1933–29 March 1985), also known as 'Jeannine'. Within Belgium's Catholic Dominican Order, she was Sister Luc Gabriel. She rose to fame in 1963 with her rendition of the popular French-language song 'Dominique', about a priest of her order, which was a hit in several countries and which topped the US *Billboard* Hot 100. Her extraordinary story had a tragic ending. An unfavourable recording contract led to penury, the experience challenged her faith, and she withdrew from the order, only to commit suicide with long-term friend Annie Pécher at the age of fifty-two.

CHAPTER 10

[1] Cynthia Lennon writing in her second memoir, *John* (Hodder & Stoughton, 2005).

CHAPTER 11

[1] The Toby Jug in Tolworth, Surrey, was a must-play on the rock circuit during the 1960s and 1970s, and hosted many now-famous acts: Muddy Waters, Led Zeppelin, Yes, Jethro Tull, the Yardbirds, Ten Years After, King Crimson, Fleetwood Mac and, later, the Stranglers, Squeeze, the Fabulous Poodles, the Damned, Ultravox and many more. David Bowie glammed there in 1972, on what became known as the Ziggy Stardust Tour.

Despite biogs and docs always citing the Toby Jug as having presented 'the first' Ziggy Stardust gig, Spiders keyboard player and Mainman (Bowie's management company) executive Nicky Graham disagrees: 'The Ebbisham Hall, Epsom gig, MC'd by DJ Bob Harris, is the one that those of us who were actually there regard as the very first Ziggy Stardust gig,' he insists. 'It hadn't come together until then.' The pub fell into decline during the nineties, a victim of live music's evolution, and was pulled down in 2000. RIP, pretty things.

[2] John's paternal half-brothers are David Henry Lennon, born 26 February 1969, and Robin Francis Lennon, born 22 October 1973.

[3] Pauline Lennon's *Daddy, Come Home: The True Story of John Lennon and his Father* (Angus & Robertson, 1990) is a memoir about her love for John's father and his encounters with his son. Its core content derives from Freddie's own unpublished autobiography. Pauline remarried after Freddie's death, taking the surname Stone.

CHAPTER 12

[1] A quote attributed to a wide variety of public figures, from film producer Samuel Goldwyn to golfer Gary Player. It probably started with Thomas Jefferson, American founding father and third president, who said, 'I'm a great believer in luck, and I find that the harder I work, the more I have of it.'

[2] This attendance record held for eight years, until it was broken by Led Zeppelin, who clocked up 56,800 fans at Tampa Stadium, Florida in 1973.

Shea Stadium was named after William Shea, the New York lawyer who returned National League baseball to the city. It opened for business on 17 April 1964. It welcomed the Beatles back on 23 August 1966; the Summer Festival for Peace fundraiser was held there in August 1970, starring Paul Simon, Janis Joplin, Steppenwolf, Creedence Clearwater Revival and more; Grand Funk Railroad supported by Humble Pie in 1971 out-did the Beatles fastest-ticket-sales record. Like London's Wembley Stadium, Shea became a standard stadium concert venue, welcoming Jethro Tull, the Who, Simon & Garfunkel, the Police – 'We'd like to thank the Beatles for lending us their stadium,' cried Sting from the stage. There was Pope John Paul II in October 1979, six nights with the Stones in October 1989, and Elton and Clapton in August 1992. After the 2001 9/11 atrocities, Shea was used as a rescuers' HQ, storing medical supplies, food and water, and offering sleep shelter to relief workers.

Springsteen and his E Street Band performed there in October 2003. Its final concerts, 'The Last Play at Shea', featured Billy Joel in 2008, when he was joined by Tony Bennett, Steve Tyler, Don Henley and more. Paul McCartney, poignantly, stepped up to perform 'Let It Be'. The stadium was demolished in 2009.

[3] Linda Eastman married Paul McCartney in London in 1969. Born Linda Eastman on 24 September 1941 in Scarsdale, NY, her entertainment lawyer father's original name, coincidentally, was Leopold Epstein, which he anglicised to Lee Eastman. Linda had lost her mother three years earlier, in the American Airlines Flight 1 crash in Queen's, March 1962. She had been divorced for just a few weeks when she attended the gig, from first husband Melville See, Jr, with whom she had a three-year-old daughter, Heather. The college graduate was now working as a photographer, and was permitted backstage at Shea Stadium. She met Paul again in London in May 1967, during a Georgie Fame gig at the Bag O' Nails club. She and Paul hooked up at Brian Epstein's house four days later, at a launch party for the *Sgt. Pepper* album; and again in New York a year on, when John and Paul were there to launch Apple Records. Their marriage on 12 March 1969 infuriated

fans and earned her abuse, because she had nabbed the 'last available Beatle'. John married Yoko Ono in Gibraltar eight days a week later, on 20 March. Both women were widely blamed, ridiculously, for the break-up of the Beatles. Linda died from breast cancer on 17 April 1998, aged fifty-six.

Actress and model Barbara Bach became Mrs Ringo (now Lady Starkey) 27 April 1981, soon after they met that year during the filming of *Caveman*. A Rosedale, Queens, girl born Barbara Goldbach on 27 August 1947, she became world-famous as a Bond girl in 1977 opposite Roger Moore in *The Spy Who Loved Me*. Her sister Marjorie is the fifth wife of the Eagles' Joe Walsh.

[4] From 'Getting Better', on *Sgt. Pepper*.

[5] **The Beatles children:**

Ringo: Zak Starkey born 13 September 1965, drummer (the Who, Paul Weller, the Waterboys, Oasis etc.); Jason Starkey, 19 August 1967; Lee Starkey, 11 November 1970.

Paul: Heather McCartney (Linda's daughter, whom Paul adopted), 31 December 1962; Mary McCartney, photographer, 28 August 1969; Stella McCartney, fashion designer, 13 September 1971; James McCartney, musician, 12 September 1977; Beatrice McCartney, his daughter with second wife Heather Mills, 28 October 2003.

John: Julian Lennon, musician and photographer, 8 April 1963; Sean Ono Lennon, musician, 9 October 1975.

George: Dhani Harrison, born 1 August 1978, with second wife Olivia.

[6] New Yorker Veronica 'Ronnie' Bennett, the 'Bad Girl of Rock'n'Roll', was lead singer of hugely popular girl group the Ronettes which also featured her sister Estelle and cousin Nedra. Although seriously tempted towards John, who was equally smitten, Ronnie married their producer Phil 'Wall of Sound' Spector in 1968. She suffered years of domestic abuse, even imprisonment and being held at gunpoint, as well as her husband's sabotage of her career. Because he confiscated her shoes to prevent her from leaving, she was forced to escape the marriage through barbed wire and guard dogs barefoot, with the help of her mother, in 1972. Her memoir *Be My Baby: How I Survived Mascara, Miniskirts and Madness, Or My Life as a Fabulous Ronette*

(Harmony 1990), with a foreword by Cher and an intro by Billy Joel, is a hell of a read.

Spector was later appointed to work on the *Let It Be* project. John hired Spector in 1973 to produce his collection of covers of cherished fifties and sixties songs, *Rock'n'Roll*. The album was eventually released (after shenanigans involving Spector making off with the masters, a motorbike accident, and a legal wrangle with fearsome American music executive Morris Levy, who was suing John for infringement of copyright over a line in the song 'Come Together') – in 1975. The famous sleeve shot of leather-jacketed John standing in a brick doorway was taken in Hamburg in April 1961 by Beatles friend Jürgen Vollmer, and only turned up years later. Said John of Spector, 'I'm fond of his work a lot. His personality I'm not crazy about.'

CHAPTER 13

[1] The old stadium, which stood on the gusty west shore of San Francisco Bay, was named after the so-called candlestick birds, a variety of curlew also known as the sicklebird, long common to the area.

Paul McCartney gave the last-ever gig there in August 2014, before the stadium was demolished. Firsts and lasts: Paul's favourite.

[2] From 'The Hollow Men', T.S. Eliot.

[3] The *geta* is the traditional wooden platform shoe, like a cross between a flip-flop and a clog, worn by the Japanese.

CHAPTER 14

[1] Johann Wolfgang von Goethe, German poet, philosopher, novelist, playwright, statesman, creator of *Faust*, leading figure of the eighteenth-century Sturm und Drang (storm and stress) literary movement, the main thrust of which was expression of extreme human emotion in creative works, especially music and literature.

[2] EMI recording engineer Ken Townsend invented ADT (Artificial/Automatic DoubleTracking) early in 1966, at John's express request. Lennon couldn't stand the laborious process of double tracking/

overdubbing during recording sessions, and kept pestering the technicians to come up with some mechanised way of achieving enhancement. It was Townsend who had the brainwave of using tape delay added to the first 'flat', 'straight', recording to 'fluff up' John's vocals, which had an effect comparable to using hair thickener before blow-drying! Tape delay fattened and enriched the sound. The Beatles began using it on instrumental recordings too. That's actually manual double tracking on 'Tomorrow Never Knows', but the rest of the *Revolver* album does benefit from ADT. Check out the dreamy reverse guitar played by George on 'I'm Only Sleeping', and his lead guitar on 'Taxman'. Also, 'Within You, Without You', 'Being for the Benefit of Mr. Kite!', 'Blue Jay Way' and 'I Am the Walrus'. Many other musicians picked up on the technique throughout the sixties and seventies. Its popularity faded with the advent of digital technology in the eighties. Previously unimaginable techniques can now easily be achieved with simple computer software.

[3] *All You Need is Ears*, George Martin with Jeremy Hornsby, 1979.

[4] Barbershop standard 'Wedding Bells' from the 1920s, lyrics by Willie Raskin and Irving Kahal, music by Sammy Fain. Paul was probably familiar with the 1954 recording by the Four Aces.

[5] New Testament of the Holy Bible, 1 Corinthians 13:11, Paul's First Epistle to the Corinthians (KJV). The inference there was that the same will happen for believers when Christ returns, and when our partial understanding of God will become full, mature and 'knowing'.

[6] PPL PRS Ltd is the UK's music licensing body, combining the organisations that protect music performance rights and collect royalties on behalf of artists. www.pplprs.co.uk

[7] The Beatles' *One World* sequence was subsequently computer-colourised, to modernise it for the *Anthology* documentary series.

[8] John's 1970 interview with *Rolling Stone*.

CHAPTER 15

[1] An ashram spiritual retreat is usually remote from other human settlements, set in peaceful, natural surroundings, welcoming those

seeking guidance and enlightenment. Attendees are required to live simply without the trappings of their usual lifestyles, and to relinquish 'bad' habits and indulgences such as cigarettes, alcohol and drugs.

Rishikesh in northern India, regarded as one of Hinduism's holiest places, is situated in the mountains at the emergence of the Ganges. It is the yoga capital of the world, hosting the annual international yoga festival each March.

[2] Their Irish-American actress mother Maureen O'Sullivan, the star of more than sixty Hollywood films, played Jane to Johnny Weissmuller's Tarzan in the great 'ape man' films of the 1930s and 1940s. She and her director husband John Villiers Farrow had seven children together.

[3] John's interview with *Playboy*, published in 1981. Prudence Farrow Bruns published her memoir *Dear Prudence: The Story Behind the Song* in 2015. Prudence quoted in a *Rolling Stone* interview, September 2015.

[4] Although Jenny had met Mick Fleetwood when she was sixteen, they had a long on-off relationship before marrying in 1970, divorcing six years later. She remarried the Fleetwood Mac drummer the following year, and divorced him again the year after that. The couple had two daughters. She became a rock wife a third time when she married drummer Ian Wallace (Bob Dylan, Bonnie Raitt, King Crimson, Crosby Stills and Nash, Don Henley), but that, too, ended in divorce. During the late 1980s, she enrolled as a mature student at UCLA, earning a PhD in Human Behaviour. She became a clinical consultant, writer and author. Her published books include *It's Not Only Rock'n'Roll* and *Jennifer Juniper: A Journey Beyond the Muse*.

[5] Donovan, *Rolling Stone* interview, 2012.

[6] As quoted in *Lennon Remembers*, Jann S. Wenner.

[7] *A Tale of Two Cities*, Charles Dickens.

[8] In 2019, it was announced that *The Lord of the Rings* director Peter Jackson had been commissioned to turn 58 hours of archival footage and 140 hours of audio recordings, plus the live-on-the-roof footage, into a new *Let It Be* documentary. A reissue of the original *Let It Be* may follow Jackson's film in 2020, to commemorate its fiftieth anniversary.

[9] 'Hey Jude' began life as 'Hey Jules', written for Julian Lennon, to help him feel better after his parents split up. It was the first Beatles record to be recorded on eight-track, at the now-defunct Trident Studios, St Anne's Court, London's Soho. At seven minutes and eleven seconds, it was the longest single to date ever to reach Number One in the UK. Compare this to Don McLean's 'American Pie', 8.5 mins, *but* divided in half by the record company; Clapton's 'Layla', 7:08 mins, the album version; Queen's 'Bohemian Rhapsody', a 6-minute single; 'MacArthur Park' recorded by Richard Harris, 7:21; and the Doors' 'Light My Fire', 7:06 on the album.

Julian discovered only in his teens that Paul had written 'Hey Jude' for him.

[10] Paul quoted in *Paul McCartney: Many Years from Now*, Barry Miles.

[11] Julian quoted in *A Hard Day's Write: The Stories Behind Every Beatles Song*, Steve Turner.

[12] Cynthia was married to hotelier Roberto Bassanini, 1970–73; to Lancashire engineer John Twist, 1976–82; she lived with Liverpool chauffeur Jim Christie for seventeen years, until their separation in 1998; her final, fourth, marriage, to Barbadian nightclub owner Noel Charles, lasted from 2002 until his death from cancer in 2013. Cynthia also died of cancer, in 2015.

[13] 'The Ballad of John and Yoko', Beatles single, May 1969: their seventeenth single, the first Beatles record released in stereo, and their last British Number One. John wrote the song in Paris. Only two Beatles appear on the recording: John playing lead guitar, and Paul playing drums and bass.

CHAPTER 16

[1] Interview with the author.

[2] 'Goin' Back', the hit song by Gerry Goffin and Carole King, 1966. Recorded by many, not least by Dusty Springfield, the Byrds, Freddie Mercury as Larry Lurex, and by Carole herself.

[3] Aunt Mimi's bungalow stood on a plot that has since become one of the

most valuable pieces of coastal real estate in the world, the domain of the rich and famous. It was sold by Yoko Ono after Mimi's death, and later demolished. The property that now occupies the same plot was recently renovated, and renamed 'Imagine'. It was valued at £7.2 million.

Mimi Smith interviewed by Christopher Peacock for Southern Television in 1981, her only TV interview.

[4] The Beatles had known Maureen since Cavern Club days. She was only sixteen when she started dating Ringo. She was as good as a sister-in-law to John, Paul and George, hence John's widely quoted rebuke.

Pattie Boyd inspired ten songs: 'I Need You', 'Something' and 'For You Blue', the Beatles. 'Layla', Derek and the Dominos (Clapton). 'Mystifies Me' and 'Breathe on Me', Ronnie Wood. 'So Sad', George Harrison. 'Wonderful Tonight', 'She's Waiting' and 'Old Love', Eric Clapton.

[5] Pete Shotton speaking exclusively to David Stark in 1983, in a taped interview never previously published. Shotton died from a heart attack at home in Cheshire, on 24 March 2017, aged seventy-five.

[6] The teenager in question, Gail Renard, had talked herself into the room with a present for Yoko's five-year-old daughter Kyoko. Although she spent the entire week there, she was sent home every night. She auctioned the hand-written lyrics to 'Give Peace a Chance', gifted to her by John, in 2008, to repair her leaking roof.

Roger Scott went on to create countless Beatles documentaries for the US radio syndication company Westwood One, including nine-part series *Sgt. Pepper's Lonely Hearts Club Band – a History of the Beatle Years 1962–1970*, co-produced by Beatles historian Mark Lewisohn. Roger died on 31 October 1989, aged forty-six. A memorial concert on 7 December that year, featuring Chris Rea, Mark Knopfler, Dave Edmunds, Nick Lowe and others, was held at Abbey Road. The singer who had first inspired Roger's love affair with music, Cliff Richard, sang the song that had ignited Scott's passion: 'Move It'. Said 'Whispering Bob' Harris, 'Roger Scott was the best DJ who ever walked the planet.'

CHAPTER 17

[1] John and Yoko interviewed by Tariq Ali and Robin Blackburn for underground newspaper *Red Mole*, January 1971.

John speaking to his friend Roy Carr, the Executives musician, Beatles author, staffer at the *NME* from 1970, and its eventual editor, in 1972.

[2] Tony Cox talking to US magazine *People* in February 1986.

[3] The 'film about bums' is a short, *Film No. 4. 1966–67*, aka *Bottoms* or 'the Bottoms film'. Consisting entirely of close-ups of the bottoms of famous people, it was intended by Yoko to 'encourage dialogue for world peace'.

[4] Reported by British journalist Sharon Churcher in the US Cult Education Institute's *Advertiser*, January 2001.

CHAPTER 18

[1] The former Immigration and Naturalization Service (INS) was terminated on 1 March 2003 as part of the overhaul that followed the 2001 9/11 terrorist attacks. The three new sub-departments created under the Department of Homeland Security (DHS) are USCIS – US Citizenship and Immigration Services; ICE – US Immigration and Customs Enforcement; and CBP – US Customs and Border Protection.

[2] A phrase coined by American author Erica Jong in her 1973 feminist novel *Fear of Flying*, to denote sexual intercourse for the sake of it between hitherto unacquainted partners who are not emotionally involved with each other. Jong, now seventy-eight, describes such sex as 'zipless' because 'when you came together, zippers fell away like rose petals, underwear blew off in one breath like dandelion fluff. For the true ultimate zipless A-1 fuck, it was necessary that you never got to know the man very well.' The book struck a chord with unfulfilled women everywhere, and sold twenty million copies!

[3] Greta Garbo, 18 September 1905–15 April 1990, Swedish-born Hollywood actress of the twenties and thirties, who famously 'wanted to be alone'.

[4] Now the Grand Hyatt New York.

[5] Although John had been the first former Beatle to release a solo single – his and Yoko's 'Give Peace a Chance', in 1969 – he was the last to score a Number One. George Harrison, 'My Sweet Lord', 1970. Paul McCartney, 'Live and Let Die'; Ringo Starr, 'Photograph' and 'You're Sixteen', all 1973. John's '(Just Like) Starting Over' reached the top slot in late December 1980, three weeks after his death.

[6] John talking to David Sheff, 1980.

CHAPTER 19

[1] Yoko Ono interviewed by Philip Norman for *John Lennon: The Life*. (HarperCollins, 2008)

CHAPTER 20

[1] Captain Hank Halstad, Tyler Coneys and his cousins Ellen and Kevin were John's crew.

The phenomenon of the 'deadly Bermuda Triangle', an area of the North Atlantic in which ships and planes are said to have vanished, never to be found. Many notable disappearances have been disproved, but the conspiracy theory alleging paranormal activity persists.

CHAPTER 21

[1] In 2017, the NMPA (National Music Publishers Association) of America announced plans to acknowledge Yoko as co-writer of 'Imagine', correcting 'an historical oversight' that John admitted in his interview with Andy Peebles was his own fault. Yoko later accepted a Centennial Award from the NMPA, saying, 'This is the best time of my life.'

[2] Pete Shotton quoting George Harrison in his interview with David Stark.

IN OTHER WORDS

'Don't you think that the Beatles gave every soddin' thing they've got to be the Beatles? That took a whole section of our youth – that whole period – when everybody else was just goofin' off, we were workin' twenty-four hours a day!'

John Lennon

'In today's pop music, there are only two things that interest me: rock'n'roll and avant-garde poetry. Only one group today is of interest to me, Marc Bolan and T. Rex. He is the only one who has excited me, and I look forward to meeting him again. His music is good rock'n'roll; it has good beat, and it really swings. But it is mainly his lyrics that amaze me. His way of writing is new, and I have never read lyrics as funny and as real as his. Apart from few American exceptions, Marc Bolan is the only one that has caught my attention, and I believe his mythology is real as well. He will release a book of poetry in the near future, and I look forward to read it again and again. Marc Bolan is the only one who can succeed to the Beatles.'

John Lennon

'They gave the British the illusion that they meant something again. We love hearing that. *Boy* do we love hearing that.'

David Bowie

'What kept the Beatles head and shoulders above everyone else is that they were prepared to change, do different things. No one record was a carbon copy of another. We never fell into the *Star Wars II* syndrome, remaking something under a new title.'

Sir George Henry Martin CBE

'In my country, the Beatles took society and changed its direction. We had come out of the gruelling endurance of World War II, and the Beatles said, "Not anymore." It created a belief system that wasn't about money – although money obviously has a part to play in it – or religion or war. It was about culture driving society and being young and not being our parents. It was about loveliness and pleasure and enjoyment. It was about love.'

Danny Boyle, director, *Yesterday*

'My model for business is the Beatles. They were four guys who kept each other's negative tendencies in check. They balanced each other, and the total was greater than the sum of the parts. And that's how I see business. Great things in business are never done by one person, they are done by a team of people.'

Steve Jobs

'We were driving through Colorado, we had the radio on, and eight of the Top 10 songs were Beatles songs – 'I Wanna Hold Your Hand', all those early ones. They were doing things nobody was doing. Their chords were outrageous, just outrageous, and their harmonies made it all valid … I knew they were pointing the direction of where music had to go.'

Bob Dylan

'I love the Beatles. What more can I say? I'm not gonna lie to you. I love 'em. They make me happy. And I think they were the best, and still are.'

Liam Gallagher

'I don't think anybody comes close to the Beatles, including Oasis.'

Brian May

'This was different, [it} shifted the lay of the land. Four guys, playing and singing, writing their own material … Rock'n'roll came to my house where there seemed to be no way out … and opened up a whole world of possibilities.'

Bruce Springsteen

'That one performance [*The Ed Sullivan Show*] changed my life … Up to that moment, I'd never considered playing rock as a career. And when I saw four guys who didn't look like they'd come out of the Hollywood star mill, who played their own songs and instruments, and especially because you could see this look in John Lennon's face – and he looked like he was always saying: "F-you!" – I said, I know these guys, I can relate to these guys, I *am* these guys. This is what I'm going to do: play in a rock band.'

Billy Joel

'His bluff was all on the surface. He used to take his glasses down, those granny glasses, and say, "It's only me!" They were like a wall, you know? A shield. Those are the moments I treasure.

'I talked to Yoko the day after he was killed, and the first thing she said was, "John was really fond of you."'

Sir James Paul McCartney, CH, MBE

'A lot of people were just as shocked as I was … I was in New York at his home, the Dakota. He was nice. He was running round the house making dinner and playing a lot of Indian music, which surprised me … he grew into it.

'The thing is, I hadn't seen him for so long. I mean, for all I knew, he could still be there now, you know, because I didn't see him for two years anyway. And occasionally maybe, he'd send a postcard. And it's knowing that he's on the other end of a telephone if you do want to call. That's the difference. Now, you need the big cosmic telephone to speak to him … I believe that life goes on. And so, to me, I can't get sad … we all meet again, somewhere down the line.'

George Harrison, MBE

'I still well up that some bastard shot him.

'We got a plane to New York, and we went to the apartment. "Anything we can do?" And Yoko just said, "Well, you just play with Sean. Keep Sean busy." And that's what we did.

'I miss his friendship. I miss hanging. I miss … just that we're not together right now. That's what I miss. I go to New York a lot, I say hi to Yoko, and it sucks, you know? But he's still in my heart.'

Sir Richard Starkey, MBE (aka Ringo Starr)

'As far as the music was concerned, John Lennon was always looking for the impossible, the unattainable. He was never satisfied.'

Sir George Henry Martin, CBE

'Dad could talk about peace and love out loud to the world, but he could never show it to the people who supposedly meant the most to him.'

Julian Lennon

'I have a lot of memories of just talking with him, hanging out and watching TV. Saying "Goodnight" to me was an intimate moment. It was just me and him. There was something so soothing about his voice. And he did this really cute thing: He would flick the lights on and off in rhythm to whatever he would say. He would say, "Good night, Sean," and the lights would go [he makes clicking noise]. It just made me feel so cozy.'

Sean Lennon

'The fact that he was too honest may have offended some people … he was very upfront, extremely open to people. I think that sometimes you have to pay a high price for this … and he gambled on it, I think.'

Yoko Ono Lennon

'I think he found his space. I don't think he found the complete satisfaction in life because I think he was always searching, always looking for it, always wanting something new. I mean, he was due to come back to England near the end, just before he died. So he was constantly changing and looking for new quests. But whatever he did, it was totally honest and wholehearted.'

Cynthia Lennon

'Lennon was a most talented man, and above all, a gentle soul. John and his colleagues set a high standard by which contemporary music continues to be measured.'

Frank Sinatra

'Forty is an early age to have to leave this planet, but as a performer, the way Lennon was killed is very frightening and tragic to me. He was truly one of the world's greatest musical innovators, and I'm sure he'll be missed and mourned by many, especially those of us who are his peers.'

Smokey Robinson

'I first met him in London in 1963. The Ronettes were the top group in England at that time. He saw us and got in touch with our manager, and there was this party and we danced all night with all the fellas, taught them the New York dances. He liked me for more than just my voice … I was just nineteen years old, and starting to make it big, and he knew things … I met him in the street, years later. He called my name – "Ronnie!" – and I turned around; it was so fucking cool … he got shot right after that … I was so devastated, I stayed in bed for a week. It broke my heart. I always think of John Lennon every time I'm in the recording studio. I can't help it. He's my spirit talking to me, saying, "Don't give up."'

Ronnie Spector

'The weekend we went to Bangor [Wales, where Maharishi was delivering a lecture] was very intense because we all went on the train there: the Beatles and me and Mick Jagger and the Maharishi. Then, over the weekend, we got the news that Brian Epstein had overdosed. John was devastated. I wish I'd gone on the retreat in India – not because I liked the Maharishi, because I didn't. Just to be there to hear Lennon's asides and to watch the whole thing unravel – because it did. I would have loved to be there for that. His legacy? It's hard to put into words. I mean, it's nothing, really. He just changed the face of popular music forever, didn't he.'

Marianne Faithfull

'I liked John a lot. He was the one I really got on with the most. We weren't buddy-buddies but we were always friendly. But after the Beatles and the Stones stopped playing clubs, we didn't see each other that much until he separated from Yoko, around 1974. We got really friendly again. And when he went back with Yoko, he went into hibernation … when I went to visit someone in the Dakota, I'd leave him a note saying, "I live next door. I know you don't want to see anyone, but if you do, please call." He never did.'

Sir Michael Philip Jagger

'It's really hard to remember when I actually met John. It must have been middle '74-ish … we started knocking around with each other. He was one of the brightest, quickest-witted, earnestly socialist men I've ever met in my life. Socialist in the true definition, not in a fabricated political sense. A real humanist. And a really spiteful sense of humour, which of course, being English, I adored. I just thought we'd be buddies forever and get on better and better. Yeah. Fantasy.'

David Bowie

'I really loved John. And when you love someone that much, I don't think you ever quite get over their death.'

Sir Elton Hercules John, CBE

'I remember hearing about the death of John Lennon [when I was] in Florida. I was waking up after a very late-night session at Criteria Studios. I regret to this day not abandoning recording and going to pay my respects outside the Dakota building. He was my absolute hero.'

Barry Blue

'What he wrote was what he felt. He always wrote the truth. He always said, "I write the truth and make it rhyme." He was his music. He was also extremely generous. I don't mean in a monetary way, although he was. But in a way that, if he liked you and trusted you … he really gave you something of himself … that you were able to carry forever.'

Jack Douglas, engineer on *Imagine*, producer on *Double Fantasy*

'Numb with disbelief and sadness, my BFF Hilary and I climbed into bed with a bottle of Bailey's and watched hours of footage on TV. What else could we do …'

Miriam Stockley, British-South African singer/composer

'I met John several times in Los Angeles and New York, sometimes socially in that he just happened to be where I was, out on the town, and he didn't mind if I joined him and whoever he was with. On about the third occasion, after I'd done one long interview [with him] for *Melody Maker*, I was a bit cheeky and asked him for his phone number. He said he didn't know it. Yoko looked after that stuff. But he said that if I wanted to get in touch with him, I should send him a cable [telegram] to [the Dakota] and mention my number. If he was there, he'd call me back. We did this three or four times. I arranged two interviews that way, never through PRs. Ray Coleman [writer] would ask me to get a quote from him on this or that. Another time, we discussed his immigration situation. "Hello, Chris, it's Johnny Beatle here," he would say when he called. Eventually, he gave me a number for his private office. I still have it in my old phone book from those days. I went to his Green Card hearing, and the last time I ever saw him was on the street outside afterwards. He was holding it up, and I mentioned to him that it wasn't green, it was blue! He laughed. He was so happy that day. The last time I sent him a cable was shortly after this. He didn't call me back, but he sent me a postcard. I still have it.'

Chris Charlesworth, journalist, author and
former Managing Editor of Omnibus Press

'John Lennon is the most iconic figure in music since the 1950s. He is the highest-regarded: above Michael Jackson, above Elvis Presley, above all of them. This is not necessarily fair. Paul McCartney is undeniably the better songwriter. He creates exquisite melodies. John's composing is more functional. If you put all of John's music together, there is not actually a huge amount. Of course his enduring popularity has to do with having been assassinated. It boosts the whole romance of it. But would he be so revered today, had he not died? I'm not so sure. Which is not to underestimate or pour scorn on his intelligence, his incredible knowledge and understanding of contemporary music, and his ability to play the industry – and indeed the world – at its own game. John was undoubtedly the leader in all things the Beatles did that were new and experimental. And he was the only one in the group who was interested in how the music business worked.'

Simon Napier-Bell, record producer, songwriter,
artist manager, author and filmmaker

* To fight document fraud, INS (Immigration & Naturalization Service) redesigned the Green Card seventeen times between 1952 and 1977, according to the American Immigration Lawyers Association (AILA). In 1964, for example, it changed to pale blue. These colour changes helped immigration officials to identify new and expired versions more quickly.

SOME TRIBUTE SONGS TO JOHN

'Here Today' – Paul McCartney, on *Tug of War*, 1982

'I'm Outta Time' – Oasis, from *Dig Out Your Soul*, 2008*

'Edge of Seventeen' – Stevie Nicks, from her debut solo offering
    Bella Donna, 1981

'All Those Years Ago' – George Harrison, on *Somewhere in England*, 1981

'Life is Real' – Freddie Mercury, on Queen's *Hot Space*, 1982

'11:07pm' – Dizzy Mizz Lizzy, 1996

'I Just Shot John Lennon' – the Cranberries, from *To the Faithful
    Departed*, 1996

'Ballad of John Lennon' – the Elect**, 1997

'Roll on John' – Bob Dylan, on *Tempest*, 2012

'Empty Garden (Hey Hey Johnny)' – Elton John, featured
    on *Jump Up!*, 1982

'Moonlight Shadow' – Mike Oldfield*** (1983)

* Echoing John's 'Jealous Guy' and the Beatles' 'A Day in the Life', it features not only a mellotron and Ringo's son Zak Starkey on drums, but also John speaking in a clip lifted from one of his 1980 interviews: 'As Churchill said, it's every Englishman's inalienable right to live where the hell he likes. What's it going to do, vanish? Is it not going to be there when I get back?'

** A band from Lusaka, Zambia, formed in 2009.

*** This song is widely regarded as being about John's murder. When asked about it in a 1995 interview, Oldfield said: 'Not really … well, perhaps, when I look back on it, maybe it was. I actually arrived in New York that awful evening when he was shot, and I was staying at the Virgin Records house in Perry Street, which was just a few blocks down the road from the Dakota building where it happened, so it probably sank into my subconscious …'

MUSIC

The Beatles' entire twelve-album oeuvre (some say eleven, discounting the *Yellow Submarine* film soundtrack, while others state thirteen, to include the *Magical Mystery Tour* EP, which was not recorded as an album but which was later released as one in some territories) was recorded over a period of just seven years.

BEATLES ALBUMS

(All UK release dates)

Please Please Me (1963)
With The Beatles (1963)
A Hard Day's Night (1964)
Beatles For Sale (1964)
Help! (1965)
Rubber Soul (1965)
Revolver (1966)
Sgt. Pepper's Lonely Hearts Club Band (1967)
The Beatles (the 'White Album) (1968)
Yellow Submarine (1969)
Abbey Road (1969)*
Let It Be (1970)
Magical Mystery Tour was originally released as a double 7" EP in the UK in 1967, but appeared as a full-length album in the US and other territories.

THE BEST OF THE REST

Red Album 1962–1966 (1973)
Blue Album 1967–1970 (1973)
The Beatles at the Hollywood Bowl (1977)
The Beatles Past Masters (1988–2009)
The Beatles Live at the BBC (1994)
Anthology 1 (1995)
Anthology 2 (1996)
Anthology 3 (1996)
1 (One) (2000)**
Love (2006)

JOHN LENNON ALBUMS

Unfinished Music No. 1: Two Virgins (1968)
Unfinished Music No. 2: Life with the Lions (1969)
Wedding Album (1969)
Live Peace in Toronto - The Plastic Ono Band (1969)
John Lennon/Plastic Ono Band (1970)
Imagine (1971)
Some Time in New York City - with Yoko Ono (1972)
Mind Games (1973)
Walls and Bridges (1974)
Rock 'N' Roll (1975)
Shaved Fish (1975) – featuring all of John's singles as a solo artist released in the US until then (except 'Stand by Me', released earlier). This was the only compilation of his non-Beatles recordings released during John's lifetime, and his final album on the Apple label.
Double Fantasy - with Yoko Ono (1980)
Milk and Honey - with Yoko Ono (1984)

THE BEST OF THE REST

Live in New York City (1986)
Menlove Ave (1986)
John Lennon Anthology (1998)

Wonsaponatime (1998)
Acoustic (2004)
John Lennon Signature Box (2010)

THE AUTHOR'S FAVOURITE
BEATLES SONGS

I can list only my own favourites. We would be here forever otherwise. One of the wondrous things about Beatles music is that there is something for absolutely everyone. Tweet me yours, to **@LAJwriter**. We can compare notes.

There were how many songs in total, exactly? That depends. Although a core catalogue of 213 songs (a few of which are different versions) is generally given, 188 of which are originals and twenty-five of which are covers, ultimateclassicrock.com reckons they recorded 227 songs that were officially released, not including BBC or live tracks. More made it to market after their dissolution, including live numbers never captured in the studio and a feast of outtakes and demos, which can be found on compilations, live albums, special editions and remix packages galore. Lots, anyway. Perhaps there are more to come.

Simplicity ruled. They kicked off with a limited vocabulary. Their early songwriting focused primarily on universal sentiments, plainly expressed. They rarely used words of more than three syllables. Notable are 'balalaikas' ('Back in the USSR'), 'kaleidoscope' ('Lucy in the Sky with Diamonds'), and 'Montélimar' ('Savoy Truffle'). The five most common words in their lyrics are single-syllable. 'You' occurs the most frequently (2,262 times), followed by 'I' (1,736), 'the' (1,355), 'to' (1,097) and 'me' (1,060). They deployed 'girl' a mere 170 times (I would have guessed more), 'baby' 300 times, and 'love' a relatively restrained 613 times ... although emotion is implied if not blurted in almost every song.***** Talking of which, girls' names are writ large in songs they both created and borrowed: Michelle, Eleanor, Rita, Madonna; Prudence, Martha, Sadie, Julia; Maggie Mae, Anna, Pam, Lizzy (dizzy miss) and Sally (long, tall); Lucy, Lucille, Carol, Clarabella and Penny; Mary Jane, Molly, Yoko, Loretta and Lil (but everyone knows her as Nancy).

Among the more unusual word choices are 'scrimp' ('When I'm Sixty-Four'), 'dovetail' ('Glass Onion'), 'summersets' (acrobatic flips) and 'hogshead' ('Being for the Benefit of Mr. Kite!'), 'hoedown' ('Rocky Racoon'), 'boatswain' ('Yellow Submarine'), 'meander' ('Across the

Universe'), 'chapattis' (What's the New Mary Jane') and 'plasticine' ('Lucy in the Sky with Diamonds'). There is a plethora of gorgeous absurdity, from the brown-underpant-wearing Welsh Rarebit (which in the real world is cheese on toast) in 'Revolution 9', the contradiction of letting it out and letting it in ('Hey Jude'), the eggman, the goo goo g'joob-ing and the semolina pilchard climbing up the Eiffel Tower (*what?*) of 'I Am the Walrus', and the majesty of an octopus's garden to Polythene Pam (*Abbey Road*), the rich man with brown-bagged money in a zoo ('Baby You're a Rich Man'), a week comprising eight days and the sun turning out his light ('Good Night'). There are numerous quintessentially British references: the House of Lords, the Albert Hall and Blackburn, Lancashire, of 'A Day in the Life'; the National Health Service ('Dr. Robert'); the ten-bob note in 'Mean Mr. Mustard' the wonky finger, sideboard, gumboots, wellies, spinal cracker (osteopath?), toe jam (don't go there) and the rest ('Come Together'). If we get into helter skelter (eponymous), the National Trust ('Happiness is a Warm Gun'), and the Mackintosh raincoat, portrait of the Queen and the four of fish and finger pies ('Penny Lane'), we could be here all year.

So, yes: more innovative, experimental, influential and enduring than any other group of their era. Of their century. Reduce the entire catalogue to a mere handful? Honey, I tried.

'P.S. I Love You' – B-side of their debut single 'Love Me Do'
He had me from 'You, you, you'. Released 5 October 1962, 'PSILY' also appeared on the first album, *Please Please Me*. Paul wrote most of the song in Hamburg earlier that year, possibly as a missive to his sweetheart of the moment, Dot Rhone. Macca has contradicted this, insisting that it was just a generic love-letter song; and anyway, John chipped in his two penn'orth. Scottish session drummer Andy White replaced Pete Best as percussionist, although the band had already appointed Ringo … who also turned up to the session and shook maracas (not a euphemism). Starr later played on the BBC session recordings of the song. Love the boys' coy pose on the original single bag.

'Money (That's What I Want)' – from *With the Beatles*
An R&B cover, written by the Tamla and Motown labels' founder Berry Gordy with American songwriter Janie Bradford. Recorded originally by

Barrett Strong in 1959 for the Tamla label. Also covered by the Rolling Stones on their first British EP, and by many others, notably the Searchers. The Doors' version, on their 1970 *Live in New York* album, is worth a listen. The Beatles' live recording of it, made in Stockholm, October 1963, is on their *Anthology 1*. Quintessentially screaming Lord Lennon, on a razor-blade snack and ripping his throat to shreds. Primal, wild and let-rip. Even better, IMHO, than their cover of 'Twist and Shout'.

'I Saw Her Standing There' – from *Please Please Me*

Penned mostly by Paul, who at first called it 'Seventeen', with input from John. The opener of their debut album. Said to have been inspired by girlfriend Celia Mortimer, who was that age at the time (October 1962). Paul confessed to having plagiarised the bass riff on Chuck Berry's 'Talkin' About You' (the Beatles used to play that song, too: their version can be found on their double album *Live! At the Star-Club in Hamburg, Germany; 1962*). In the sleeve notes for *Please Please Me*, the writing credit on this song is given as 'McCartney–Lennon'.

'If I Fell' – from *A Hard Day's Night*

A hugely underrated 'we've all been there' song. A song about hurt and love and taking chances, mainly written, and sung, by John, who described it as his first attempt at a 'ballad proper'. Mellifluous, Everly-esque harmonies and complex key changes. Interestingly, they performed it at a pacier tempo live than when they recorded it; and singing it made giggle-arses of John and Paul. The track was also pressed as a single in December 1964, with 'Tell Me Why' on the B. This was an export single, but it wound up being shipped back into Britain and sold over the counter. It didn't chart, and is not usually counted as a proper UK single release.

'Things We Said Today' – from *A Hard Day's Night*

Also the B-side of the 'A Hard Day's Night' UK single. Written by Paul while cruising the Caribbean with his actress partner Jane Asher in May 1964, it reflected their challenged romance. Both successful at a young age, they were kept apart by their respective schedules. The separations were taking their toll. This solemn song has a real sense of foreboding, of bad times a-coming. Its tempo changes are wondrous.

'I'll Follow the Sun' – from *Beatles for Sale*
Written by Paul when he was about sixteen, at his Forthlin Road home. It has also appeared on bootlegs, EPs and B-sides. A conscious effort by McCartney to ensure that every next song was 'different' from the last. The track features Ringo knee-slapping. A pure, upbeat, carpe diem song that lacks the majesty of their other 'sun song', George's 'Here Comes the Sun', as well as that trace of sorrow between the lines of the latter's optimistic lyric.

'I Feel Fine' – single, backed by 'She's a Woman'
Notable for being the first time that feedback was ever used purposefully as a recording effect. John sings the song that he wrote himself, admitting that its riff was inspired by Bobby Parker's 'Watch Your Step' (1961), which the Beatles had covered live. Paul added that Ray Charles's 'What I'd Say' (1959) influenced the drums on the track. Fifties pop cutie Alma Cogan covered it on her 1967 album *Alma*.

'I Need You' – from *Help!*
That is indeed Ringo drumming on the back of a Gibson Jumbo acoustic guitar (as well as dinging a cowbell), with John on the snare drum. It's George's double-tracked vocal, and he's playing an acoustic rhythm guitar *and* a twelve-string lead guitar. He also wrote this somewhat anxious and despondent song – perhaps about his love for model Pattie Boyd, whom he met on the set of *A Hard Day's Night* and later married, in January 1966.

'You've Got to Hide Your Love Away' – from *Help!*
John, baring his soul again, just as he'd found the courage to do on 'Help!' and 'I'm a Loser'. The song is both specific and obscure, with a psychological sophistication belying his twenty-four years. Some have speculated that it is about his frustration at having to keep his wife under wraps, for fear that her known existence would compromise his reputation as a Beatle; others that it hinges on a secret love affair with an unnamed woman; still others that it exposes damage done to him by fame and fortune. Or was it, in fact, a song about the band's manager, closet homosexual Brian Epstein? Whatever, Paul's take was that this was John doing a Bob Dylan – with tenor and alto flute in place of harmonica. The 'Hey' was Pete Shotton's idea.

'Nowhere Man' – from *Rubber Soul*
Written and sung by John. Released as a single outside the UK, it also features in their film *Yellow Submarine*. This is Lennon at his most directly self-analytical, writing about himself in the third person, stepping away from the she-loves-me-I-love-her framework to go deeply within. He lays himself bare. Sitting around at home, under pressure to come up with another song against the clock for *Rubber Soul,* and frustrated by lack of inspiration, he threw aside his efforts and went for a lie-down. At which point the muse delivered the entire song to him, music and words. When John later discussed this period with interviewers, he described a state of almost textbook catatonia – a serious psychiatric condition affecting sufferers of depression, or of what we now call bipolar disorder, and of schizoaffective disorder. The catatonic individual withdraws from their environment, sits or lies staring into space, may display such symptoms as rigidity or stupor, and be unwilling or unable to speak, respond or even move much. The state can endure for days. Sufferers may also experience delusions, hallucinations and echolalia: one of the most beautiful words in the English language, signifying repetitive speech or the echoing of sounds, phrases and words.

'And Your Bird Can Sing' – from *Revolver*
A jangly pop/rock, pre-Allman Brothers Band/Lynyrd Skynyrd sound. Primarily John's, which he later shrugged off as 'another of my throwaways … fancy paper around an empty box'. His raw vocal is cushioned in sublime harmonies. Both Paul and George play lead guitar on this moreishly multi-layered track.

'Eleanor Rigby' – from *Revolver* (also released as a double A-side with 'Yellow Submarine')
This Greek tragedy of a song, with its bleak themes of ageing, loneliness and death, transcended the conventions and shape of pop and rock at the time, and broadened the band's appeal. All four Beatles and Pete Shotton came up with contributions. No Beatle played any instrument on the track: its backing is a string ensemble. The score was composed by George Martin. The song is sung by Paul; John and George sing harmonies with him. Angelic. Sublime.

'Ticket to Ride' – from *Help!*

Also in the film, and a single backed by 'Yes It Is'. Ah, George's Rickenbacker twelve-string riff. Despite which, I tend to think of the Carpenters' haunting cover first, though it was recorded by, among others, Mary Wells (whom the band adored), John's lover Alma Cogan, and the Beach Boys. Again, John and Paul contradicted one another as to who contributed what, though it is more likely John's song. He liked to describe it as 'the first heavy metal record ever made.' He said it was about the Hamburg prostitutes they met during their stays there, who were obliged to produce cards proving themselves STD-free before they could engage in sexual intercourse, or 'a ride'.

'Rain' – single B-side

Anthemic, psychedelic, echoey, experimental, detached, with exotic melodies and speed-up-slow-down recording. Notable for John's lead vocal and Ringo's exceptional drumming. This is the B-side of the single 'Paperback Writer', so often singled out as their finest flip. Recorded during the *Revolver* sessions (though neither track made the LP). It features early 'reverse lyrics', the backward technique also adopted on *Revolver*'s 'Tomorrow Never Knows'. Widely regarded as 'Ringo's greatest hit'. Ringo would later comment that he was 'possessed' during recording. His bass drum was given more boom by George Martin's assistant Geoff Emerick, with a closer mic and a knitted jumper inside to muffle the sound. Tempo at times puzzling, yet still awesome. Perhaps drug-inspired, more likely prompted by the wet weather that greeted them when they landed in Sydney during their first and only jaunt around Australia in 1964 (as part of their first world tour). Oasis may have listened to this a few times.

'Strawberry Fields Forever'/'Penny Lane' – double A-side single

Two of the most important songs that they ever wrote would go down in history as George Martin's greatest regret. Not because they were inferior, but because he recognised them as the best songs Paul and John had (until then) ever written, but they were 'thrown away' as singles. Both should have had a place on *Sgt. Pepper's Lonely Hearts Club Band* – but for the record company's demand for a single to appease the fans until the next album. Anxious to avoid accusations of short-changing them, the producer maintained that anything released as a single should not also appear on an album. The record-buying public had to feel that they were getting value for money (imagine trying to impose such a standard today). These songs mark a distinct turning point, being their first new music since the announcement that the Beatles were retiring from the road. John wrote 'Strawberry Fields' first. His nostalgic dream prompted Paul to retaliate with 'Penny Lane'. The latter is the more inclusive, accessible, charming and commercial of the two, while the former is elite, mysterious and avant-garde.

Inspired by Dylan Thomas's poem *Fern Hill* and by the Beach Boys' *Pet Sounds*, Paul took a surreal, hallucinogenic walk back through his blue-suburban-skied childhood in the pouring rain. Very strange. In so doing, he created the ultimate sentimental experience. It's worth noting that 'Penny Lane' refers to both a neighbourhood of south Liverpool and an actual street, a central feature of which was the bus terminus referred to as the 'roundabout'. It's still there – as is the barber shop where John, George and Paul had their hair cut when they were kids. Now Tony Slavin's, the salon still owns the wooden plank on which the boys sat, above the barber's chair, to bring them up to the correct height. I have seen it. Adele, the manageress, allowed me to hold it. Harry Bioletti's initials are engraved on it, and it is used in the shop to this day.

Listening to the song, we are forced to confront apparent memories of our own childhood. Was it really that way? Were those places just as we remember them, and were those people exactly who we think they were – or are we deluding ourselves?

Session musician David Mason, whom Paul enlisted after watching him perform on television, deserves a mention for his exuberant and enchanting piccolo trumpet solo.

The more bewildering and psychedelic 'Strawberry Fields', originally entitled 'It's Not Too Bad', was named for the Liverpool Salvation Army children's home close to John's childhood home in Woolton. John once played in its woods and gardens with his gang, despite Aunt Mimi's admonishments that they were not to. He regarded this as his best Beatles offering. He wrote it while reeling from the death of singer Alma Cogan, with whom he had fallen in love behind his wife Cynthia's back. The song's obscure references reflect philosophical and religious works that he was reading at the time. John would later talk about it as a musical interpretation of how 'different' from everyone else he had felt all his life, and said that it was 'psychoanalysis set to music'. Paul, however, regarded it as John's homage to Lewis Carroll and his love of that author's poem 'Jabberwocky' John reminisces in the song, bottom line. It is both nostalgic for real-life places and detached from them; both impressionistic and precise; both LSD-fuelled and whistle-clean. Its mellotron intro, trumpets and cellos haunt. One of the trumpeters, Derek Watkins, achieved fame in his own right for having played on the theme of every Bond film from *Dr. No* to *Skyfall*.

The promo films for both tracks, along with the sequences for 'Paperback Writer' and 'Rain', were among the earliest music videos, as such pieces would come to be known. With impressive vision, McCartney commented that all future pop music would be about visuals as well as sound. 'Strawberry Fields' was filmed in the Deer Park at Knole in Sevenoaks, where I lived for years and where I walked with my eldest daughter Mia every day after school.

John's Central Park, New York memorial garden is named in honour of the song.

'A Day in the Life' – the final track on *Sgt. Pepper's Lonely Hearts Club Band*
Mostly written by John, this epic piece is the Beatles' magnum opus, and universally acclaimed as one of the most innovative and influential pop recordings of all time. News-inspired, psychedelic, surreal, inexplicable, cacophonous, chilling and probably LSD-driven. It established art rock as a mainstream genre, and inspired Freddie Mercury to write Queen's masterstroke 'Bohemian Rhapsody'.

'She's Leaving Home' – also from *Sgt. Pepper's Lonely Hearts Club Band*
Based on the true story of seventeen-year-old Melanie Coe, whom Paul had read about in the *Daily Mirror*.

Like 'Eleanor Rigby', one of the few Beatles songs on which none of them played. (Hear, also, 'Within You Without You' on *Sgt. Pepper* – which does feature George, but not playing guitar. Indian instruments the sitar, tabla and dilruba are played, mostly by the North London Asian Music Circle; 'Good Night', from the 'White Album' – and only Ringo sings on it, none of the others, against an orchestra conducted by George Martin; and, er, 'Yesterday': Paul sings, only strings, and it's drumless.)

'While My Guitar Gentle Weeps' – from the 'White Album'
Written by lead guitarist George Harrison, who had found his feet as a songwriter, this is a philosophical reflection on the state of relationships

among the four after they returned home from the Maharishi's ashram in India in 1968. It features guitar by Eric Clapton, who is not credited. George said the song was inspired by the ancient Chinese text *I Ching*. Disillusioned with how the band's spiritual journey had panned out, George also acknowledges the greater theme of universal love, and laments the fact that mankind has not seen the light. One of the greatest love songs ever, paradoxically conceived during a moment of despair.

'Julia' – from the 'White Album' (also the B-side of their 1976 single 'Ob-La-Di, Ob-La-Da')
'When I cannot sing my heart, I can only speak my mind' ... does it get more agonising? John wrote this wistful song about his mother while at the Maharishi's ashram in Rishikesh. Folk-pop artist Donovan, also present in India, taught him new ways to finger-pick the guitar. He also assisted him with the lyrics, mindful of John's desire to evoke an *Alice in Wonderland* mood. I've long wondered whether the lines borrowed from Kahlil Gibran and bent a little were Donovan's idea or John's. This is just John and his acoustic, his only solo effort on any Beatles song. He stirs Yoko into the imagery – her first name means 'child of the sea' – because we know he was inclined to call her 'Mother'. In which case, we can and should read all kinds into this. Because his feelings for Julia were confused to say the least. Because every meaningful relationship he had with a woman after her death was effectively mother replacement therapy.

'Back in the USSR' – from the 'White Album' (also released as a single in 1976 with 'Twist and Shout' on the B-side.) A send-up of 'California Girls' by the Beach Boys? Wish they all could be. Paul twisted it, ripped off 'Back in the USA' by Chuck Berry and mixed that in too, for good measure. An irresistible slice of satire and a banger of a rock'n'roller, which also attracted criticism for its apparent political stance. Oh well. Love that jet-engine screech. Macca did actually get to perform it in Red Square, Moscow, post-fall of Communism, in 2003. Which must have been a trip. A pity that the British Overseas Airways Corporation didn't live to see it. Ringo was not a Beatle at this point, having stalked out in protest. Yes, he was a good enough drummer. He came back.

'Across the Universe' – from *Let It Be*

You wondered for years too, right? Jai Guru Deva Om. We couldn't look things up in those days. We kept lifting the needle and putting it back and back, scribbling down the lyrics and trying to work out what John was on about. Nope. Who knew that it was a Sanskrit mantra, meaning 'Hail to the divine guru.' Something like that. We didn't know what TM (Transcendental Meditation) was, either. We were only kids. The song first appeared on the multiple-artist compilation *No One's Gonna Change Our World*, and was restyled for *Let It Be*. John said that it was inspired by Cynthia moaning about something. A wifely nag, transformed into poetic splendour which belied John's dissatisfaction with it. Between Lennon and McCartney, the knives were out.

'The Abbey Road Medley'

Shakespearian in its diversity, spilling tragedy and comedy, poetry and dramaturgy, exquisite highs and desperate lows, culminating in 'The End'. Truly intoxicating. A masterpiece. May I be played out to this.

THE AUTHOR'S FAVOURITE
JOHN SONGS

'Instant Karma!' – single

We all shine on! My friend Chris Welch wrote this of it in the *Melody Maker*: 'Instant hit! John Lennon is singing better than ever. With a beautiful rock'n'roll echo chamber on his mean but meaningful vocals and some superb drumming, it makes up the Plastics' best piece of boogie yet.'

For every action, a reaction. Cause, effect. A bit of Buddhism here, the looming of karma there. Which is a thing. John, still a Beatle at the time, was inspired to write it after spending time with Yoko's former husband Tony Cox, their daughter Kyoko, and Cox's new lady, Melinda Kendall, who filled his head with a sprinkling of new spiritual ideas. It was produced by Phil Spector, fresh out of retirement and visiting London, and brims with his 'Wall of Sound' sound. Klaus Voormann and George Harrison join in. John has had a haircut, though the shearing is silent. So is Yoko's (but flip to the B-side).

'God' – from *John Lennon/Plastic Ono Band*

The dream is over. John means the sixties, and the fruitless indulgence in doctrines and idolatry supposed to guide us live a meaningful life. To embellish his point, he lambasts everything from royalty to rock idols, Buddhism to Hinduism, Christianity to politics to ancient texts and sects, bundling it all into the same bag. He was the dreamweaver and the walrus, but now he's John. 'I just believe in me. Yoko and me.' All he is saying is, look inwards. As if he knows that 'God' and 'Heaven' have always been within.

'Mother' – from *John Lennon/Plastic Ono Band*

McCartney majored in this theme, with 'Lady Madonna', 'Your Mother Should Know', 'Let It Be' (featuring his Mother, Mary), 'Mother Nature's Son', 'Only Mama Knows' and 'I Lost My Little Girl'. Here's John's howler to eclipse them all – even his own 'Julia'.

Oh, Lord. From its opening death knell to its concluding screeches, which heave with all the agony of a terrified toddler, this primal, Janov-inspired piece is a blood-curdling wail of rejection and grief. To be fair, John blasts both parents, his mother for giving him away and his father for abandoning him. He needed them both, he acknowledges – but evidently, they didn't need him. To hell with them, then. He doesn't mean that. The pain-wracked pleading of the closer 'Mama don't go, Daddy come home' demonstrates starkly and overwhelmingly that he never got over what they did to him.

'Jealous Guy' – from *Imagine*

A lot of people thought Bryan Ferry wrote this, so big was Roxy Music's (inferior) hit version ten years after the original. Raw, shivery and pain-riven, the song was conceived in India, where it began life as 'Child of Nature'. It was later demo'd by the Beatles, but did not progress at that time. Eventually, John was dreaming of the past, as he so often was, and look what emerged. It is an acknowledgement of his shedding of chauvinistic attitudes, and of his enlightenment regarding women. There was never danger, of course, of Yoko allowing him to own and possess her to death.

This was the last song John sang live, unannounced and unaccompanied, on an acoustic, in the deserted bar of a Japanese hotel. Anti-climactic, like. This is the way the world ends. Not with a bang but with a whimper. Hollow, goodbye.****

'How Do You Sleep?' – from *Imagine*

With the Beatles flailing to a close, the primary songwriting partnership disintegrating and so much resentment flying about, John wrote this in retaliation. Paul's album *Ram* inflamed him, featuring as it did some flagrant attacks on Lennon, particularly in the song 'Too Many People'. 'Sleep' is a great song, but it goes too far and hits below the belt. For example? All these rumours about Paul being dead were right, John claims; he's just a pretty face; he surrounds himself with yes-men; the only song of any worth he ever wrote was 'Yesterday' – a play on words, dismissing Paul as a has-been; John even derides McCartney's oeuvre as 'muzak to my ears'. It was shabby of John to write and record this embittered sneer. It was understandable of Paul to feel affronted. Losers all round. John later excused it as 'good clean fun'. Right. A cool piece of music, though.

'Happy Xmas (War is Over)' – single

Yes, yes, I've seen the 'White Christmas' sales figures. Bing can sling. Infuriating abbreviation aside, John'n'Yoko's standard, together with the Pogues/Kirsty MacColl's 'Fairytale of New York', is definitive. It's right up there with Dora Bryan's 'best bad record of 1963', 'All I Want for Christmas is a Beatle' ('Oh, that fab 'airdo').

A protest song, foremost. An anthem to peace, rendered Yule-ish. Something for everyone: the Harlem Community Choir and Children's Choir, May Pang on BVs, plaintive whispered messages to estranged offspring Kyoko and Julian, tinkling sleigh bells, production by snow plough Phil Spector. John's voice is truly lovely on this, and Yoko sings in tune. War is over. If you want it.

'Out the Blue' – from *Mind Games*

Oh, Yoko. You inspired some hefty ballads. This is a sublime and deceptively simple love song. An ode to joy. A few cranky metaphors aside, it tidal-waves through the genres as if unsure to begin with as to what kind if song it actually is, before concluding with confidence. It's the music of our dreams. Because it's all any of us wants, isn't it. The one true love. Two minds, one destiny. If only.

'#9 Dream' – from *Walls and Bridges*

'Ah! böwakawa poussé, poussé'. It means nothing to me. It meant nothing to them, either. John dreamed the song, and these indecipherable lyrics, which are in no man's language. May Pang and fairy friends deliver the backing vocals, and she murmurs her lover's name. One of the hardest Lennon songs to listen to when feeling sad, nostalgic and angry about his death. It's final and tragic.

'Watching the Wheels' – from *Double Fantasy* (also released as a single after John's death, backed by 'Beautiful Boy (Darling Boy)', his song for little Sean). He just had to let it go. He quit the big time, got off the merry-go-round, turned his back on the fame thing and slunk back to reality. He had everything that mattered. He reset his priorities. He stayed home to be the daddy and cook the dinner. People didn't get it. They do now.

'Grow Old With Me' – from *Milk and Honey*

There's all sorts going on here. John demos a song in Bermuda based on a poem by Robert Browning. Back in New York, Yoko happens upon an old poem by Browning's tragic wife, Elizabeth Barrett Browning. She pens a song inspired by it, entitled 'Let Me Count the Ways', and a lilt stirs in her head. Were John and Yoko the reincarnation of the Brownings? Well. Their two separate songs might have made it side by side onto *Double Fantasy*, but for a race against release date. They entwine instead, to become 'Grow Old With Me'. Much as their authors did – or intended to do. The best being yet to be.

Abbey Road, which came out on 26 September 1969, was the final Beatles album ever to be recorded, but not their last album to be released. *Let It Be*, most of the tracks for which were recorded during January 1969, eventually appeared in May 1970, along with the eponymous film. Debate has raged for decades as to which was the 'last' Beatles album. There are many 'fors' and 'againsts'. *Abby Road's* 'I Want You (She's So Heavy)' marked the final time that all four Beatles played in the studio together. *Let It Be* is more movie soundtrack than pure music album, and perhaps only became an official studio album because the four members had already gone their separate ways. However, *Let It Be* is technically the final Beatles album, while *Abbey Road* is the one that historians, experts and most fans think of as 'the end of the Beatles'. On 26 September 2019, fifty years to the day since the original appeared, *Abbey Road* was re-released in a variety of formats, freshly mixed by producer Giles Martin and engineer Sam Okell, and featuring many extras, including additional tracks, memorabilia and previously unseen images. Commented Martin in the notes (who was guided in his work by the original stereo mix of his father, Beatles producer George Martin): 'The magic comes from the hands playing the instruments, the blend of the Beatles' voices, the beauty of the arrangements. Our quest is simply to ensure everything sounds as fresh and hits you as hard as it would have on the day it was recorded.'

* A worldwide chart-topper, the must-have compilation *1* (*One*) includes more or less all their Number One singles in the UK and US between 1962 and 1970. Released 'on the thirtieth anniversary of the band's official demise' – although this is arguable.

The remaining three Beatles got back together for the *Anthology* project in 1994, using John's 'Free As a Bird' and 'Real Love' as the foundation for new songs that they recorded and released as 'The Beatles'.

*** Data source: *Guardian*, 2010.

**** With a nod to T.S. Eliot, author of the poem 'The Hollow Men'.

SELECT BIBLIOGRAPHY & RECOMMENDATIONS

The Holy Bible, King James Version, Oxford University Press.

Baird, Julia and Giuliano, Geoffrey, *John Lennon My Brother*, Grafton Books, 1988.

Baird, Julia, *Imagine this: Growing up with my brother John Lennon*, Hodder & Stoughton, 2007.

The Beatles Book, Omnibus Press, 1985.

The Beatles Lyrics, Futura Publications, 1974.

Bedford, Carol, *Waiting for the Beatles*, Blandford Press, 1984.

Best, Pete and Doncaster, Patrick, *Beatle! The Pete Best Story*, Plexus Publishing Ltd, 1985.

Bramwell, Tony, *My Life with the Beatles*, Thomas Dunne Books, 2005.

Brown, Peter and Gaines, Steve, *The Love You Make*, MacMillan, 1983.

Burger, Jeff, *Lennon on Lennon: Conversations with John Lennon*, Chicago Review Press, 2016.

Clayton, Marie, and Thomas, Gareth, *John Lennon Unseen Archives*, Paragon/Daily Mail/Atlantic Publishing, 2002.

Coleman, Ray, *John Winston Lennon, Vol. 1*, Sidgwick & Jackson, 1984.

Coleman, Ray, *John Ono Lennon, Vol. 2*, Sidgwick & Jackson, 1984.

Connolly, Ray, *Being John Lennon*, Weidenfeld & Nicolson, 2018.

Davies, Hunter, *The Beatles*, Heinemann London, 1968.

Davies, Hunter (ed.), *The John Lennon Letters*, Weidenfeld & Nicolson, 2012.

Edmunds, Richard A., *Inside the Beatles Family Tree*, A.R. Heritage Publishing, 2018.

Epstein, Brian, *A Cellarful of Noise*, Souvenir Press, 1964.

Faithfull, Marianne, *Faithfull*, Michael Joseph, 1994.

Giuliano, Geoffrey, *The Beatles A Celebration*, Sidgwick & Jackson, 1986.

Giuliano, Geoffrey, *Blackbird: The Unauthorised Biography of Paul McCartney*, Smith Gryphon, 1991.

Goldman, Albert, *The Lives of John Lennon*, Bantam Press, 1988.

Goodden, Joe, *Riding So High, the Beatles and Drugs*, Pepper & Pearl, 2017.

Hamp, Johnnie, *It Beats Working for a Living*, Trafford Publishing, 2008.

Harris, Bob, *The Whispering Years*, BBC Worldwide, 2001.

Harris, Bob, *Still Whispering After All These Years*, Michael O'Mara Books, 2015.

Harry, Bill, *The McCartney File*, Virgin Books 1986.

Hoffman, Dezo, *With the Beatles: The Historic Photographs*, Omnibus Press, 1982.

Jones, Kenney, *Let the Good Times Roll*, Blink Publishing, 2018.

Jones, Ron, *The Beatles' Liverpool*, Liverpool History Press, 1991.

Lennon, Cynthia, *John*, Hodder & Stoughton, 2005.

Lennon, John, *In His Own Write*, Jonathan Cape, 1964.

Lennon, John, *A Spaniard in the Works*, Jonathan Cape, 1965.

Lennon, John, *Skywriting by word of Mouth*, Vintage, 1986.

Lewisohn, Mark, *The Beatles Live!*, Pavilion Books Ltd, 1986.

Lewisohn, Mark, *The Beatles, Tune In*, Little, Brown, 2013.

MacDonald, Ian, *Revolution in the Head*, Fourth Estate, 1994.

Marion, Bob, *The Lost Beatles Photographs*, HarperCollins, 2011.

Martin, George, *Making Music*, Pan Books, 1983.

Martin, George, *All You Need is Ears*, Macmillan London, 1979.

McCabe, Peter and Schonfeld, Robert D., *John Lennon: For the Record*, (from an interview recorded in 1971), Bantam USA, 1984.

McCartney, Paul, *Blackbird Singing Lyrics & Poems 1965–1999*, Faber & Faber, 2001.

McKinney, Devin, *Magic Circles: the Beatles in Dream and History*, Harvard University Press, 2003.

Napier-Bell, Simon, *You Don't Have to Say You Love Me*, New English Library, 1982.

Napier-Bell, Simon, *Ta-Ra-Ra Boom De-Ay*, Unbound, 2014.

Norman, Philip, *Shout! The True Story of the Beatles*, Hamish Hamilton, 1981.

Norman, Philip, *The Stones*, Hamish Hamilton, 1984.

Norman, Philip, *Elton*, Hutchinson, 1991.

Norman, Philip, *John Lennon The Life*, HarperCollins, 2008.

Norman, Philip, *Paul McCartney The Biography*, Weidenfeld & Nicolson, 2016.

Pang, May and Edwards, Henry, *Loving John*, Transworld, 1983.

Peebles, Andy and the BBC, *The Lennon Tapes*, BBC, 1981.

Rogan, Johnny, *Lennon: The Albums*, Calidore, 2006.

Salewicz, Chris, *McCartney The Biography*, Macdonald & Co. (Publishers), 1986.

Scott, Neil and Foster, Graham, plus various artists, *Lennon Bermuda* (book and box set), Freisenbruch Brannon Media, 2012.

Sheff, David, *Last Interview*, Sidgwick & Jackson, 2000.

Spitz, Bob, *The Beatles: The Biography*, Little, Brown & Co., 2005.

Swern, Phil, *Sounds of the Sixties*, (featuring fifty-nine cover versions of songs written by John Lennon and Paul McCartney or George Harrison), Red Planet, 2017.

Wald, Elijah, *How the Beatles Destroyed Rock'n'Roll*, Oxford University Press, 2009.

Wenner, Jann S., *Lennon Remembers*, Straight Arrow Books, 1971.

WEBSITES

www.thebeatles.com
www.johnlennon.com
www.beatlesbible.com

RECOMMENDED

London Beatles Walking Tours by Richard Porter: five scheduled group tours a week, plus private tours. Abbey Road and more. Full details at www.beatlesinlondon.com or email beatlesinlondon@gmail.com

Stefanie Hempel's Beatles –Tour of Hamburg: a musical journey of the red light district of St Pauli and original Beatles sites. Group and private tours.
www.hempels-musictour.de/en

Fab Four Taxi Tours
54 St James St
Liverpool, L1 0AB
www.fab4taxitours.com
info@fab4taxitours.com
Eddie Connor (cab name 'Penny [Lane]') was our excellent, superbly
informed driver and guide.

National Trust combined tour of John's and Paul's childhood homes
Mendips and 20 Forthlin Road: the only way of gaining access to the
interiors of these extraordinary time warp houses. Even Bob Dylan and
Debbie Harry have done this one!
www.nationaltrust.org.uk/beatles-childhood-homes

Philharmonic Dining Rooms
36 Hope St
Liverpool, L1 9BX
www.nicholsonspubs.co.uk/restaurants/northwest/
thephilharmonicdiningroomsliverpool
A favourite Beatles haunt, with Grade I Listed gents' toilets, it featured
memorably in James Corden's *Carpool Karaoke* episode with Paul
McCartney on *The Late Late Show* (CBS).

ACKNOWLEDGEMENTS

So many have been so helpful during the research and writing of this book that to single out a handful for special praise feels unfair. Still, I wish to highlight those who went beyond.

Having worked with the same agent since 2003, I found the prospect of seeking a new one so daunting that I ignored the need to do so for more than a year. When I met Clare Hulton in 2019, we bonded instantly. She personifies the contradictions I most admire. She steams in, no-nonsense. She understands writers. She lets us get on with the words.

Kelly Ellis and I were on the same page when we discussed the possibility of a new study of John Lennon. She agreed that the point was not to churn out yet another biography for the sake of it in a major commemorative year; but that a new interpretation based on my own research and interviews would be worthwhile. She acquired the book with such enthusiasm, and was so personally supportive, that I cried when she left Bonnier/John Blake for another publishing house. I need not have worried. James Hodgkinson is her noble and cool replacement. I love working with him.

Martin Barden and Ray Cansick accompanied me to Hamburg on a whirlwind research trip, managing our schedule with quiet professionalism, kindness and humour. I could not have done it without them. We were chaperoned, supported and translated-for by Jörg and Dörte Günther, who were just as helpful, generous and lovely. I owe them all.

Ed Phillips was my indispensable Man Friday in Liverpool. He did everything, including the driving. His complete photographic record of our visit proved invaluable during the remote re-treading of the trail.

Mia Jones was my willing and able assistant on three return trips to New York. She also spent many hours delving into the archive to retrieve the obscure and the long-forgotten. Hearing and seeing things afresh through her previously un-Beatled ears and eyes has been enlightening.

Aurora Benting has done everything else, from fridge-stocking to stamp-sticking.

There are countless reasons for which to thank David Stark: not least for having taken me back to Merseyside for the Summer 2019 LIPA Graduation at Sir Paul McCartney's Liverpool Institute for the Performing Arts, housed in Macca's own former grammar school. It was there that I was able to converse with Paul one-to-one, sharing stories (and a couple of secrets) with him. I'd never imagined that I would be blessed with such an opportunity. David also provided a recording of a lost interview, never previously published or aired, that he'd conducted himself with the late Pete Shotton, John's lifelong best friend from the age of six.

Grateful thanks are due to the Hope Street Hotel Liverpool, NH Collection Hamburg City, and Soho House New York.

I am deeply obliged to Jacob Nordby for kind permission to use his quotation on the title page. www:blessedaretheweird.com/jacob-nordby/

I will always owe Andy Peebles for having made it possible for me to become, as far as we both know, the first if not the only writer in the world ever to have heard the entire, unedited, three-hour, twenty-two-minute interview that he conducted with John and Yoko at the Hit Factory recording studio in New York, on 6 December 1980. It was the first time in a decade that John had agreed to be cross-examined by BBC radio; since the Beatles had disbanded, in fact. It turned out to be John's last-ever exchange with a British broadcaster. As in any interview with Lennon, it leaves us with more questions than it answered. But that feels right. They are the questions that shaped this book.

Nor could I have written about John without the help of many willing and helpful others – a sizeable number of whom spoke to me on the assurance of anonymity, and so are between the lines here. As for the following, such remembrances to cherish. Thank you from my heart:

Frank Allen

Keith Altham

David Ambrose

Dan Arthure

Judy Astley

Mike Batt

Julianne Batt

Brian Bennett

Warren Bennett

Ed Bicknell

Francis Booth

Jenny Boyd

Clare Bramley

Fenton Bresler, R.I.P.

Clem Cattini

Chris Charlesworth

Chips Chipperfield, R.I.P.

Dominic Collier

Eddie Connor

Jeff Dexter

Kuno Dreysse

Marianne Faithfull

Paul Gambaccini

Brian Grant

Dörte Günther

Jörg Günther

Cosmo Hallström

Johnnie Hamp

David Hancock

Stefanie Hempel

Andy Hill

Jackie Holland

Richard Hughes

James Irving

Debbie Jones

Trevor Jones

The Revd Canon Dr Alison Joyce

Berni Kilmartin

Simon Kinnersley

Cynthia Lennon, R.I.P.

Julian Lennon

Steve Levine

Mark Lewisohn

Sir George Martin, R.I.P.

Linda McCartney, R.I.P.

Sir Paul McCartney

Tom McGuinness

Leo McLoughlin

Scott Millaney

Jonathan Morrish

Paul Muggleton

Mitch Murray CBE

Simon Napier-Bell

Philip Norman

May Pang

Anne Peebles

Allan Pell

Meredith Plumb

Richard Porter

David Quantick

Sir Tim Rice

Leo Sayer

Roger Scott, R.I.P.

Paul Sexton

Pete Shotton, R.I.P.

Earl Slick

David Stark

Maureen Starkey, R.I.P.

Andy Stephens

Phil Swern

Judie Tzuke

Klaus Voormann

Johnnie Walker

Michael Watts

Adrienne Wells

John Wells

Stuart White

Tom Wilcox

Suki Yamamoto

This book is dedicated to my mother, Kathleen; to Henry, Bridie and Mia; and to Cleo and Jesse, Nick, Alex and Christian, Matthew and Adam. P.S., I love you.

L-AJ, London, September 2020

INDEX